Critical Essays on

ANGELA CARTER

CRITICAL ESSAYS
ON
BRITISH LITERATURE

Zack Bowen, General Editor

University of Miami

Critical Essays on

ANGELA CARTER

edited by

LINDSEY TUCKER

G. K. Hall & Co.
An Imprint of Simon & Schuster Macmillan
New York

Prentice Hall International
London   Mexico City   New Delhi   Singapore   Sydney   Toronto

G. K. Hall & Co.
An Imprint of Simon & Schuster Macmillan
1633 Broadway
New York, NY 10019

Library of Congress Cataloging-in-Publication Data

Critical essays on Angela Carter / edited by Lindsey Tucker.
     p. cm.—(Critical essays on British literature)
  Includes bibliographical references and index.
  ISBN 0-7838-0047-9 (alk. paper)
  1. Carter, Angela, 1951– —Criticism and interpretation.
 2. Women and literature—England—History—20th century.
 I. Tucker, Lindsey, 1936– . II. Series.
 PR6053.A73Z57   1998
 823'.914—dc21   98-35179
                                     CIP

This paper meets the requirements of ANSI/NISO Z39.48-1992 (Permanence
of Paper).
10 9 8 7 6 5 4 3 2 1

Printed in the United States of America

Contents

◆

General Editor's Note

◆

The Critical Essays on British Literature series provides a variety of approaches to both classical and contemporary writers of Britain and Ireland. The formats of the volumes in the series vary with the thematic designs of individual editors and with the amount and nature of existing reviews and criticism, augmented, where appropriate, by original essays by recognized authorities. It is hoped that each volume will be unique in developing a new overall perspective on its particular subject.

Lindsey Tucker's volume represents the first full-length scholarly/critical attempt to place the work of Angela Carter in a comprehensive perspective. Using Carter's own words, Tucker's introduction goes to the essence of the writer's highly individualistic philosophy and methodology and then offers substantial examples from Carter's fiction in support of the evolving interpretation. While placing Carter's works in a contextual framework, Tucker analyzes their effects on critics reacting to such literary models as parody, Gothic grotesque, pornography, and the fairy tale, all reconceived in postmodern, largely psychoanalytic terms.

The selected essays were all published in the last 15 years, the preponderance in the last 5, reflecting the recent explosion of critical interest in Carter's work. A selected bibliography of primary and secondary works is appended.

ZACK BOWEN
University of Miami

Publisher's Note

◆

Producing a volume that contains both newly commissioned and reprinted material presents the publisher with the challenge of balancing the desire to achieve stylistic consistency with the need to preserve the integrity of works first published elsewhere. In the Critical Essays series, essays commissioned especially for a particular volume are edited to be consistent with G. K. Hall's house style; reprinted essays appear in the style in which they were first published, with only typographical errors corrected. Consequently, shifts in style from one essay to another are the result of our efforts to be faithful to each text as it was originally published.

Introduction

Lindsey Tucker

Angela Carter's death from cancer at the age of 51 was especially tragic because it ended the career of one of Britain's most original, iconoclastic, and learned writers. One cannot help but speculate on what she might have done, for she already had to her credit nine novels, four collections of short stories, two collections of prose, as well as her cultural study of pornography and several translations and editions. "She hadn't finished," Salman Rushdie concludes in his introduction to the posthumously published *Burning Your Boats: The Collected Short Stories,* and most readers would agree, although they would doubtless remain at odds about most other aspects of her work.[1] For the writer whom Rushdie describes as "formal and outrageous, exotic and demotic, exquisite and coarse, precious and raunchy, fabulist and socialist, purple and black" left behind a body of writing that is just as complex and contradictory as she was (ix).

Indeed, the work of Angela Carter has something of the shape and manner of her most memorable protagonist, Fevvers, the birdwoman aerialist of *Nights at the Circus* (1984). Described as a "big girl" with gargantuan appetites and a face of "Brobdingnagian symmetry," Fevvers is marked with a grotesqueness that would seem to belie her popularity as Europe's favorite celebrity.[2] If Fevvers's performance takes place on high, she is also equally at home in the low; and it is interesting that Walser's first meeting with her occurs in her malodorous dressing room, where her gustatory exuberance is punctuated by belches and other down-to-earth affronts to his masculinist assumptions about women. In Carter's work we find not only that which is dazzling and erudite but also that which revels in the representation of bodily functions. Carter's interest in and deployment of the grotesque in terms of both content and form suggests that she shares with Bakhtin an interest in the body composed of orifices, lumps, and protrusions—the grotesque body, which, says Bakhtin, functions as a violator of boundaries and as resistance to closure. Carter's narrative strategies also reflect this affinity for the grotesque

1

in the ways in which she mangles generic forms, denies closure to her narratives, and oftentimes empties their content while constructing a second narrative edifice over the first one.[3] Her later fiction, especially, shows her use of the grotesque to raise interesting questions about the construction of gender.[4]

Carter's work also shares with Fevvers a love of spectacle and performance. A bizarre performer at best, Fevvers appears to defy "the laws of projectiles" in her trapeze act, while on the ground she walks (clumsily) a narrow line between natural anomaly and wondrous harbinger of the new century—freak or hoax, fact or fiction. It is no secret that Carter loves carnival spaces, but her fiction is also dominated by other aspects of the theatrical—tableaux, peep shows, filmic conventions. Even her serious, full-length study on pornography, *The Sadeian Woman* (1979), brings Sade on stage with a rousing introduction and closes with a "speculative finale."[5] Her final novel, *Wise Children* (1991), the autobiographical narrative of a chorus girl, is also presented as a kind of song and dance. It has five chapters that clearly evoke the dramatic structure of acts, and it concludes with a "Dramatis Personae." In *Night at the Circus,* spectacle also extends to drag; Walser, at one point, is forced to ask himself whether Fevvers is not, after all, a man (*NC,* 35). Carter has more than once described her early writing as male impersonation, and at least one critic has seconded that description, suggesting that she writes like "a female in male chauvinist drag."[6] Although this comment was intended as criticism, a number of feminist critics have identified her use of cross-dressing and masquerade as important narrative strategies for critiquing and parodying the constructed nature of gender. In sum, like Fevvers, Carter's work is both grand and vulgar; its deployment of intertextuality is daunting, but it revels in the smells of carnival and the many representations of physicality.

Carter's work is as political and materialist as it is feminist, but as an artist Carter is always in a state of transformation and growth. To some readers and critics, her textual practices have suggested a failure to find the right form, but as Elaine Jordan has rightly observed, "Angela Carter's fictions are a series of essays: attempts, trials, processes"[7] that should be understood as a demonstration that her art is not dissociated from her politics. I think that we better appreciate Carter when we understand both her ideological and artistic concerns as dictating this more open and experimental approach to fiction.

Her preference for the picaresque is one example of her interest in open forms, useful because, in her words, it is "where people have adventures in order to find themselves in places where they can discuss philosophical concepts without distractions."[8] It is also a form with "an inbuilt narrative drive," she says, adding, "And you can always get out of places very quickly."[9] She has always expressed a suspicion about mimetic practices, arguing that while they appear to ground us in the material reality, which is for her the starting point, creating a "credible illusion" is different from the story that "is always real *as* story" (Haffenden, 80). Thus, Carter does not intend her often extravagant fictions as an evasion of reality but as a means of making reality more accessible.

She is perhaps best known for her short stories, which are often reworkings of both folklore and fairy tale, while her longer fictions are, in their expansiveness and variety, difficult to categorize. She has been called a fantasist, and a number of her novels have attracted the attention of science fiction critics. Some critics would prefer to call her fictions speculative (Jordan, 19–40). She has also been described as a magic realist. David Punter, for example, argues that her tendency to venture beyond the bounds of convention, "to depict 'magical' boundary breaking events as part of the texture of everyday experience," places her within this tradition.[10] Carter, however, has been reluctant to describe her work in this way, arguing that British writers lack not only the social forces that have operated on Latin American countries but also "an illiterate and superstitious peasantry with a very rich heritage of abstruse fictional material"; British writers are thus forced "to invent much more" (Haffenden, 82).

Also important to an understanding of her work is her own interest in the surrealists. In a piece entitled "The Alchemy of the Word," written in 1978, Carter seems more critical than celebratory. Describing surrealism as "the latest, perhaps the final, explosion of romantic humanism in Western Europe" and therefore doomed to fail, she claims to have become disenchanted with surrealist misogyny and realized "that surrealist art did not recognize I had my own rights to liberty and love and vision as an autonomous being."[11] Nevertheless, when she speaks of some surrealist practices as "a reactive negation of destruction" (*ED*, 72) and recalls from the *First Manifesto of Surrealism* the declaration that "the marvelous alone is beautiful," we sense her emotional connection to much surrealist thinking. Her comment on surrealist beauty, not as an aesthetic abstraction or a universal Truth, is revealing. Claiming that the beautiful does not exist as such, she argues instead that

> what do exist are images or objects that are enigmatic, marvelous, erotic—or juxtapositions of objects, or people, or ideas, that arbitrarily extend our notion of the connections it is possible to make. In this way the beautiful is put at the service of liberty. (*ED*, 73)

Certainly Carter's remark that "I tend to regard all of western Europe as a great scrap-yard from which you can assemble all sorts of new vehicles" suggests affinities with surrealist interests in hybrid art forms.[12] The surrealist attraction to the scatological, to irreverent rewritings of traditional texts and images, must have had some influence as well.

Most recent criticism seems to regard Carter's work as postmodernist, even though she did not seem happy with the term and tended to regard as "mannerist" the reflexivity of writers who write books about books.[13] Nonetheless, her opposition to humanism and bourgeois individualism, her use of intertextual frames, her critique of western (and patriarchal) representational practices, and her view of her own fictions as "a kind of literary criticism" place her work with the postmodernists (Haffenden, 79). Linda Hutcheon, one critic who argues for Carter as a postmodern writer, cites in particular Carter's interest in "ex-centric" subjects and her engagement in a "complicitous critique," that is, a way of writing that exposes its own position within the cultural hegemony at the same time that it undermines it. It is perhaps this difficult practice that has given some of Carter's readers so much trouble.[14] Hutcheon also links Carter with such writers as Christa Wolf, Susan Daitsch, Audrey Thomas, and Maxine Hong Kingston as practitioners of "de-doxification"—a term she uses to describe western and capitalist practices that strive to normalize signs and images (7, 20).

Robert Rowdon Wilson, using one of Carter's tales as a paradigm, sets up the conflicting discourses of postmodernisism as belonging to two separate camps—what he describes as two distinct archives. According to Wilson, one archive "constructs postmodernism to embrace culture and the economic forces that have constructed it according to the logic of commodification." The second archive is composed of discourses of a more analytic and descriptive nature that function to "isolate conventions, devices and techniques."[15] As Wilson has argued, it is useful to think of Carter's work as responding to the concerns of both, in that much of her work critiques commodification and examines culture from a materialist view, while her narrative strategies can be identified with postmodernist practices, especially those dealing with representation as political. In any event, Carter's representational practices are characterized by a resistance to containment in older forms and traditions. These she often will seek to hybridize, even as she undermines any move toward a new totalizing system (Hutcheon, 20). Her later works evidence another important component of postmodern fiction, for as she moves further away from realism, she becomes more interested in destabilizing the ontological planes, which—if Brian McHale is right—mark the difference between postmodernist and modernist practices.[16]

I would argue that it is Carter's fondness for parody that most strongly places her among the postmodernists. Early critics made note of the parodic element in her work but at the same time saw that quality as a mark of her failure, possibly because parody is often viewed as more of an eighteenth-century phenomenon and involves notions of satire and ridicule, which, practiced in the late twentieth century, have come to be seen as pastiche, a play with empty forms. Postmodern parody, however, is seriously political and critical, even if it possesses the characteristics of play. Nor does it imitate earlier art forms in any nostalgic way but intends, rather, to expose structures of power, undermining western assumptions about artistic originality and the consumerist preoccupations attendant upon them. Parody is most importantly deployed to show, in Hutcheon's words, "how present representations come from past ones and what ideological consequences derive from both continuity and difference" (93). In any event, as we shall see, critics tend to agree that some kind of parody is present in almost all of Carter's work—which is not to say that it takes repetitive or predictable forms.

THE STORIES

Carter produced four story collections—*Fireworks* (1974), *The Bloody Chamber* (1979), *Saints and Strangers* (1985), and *American Ghosts and Old World Wonders* (1993), and it may be for these that she is best known.[17] As mentioned earlier, the tale has been one of her preferred narrative forms, different from the short story because "it makes few pretenses at the imitation of life" and therefore "cannot betray its readers into a false knowledge of everyday experience."[18] Having affinities with pornography and dream, a vehicle for the surfacing unconscious, the tale is, for Carter, a form in which she can also explore most fully her interest in the Gothic. While the Gothic appears in much of her work, her short fiction abounds with labyrinthine spaces, menacing forests, uncanny figures, both living and inanimate (or a mix of both), and themes of incest.

Fireworks contains material begun during the period of her stay in Japan and was written between 1970 and 1973. Although this collection has not yet received the study it deserves, a couple of stories—"Flesh and the Mirror" and "The Loves of Lady Purple" have attracted attention, perhaps because in the case of the former, Carter's interest in mirrors is in evidence, while the latter displays her creative conflation of a puppet narrative with questions about female sexuality and prostitution. "Flesh and the Mirror"— one of her so-called Japanese tales—foregrounds the problematics of the mirror image that grants a woman an identity even as it assures her alienation from the immediacy of the flesh.[19] "The Loves of Lady Purple" anticipates Carter's interest in the construction of women as simulacra. Lady Purple is a puppet and the greatest achievement of the puppet master because of her lifelikeness. This ability to mimic the real finally enables her to transcend her dependency on her creator, but her freedom to return to the brothel (she is a replica of a real-life prostitute) reveals the literalizing strategies of Carter, whose point seems to be that since prostitutes are only abstractions of women constructed by male fantasy, they are never "real."[20] A third story, "Penetrating to the Heart of the Forest," introduces another of Carter's favorite topics, an Edenic space (here ironically populated by a community of ex-slaves). It is also a sanctuary for the French botanist who retreats into his prelapsarian world to become *homo silvester* but cannot prevent his two incestuous children from venturing out of Eden and assuring their fall into the condition of *homo sapiens*.

The Bloody Chamber is Carter's second and most well-known collection. Described by Rushdie as her masterwork, it has doubtlessly received the most critical attention, in part because, as "stories about fairy stories," to use Carter's words, the collection offered some suggestive feminist revisionary work.[21] Indeed, while Carter's researches into the genealogies of the Perrault and Grimm collections are serious and extensive, it was against the psychoanalytic readings of Bruno Bettelheim that Carter, in the main, directs her own, very political creative efforts. Three clusters of fairy tales in particular are of interest to her: Bluebeard, Beauty and the Beast, and Red Riding Hood. In the title story, Carter challenges Bettelheim's argument that the moral of the Bluebeard tale is that women should refrain from sexual curiosity. Therefore, in "The Bloody Chamber" Carter introduces several plot revisions. The most important change, as Robin Ann Sheets had noted, is Carter's construction of her Bluebeard figure as a pornography connoisseur; she also chooses to have the young woman narrate her own story, she introduces an unusual second husband, and she inserts the mother into the role of rescuer.[22]

The two "Beauty and the Beast" stories show Carter engaging in a double revisioning process. "The Courtship of Mr. Lyon" operates as what Sylvia Bryant describes as an "overt expose" of contrived gender differences, while a second tale, "The Tiger's Bride," narrated this time by the "heroine," explores the ways that commodification and exchange operate as the tale's subtext.[23] While Bettelheim reads these tales (in opposition to Bluebeard) as tales of true love that help to resolve childhood fears about sexuality, Carter's version shows the Beast as benign, not when he dons his human mask, but when stripped of it, while the narrator, thanks to the ministrations of the wolf, uncovers beneath her skin "a nascent patina of shining hairs."[24]

Carter's three Red Riding Hood tales show a similar progression. "The Werewolf" reveals the grandmother and the wolf to be one; in "The Company of Wolves" a kind of mating ceremony provides the denouement. "Wolf Alice," on the other hand, may be, as Ellen Cronan Rose has argued, Carter's own. Here the wolf child exists in her unmediated flesh until her encounter with her own mirror image.[25]

The stories of the final two collections are as much alike as they are different from the stories of *The Bloody Chamber*. Rushdie sees in these collections Carter's abandonment of the fantasy world for the real, where an interest in portraiture dominates (xiii). While *Saints and Strangers* does contain stories with historical people—Lizzie Borden, Edgar Allan Poe, and Jeanne Duval, the mistress of Baudelaire—these stories are also notable for their metafictional character. For example, in a story from *American Ghosts and Old World Wonders* entitled "John Ford's '*Tis a Pity She's a Whore*," Carter juxtaposes a western incest narrative as it might have been filmed by American director John Ford, against John Ford's 1683 drama. Carter also rewrites the captivity narrative, creating, in "Our Lady of the Massacre," a speaker who is no maiden but instead an English prostitute who finds her life among the Indians a civilizing experience, while her rescue by the Puritan "community of Saints" is characterized both by violence and intolerance.

Carter's politics is evident in these stories; Puritan materialism is one of her targets in "The Fall River Ax Murders" and in a later story, "The Ghost Ships: A Christmas Story," where she does a satirical exegesis on the fate of the three Christmas ships of the well-known carol and the vicissitudes of their perilous transatlantic journey to New England. "Black Venus" indicts not only Baudelaire for his manipulative reduction of this Francophone Caribbean woman to Muse but also the colonialist imprint on the art, literature, and sciences of Baudelaire's time that had both coded and recoded the "colonized territory of the female body" as black and diseased (Hutcheons, 149). Still, Carter's stories are complex and highly allusive and these last two collections are especially in need of much fuller study.

THE SIXTIES NOVELS

Her early novels may have introduced, in the words of Punter, "an evolution of a single albeit elaborate image stock and a set of variations on a theme," yet while these novels have something of the same texture, and engage several stylistic and thematic concerns that will be more fully explored in her later work, they only hint at the imaginative directions that her later work will take.

The novels that can be usefully grouped together are the five that were written in the sixties—*Shadow Dance* (1966), *The Magic Toyshop* (1967), *Several Perceptions* (1968), *Heroes and Villains* (1969), and *Love* (written in 1969, but published in 1971). They reveal Carter's interest in the world of surfaces, in the constellation of power relations centered on sexuality, and in the hippie culture that has impacted upon appearance, art, and sexuality. While each novel ventures in a somewhat different direction, each shares a similar adherence to realism. All are set in recognizable South London and Bristol environs. Each depicts the gritty, sometimes sinister underside of the bohemian culture of the sixties with all of its flaunted sexual freedom and narcissism—and violence.

Though not all critics would view them as realistic, they remain grounded in realities of sixties urban living, even though—and this constitutes their second shared characteristic—that reality is strongly refracted through the lens of the Gothic. Indeed, the Gothic texture of these novels has perhaps been their most notable quality, although the emphasis on Gothic material is different. While the usual Gothic elements are present—labyrinthine spaces, mirror imagery, vulnerable and virginal women, male predators—the emphasis in the novels is more on sexual themes involving incest and rape.

While critics like Leslie Fiedler and Norman Holland have read Gothic material against an Oedipal plot that focused on the male hero-villain, and

Gothic spaces as maternal and potentially incestuous, Claire Kahane, noting the popularity of the Gothic among female readers (and writers), saw the need to examine more fully the heroine. She argues that the Oedipal plot is more of a "surface convention," whereas what is actually in the center is the "spectral presence of the dead-undead mother, archaic and all encompassing; a ghost signifying the problematics of femininity which the heroine must confront."[26] All these paradigms are relevant to Carter's Gothic fictions, yet none seems to satisfactorily describe her practices.

For example, it is difficult to argue that Carter is following more recent feminist revisionary Gothic conventions or that in the early sixties she was particularly conscious of any feminist revaluation of Gothic. Only two of these novels have female protagonists—*The Magic Toyshop* and *Heroes and Villains*—and it is questionable whether these characters fit Kahane's more proactive figures of female desire and aggressivity, although it certainly is true that mothers are absent in both.[27] Lorna Sage describes Carter's basic plot for these novels as follows: "a middle class virgin bewitched and appalled by the fictions of femininity, falls in love with a working class boy, a dandified, dressed up tramp who's meant to make sense of her desires but doesn't."[28] Indeed, both Melanie in *Magic Toyshop* and Marianne in *Heroes and Villains* are from affluent middle-class backgrounds. Melanie can be seen as a Gothic heroine, who, having been orphaned at the age of 15, is forced to move from her comfortable country surroundings to a South London apartment of her dour and abusive uncle. Here Gothic space becomes related to class, and Melanie, forced to live in "melancholy, down-on-its-luck South London" in a seedy apartment over the puppet master's shop, is more threatened by the "ferocious, unwashed animal reek" of her cousin Finn and the "poverty-stricken slum smell" of the household than by the truly dangerous uncle who terrorizes it (*MT,* 36). Here Carter's more parodic use of the Gothic is deliberately introduced into a historically and culturally specific context in order to better expose power relations within the family. Gothic exaggeration of the usually hidden violence of father-daughter relations in a patriarchal context may be a less obvious Gothic feature, but when it is combined, as it so often will be in Carter's work, with a rewriting of long-standing and hence anachronistic narratives of male desire, the effect is often one of useful disorientation.

The second novel with a female protagonist is *Heroes and Villains*, a dystopic novel that takes place in some future where Professors exist in a state of siege while the world around them swarms with Barbarians and Out People. Gothic spaces in this postapocalyptic time are represented by the abandoned and ruined houses of the rich, which serve as temporary housing for the Barbarians. Marianne, whom Sage describes as one of Carter's heroines with "brittle mirrored personalities," is nevertheless a bit more resilient than Melanie (178). As a Professor's child, and of necessity separated from the world of the Barbarians, Marianne spends her girlhood looking down on the violence with "sharp cold eyes" (*HV,* 1). Her later experience among them also involves an immersion in the materiality and violence of survival. It would seem, then, that Carter finds the Gothic useful for critiquing bourgeois culture.

The other three novels contain male protagonists and in general present a picture of victimized women. Both *Shadow Dance* and *Love* are similar in that they center on erotic triangles that suggest not only Carter's ambivalence toward female characters but also her interest in another less obvious feature of Gothic, namely, its concern with male homosocial desire. As Eve Kosofsky Sedgwick has noted, the Gothic novel "was the first novelistic form to have close, relatively visible links to male homosexuality."[29] Hence the male protagonists in these novels appear sensitive and suffering, involved only peripherally and unsuccessfully with women but bonded with flamboyant, dandified, hypermasculine alter egos whose penchant for violence masks their own sexually ambiguous desires. In these works Carter seems intent on exploring male bonding, gender asymmetry and its links to violence against women within an exchange-of-women framework that has been explored largely by Claude Levi-Strauss and Gayle Rubin.

Her first novel, *Shadow Dance,* offers the most violent of these erotic triangles. Morris, although shocked by Honeybuzzard's "flamboyant and ambiguous beauty," is also described watching his "Fancy Dress Honey" dance "with great pleasure."[30] Morris's wife hardly appears on the scene at all, and the plot focuses instead on the anguish Morris experiences over the brutally disfigured girlfriend Ghislaine, who bears a long facial scar from the knife-wielding Honeybuzzard. The fact that Morris feels less complicity in this act than he does a horror of Ghislaine is obvious when Honeybuzzard playfully bites him in the throat one night and Morris imagines him to be Ghislaine. In *Sadeian Woman* (1979), Carter writes fully on women and wounding, arguing that erotic violence perpetrated by males awakens "the memory of the social fiction of the female wound, the bleeding scar left by her castration, which is a psychic fiction . . . deeply at the heart of Western culture" (*SW,* 23).

The underlying exchange-of-women structure is often literalized in both *Love* and *Shadow Dance.* Ghislaine is not the only woman the two men share; later in the novel Morris sleeps with another of Honeybuzzard's girlfriends and considers the act "something of an achievement" (*SD,* 150). In *Love,* the erotic triangle involves two brothers—the sensitive Lee and his darker, sartorial knife-wielding brother, Buzz. In this novel the sharing of Annabel has an additional element of incest, but the homosexuality of the two brothers is also strongly suggested. For example, Lee decides to sleep with Annabel only after he mistakes her for Buzz.[31] Here Carter seems to be interested in the relationship of maleness to costuming. Even Lee wears his attractiveness as a costume, and decked out in his "wardrobe of smiles," appears more benign than he actually is.[32]

THE NOVELS OF THE SEVENTIES:
CARTER'S CRITIQUE OF MYTH, PORNOGRAPHY, AND FILM

It is interesting that in her 1987 afterword to *Love,* written to suggest "how I feel about it after nearly twenty years," Carter admits instead her awareness of the novel's "almost sinister feat of male impersonation" and "its icy treatment of the mad girl" (*L,* 113). Certainly Carter's feminism developed over time, as she has admitted in many interviews and in her writings. "Growing into feminism," she says, "was part of the process of maturing."[33] If Carter's representation of women in the early novels is more susceptible to re-presenting stereotypes than in deconstructing them, it is a more complex and sophisticated feminism that emerges in the novels of the late seventies. These works have attracted considerable scholarly attention—and some controversy. I am thinking of *The Infernal Desire Machines of Doctor Hoffman, The Passion of New Eve* (1977), and especially *The Sadeian Woman.*

Desire Machines was in many ways a departure from the early novels. It is the first of her picaresque works, an elaborate, surreal journey taken by Desiderio, who is also the narrator. It has been read as an allegory of the unconscious, a Manichean struggle between Apollonian and Dionysian modes of consciousness, a battle between pleasure and reality principles, a narrativization of epistemological struggles that evoke such sixties "fathers of liberation" as Wilhelm Reich, Norman O. Brown, and Herbert Marceuse.[34] It is heavily intertextual, most clearly evoking, in one chapter, *Gulliver's Travels.* Here Carter recasts Swift's Houyhnhnms as centaurs whose puritanical society lives by a group of rites and mythologies that are wicked parodies of Judeo-Christian religious practices.

Some critics objected to Carter's predilection for sexual violence and were puzzled by her use of a male narrator. Other, more recent discussions have perhaps better understood Carter's purposes as having to do with a nonessentialized and constructed subject. *Desire Machines* does appear to reflect Carter's developing interest in gender issues. Sally Robinson argues that Carter's use of a male narrator is a function of mimicry deployed by Carter to politicize desire in order to expose its complicitous relationship with dominance; thus the "overt" masculinity of the narrative serves to undermine rather than enhance reader identification.[35]

Reader identification was put to an even more severe test in *The Passion of New Eve* once readers discovered that no "newly born woman"—certainly no *woman* named Eve—was to be found in the text.[36] For this novel, Carter has once again chosen to work with the picaresque form and a first-person male narrator, but in this work her interest in the fluidity of gender categories took her in quite a different direction. As Carter has noted in more than one interview, *Eve* was largely misunderstood. Rather than a feminist tract, she explains, she had embarked upon a "quite careful and elaborate discussion of femininity as commodity."[37] In any event, the novel contains as its central characters a narrator named Evelyn—later reconstructed as a woman—and a Hollywood film idol from Evelyn's boyhood named Tristessa—later revealed to be a man. What was also prominent in the novel were the ever proliferating evocations of mythic material, especially that related to the mother goddess. Set in some futuristic America, the novel consists of three definable geographic spaces, all of which are evoked in both realistic and archetypal terms.

Some critics understood Carter to be debating the theories of androgyny that were taking place in some feminist circles at the time, while others were dubious about Carter's success in critiquing narratives of sexual domination and submission and felt that she remained entrapped within them, or that she failed to render up a radical vision of a truly "newly born woman." Despite the essentialist assumptions that surface in these critiques, Carter's interest in the construction of gender is very creatively engaged in this text and tends to render problematic the definitions of androgyny and transsexuality. The very lack of any clarification of such identity categories makes *New Eve* less a "model for a kind of eroticism," to use Suleiman's words, than a kind of postmodernist and feminist fictional strategy that is based on "the multiplication of narrative possibilities rather than on their outright refusal" (Suleiman, 139). The multiplication of such possibilities is replicated in the number of identity categories that the text generates.

To that end, the construction of a character with the sexually ambiguous name of Evelyn gives Carter the opportunity to explore the relationship between the body as sexed and the body as gendered. While it might be agreed that Evelyn is rendered a transsexual in the course of the narrative, critics usually tend to describe him as castrated. Jean Wyatt has argued that castration is the point: "Carter seems to be giving body to Freud's myth of woman as a castrated man—and so reinforcing it—until it becomes evident that Eve, the perfect woman, is constituted according to the specifications of male desire."[38] While I agree that Carter has indeed embarked on another of her arguments with Freud, I also wonder if she may have intended to play on the reader's susceptibility to the myth of woman's castration, and having exposed its mythic status, forced us to alter our perceptions about whether Evelyn's surgery is an amputation or addition. Certainly, we see an Evelyn that has been reconstructed, since his surgery—a combination of cosmetic reconstruction and organ transplant—has added to his body some previously missing parts—breasts, a clitoris, a uterus. Also, when practiced on women, reconstructive surgery is never viewed as a taking away. For Evelyn, however, a castration has occurred and the absence of a penis signals only loss, "a void, a noisy silence."[39] *The Passion of New Eve* may be Carter's most subversive novel, an attempt to textualize the truly indeterminate and fluctuating directions of gender construction.

It was *Sadeian Woman,* (subtitled *An Exercise in Cultural History* in the British edition) that proved the most controversial work of this period, at least with early critics. For one thing, its publication coincided with the early pornography debates, which were going on in the United States.[40] Attacks on Carter's work derived from feminists that saw porn as violent and inevitably aggressive because it represented male sexuality. Sheets has countered that some antipornography feminists tend to conflate pornography with "reality" and has suggested that the subject of pornography is better approached through the work of feminist film theorists who have been engaged in discussions of representation and spectatorship (639).

The Sadeian Woman was, in any event, a work that was easy to misunderstand, especially since discussion focused primarily on Carter's description of a kind of "moral pornographer" who, she writes, "might use pornography as a critique of current relations between the sexes."[41] Unfortunately, the term "moral pornographer" became bandied about as the sum and substance of the text, and some critics claimed to see Carter's "fascination" with Sade and her attraction to violent eroticism as deeply troubling. I would argue that to focus on Carter's speculation on the function of the "moral pornographer" is to neglect the context of this discussion, since it is clear from the rest of Carter's "Polemical Preface" that she is under no illusion about pornographic practices as dangerous to women. Her "fascination" with Sade derives from her view of him as a "monstrous, and daunting cultural edifice" (*SW,* 37) whose influence is still with us—especially in the filmic production of the Hollywood iconography—since Sade's heroine, the virtuous and totally victimized Justine, becomes for Carter "the prototype of two centuries of women" and "the start of a kind of self-regarding female masochism" (*SW,* 57).

"Pornography," Carter writes, "must always have the false simplicity of fable," which creates of the flesh an abstraction and "reduces the actors in the sexual drama to instruments of pure function, so the pursuit of pleasure becomes in itself a metaphysical quest" (*SW,* 16). I would argue that *Sadeian Women* is a good deal more than a lapse of good taste, a reinscription of patriarchy, or a muddled feminist manifesto inimical to feminist interests. I think that it remains instead a useful guide to some of Carter's overriding feminist and political concerns, especially as they manifest themselves in the works of this period. *Sadeian Woman* introduces three areas that seem especially important to Carter's work: myth, pornography, and film. While issues involving pornography have remained in the foreground of discussion, Carter's critique of myth offers us a context for her interest in pornography, while pornography itself is useful for what it can tell us about gender and social fictions in the present time, including those generated by film. There is little doubt about the interrelatedness of the three areas in *Sadeian Women;* Carter describes pornographic fiction and photography as the "pure forms of sexual fiction, of the fiction *of* sex" (*SW,* 17).

Carter is also quick to assert the connection of pornography to myth, and writes in her preface that since "all pornography derives directly from myth, it follows that its heroes and heroines, from the most gross to the most sophisticated, are mythic abstractions" (*SW,* 6). Given the number of pages that Carter spends critiquing myth, it is perhaps more useful to focus on the ways in which this critique is manifested in her fictions. As "false universals" to be found in abundance in western narratives, myths constitute a body of collective wisdom deployed in the main for the enslavement of women. Carter's antipathy for the abstractions that produce metaphysical systems is due to her belief that such systems belie the actuality of the flesh. Such false universals dull the pain of the particular, the cultural specificity that repeats a history of subjugation and economic dependence (*SW,* 5). Nor is she appeased by the supposedly empowering figures of the goddess. These she regards as "consolatory nonsense," since "mother goddesses are just as silly a notion as father gods" (*SW,* 5). In the end any such sanctifying of Woman sets up women as both victim and villain.

We can see Carter's emergent hostility to myth and the creative ways she deploys to dismantle it by comparing her use of Leda and the Swan in *The Magic Toyshop* and *Nights at the Circus.* In the earlier novel, the myth is written into a puppet show and Carter, while claiming to be ignorant of what she was about, nevertheless made the swan "an artificial construct, a puppet and somebody, a man, was pulling the strings."[42] However her attack on this myth is more sophisticated than she allows. First, Phillip, the puppet master and uncle of Melanie (who is to play Leda), is disappointed in the emergent breasts of Melanie, because he has conceived of Leda as a "little girl." Then, in the actual enactment of the myth, Melanie finds herself under attack, not by the "wild phallic bird of her imaginings" but by what she labels "a grotesque parody" (*MT,* 143). What Melanie does see in very concise detail is the swan as *structure*—as plywood, glued-on feathers, a rubber neck, eyes of black glass, head and beak carved of wood, wings that are "arched struts" covered with paper. Yet the rape becomes a real and terrifying event to her. Melanie's total awareness of the constructed nature of the bird does not guarantee her escape from the puppeteer's plot, just as narratives of erotic violence as "the convulsive form of the active, male principle" (*SW,* 22) can still lead to victimization, even when the victim sees the plot for what it is.

In *Nights at the Circus* Fevvers is allowed to construct her own myth, using the birth of Helen of Troy as her own originary narrative. Declaring herself "hatched," Fevvers has based her own myth of origins on a Titian rendering of Leda and the Swan that hangs above the brothel fireplace. This and other "classical" artworks are owned by Ma Nelson, the whorehouse madame, and although they are displayed on her walls as payment for services rendered, their representations have, in effect, been subverted, becoming unreadable over time, "so crusted with age that the painted scenes within the heavy golden frames seemed full of the honey of ancient sunlight" that has "crystalized to form a sweet scab" (*NC,* 28). Declaring that father time's "invisible hand must be respected at all costs," Ma Nelson undermines the power of the abstracting fictions of western art by giving "father time" his literal due and subordinating him to process.

The Passion of New Eve is Carter's most extended critique of myth. Described by Carter as "anti-mythic," the novel is constructed largely out of myths that get a drastic literalization in Evelyn's quest narrative. In the section where Evelyn finds himself in the gynocratic society of Beulah, Carter offers up a Great Mother that seems blatantly overcoded. This configuration combines not only a chthonic deity, a many breasted Artemis, and a Cybellian priestess but also goes by the name of every goddess to be found from the Ancient Near East to Northern Europe and the British Isles. Evelyn's description of Mother as having a head "as big and as black as Marx's head in Highgate Cemetery," a beard "like Queen Hatsheput," and "breasted like a sow" (*E,* 59) not only parodies celebratory studies of the goddess but also reveals the role of Evelyn's own cultural and educational background in the construction of his encounter. When this bizarre being declares to the now castrated Evelyn, "I am the Great Parricide, I am the Castratrix of the Phallocentric Universe, I am Mama, Mama, Mama!" it becomes clear that Carter is taking a strongly comedic tack in this work (*E,* 67).

If Carter deuniversalizes myth by parodying its pretenses to discursive power, she also takes on the secondary production of myth, namely, pornography. Indeed, it might be argued that *Desire Machines* is her most pornographic novel, or to put it another way, the novel in which she appears most interested in reconstituting pornography. While critics have debated on just how effectively she dismantles this rather daunting and troublesome subject, it is useful to read this work through the lens of the common postmodernist technique of denaturalization.

Arguing against the supposition that pornography responds to human nature, that sex is "an external fact, one as immutable as the weather," Carter reconstructs the fictions of Sade and his libertines in such a manner that their "unnaturalness" is exposed (*SW,* 3–4). Thus in the section of *Desire Machines* entitled "The Erotic Traveller," Carter depicts a typical Sadeian libertine. Like all Sade's protagonists who are tyrannical statesmen, princes, and popes, the Count's brutal and egomaniacal nature is linked always to his sexuality (*SW,* 26). Sade's "absolutely sexualized view of the world" is represented in the Count's obsessive journey, which is undertaken without a compass but is set instead "by the fitfulness of fortune" and guided by "the inextinguishable flame of my lusts."[43] Because of the repressive nature of the society in which Sade lived, all sexuality was experienced, says Carter, as necessarily violent. Thus for the Sadeian libertine sex is always between unequals. The first sexual act we witness in *Desire Machines* is the Count's rape of his valet, an act that reflects Carter's view that Sadeian pleasure consists not only of submission but also of the "annihilation of the partner" as sufficient proof of the ego (*SW,*

142). The rape of the valet also parodies the Sadeian orgasm that is always experienced as fury because it is linked to nature, becoming, in Carter's words, "like the visitation of the gods of Voodoo, annihilating, appalling" (*SW,* 149). An astonished Desiderio describes "the count's lengthy progress towards orgasm" as follows:

> The vault of heaven above us darkened and all the time the frightful cries and atrocious blasphemies issued from the Count's throat. He whinnied like a stallion; he cursed the womb that bore him; and finally the orgasm stuck him like an epilepsy. (*DM,* 125)

The House of Anonymity perhaps best announces itself as a Sadeian intertext, a replication of the Sadeian orgy, but with its dynamics of reification no longer masked. Carter has commented that desire in porn is a function of the act, whereas the act should be a function of desire. Desire in the House of Anonymity is therefore constructed as spectacle, and even the Count and Desiderio are costumed. But in spite of their "priapic attire (they are costumed so that their genitalia are exposed but their faces hidden), they become reduced to 'undifferentiated parts,' thereby exemplifying Carter's contention that pornography reduces human sexuality to its formal elements" (*DM,* 130; *SW,* 4). Nor do the caged goddesses that are an important part of the House's spectacle create desire, as Desiderio quickly perceives. Having been reduced not only to iconography but also to an "undifferentiated essence of the *idea* of the female," these women lack all humanity and become to Desiderio "sinister, abominable, inverted mutations" (*DM,* 132).

Finally, Sadeian pornography is useful because it offers us what Carter describes as "an exercise of the lateral imagination" (*SW,* 37). What I take her to mean is that Sade is not to be read as a historical oddity but that Sadeian pornography can be placed alongside contemporary representational practices for constructive comparison. One such practice is film. Film not only confirms the relevancy of Sade but also demonstrates the tenacious influence of Sade's heroine, Justine, on Hollywood cinema. Indeed, Carter has argued that Justine is the patroness of classic Hollywood heroines, and she adds that the public sexual ideology of Hollywood that "formulated itself in the 1940s was a version of Justine's own" (*SW,* 60, 62).

Of compelling importance to Carter is the commodification of women and the fact that in filmic representation the collusion between values based on looks and the sale of sex as commodity is exposed. For Justine and her sisters, sex is never recognized as a commodity; therefore, they can never make themselves their own capital investment. Instead, that investment is inevitably taken from them so that, while remaining victims, they will also remain blameless. Since film production—what Carter refers to as "the celluloid brothel"—allows for the constant viewing of merchandise that can never be purchased, female beauty can be admired while the sexuality responsible for the beauty is denied (*SW,* 60). This is the dynamics that Carter discusses so fully in *Sadeian Woman* and explores in her fictions.

Of special interest to her are the Good Bad Girls, the femmes fatales, and the Mae West figure. The first—represented by the likes of Judy Holiday, Jayne Mansfield, and especially Marilyn Monroe ("the living image of Justine" [*SW,* 63])—are "connoisseurs of the poetry of masochism." They appear not to be aware of their sexuality, or are somewhat mystified by it, and project a fragility that disguises the underlying masochism that characterizes them and their fates. The second type—the femme fatale—is of great interest to Carter. The femme fatale is best represented by Dietrich or Garbo and derives her appeal in part from her European origins that lend her an air of sexual knowledge and transgressiveness. She is "fatal," says Carter, because "she lives her life in such a way that her freedom reveals to others their lack of liberty" (*NS,* 123).

While the masochistic Good Bad Girl is present in the construction of Tristessa in *New Eve,* it is the femme fatale upon whom this character is mostly modeled. She is interesting in part because of the severity of her facial features—her hollow cheeks, hooded eyes, and especially her androgynous quality, which also extends to her tendency to appear in drag (*SW,* 121; *NS,* 91). Carter also notes that because the femme fatale appears today as a somewhat anachronistic figure, she is better played by a female impersonator. Clearly the figure of Tristessa evolved from these concerns.

The importance of the scopic regime to *New Eve* and to Carter's argument regarding the power of the image not only to mediate but also to govern the subject's trajectory of desire is introduced in the opening lines of the novel where Evelyn, addressing his thoughts to his beloved film idol, describes having sex with a nameless girl during a rerun of an old Tristessa film and of paying to Tristessa "little tribute of spermatoza" (*E,* 5). Evelyn's bondage to a mediated reality where flesh is subordinated to image is thus early established.

Tristessa's image appears in every subsequent geographical space in the novel. For example Evelyn's pursuit of Leilah in the "Siege of Harlem" section comes to an end when his "prey" stands beneath the lighted theater portico between a life-sized face of Tristessa on one side and a "red painted column" on the other. This tableau includes Leilah's offering of her "crotchless knickers" to the violently desirous Evelyn. The mix of image and fetishistic reassurances is not accidental. Tristessa's image is later evoked as part of the altered Evelyn's programming in Beulah, where the women are aware of her power to represent "every kitsch excess of the mode of femininity" (*E,* 71).

Even in Zero's patriarchal space Tristessa's image—this time a large poster of the idol wearing "the bloody nightdress of Madeline Usher"—serves as an object of Zero's desecration, a text upon which Zero writes his own countering discourse (*E,* 90). Particularly threatening to Zero as the cause of his infertility, she is actually demonized, not for her "femaleness" but for an imagined lesbianism. Zero becomes an interesting configuration of the male imaginary since, besides being a jealous and brutal misogynist, he sports a missing eye and amputated limb. It is these markers of castration that he needs to displace onto women. Carter's intertextual joke involves not only her parody of *The Story of O* but her comic literalization of her own remark that, in the language of pornography, "between [the woman's] legs lies nothing but zero" (*SW,* 4).

Carter's third film type—the Mae West figure—is clearly one that has appealed to her, and she has written at some length about the subversive nature of West's performance. In Carter's view, Mae West attained a degree of explicitly sexualized freedom because she was middle-aged. Unlike Justine and her sisters, Mae West was happy to be in charge of herself as a business, writing her own scripts and inventing her own dramatic persona. She was able to effect what Carter describes as a "double bluff"—remaining sexually free, even as she masqueraded as a dangerous and slightly castrating presence. She managed to become, in other words, a skillful female impersonator. Says Carter, "she made her own predatoriness a joke and concealed its power while simultaneously exploiting it" (*SW,* 61). We know, of course, that Mae West was the model for Fevvers, who, like her predecessor, is able to scheme for "libidinal gratification, even while adding up her bank accounts" (*SW,* 61). By the time Carter is writing her final novels—*Nights at the Circus* and *Wise Children*—film as well as spectacle and masquerade have become important thematic concerns.

THE LAST NOVELS: SPECTACLE AND MASQUERADE, ORGASMIC FINALES

In her final novel, *Wise Children,* Carter offers up a remarkable theatrical family comprised of two branches—the Hazards and the Chances. As might be expected, their names, although seemingly synonymous, carry different connotations, with "Hazard" suggesting, in more elegant diction, contingency with an element of danger, and "Chance," in a more commonplace discourse, signifying luck and happenstance. The Hazards are linked to Shakespeare, and especially Shakespearean tragedy, while the Chance sisters are chorus girls who thrive in a comedic world where Shakespeare, if performed at all, is burlesqued. "The Hazards would always upstage us," Dora observes, "tragedy, eternally more class than comedy."[44]

Their names also hint at the indeterminacy of bloodlines and thus the fictions of patrilineage, as Carter, using plots of Shakespearean comedy (especially those of *A Midsummer Night's Dream, Twelfth Night,* and *As You Like It*) as grist for her irreverent creativity, has another go at Freud and the oedipalized subject, or, in this instance, the oedipalized family. The motif of incest is everywhere, but Carter has reinvented the Oedipal plot as comedy. If the incestuous coupling of Oedipus is responsible for the abolition of difference—of the very collaspe of "culture" back into "nature"—Carter's revisionary plot is willing to risk such dangers in the celebration of fertility. Oedipus, through accident and ignorance, may have connected with Jocasta, but the Hazards are less innocent and also much luckier.

For example, Melchior and Peregrine Hazard, the eldest of several sets of twins that proliferate in this novel, get around—at least around each other's sexual partners—so that Melchior's chance relationship with a nameless Brixton girl results in the birth of Dora and Nora, who, unclaimed by their biological father, Melchior, are instead "fathered" by Peregrine. Lady A, Melchior's first wife, gives birth to another set of twins named Saskia and Imogen, whose biological father is not Melchior but Peregrine. Nora and Dora grow up infatuated with their absent but famous father, while Saskia proceeds to have an affair with the son of Melchior's third wife. Saskia is not only twice the age of Tristram but also his half sister, although, since Tristram really is Melchior's biological son and she is really the biological daughter of Peregrine, she is not really guilty of incest. And so on, until the final, celebratory coupling of the 75-year-old Dora with her beloved uncle Peregrine on the eve of his and Melchior's 100th birthday.

Of some significance, I think, are the similarities between Fevvers and Dora Chance. As Beth Boehm has noted, Carter seems to have resurrected both the voice and narrative style of her earlier heroine.[45] Indeed, both novels depict female subjects whose control over their own narratives seems linked to their ability to enunciate desire, to live as sexual beings beyond the binding conventions of patriarchal plots. Their successes, however, seem to derive from the rather paradoxical fact that they have careers as performers. Because spectatorial desire is linked with fetishism and voyeurism, the structure of the look is argued to be masculine. For women to "make spectacles of themselves" is therefore dangerous, as Russo has argued, liable to enact boundary violations, to invite fear, contempt, and an acknowledgement of the female body as a possible "site of dangerous excess" (67). Yet like Mae West, both Fevvers and the Chance sisters manage as spectacles because, like her, they take part in the production process.

To understand the extent of Carter's subversive strategies, both Russo and Robinson have turned to theories of masquerade that have their beginnings in the 1929 article by Joan Rivere, who argued that femininity itself was a performance, a strategy on the part of some women to disguise their "possession of masculinity."[46] More recently, Mary Ann Doane has argued for masquerade as a distancing strategy, whereby the female subject separates herself from the conflation of "femininity as presence" with a surface image of Woman that tended to leave the subject trapped within the look (Doane, 25). In so doing she is able to defamiliarize female iconography.

Carter's insistence on the nature of femininity as impersonation echoes some of these arguments, but in her final novel she seems to call upon perfor-

mative strategies to undermine not only gender but also the fiction of relationships presumably grounded in biology. Thus, her last two novels reveal a
reverence for comedy that is consistent with her materialist view of the world.
For the comic rhythm acknowledges the human condition as all there is and,
by favoring cyclical rhythms over linear progression, comedy also privileges
mortality over transcendency, generational continuity over the individual
myths of origin and ascent. Finally, whereas tragedy is structured within
time, comedy escapes it, at least momentarily.

For Carter, this ability to stave off death is part of the function of the
writer. In the introduction to her final collection of essays, *Expletives Deleted,*
she outlines the relationship of time to the writer as follows:

> All writers are inventing a kind of imitation time when they invent the time in
> which a story unfolds, and they are playing a complicated game with our time,
> the reader's time, the time it takes to read a story. A good writer can make you
> believe that time stands still.[47]

Yet she continues, the end of all narrative, "even if the writer forebears to
mention it, is death. . . . we travel along the thread of narrative like high-wire
artists. That is our life" (*ED,* 2).

Aware as she must have been in these last years of her own impending
death, Carter the writer opted to keep her readers—and possibly herself—
atop the high wire. Comedy was her genre of choice, but she also knew that
at the heart of comedy, the mover of the comic rhythm, was sexuality. Thus,
to conclude these remarks, I would like to turn to what I will call the orgas-
mic finales of these novels, all the sexual couplings that are intended to celebrate not the resolution of the story but the possible beginnings of the many
new ones.

"The erotic clock halts all clocks," muses Evelyn, now Eve, during his
erotic encounter with Tristessa in the final section of *New Eve* (148). But the
labels of "transsexual" and "transvestite" have been rendered not only meaningless but silent before "the mute speech of flesh." At this point, although
still haunted by "fragments of old movies playing like summer lightening on
the lucid planes of [Tristessa's] face," Eve recognizes these fragments for what
they are—"a shadow show" (*E,* 149). Meanwhile, in lovemaking that defies
gendering, "the glass woman" that was Tristessa is, through Eve's active role,
broken into fragments, which then "recomposed themselves into a man who
overwhelmed me" (*E,* 149).

In *Nights,* Fevvers imagines time to be running out and herself to be
diminishing until she happens upon the newly "hatched" Walser. In making
love on the Shaman's brass bed just at the midnight hour that marks the
beginning of the new century, their coming together seems to inaugurate
time, to initiate a new cyle. Fevvers's carnivalesque laughter seems to be the
dominant force in this instance, first causing the "tin ornaments of the tree

outside the god-hut to shake and tinkle," and finally becoming a "spiralling tornado that covers the globe, as if in spontaneous response to the giant comedy that endlessly unfolded beneath it, until everything that lived and breathed, everywhere, was laughing" (*NC,* 295).

The lovemaking of Dora and Peregrine also marks and is marked by a special time. Occurring during the 100th birthday of the Hazard brothers— and on Dora's own 75th—it is directly a stay against death. Peregrine, says Dora, is "not the love of my life but all the loves of my life at once, the curtain call of my career as lover" (*WC,* 295). Although less cosmic in its effects than the scene that inspires Fevvers's laughter, Dora and Peregrine's lovemaking becomes the center of the comic celebration going on downstairs—literally. Because the chandelier over which their lovemaking occurs is also the center of the ballroom in which the celebration continues, the bouncing bed of the two antiquarians generates its own fireworks. While at first the tinkling glass of the chandelier serves as an accompaniment to the music, things soon get out of control until "the tiers of glass began to sway from side to side, slopping hot wax on the dancers below, first slowly, then with a more and more determined rhythm until they shook like Josephine Baker's bottom" (*WC,* 220). Since the guests are hardly oblivious to the goings-on upstairs, it would seem that both Dora and Peregrine remain true to their performative selves, becoming the main players in a fertility ritual.

The critics whose articles appear in the following pages have already lent supporting voices to these introductory pages. While some of their work appeared in the 1980s, most has been published in the last several years, suggesting that much remains to be done. Certainly more study is needed on the earlier novels, all the stories, and Carter's most recent novel, *Wise Children.* Contemplating the loss of this gifted writer, I take some comfort in knowing that, in the study of her work, we are only at the beginning.

Notes

1. Salman Rushdie, introduction to *Burning Your Boats: The Collected Short Stories,* by Angela Carter (London: Chatto and Windus, 1995; New York: Henry Holt, 1996), xiv; hereafter cited in text.

2. Angela Carter, *Nights at the Circus* (London: Chatto and Windus, 1984; New York: Penguin, 1985), 35; hereafter cited in the text as *NC.*

3. Mikhail Bakhtin, *Rabelais and His World,* trans. Helene Iswolsky (1965; Bloomington: Indiana University Press, 1984), 316–17. Bakhtin writes, "the artistic logic of the grotesque image ignores the closed, smooth, and impenetrable surface of the body and retains only its excrescences . . . and orifices" (317–18).

4. Mary Russo, *The Female Grotesque: Risk, Excess and Modernity* (New York: Routledge, 1994), 53–70. Russo's work on the female grotesque is a useful counter to the views of the carnivalesque as both liberating and subversive. Russo notes that Bakhtin seems unaware that his

use of the hag as the most compelling representation of the grotesque body raises troubling issues about the role of gender in carnivalization.

5.   Carter concludes her "Polemical Preface" as follows:

> And give the old monster his due; let us introduce him with an exhilarating burst of rhetoric:

> Charming sex, you will be free: just as men do, you shall enjoy all the pleasures that Nature makes your duty, do not withhold yourselves from one. Must the more divine half of mankind be kept in chains by the others? Ah, break those bonds: nature wills it. (*The Sadeian Woman and the Ideology of Pornography* [New York: Pantheon 1979; New York: Harper Colophon, 1980], 37; hereafter cited in the text as *SW.*)

6.   Robert Clark, "Angela Carter's Desire Machine," *Women's Studies* 14 (1987): 158.

7.   Elaine Jordan, "Enthrallment: Angela Carter's Fictions," in *Plotting Change: Contemporary Women's Fiction,* ed. Linda Anderson (London and Melbourne: Edward Arnold, 1990), 27; hereafter cited in text.

8.   John Haffenden, *Novelists in Interview* (London and New York: Methuen, 1985), 87, hereafter cited in text.

9.   Angela Carter, "Interview: Angela Carter," interview by Kerryn Goldsworthy, *Meanjin Quarterly* 44, no. 1 (1985): 12.

10.   David Punter, "Essential Imaginings: The Novels of Angela Carter and Russell Hoban," in *The British and Irish Novel since 1960,* ed. James Acheson (New York: St. Martin's Press, 1991), 142.

11.   Angela Carter, *Expletives Deleted: Selected Watings* (London: Chetto and Windus, 1992; New York: Vintage, 1993), 73; hereafter cited in the text as *ED.*

12.   Haffenden, *Novelists in Interview,* 92. See also Susan Rubin Suleiman, *Subversive Intent: Gender, Politics, and the Avant-Garde* (Cambridge and London: Harvard University Press, 1990), 240, n. 47; hereafter cited in text. Suleiman makes a strong case for the influence of the surrealists on Carter's work, suggesting that Carter's "affinities with Surrealism are quite clear" but are in need of more detailed study. She does suggest some interesting links between Robert Desnos and Carter's borrowings. Max Ernst, whom Suleiman argues to be the "greatest and most consistent Surrealist practitioner of collage as an art form," is also admired by Carter, who describes him as "the most literary of painters" (*ED,* 71).

13.   In her interview with Haffenden she speaks of "books about books" as "fun but frivolous" (79).

14.   Linda Hutcheon, *The Politics of Postmodernism* (London and New York: Routledge, 1989), 13; hereafter cited in text. Hutcheon also notes that Carter's practice of treating subjects in historically and culturally specific situations leads her to construct subjectivity as a process.

15.   Robert Rawdon Wilson, "SLIP PAGE: Angela Carter, In/Out In the Postmodern Nexus," *Ariel* 20, no. 4 (October 1989): 100–103. Wilson's two archives are useful because he resists leaving them as isolated and dichotomous categories. Noting that postmodernism engages "the problem of boundaries and slipping categories: collapsing borders, fuzzy sets and unmappable zones" (104), Wilson offers an analysis of Carter's story "Lady of the House of Love" as the "nexus of intersecting archives" (105).

16.   Brian McHale, *Postmodernist Fiction* (New York and London: Methuen, 1987), 9. McHale argues that postmodernism represents a shift away from the modernist interest in epistemological questions regarding ways of knowing, to the postmodernist concern with "modes of being," with ontological pluralities and with a consequent destabilization of ontological certainties.

17.   Angela Carter, *Fireworks: Nine Stories in Various Disguises* (London: Quartet, 1974; New York: Harper Colophon, 1982); *The Bloody Chamber and Other Adult Tales* (London: Gollanez, 1979; New York: Harper Colophon, 1981); *Saints and Strangers* (London: Chatto and

Windus, 1985; New York: Penguin Books, 1987); *American Ghosts and Old World Wonders* (London: Chatto and Windus, 1993).

18.　Carter, afterword to *Fireworks*, 133.

19.　See Russo, *The Female Grotesque*, 162–64, where she discusses the protagonist of this story as a point of departure for the figure of Fevvers in *Nights at the Circus*.

20.　See Hutcheon, *The Politics of Postmodernism*, 32–33, for commentary on Carter's use of literalization in this story.

21.　Rushdie, introduction, xi; Angela Carter, "Notes from the Front Line," in *On Gender and Writing*, ed. Michelene Wandor (London: Routledge, 1983), 71; hereafter cited in text.

22.　Robin Ann Sheets, "Pornography, Fairy Tales, and Feminism: Angela Carter's 'The Bloody Chamber,' " *Journal of the History of Sexuality* 1, no. 4 (April 1991): 633–67; hereafter cited in text.

23.　Sylvia Bryant, "Re-Constructing Oedipus through 'Beauty and the Beast,' " *Criticism* 31, no. 4 (Fall 1989): 439–53.

24.　Carter, *The Bloody Chamber*, 83.

25.　Ellen Cronan Rose, "Through the Looking Glass: When Women Tell Fairy Tales," in *The Voyage In: Fictions of Female Development*, ed. Elizabeth Abel, Marianne Hirsch, and Elizabeth Langland (Hanover and London: University Press of New England, 1983), 226.

26.　Claire Kahane, "The Gothic Mirror," in *The (M)other Tongue: Essays in Feminist Psychoanalytic Interpretation*, ed. Shirley Nelson Garner, Claire Kahane, and Madelon Sprengnether (Ithaca: Cornell University Press, 1985), 336.

27.　Angela Carter, *The Magic Toyshop* (London: Heinemann, 1967; New York: Penguin, 1996); *Heroes and Villains* (London: Heinemann, 1969; New York: Penguin, 1981); hereafter cited in the text as *MT* and *HV*.

28.　Lorna Sage, *Women in the House of Fiction: Post-War Women Novelists* (New York: Routledge, 1992), 170; hereafter cited in text.

29.　Eve Kosofsky Sedgwick, *Between Men: English Literature and Male Homosocial Desire* (New York: Columbia University Press, 1985), 91.

30.　Angela Carter, *Shadow Dance* (London: Heinemann, 1966; New York: Penguin, 1996), 55, 78; hereafter cited in the text as *SD*. As partners in an antique business, their activities are also telling, since their greatest satisfaction seems to involve the nightly explorations of derelict houses, and "the pleasure of creeping through the abandoned dark, of prying and poking" (*SD*, 90).

31.　Patricia Juliana Smith, in "All You Need Is *Love*: Angela Carter's Novel of Sixties Sex and Sensibility," *Review of Contemporary Fiction* 14, no. 3 (Fall 1994): 27, writes, "it is hardly an accident that their delayed consummation finally occurs when Lee returns home to find Annabel dressed in the absent Buzz's clothes." Smith focuses on the homosexual ingredient as symptomatic of sexuality in the sixties, but I think that Carter is less interested in representing sixties sexuality than she is in the relationship between gendering and costume. In *Several Perceptions* the protagonist sleeps with his best friend's mother.

32.　Angela Carter, *Love* (London: Rupert Hart-Davis, 1971; rev. ed. New York: Penguin, 1988), 19; hereafter cited in the text as *L*.

33.　Angela Carter, "Notes from the Front Line," 69.

34.　See David Punter, "Supersessions of the Masculine," *Critique* 25, no. 4 (Summer 1984): 209–21; McHale, *Postmodernist Fiction*, 143; and Ricarda Schmidt, "The Journey of the Subject in Angela Carter's Fiction," *Textual Practice* 3, no. 1 (1989): 56–75.

35.　Sally Robinson, *Engendering the Subject: Gender and Self-Representation in Contemporary Women's Fiction* (Albany State University of New York Press, 1991), 104.

36.　See Roberta Rubenstein's useful comparison of Catherine Clemont and Helene Cixous's *la jeune nee*—a model whose mythic ancestors were the sorceress and the hysteric—with Carter's Evelyn. Rubenstein focuses in particular on the bisexual nature of the hysteric and also draws on Sandra Gilbert's work on transvestism as backgrounds for *Eve* ("Intersexions:

Gender Metamorphosis in Angela Carter's *The Passion of New Eve* and Lois Gould's *A Sea Change*," *Tulsa Studies in Women's Literature* 21, no. 1 [1993]: 103–18.)

37. Haffenden, *Novelists in Interview*, 86. Carter also says, "I created this person [Evelyn] in order to say some quite specific things about the cultural production of femininity," thus offering further evidence of her opposition to any essentialized idea of the feminine.

38. Jean Wyatt, "The Violence of Gendering: Castration Images in Angela Carter's *The Magic Toyshop, The Passion of New Eve,* and 'Peter and the Wolf,' " *Women's Studies* 25 (1996): 552. Despite the grim section of this novel, and the seriousness with which Carter conceived of the subject matter, she also describes the work as a dark comedy, a remark that has not been taken enough to heart. Evelyn's narrative is, after all, his own and is marked by the myths of gender that have constituted him. Living a literal experience of such myths has its comical side, certainly in evidence when "Eve" in a flash of insight understands he has become his own "masturbatory fantasy" and that "the cock in my head still twitched."

39. Angela Carter, *The Passion of New Eve* (New York: Harcourt Brace Jovanovich, 1977), 75; hereafter cited in text as *E.*

40. For the most helpful discussions of Carter's interest in pornography, see Robin Ann Sheets, "Pornography, Fairy Tales, and Feminism: Angela Carter's 'The Bloody Chamber,' " 633–57; also Elaine Jordan, "The Dangers of Angela Carter," in *New Feminist Discourses: Critical Essays on Theories and Texts,* ed. Isobel Armstrong (London and New York: Routledge, 1992), 119–31.

41. The quotation goes on to describe the function of such a person: "His business would be the total demystification of the flesh and the subsequent revelation, through the infinite modulations of the sexual act, of the relations of man and his kind. Such a pornographer would not be the enemy of women, perhaps because he might begin to penetrate to the heart of the contempt for women that distorts our culture even as he entered the realms of true obscenity as he describes it" (*SW,* 19–20).

42. Angela Carter, "An Interview with Angela Carter," interview by Anna Katsavos, *Review of Contemporary Fiction* 14, no. 3 (Fall 1994): 12.

43. Angela Carter, *The Infernal Desire Machines of Doctor Hoffman* (London: Rupert Hart-Davis, 1972; New York: Penguin, 1994), 123; hereafter cited in the text as *DM.*

44. Angela Carter, *Wise Children* (London: Chatto and Windus, 1991; New York: Penguin Books, 1993), 58; hereafter cited in the text as *WC.*

45. Beth A. Boehm, "*Wise Children:* Angela Carter's Swan Song," *Review of Contemporary Fiction* 14, no. 3 (Fall 1994): 84.

46. Joan Rivere, "Womanliness as a Masquerade," quoted in Mary Ann Doane, *Femmes Fatales, Feminism, Film Theory, Psychoanalysis* (New York: Routledge, 1991), 25; hereafter cited in text.

47. I am indebted to Boehm's discussion of time and death in "*Wise Children:* Angela Carter's Swan Song," 85–86.

Notes from the Front Line

Angela Carter

I've just scrapped my sixth attempt to write something for this book because my ideas get quite out of hand the minute I try to put them down on paper and I flush hares out of my brain which I then pursue, to the detriment of rational discourse. To try to say something simple—do I "situate myself politically as a writer"? Well, yes; of course. I always hope it's obvious, although I try, when I write fiction, to think on my feet—to present a number of propositions in a variety of different ways, and to leave the reader to construct her own fiction for herself from the elements of my fictions. (Reading is just as creative an activity as writing and most intellectual development depends upon new readings of old texts. I am all for putting new wine in old bottles, especially if the pressure of the new wine makes the old bottles explode.)

The Women's Movement has been of immense importance to me personally and I would regard myself as a feminist writer, because I'm a feminist in everything else and one can't compartmentalise these things in one's life. My work *has* changed a good deal in the last ten or fifteen years; it would have been rather shocking if it hadn't, since, during that time, I've progressed from youth to middle age, and, for me, growing into feminism was part of the process of maturing. But when I look at the novels I wrote in my twenties, when I was a girl, I don't see a difference in the emotional content, or even in the basic themes; I recognise myself, asking questions, sometimes finding different answers than I would do now. I also see myself expressing myself in quite different ways now that I'm capable of subjecting to critical analysis problems that, when I was younger and perhaps bruised more easily, I perceived and interpreted in a much more intuitive and also much more self-defensive way. For example, I used the strategy of charm a good deal—I attempted to disarm with charm, in a way that makes me feel affectionately indulgent and maternal to the young person I was, who wanted so much to be loved.

I'm forty-two now; therefore I was a young woman during the 1960s. There is a tendency to underplay, even to completely devalue, the experience

From *On Gender and Writing,* ed. Michelene Wandor (London: Pandora Press, 1983), 69–77.© 1983 Angela Carter. Reprinted by permission.

of the 1960s, especially for women, but towards the end of that decade there was a brief period of public philosophical awareness that occurs only very occasionally in human history; when, truly, it felt like Year One, that all that was holy was in the process of being profaned and we were attempting to grapple with the real relations between human beings. So writers like Marcuse and Adorno were as much part of my personal process of maturing into feminism as experiments with my sexual and emotional life and with various intellectual adventures in anarcho-surrealism. Furthermore, at a very unpretentious level, we were truly asking ourselves questions about the nature of reality. Most of us may not have come up with very startling answers and some of us scared ourselves good and proper and retreated into cul-de-sacs of infantile mysticism; false prophets, loonies and charlatans freely roamed the streets. But even so, I can date to that time and to some of those debates and to that sense of heightened awareness of the society around me in the summer of 1968, my own questioning of the nature of my reality as a *woman*. How that social fiction of my "femininity" was created, by means outside my control, and palmed off on me as the real thing.

This investigation of the social fictions that regulate our lives—what Blake called the "mind-forg'd manacles"—is what I've concerned myself with consciously since that time. (I realise, now, I must always have sensed that something was badly wrong with the versions of reality I was offered that took certain aspects of my being *as* a woman for granted. I smelled the rat in D. H. Lawrence pretty damn quick.) This is also the product of an absolute and committed materialism—i.e., that *this* world is all that there is, and in order to question the nature of reality one must move from a strongly grounded base in what constitutes material reality. Therefore I become mildly irritated (I'm sorry!) when people, as they sometimes do, ask me about the "mythic quality" of work I've written lately. Because I believe that all myths are products of the human mind and reflect only aspects of material human practice. I'm in the demythologising business.

I'm interested in myths—though I'm much more interested in folklore—just because they *are* extraordinary lies designed to make people unfree. (Whereas, in fact, folklore is a much more straightforward set of devices for making real life more exciting and is much easier to infiltrate with different kinds of consciousness.) I wrote one anti-mythic novel in 1977, *The Passion of New Eve*—I conceived it as a feminist tract about the social creation of femininity, amongst other things—and relaxed into folklore with a book of stories about fairy stories, *The Bloody Chamber,* in 1979. It turned out to be easier to deal with the shifting structures of reality and sexuality by using sets of shifting structures derived from orally transmitted traditional tales. Before that, I used bits and pieces from various mythologies quite casually, because they were to hand.

To return to that confused young person in her early twenties attempting to explicate the world to herself via her craft, the person in the process of becoming radically sceptical, that is, if not free, then more free than I had been. Apart from feeling a treacherous necessity to charm, especially when, however unconsciously, I was going straight for the testicles, I was, as a girl, suffering a degree of colonialisation of the mind. Especially in the journalism I was writing then, I'd—quite unconsciously—posit a male point of view as a general one. So there was an element of the male impersonator about this young person as she was finding herself. For example, in a piece about the suburb of Tokyo I lived in in 1969, I described the place thus: "It has everything a reasonable man could want. . .massage parlours and, etc." I used the phrase, "a reasonable man," quite without irony, although, reading the piece in 1982, it is, ironically, most fitting—the suburb *did* boast all the conveniences a "reasonable man" might want, although a reasonable woman might have found them inessential, to say the least.

When the piece was republished in a collection of essays last year, I wondered whether to insert "sic" in brackets after that "reasonable man" but then I thought, no; that's cheating. Because my female consciousness *was* being forged out of the contradictions of my experience as a traveller, as, indeed, some other aspects of my political consciousness were being forged. (It was a painful and enlightening experience to be regarded as a coloured person, for example; to be defined as a Caucasian before I was defined as a woman, and learning the hard way that most people on this planet are *not* Caucasian and have no reason to either love or respect Caucasians.)

By the way, I make my living as a writer and have done so most of my adult life. This is no big deal and doesn't mean I always made much money. It has always been easier for me to cut my life-style to suit my income than the other way round so it's always been possible to manage. On the rare occasions when I've attempted to work within a hierarchical framework, when you have to get to an office on time and so on, and be nice to people you don't actually like, much, things have always gone badly. Because I've almost always been self-employed, I've had very little experience, as a woman, of the hurly-burly of mixed-sex working life. I get messages through from the front line that fill me with grief and fury for my sisters out there but this is different from personal experience. For some reason, I've almost always worked with women editors at my various publishing houses, and, even when one is dealing with a woman with zero feminist consciousness, there *is* a difference. Since it was, therefore, primarily through my sexual and emotional life that I was radicalised—that I first became truly aware of the difference between how I was and how I was supposed to be, or expected to be—I found myself, as I grew older, increasingly writing about sexuality and its manifestations in human practice. And I found most of my raw material in the lumber room of the Western European imagination.

Let me explain this. It seems obvious, to an impartial observer, that Western European civilisation as we know it has just about run its course and the emergence of the Women's Movement, and all that implies, is both symptom and product of the unravelling of the culture based on Judeo-Christianity, a bit of Greek transcendentalism via the father of lies, Plato, and all the other bits and pieces. As a Japanese friend of mine once said, the spotlight of history is moving inexorably away from Europe towards Asia and Africa—societies that we (and white women can't get out of our historic complicity in colonialism, any more than the white working class can) comprehensively screwed, that owe us nothing and expect nothing whatsoever from us, which is just as well as the idea we might actually owe *them* something, like cash, doesn't go down too well, certainly in Britain. It is possible, assuming Western Europe is permitted to sidle out of the spotlight of history rather than going up with a bang, that, for the first time for a thousand years or so, its inhabitants may at last be free of their terrible history.

The sense of limitless freedom that I, as a woman, sometimes feel *is* that of a new kind of being. Because I simply could not have existed, as I am, in any other preceding time or place. I am the pure product of an advanced, industrialised, post-imperialist country in decline. But this has very little to do with my ability to work as I please, or even to earn a living from writing. At any time up to the early twentieth century, I could have told as many stories as I wanted, and made them as wonderful and subversive as I wished, had I survived the births of my children or the hazards of working-class or peasant life to a sufficient age to have amassed a repertoire of orally-transmitted fiction. If I'd been born an aristocrat, I could certainly have become very famous and honoured as an actual writer in medieval Japan, where there were many women writers of fiction and poetry, and where human ingenuity in sexual practice (unrestricted by the Judeo-Christian ethic, which they knew nothing about) certainly seems to have made sexual intercourse less onerously fruitful than in the West. I could have been a professional writer at any period since the seventeenth century in Britain or in France. But I could *not* have combined this latter with a life as a sexually active woman until the introduction of contraception, unless I had been lucky enough to have been born sterile, as George Eliot must have been. Even if I had been rich enough to afford child care, wealth was no protection against puerperal fever, and being pregnant most of the time is tiring, enfeebling, and a drain on one's physical and emotional resources. In fact, most women were *ill* most of the time until the introduction of contraception and efficient post- and ante-natal care and you need to be quite strong and healthy to write big, fat books. (You do also need to have been around.)

And, just as I write this, I recall a bizarre contradiction. For the past three centuries in Europe, women have excelled—and been honoured for it—in the performing arts. Acting, singing, dancing, playing musical instruments. For some reason, the Women's Movement tends to overlook all that, perhaps because it seems less "creative" to play somebody else's piano concerto beautifully than it is to write the thing. But it certainly takes a good deal more physical energy to perform a piano concerto than it does to write one, and weak, feeble women have been strumming away, sometimes in the last stages of pregnancy, ever since they were let up on the podium. It *is* odd. Like so many girls, I passionately wanted to be an actress when I was in my early teens and I turn this (balked, unachieved and now totally unregretted) ambition over in my mind from time to time. Why did it seem so pressing, the need to demonstrate in public a total control and transformation of roles other people had conceived? Rum, that.

However. A "new kind of being," unburdened with a past. The voluntarily sterile yet sexually active being, existing in more than a few numbers, *is* a being without precedent and, by voluntarily sterile, I don't necessarily mean permanently childless; this category includes women who are sterile not all, just most of the time, after all. I/we are not the slaves of the history that enslaved our ancestors, to quote Franz Fanon (although he meant specifically chattel slavery).

So I feel free to loot and rummage in an official past, specifically a literary past, but I like paintings and sculptures and the movies and folklore and heresies, too. This past, for me, has important decorative, ornamental functions; further, it is a vast repository of outmoded lies, where you can check out what lies used to be à la mode and find the old lies on which new lies have been based.

There are one or two lies in the lumber room about the artist, about how terrific it is to be an artist, how you've got to suffer and how artists are wise and good people and a whole lot of crap like that. I'd like to say something about that, because writing—to cite one art—is only applied linguistics and Shelley was wrong, we're *not* the unacknowledged legislators of mankind. Some women really do seem to think they will somehow feel better or be better if they get it down on paper. I don't know.

Writing—the only art form I know too much about, as practice—certainly doesn't make better people, nor do writers lead happier lives. How can I put it; although I might have liked to write poetry like Baudelaire's, I certainly would not, for one single minute, have wanted the kind of life that Baudelaire lived. His poetry is the product of terminal despair, and he was a shit, to boot. It is easy to forget that most of the great male geniuses of Western European culture have been either depraved egomaniacs or people who led the most distressing lives. (My two male literary heroes, Melville and Dostoievsky, were both rather fine human beings, as it turns out, but both of them lived so close to the edge of the existential abyss that they must often, and with good reason, have envied those who did not have enquiring minds.) I'm not saying it's great to be a cow, just keep on chewing the cud, although I have nothing against cows nor, for that matter, against enquiring minds. Only, that posthumous fame is no comfort at all and the actual satisfactions of artistic production are peculiarly lonely and solipsistic ones, while the work itself has the same compensations as those of any self-employed worker, no more.

To backtrack about the bit about "applied linguistics." Yet this, of course, is why it is so enormously important for women to write fiction *as* women—it is part of the slow process of decolonialising our language and our basic habits of thought. I really do believe this. It has nothing at all to do with being a "legislator of mankind" or anything like that; it is to do with the creation of a means of expression for an infinitely greater variety of experience than has been possible heretofore, to say things for which no language previously existed.

One last thing. So there hasn't been a female Shakespeare. Three possible answers: (a) So what. (This is the simplest and best.) (b) There hasn't been a *male* Shakespeare since Shakespeare, dammit. (c) Somewhere, Franz Fanon opines that one cannot, in reason, ask a shoeless peasant in the Upper Volta to write songs like Schubert's; the opportunity to do so has never existed. The concept is meaningless.

The novel, which is my chosen form, has existed as such in Europe for only two or three hundred years. Its existence is directly related to the history of the technology of printing and to the growth of a leisure class with time to read. Much of that leisure class was female and the novel in Western Europe—unlike the forms it has taken when it has been exported to Latin America and Africa in this century—has tended to reflect the preoccupations of the lives of leisured women. Perhaps that's why so many great European novels are about adultery, especially when written by men (*Madame Bovary, Anna Karenina*) who couldn't imagine what else women might get up to if they had a bit of free time. These are interesting historical facts, but they have nothing to do with me as a writer.

One important function of bourgeois fiction is to teach people how to behave in social circles to which they think they might be able to aspire. The novels of Jane Austen are basically fictionalised etiquette lessons and a lot of the fiction that has come directly from the Women's Movement performs, however unconsciously, the same functions. (Marilyn French's *The Women's Room* is really an instruction manual for the older woman post-graduate student.)

But all this bores me stiff, in fact, because it no longer seems particularly relevant to instruct people as to how to behave in a changing society, when one's very existence is instrumental in causing changes the results of which one can't begin to calculate. And I personally feel much more in common with certain Third World writers, both female and male, who are transforming actual fictional forms to both reflect and to precipitate changes in the way people feel about themselves—putting new wine in old bottles and, in some cases, old wine in new bottles. Using fictional forms inherited from the colonial period to create a critique of that period's consequences. Obviously, one is bound to mention Gabriel García Márquez, although he must be getting pretty bored, by this time, to be the white liberal intellectual's pet fabulist, but there are lots of others and some very fine writing, often in a quite conventionally naturalist mode—I'm thinking of the Black South African writer, Bessie Head, who has utilised forms utterly alien to her own historical culture to produce complex illuminations of sexual and political struggle.

But, look, it *is* all applied linguistics. But language is power, life and the instrument of culture, the instrument of domination and liberation.

I don't know. Ten years ago, I'd have said that I, myself, wanted to write stories that could be read by guttering candlelight in the ruins of our cities and still give pleasure, still have meaning. Perhaps I still think that.

All this is very messy and self-contradictory and not very coherent or intelligently argued. It's been amazingly difficult, trying to sort out how I feel that feminism has affected my work, because that is really saying how it has affected my life and I don't really know that because I live my life, I don't examine it. I also feel I've showed off a lot, and given mini-lectures on this and that, in a pompous and middle-aged way. Oh, hell. What I *really* like doing is writing fiction and trying to work things out *that* way.

But I hope this will do.

GENERAL

◆

The Dangers of Angela Carter

Elaine Jordan

She felt young and tough and brave, giving away her relics.
—The Magic Toyshop, p. 189.

The habit of sardonic contemplation is the hardest habit of all to break.
—The Infernal Desire Machines of Dr Hoffman, p. 201.

The wisest thing—so the fairy tale taught mankind in olden times, and teaches children to this day—is to meet the forces of the mythical world with cunning and with high spirits.
—Walter Benjamin, "The Storyteller"
(*Illuminations,* Fontana Books, 1973, p. 102).

My title sounds as though I am joining the attack which in fact I mean to counter by offering this paper—riding to the rescue of a woman writer in danger. But, every Pauline her own saviour from Perils—Angela Carter doesn't need me. What gets me going is of course what Carter's critics (Patricia Duncker, Susanne Kappeler, Robert Clark) make of me as someone who not only loves reading her work, but put it on my reading lists and in the way of my teenage daughter, and my sons. Patricia Duncker here signifies lesbian, woman-identified criticism; Clark an old-fashioned if Althusserian Marxism that wants to articulate itself with the "authentic experience of women"; Susanne Kappeler represents anti-pornographic feminism, although her larger argument in *The Pornography of Representation* knows that censorship from within the existing system is merely cosmetic: she challenges representation altogether.[1]

From *New Feminist Discourses: Critical Essays on Theories and Texts,* ed. Isobel Armstrong (London and New York: Routledge, 1992), 119–131. © 1992 Elaine Jordan. Reprinted by permission.

Reading back through Angela Carter's work from the sixties on, I had my moment of horror and cold feet at what I was letting myself in for. It's true (as she acknowledges in the Afterword to the reissued *Love*) that she started out writing as a kind-of male impersonator, with a strong streak of misogyny which is very much of the period and which, since it's directed against the taste of the proper little lady, the educated daughter of the bourgeoisie or the Welfare State, is preserved in her later writing as an assault on the confining codes of "femininity."

Does she offer a knowledge of patriarchy, Robert Clark asks, as if that were something that could be simply served up on a salver; or does she, as he thinks, simply repeat the "self-alienation" imposed by the system of power relations condensed in that term? Inevitably, her work exposes a history, a process of change which involves a series of honourable attempts to be an agent of change—part of the solution, rather than contemplating a problem of which she is part—to be boldly and honestly materialist, atheist, antityrannical and feminist. I'll please no-one, least of all her, by trying to say she's not offensive. Just about everything Carter gains in her writing is at a cost: to be immediately specific, to query the political value of speaking as a victim can be only a hairsbreadth away from blaming the victim. But that space does exist. I want to assert—although in a rather schematic form here—those things which I see as constructive, productive, positive, for women and feminism, in Angela Carter's writing:

1. The questioning throughout her work (but most quickly located in the figure of Justine in *The Sadeian Woman*), of the subject position of the virtuous victim, and its adequacy as a position from which to resist oppression. Justine's preservation of her purity and innocence in an awful world is not, Carter writes, "the continuous exercise of a moral faculty" but "a sentimental response to a world in which she always hopes her good behaviour will procure her some reward, some respite" (p. 54). This position needs, not just a sympathetic audience of other victims, but the supposition of some benign authority that can make it all better. Carter's position is a dangerous one, because given the actual situation of many women they are quite likely to speak or write against it as victims, in some degree. Nevertheless, she alerts us to the limitations of this mode of resisting the systems of power that produce suffering.

2. Conversely, she queries Juliette, the career woman of power who avoids slavery by embracing tyranny. In *The Pornography of Representation* Susanne Kappeler assumes that Angela Carter is offering Juliette as a model, and ignoring her complicity with a system that oppresses women. Carter is in fact stating a position like Kappeler's: "A free woman in an unfree society will be a monster" (*The Sadeian Woman*, p. 27). Kappeler ignores this solidarity, as she ignores Carter's final rubbishing of Sade, once she's used his writing as a springboard for whatever she can get from it for women—that is, an analysis

of the virtuous victim and the woman of power, as well as Sade's liberating refusal to consider sexual pleasure as secondary to the business of reproduction. Like Donally in *Heroes and Villains* and the Count in *The Infernal Desire Machines of Dr Hoffman,* Sade cannot abide reciprocity, or even the freedom he means to desire, "still in complicity with the authority which he hates" (*The Sadeian Woman,* pp. 132, 141, 136). Work like Carter's is crucial if we are to both use, and differentiate ourselves from, "traditions" of liberation and the surreal.

The rejection of the types of behaviour figured in Justine and Juliette, and elaborated through twentieth-century instances, implies a general struggle towards something else, towards free and fair human relations, and love that can be "a reciprocal pact of tenderness" (*The Sadeian Woman,* p. 8). This may involve acknowledging some of the advantages that are side-effects of subordination, and letting go some defences and justifications; and that is why Carter's writing can baffle, or be experienced as an assault. I was astonished to find some aspects of myself in both Justine and Juliette, which provoked me to question my ways of relating myself as I had never done before. In this respect I find it useful to lean on the idea of the discomposing or decomposition of the reader, in Linda Williams's paper, "Happy Families? Feminist Reproduction and Matrilineal Thought." If books can change lives at all, they must do so by unsettling identities and fixed positions. I plead, against Clark, Duncker and Kappeler, that readers should attend to the whole argument of Carter's fictions and at least think twice before deciding that there is nothing positive for them and for feminism, when their predispositions are offended. This does not mean that I am asking for passive submission to the author's goading; it is the moment of disturbance and anger which may produce a new consciousness and a new order of things.

3. One knowledge or exploration Carter does genuinely offer is of narcissistic desire, self-preoccupied fantasies which interfere in the possibility of relation between people who are other in themselves, not just projections of each other's desires. This is a particular concern of *Heroes and Villains,* where Marianne embodies her estranged desire in the Barbarian Jewel; it is implicated in the virgin births of Eve and Tristessa in *The Passion of New Eve,* and it is articulated in "Flesh and the Mirror" in *Fireworks,* where, like Jewel, the man is objectified:

> I suppose I shall never know, now, (how he really looked) for he was plainly an object created in the mode of fantasy. His image was already present somewhere in my head and I was seeking to discover it in actuality, looking at every face I met in case it was the right face—that is, the face which corresponded to my notion of the face of the one I should love, a face created parthenogenetically by the rage to love which consumed me. So his self . . . the thing he was to himself, was quite unknown to me. I created him solely in relation to myself, like a work of romantic art. (p. 67)

4. One of the things I'm very keen to get said is that, although such a passage may sound autobiographical, none of Carter's exploratory fictions are absolute versions of reality, although real relations—sexual, political, economic—are of immense concern to her. There are no naturalistically credible imitations of experience in her work and no role models either, not in any simple sense; choices of behaviour have to be read within a particular set-up. However much motifs are repeated from one end of her work to the other, each project is tactical and specific within a general feminist and materialist strategy—you cannot lay a grid across her work and read off meanings from it, according to a law of the same, which is what I think Duncker, Kappeler and Clark try to do.[2] To offer one example of what I mean: Patricia Duncker assumes that the blindness of the piano tuner in "The Bloody Chamber" is a symbolic castration, like Charlotte Brontë's mutilation of Mr. Rochester in *Jane Eyre*. And indeed the piano tuner does function as a cipher, as anonymous as the princess that the prince may be awarded in a fairy tale. I want Carter and myself to be allowed a transient tactical liberation from the genuine enough theoretical import of such an interpretation (though it is never *more* than an interpretation). I can't speak for the blind, being at the moment abled in that respect, but I think that if I were blind I would by now be quite weary of this sort of interpretation. The blindness of the piano tuner, the alternative husband to Bluebeard, is produced by the needs of the story's argument. The bride has already been too much seduced by seeing herself as the object of an erotic gaze, so that any other lover must be marked as "not like that," one who knows her in his heart, and can appreciate her skill as a musician. He must of course be disabled in some respect, so that it is the bride's mother not he who rescues her. But, the musical instrument which brings them together is "perfectly in tune" ("The Bloody Chamber," p. 40).

Another example: in my experience readers often assume that Eve in *The Passion of New Eve* is a role model for a new woman (it is not Carter who misleads them but the desire for role models disseminated by the empire of US sociology).[3] The title's analogy with the passion of Christ the Messiah might also suggest such a reading—but this is blasphemous not authoritative; Carter is playing with alternative theologies of the power of virginity and the androgyny of God's son. Rather, Eve/Evelyn like Desiderio in *Hoffman,* is akin to the passive hero of Scott's novels, who is put through certain phases of action for the instruction of the reader. It is the action and the commentary on it which signify. In *The Passion of New Eve* these phases are modelled on those of the alchemical search: first *nigredo,* the melting of the metals, as in the chaos of New York where blackness actually holds a promise for the future as yet unseen; then the whitening phase in which elements separate out, as in the fragments of American lifestyles Eve encounters; and finally *rubedo,* the red fire of revolution which may produce pure gold. The Czech alchemist in New York is one pointer to such a reading; and given this story's concern with cinema, one model could have been Sergei Eisenstein's notion of combining alchemy with dialectical materialism, in montage.[4] So all this demands special knowledge? Yes, why not? Curiosity, as Charles Perrault said, is a charming passion. It is not essential for a feminist writer to assume naive readers, or for every reader to see all possible readings. In my mother's tenement there are many apartments, and that's not the only house there is. This may mislead readers who are not already politically aware, as Clark fears? Get away—I'm not as daft as you think, my mother always says.

Carter's fictions are serial and episodic, not hierarchical and organic. That is, they work like the speculative fictions of the Enlightenment, like *Candide* or *Gulliver's Travels,* not like Romantic works of art in which the whole significance might be read off from any sample. Her typical narrative procedure is the refusal of nostalgia, *not* keeping the home fires burning for an escape route. She burns the boats or the brothel, crashes the train, or buries the last provisional family acquired under a landslide. There's no going back, her narratives insist; you have to go somewhere else, even become someone else: "It just goes to show there's nothing like confidence," as Fevvers concludes (*Nights at the Circus*). On the one hand, that's a simple crude slogan, and Carter has a few of those, with which, as it happens, I sympathize; they manifest her general tendency unmistakably. Contrarily, it's not that simple. Confidence is a desideratum for any woman or any group in struggle, but Carter also means conning people. The rational truth teller is also a performance artiste, turning a penny or two.

That you have to let go, move on, give away your relics—the moral of all Carter's longer narratives—is violently in contradiction with the fact that in demythologizing she is also refurbishing old myths and symbols, setting them going again. And that strong linear drive of her fictions is never towards conclusion and resolution, only towards the assertion of certain principles or negations, in the light of which the struggle goes on. She has no time for Utopias or "that great commune in the sky." Confidence is all because life is struggle. "There is no way out of time. We must learn to live in this world, to take it with sufficient seriousness, because it is the only world we will ever know" (*The Sadeian Woman,* p. 110). This maxim comes as the conclusion to her rejection of Woman or Mother as the last refuge of the concept of Eternity, of escape or appeal to some other level; to me it is poignant and invigorating. It is the heart of her demystifications.

Angela Carter is a writer of contradictions. Her style (that is, her self-production as a writer, her deliberate though often ironic position—not some showy extra, as Clark seems to think) yokes disparate effects: the banal and the extraordinary, the prim and the offensive, the baroque and the offhand. The unmistakable boldness of this style is produced by its collisions, its very active dependency on previous texts, which is a reader's rewriting and the rewriting of readers. It is not out of this world. I want to examine Carter's intertextual dialogues (or polylogues) through discussion of one short fiction, the title story of *The Bloody Chamber.* I have chosen this story because it also allows me to discuss the apparent contradiction between Carter's feminist "line" and her exploitation of a dangerous reactionary fascination—heterosexual desire in thrall to soft pornography and sado-masochism.

The young pianist of "The Bloody Chamber" is the willing bride of a Bluebeard, a connoisseur of juvenile and sadistic pornography, as well as of five centuries of European art. These are his things. Carter's writing here offers the excitement of erotic anticipation even while parodying it.[5] It parodies also the poignancy of the separation of mother and daughter, a pathos which constitutes part of the erotic excitement:

> my burning cheek pressed against the impeccable linen of the pillow and the pounding of my heart mimicking that of the great pistons ceaselessly thrusting the train that bore me through the night, away . . . from girlhood . . . Oh! how he must want me! (*The Bloody Chamber,* pp. 7, 10)

The mother's regrets are imagined: "folding up and putting away all my little relics," lingering over "this torn ribbon and that faded photograph" (p. 7), while the bride herself is so seduced by the part she is playing that she does not regret "the world of tartines and maman that now receded from me as if drawn away on a string, like a child's toy" (p. 13). In context, this wonderfully evokes the sensation of pulling out of a railway station, but also, in a wider context, grandfather Freud's game of Fort/Da, here and gone—the child's overcoming of separation from the mother by calling performance and language, signification, into play.

Carter's writing may simply be consumed but can also produce *wincing* from this fascination of the girl with being acquired and seduced by a knowing and powerful man who "wants her so much"—a wincing recoil of the reader who has been at all seduced by the aroma, texture, dynamics, of erotic difference. "Was it I who wanted this? Was it this that I wanted?" The rhetorical figure that's been on my mind as I've tried to characterize Carter's writing has been zeugma, the yoking together of different objects and effects within the same syntax—a comic and explosive device. Fascination and recoil are parts of the enticements of pornography, either way. One feminist position is to condemn any truck with such available fascinations altogether.[6] Another is to face the fascination—to spring forward *from* recoil, from wincing at an acknowledged desire. (*Who* is it that acknowledges? Either the sadistic or the masochistic subject, of whatever gender. To whatever degree.)

If I read Robert Clark right, he believes that sexuality is *only* made significant by prohibition, so that Carter's experiment with "moral pornography" as a critique of current sexual relations is doomed to be part of what it criticizes: "the illicitly desiring self pulls forwards, the censoring mind pulls back preaching an exemplary sermon."[7] What then shall we do with our illicit desires? Flagellate ourselves? The notion of recoil can have an opposite value, one which does not deny or prohibit the energies of desire as they exist: a springing movement which may be experienced as active and productive, rather than a helpless captivation. Although the attitude of mind is perhaps already sufficiently widespread, I take the term recoil, or wincing, with its implication of self-overcoming ("Was it I? Was it this?"), from my notes of a particularly lively account by Charles Scott of Foucault's *Madness and Civilization* and *The Order of Things*, notes which continue:

> Genealogy is effective history, and curative science. It is not a coming to truth or health (concepts which can be used punitively and coercively), but to a knowledge of one's own contingent process, as in psychoanalysis. The curative aspect is in a knowledge that finds itself repeating and departing from the inheritance it describes. This is not true insight inspecting a false knowledge: it stays on the boundary, on the dangerous edge, as a therapeutic listening, the very opposite of a discipline of confinement.[8]

Repeating and departing from the inheritance described struck me as a good account of the processes of Carter's writing, and the strongest answer to the charge that she merely reinscribes patriarchy. Where else can you start from, if not from where you actually are? (as Voltaire wrote, and it still seems to me good political practice). Where we are may include fascinations from which a rational and ethical self recoils. My diction there gave me a long pause for thought—how many can I include in what I acknowledge about myself as a reader? "I think I'm typical," Angela Carter said in an interview with Lorna Sage.[9] And yes, she does speak to my condition as a daughter of the Second World War and the Welfare State, who has done time in Yorkshire and South London, and been nourished by Eng. Lit. and centuries of European art and taste, or versions thereof. I do feel that I know better than Robert Clark what she's up against and up to. Where I start is with the languages of my education and the responses it produced: "Kennst du das Land?" Is that song a nostalgic harking back, or a certainty that there is somewhere else to be?

I want to consider Carter's "fiction as literary criticism," as putting the educated reader on the spot.[10] "Read Angela Carter and re-read Culture?" "The Bloody Chamber" rewrites a folk/fairy story, of Bluebeard's castle and bride. But Carter's tales in fact rarely rewrite one story only. "Peter and the Wolf" in *Black Venus*, for example, suddenly reveals itself as not only a revision of Prokofiev's instruction of children but also as a blasphemous revision of Genesis, in which the gulf between human and animal is seen to yawn less wide than that between the perceived nakedness of male and female. This double gulf is bridged when the boy shocked by visible sexual difference into priesthood gets a second chance to recognize his peaceable kinship with the wolf-cousin who is simply a mother. So, the story of "The Erl-King" in *The Bloody Chamber*, which Patricia Duncker dismisses briefly as a reworking of

Goethe's ballad, *also* re-examines Hegel's dialectic of master and slave through medieval ballads such as "The Cruel Mother" and a version of Blake's "The Mental Traveller," which represents the cycle of mother/father and child—the rebel who becomes oppressive authority in her/his turn. "The Erl-King" needs to be compared to the Red Riding Hood story that Clark has a go at, "The Company of Wolves." The dank but brilliantly lit atmosphere of "The Erl-King" (which does for the vegetable, the "natural," kingdom what other stories do for the "wild" world of wolves) is evoked as a cage, a world without ambiguity: "everything in the wood is exactly as it seems" (p. 113). The resolution, in which the captivated girl will turn on her captor, is in the future tense. The shifting of tense and of grammatical subject in this story (from "always" to "now" to "will be," from "anyone" to "you" to "I") ought to be read as twistings and turnings to escape the transparent, unambiguous world of experience, the world of Locke's enlightened linguistics in which ideas are derived simply from sense-perception. This is the Enlightenment, Locke's world of locks, cages and fixities from which Blake also wanted to get out:

> A young girl would go into the wood as trustingly as Red Riding Hood to her granny's house but this light admits of no ambiguities and, here, she will be trapped in her own illusion because everything in the wood is exactly as it seems. (*The Company of Wolves*, p. 113)

So, "The Company of Wolves" must be read in the afterglow of this story, as producing a world where there are ambiguities, gaps between the signifier and the signified, so that the significance and the outcome can be changed. At some point the mother need not poison or consume her son, the girl need not kill her beloved and make him the instrument of her song of seduction and betrayal; conceivably she could just get into bed with him.

The Bloody Chamber, then, is not a coherent whole, but neither is it entirely heterogeneous and fragmentary. The fairy stories are played with and worked as different versions ("see what we can do with this one, then?"—or then, try again, as in the side-by-side versions of "Beauty and the Beast," "The Courtship of Mr Lyon" and "The Tiger's Bride," reworked again with lots of other things in "Wolf-Alice"). Carter's critics seem unable to keep up with her productive resourcefulness. The pleasure of innocent readers less disposed to disapprove may be a better guide. The next story to "The Erl-King" is very disturbing, in representing a father's sexual penetration of his daughter, but it can be made less so when it is read in this deliberately placed succession, rather than in some assumed universally valid context; "The Snow Child" follows on the argument of "The Erl-King." It has to do with breaking "archetypal" cycles of oppression. It prefaces "The Lady of the House of Love," which transforms a vampire *femme fatale,* suffering from her destined immortality which feeds on humanity, into a girl whose death establishes her reality: "I am, because I can die like anyone else" and, "because that is how I am, I desire." This appalling She becomes a human subject, not someone else's fantasy. Her lovely young lover's successful attempt to revive the baleful rose which has been her symbol dooms him to the carnage of the First World War. He would have been better advised to accept her mortality along with her love for him, and to stay with his bicycle, the anti-Gothic sign of human rationality.

The daughter in "The Snow Child" remains inhuman. She is what the father wants, as Snow White was the creature of her mother's desire. Like a customer in a brothel, sometimes he wants the virginal girl, sometimes he wants the corrupt queen, a role which the girl would take up in her turn, if she survived to age. The queen or rather Countess in "The Snow Child" exposes the truth of such masculine desires: either the love-child is ephemeral as snow, or her sexuality when matured would threaten the man—the final rose that bites, of male terror. Go on imagining women in these ways and you will destroy or disempower women as human beings, and thereby annihilate love as a mutual pact of tender passion; that's the argument, as I read it. The killing of the object of desire in these stories is not a killing of women, but a killing of masculine representations, in which some women collude. To invert their ferocity, as at the promised end of "The Erl-King" and in the threatening image of the genital rose with teeth, is one tactic but not the whole strategy. It doesn't have to be the only story that can be told.

Carter's rational arguments are produced by such strange yokings of representations. "Bluebeard" has the dubious charm of the young-girl-at-risk—*that* story, as Anne Sexton put it in *Transformations*.[11] Carter's *ingénue* is not like the wife in Margaret Atwood's "Bluebeard's Egg," who ends up knowing that she has been fooled about the secret life of a husband who is a specialist in women's bodies (a heart surgeon) and also that she has fooled herself—but doesn't know what to do about it.[12] Atwood's wife is exposed as a victim and remains so, to this reader's horror and her own. Carter's is always a girl of spirit, both an adventuress and a curious, knowing spectator of her own seductions and trials. Another comparison could be with the trials of Blanca in chapter 8 of Isabel Allende's *The House of the Spirits*.[13] Far from knowing, Allende's heroine nevertheless has the guts to get right out from there—the house of her husband's experiments in photographing sexual exploitation—even in an advanced stage of pregnancy, or probably because of that. The spiritedness of Carter's bride of Bluebeard derives from the *other* pre-text for "The Bloody Chamber," that is, the homage it pays to the turn-of-the-century writing of Colette.

This may well be obvious, in terms of the bride's style and the phenomena she encounters, but some of the connections are very precise. This title story is one which Patricia Duncker exempts from her criticism of Carter's whole collection of revised fairy stories: that the bride is rescued not by her brothers but by an indomitable and loving mother, redeems it for Duncker from the captivated heterosexism of the rest. Nicole Ward Jouve has pointed out to me that the story can be read as a version of Colette's biography, for example of "Mes apprentissages," of how her mother rescued her from her husband Willy, that titillating master of hack writers, and from the dissipations of urbane society which had made her ill; the mother, so the story goes, nursed her back to rude health in the country.

It was mean of Patricia Duncker, I think, to leave consideration of this story to the last in her article, since Carter deliberately put it first, possibly to disarm the kind of attack Duncker makes on the rest of *The Bloody Chamber*. "She couldn't imagine Cinderella in bed with the Fairy Godmother," writes Duncker.[14] The love between Mignon and the Princess of Abyssinia in *Nights at the Circus* reads like a response to such complaints, a rich, multifocal, reparation, as the black woman finds a voice, and the victim girl of Europe, Mignon, becomes first a performing artist and then a composer, through their mutual love. It is an empowering lesbian idyll which also redeems and celebrates the ecstatic and revolutionary potential within European art. *Nights at the Circus* rewrites Yeats ("The Second Coming," "Sailing to Byzantium" and "The Circus Animals' Desertion"; Yeats for all his sins learned from Blake the artisan) and Hamlet's "What a piece of work is man!," in deconstructing its sardonic observer, Jack Walser, and showing how the New Woman is constructed by Fevvers as the "Winged Eros" which Alexandra Kollontai also wanted to make real.[15] In speaking of such a reparation, I'm thinking of the twice replayed scene where Blake's Tygers, set in gold like Yeats's sages, are enchanted by the two loving women's performance of Goethe's lyric "Mignon," which begins "Kennst du das Land?" Mignon did not yearn for that land because she was uncertain of its existence. Certainly, unlike her original, she could not have wanted to go back to what her life had been, her "fatherland": Carter writes that "she said that this new land existed, and only wanted to know if you knew it too" (*Nights at the Circus*, p. 247). This is a rare instance of idyll in Carter's work. Her Paradises usually have shit in them, horse shit, and even here it's not everyone's cup of tea; the Shaman and the Finno-Ugrian tribe don't like it, because they can't read it (although they do know more than they will yet speak).

The dialogic relation of *Nights at the Circus*, narratively speaking, is also (effectively) a strong mother-daughter relation, that of Fevvers and Lizzie, fond and ratty by turns. I think the tactic in "The Bloody Chamber" which Patricia Duncker buys, is less whole-hearted, more a matter of giving them what they want to buy them off. Carter didn't after all buy Colette's late return to her mother's house (which I love)—"all that obsessive gush about Sido" (*Nothing Sacred*, p. 175). It's the bad Colette, the narcissistic performer who began writing as her husband's creature and hack, that Carter said would do women good if they were exposed to her early enough. Carter will write in a fair do for gay women; but that's not the end of it, in *Nights at the Circus*, and that's not what she's really about. She is "doing it from a feminist angle," "trying to be radical" (to use her own offhand phrases from *Nothing Sacred* and the *Women's Review* interview with Anne Smith), but she writes from and for the difficult position of being heterosexual and feminist, and it's from that position that I value and want to use her work. I might also add that although Carter hardly ever complicates her story line in a modernist manner her conclusions may offer alternative options. So *Nights at the Circus* gives us optimistic versions of Justine/Marilyn Monroe, in Mignon's story, and of Juliette/Mae West in that of Fevvers—the woman of power who not only helps Mignon but becomes more shabby, less starry, before regaining her stride differently. So in *The Passion of New Eve*, "Woman" leaves Myth and enters History, in the penultimate sequence which shows the black prostitute and victim Leilah/Lilith as a guerilla leader; but also a space is left for the fascination of what is not yet known, as the new Eve sails off to give birth to an unpredictable future.

Colette's *My Mother's House* was entitled *La Maison de Claudine* in the 1922 original, thereby linking memories of her childhood home that celebrate her mother, Sido, with the heroine of her first novels, Claudine, from whose home the mother was rigorously excised, in favour of a benignly neglectful father whose preoccupation with malacology leaves his spirited daughter free. Claudine was a version of Colette; Angela Carter's young bride, the pianist, is a version of both. If you read the first of the Claudine novels to be published in Colette's own name rather than that of her husband, *Claudine amoureuse* or *Claudine Married* (1902) you will find that the sensual feeling for Renaud, Claudine's husband (an idealization of Willy), has been evoked for the husband in "The Bloody Chamber"—the masculine whiff of tobacco and Russian leather (or, most probably, soap and aftershave—"Cuir de Russie" or Imperial Leather). Each offers his bride a ruby necklace also. Claudine sucks hers as if it were a sweetie; Angela Carter means to suggest the red neckband defiantly sported by aristocratic women facing the guillotine. Renaud fails to satisfy Claudine's desires. She wants to be deeply ravaged by passion, and is frustrated by his light-hearted licentiousness: "Alas! Are you to remain your own mistress for ever, Claudine?," she asks herself. Perforce she must rest contented that "If I have not found my master, I have found my friend and ally" (*Claudine Married*, pp. 334–5). What she has desired is the hero of romantic fiction, duplicated in soft pornography.

The strongest feminist reading of "The Bloody Chamber" is not only in terms of a mother-daughter idyll, but as a quarrel with another, intensely admired, woman writer. The dynamic and the conclusion of that argument are identical to the moment of recoil articulated by Desiderio in *The Infernal Desire Machines of Dr Hoffman*, in response to the fantasies projected by himself and Hoffman's daughter Albertina, his beloved and his alter-ego, of dismemberment and gang rape: "victims of unleashed, unknown desires, then die we must, for as long as those desires existed, we would finish by killing

one another" (p. 191). "The Bloody Chamber" is a strong answer to an existing representation, Colette/Claudine's desire to be ravaged by the other, saying "I can see the fascination, but just look where it gets you—to a spread of
pictures in the *Sun,* to a place in the series of defunct and mutilated brides."
Better the man who's a friend and ally, the blind piano tuner.

One weakness I can see in my own reading is that something much the
same could have been reached without recourse to *Claudine Married* (that in
fact would be one answer to Clark's accusation that Carter's stories may be
read one way by feminists, and otherwise by those who are not). But the invi-
tation that is there to read "The Bloody Chamber" in the light of Colette
underlines as an active process something that has to be worked through if we
are to change what we desire, the ways in which women can be complicit
with what captivates and victimizes them, even or especially in their adven-
turousness. It underlines and undoes the captivation. What Carter does in
"The Bloody Chamber" didn't come home to me fully until I read *Claudine
Married* in the light of it. My conviction that you have to go through it, and
along the line of Carter's narrative arguments to evaluate them properly (that
is, politically), needs to be argued by serious analysis of her longer fictions,
which explore the real material world of fantastic appearances, of representation. To stop short at particular sensational instances is to reproduce the titillating censoriousness of newspapers.

The spiritedness of Colette and Angela Carter gets them into dangerous
places. Both Patricia Duncker and Susanne Kappeler quote Andrea Dworkin
against Carter; but on the 1987 publicity tour for her novel *Ice and Fire*
Andrea Dworkin confessed that her models for writing were men, because of
their boldness and freedom; "feminine" modes and themes she found con-
stricting. Like Atwood's "Bluebeard's Egg," *Ice and Fire* ultimately represents
women as victims of their own desire and that of others. What I want to celebrate finally about the work of Colette and Angela Carter is that you can't
feel sorry for yourself, reading it. They may make you cross but anger ani-
mates.

Notes

1. Patricia Duncker, "Re-imagining the Fairy Tale: Angela Carter's Bloody Chambers," *Literature and History* X, I, Spring 1984; Susanne Kappeler, *The Pornography of Representation* (London: Polity Press, 1986), pp. 133–7; Robert Clark, "Angela Carter's Desire Machine,"
Women's Studies XIV, 2, 1987.

2. The notion of "the same"—judgement according to universal criteria, so that whatever you look at you can only see mirror images of yourself and the present—is drawn from the
work of Luce Irigaray.

3. "One important function of bourgeois fiction is to teach people how to behave in
social circles to which they think they might be able to aspire. . . . But all this bores me stiff, in
fact, because it no longer seems particularly relevant to instruct people as to how to behave in

a changing society, *when one's very existence is instrumental in causing changes the results of which one can't begin to calculate* [my italics]. And I personally feel much more in common with certain Third World writers, both female and male, who are transforming actual fictional forms to both reflect and to precipitate changes in the way people feel about themselves." (Angela Carter, "Notes from the Front Line," *On Gender and Writing,* ed. Michelene Wandor [London: Pandora Press, 1983] p. 76).

4.   I'm indebted to conversation with Richard Crane about his play on Eisenstein, *Red Magic,* for this analogue (the play was presented at the Edinburgh Festival Fringe and at the South Bank Museum of the Moving Image in the Summer of 1988).

5.   Though it's an article she might well want to revoke or renew, I'll cite here Susan Sontag's "The Pornographic Imagination," to the effect that pornography is already so selective and ready-made that it *can't* parody itself or be parodied (*Styles of Radical Will,* London: Secker & Warburg, 1969, p. 51).

6.   See Mandy Merck's comparison of Andrea Dworkin's *Intercourse* with the film *Fatal Attraction,* in *Feminist Review* XXX, Autumn 1988.

7.   Clark, op. cit., p. 153.

8.   Seminars at the University of Essex, May 1988.

9.   Lorna Sage, "A Savage Sideshow," *New Review* IV, 39/40, July 1977.

10.   Interview with Anne Smith, "Myths and the Erotic," *Women's Review* I, November 1985.

11.   Anne Sexton, *Transformations* (London: Oxford University Press, 1972).

12.   Margaret Atwood, "Bluebeard's Egg" in her collection *Bluebeard's Egg* (London: Jonathan Cape, 1987).

13.   Isabel Allende, *The House of the Spirits* (London: Jonathan Cape, 1985).

14.   Duncker, op. cit., p. 8. (Contrast this with Carter's account of her grandmother's story-telling, in John Haffenden, "Magical Mannerist." *The Literary Review,* November 1984.)

15.   That's not, of course, the half of it. I would and would not like to produce the annotated edition of one page of *Nights at the Circus.* Which is not to say that Angela Carter is not a highly original writer.

I would like to acknowledge my debt to discussions with graduate students at the University of Essex, Manda Ilic and Sally Keenan, and with Dr Jane Health.

Angela Carter: Supersessions of the Masculine

David Punter

Angela Carter has now been charting the unconscious processes of Western society for a number of years, principally in her series of novels but latterly also in the form of a kind of psychoanalytic journalism and in *The Sadeian Woman* (1979), a major history and interpretation of sexuality and its acculturation.[1] I propose here to try to identify a principal shift of attention in this body of texts which occurred in the 1970s, through an examination of two of her novels, *The Infernal Desire Machines of Doctor Hoffman* (1972) and *The Passion of New Eve* (1977). That change can be expressed in plain terms, although these do not do justice to the convolutions of the psyche which structure the two texts. Both novels, and indeed all Carter's work, are to do with the unconscious and its shapes, and thus to do with sexuality, and in *Doctor Hoffman* this concern reaches a peak in the interplay of Freud and Reich which forms the underpinning of the text. But that peak is also a point of division, and what is new in *New Eve* is that the issue of sexuality is linked directly to the different issue of gender; that is to say, *New Eve* speaks—and, indeed, helps to form—a language in which it is impossible to conjugate the pure term "sexuality," for the questions of ownership, agency, and power which surround our use of language have been made manifest, and now there is "male sexuality" and "female sexuality," without an assumed bridge. The intensity of focus on hermaphroditism is present in both texts, but to different purpose: in *Doctor Hoffman,* hermaphrodites are merely the object of the gaze, the Platonic linked double to be worshipped and admired: in *New Eve,* the structures of hermaphroditism operate within the perceiving subject itself, so that the gaze is dislocated at source.[2] And the dislocation of the gaze entail also a primary dislocation of plot: it is significant that *Doctor Hoffman* is intensely reliant on literary models, from the picaresque pretensions of the hero (in some of his phases) to the conventionality of the love-plot in which he is enmeshed. *New Eve,* of course, is not without models; but the relation between plot and character is more twisted, if only because of the further depths to which Carter has taken her exploration of the construction of the subject.

From *Critique* 25, no. 4 (Summer 1984): 209–21. Heldref Publications. © 1984 Helen Dwight Reid Educational Foundation. Reprinted by permission.

For both novels are dramatizations of the constructed subject, and they relate to each other precisely along the lines of the development of recent theoretical debate about such construction, and specifically about the exact point at which gender enters as a structuring principle.[3] "You could effectively evolve a persona from your predicament, if you tried,"[4] Desiderio is admonished in *Doctor Hoffman* at one point, although Carter does not here go in for easy answers. Indeed, the "answers" with which she presents us are exceedingly difficult, rather in the manner of the metaphysical speculations of Flann O'Brien;[5] and thus the question of the reality status—or, perhaps, varying reality statuses—of the "phantoms" which Hoffman unleashes on the city remains to the end a matter for conjecture. That conjecture is simultaneously a metaphysical one, about the concept of the symbol; what we might term a semiotic one, about the relation between the sign and its referent; and a sociosexual one, for it raises the questions of the ontological location of desire and of the arbitrariness of change.

Imagistically, the "question of reality"—and to give it this formulation is already to underestimate the powerful web of ironies through which Carter mediates this metaphysicalization of the political—is represented in terms of opacity and transparency, vision and shadow. A key term, cropping up throughout Desiderio's wanderings like a talisman but never subjected to the indignity of abstract "explanation," is "persistence of vision," which carries two different but related meanings. First, it is this ambiguous persistence, manifested chiefly in the emaciated and academic shape of the Doctor himself, which achieves the alchemical transmutation of desire into material manifestation and thus threatens those limits of the conceivable which Desiderio ends up by defending. But second, it is persistence of vision which maintains our illusion of continuity in the world, which moulds our discrete presence into a coherent narrative. It is the proprietor of the peepshow, which perhaps causes these transformational phenomena, who points out that there is "no hidden unity" (*Doctor Hoffman,* 126); thus, that his demonstrations of carnality and violence become coherent and intelligible only through a "persistent" trick of the eye and psyche, through a refraction of the perennial Oedipal search for origins.[6] Sexual energy is the key to the manifestation of desire; but to subdue this perpetual slow explosion to the logistics of orgasm and climax is to submit ourselves to a teleology which merely demonstrates our obsessional inability to escape from the family which gave us birth. The ultimate acrobats of desire, down in the technological hub of the Doctor's replacement universe, embody postponement, or perhaps a hidden fear of premature ejaculation; certainly it is premature ejaculation which occurs in terms of the narrative itself, as Desiderio knows: both in that, within the mutual fiction of the later course of the world which Desiderio weaves around himself and the reader, we are supposed already to know the outcome of the story through history books, and also, more concretely, in that he gives us the conclusion of the story ahead of its "natural" place, and himself bemoans the fact: "but there I go again—running ahead of myself! See, I have ruined all the suspense. I have quite spoiled my climax" (*Doctor Hoffman,* 268).

The Doctor's system, for system it is (the unconscious here is very deliberately structured like a language), operates on the basis of continuing possibility, and it is this which strikes the hard resistant material of the universe in the shape of the Minister of Determination and his Kafkasque police force. The early stages of the conflict, of which Desiderio, the "desired one," is going to become the solution, involve the Minister's attempts to prevent the Doctor's illusions from swamping the real by the use of various technological devices, none of which prove particularly effective in a world where objects may change their names, shapes, and functions from moment to moment. One of these weapons requires for its efficacy the construction of a model of the Doctor's "unreality atom," which turns out to be "bristling with projections"; but these projections, of course, are not literal bumps but the material form of the psychological projections which colour and shape our apprehension of the Other. The universe Carter portrays, however, cannot be simply predicated on the limitless power of these projections as far as the individual is concerned, for here ignorant projections clash by night; that is, projections ignorant of their own and others' origin, so that a battle of psychic power is enacted reminiscent, especially in the shape of the vampire Count, of the psychological power-struggles which lie at the root of sword-and-sorcery fiction.

Besides, since the projections teem from the unconscious, they can be *known* neither in their aetiology (the lost box of "samples") nor in their manifestation; and we remain uncertain, in particular, about the nature of Desiderio's own unconscious. He is at once an allegorical figure for the object of desire, and thus undergoes transmutation with each book of the novel; and a representation of a historically specific type of alienated consciousness, which means that despite these transmutations he possesses a residual consistency felt as boredom and disaffection. It is precisely the survival of this root of tedium which provides him with the vacant strength to quash the Doctor's schemes, and at this level we can read the text as a series of figures for the defeat of the political aspirations of the 1960s, and in particular of the father-figures of liberation, Reich and Marcuse.

But we can nonetheless plot the shapes of desire as the text envisages them by entering the kaleidoscope of what Desiderio variously becomes, even if he pulls back from the brink of immersion in these internal fictions and, indeed, never fully understands his own role in them. There is the faithful operative given a heroic mission; the visitant lover whose congress with the enervated Mary Ann precipitates her death; the compliant member of family which he becomes on the boat of the River People; the peep-show proprietor's nephew who, in a world of transitory freaks, possesses "the unique allure of the norm" (*Doctor Hoffman,* 128); the half-willing companion of the "erotic traveller"; the again heroic killer of the black chieftain of cannibals; and, of course, over all the potential lover of the elusive Albertina. But the structure which is woven from these tales remains ambivalent. It might be that the Boys' Own quality of Desiderio's incarnations reflects a paucity of imagination, perhaps specifically of male imagination, on Desiderio's part; or it might equally well be that in these largely adjuvant shapes is reflected a specific historical role for the "British" consciousness within international conflict, that the unconscious of the text, split as it is between New World and Old, has an even more precise bearing on cultural attitudes than would appear from the examination of Desiderio's attenuated psyche.[7]

It is only with River People that he claims to feel "at home," and this feeling is made the site for an appalling summary of familial claustrophobia. His putative child-bride appears at first to carry everywhere with her a doll, but this is next revealed to be a fish in doll's clothing, symbol indeed for desire and for the phallus but neatly bound up in conventional wrappings, slippery and to be toyed with as Desiderio is himself toyed with by her family. But this representation of captured "difference" finally yields its secret, and is replaced in turn by a knife, the knife which will effect the real desire which the family has invested in Desiderio and will ensure that his knowledge, severed and offered with the hunks of his meat, will pass forever safely back to the family and ensure a closed circle of deprivation and incest. From the doll to the fish to the knife, we move from pure representation through the shadowy realm of the symbolic into the ghastly manifestation of the real. It is the ambiguous realm of the fish which Doctor Hoffman's enemies suppose him, Nemo-like, to inhabit, although in the end it seems doubtful that this is the correct interpretation. Albertina, his daughter, describes the Minister's assaults on her father's efforts, and in particular that functionary's decision to "keep a strict control of his actualities by adjusting their names to agree with them perfectly":

> So, you understand, that no shadow would fall between the word and the thing described. For the Minister hypothesised my father worked in that shadowy land between the thinkable and the thing thought of, and, if he destroyed this difference, he would destroy my father. (*Doctor Hoffman*, 249–50)

The Minister employs a team of logical positivists to embark on this great work of classification, on the construction of a philosophy of identity, and, indeed, through the agency of Desiderio he is in the end successful and the forces of order inflict another crushing defeat on the uprising of the imagination; but then, Desiderio is the "new youth," has himself been formed by the Minister's society, by the society of apparent institutional order and totalitarian conformism. How, then, could it be otherwise? To Desiderio, even the form of the Doctor himself, which we may presume to be as malleable for the perceiving subject as that of his daughter, appears only as another grey-suited seeker after power, and Desiderio's cynicism brooks no culmination but a restoration of the "absence" which bred him.

Doctor Hoffman, then, attempts a subversion of narrative, on the grounds that narrative is itself ideological in form, even before we begin to consider its content; in other words, that narrative attempts to bind together and naturalize the disunited subject and that this attempt is made at the service of specific societal interests. But this places us, of course, in the hall of mirrors: "Desiderio," the desired *one,* is also anagrammatically ambivalent: the name contains the "desired I," but also the "desired O," and this encapsulates the problems of subjectivity which the text explores. Desiderio reverses the tradition of the search, or rather he displays the ambivalence of that search. Alongside the seeking for self lies always the hunt for the zero, for the still point, the thanatic impulse which requires him to set all things at nought and thus to represent the "limits" of consciousness in their most extreme form, as a closing in and closing down. What gives him privilege is his apparent lack of interest in the unification of the self; but this is associated throughout with a negation of value, and thus the final consummation with Albertina is turned almost accidentally into a series of deaths as Desiderio makes real the point of resistance which brings all the efforts of fantasy to emerge into the world down to dust.

The parallel between the operations of the psyche in its ambivalent dealings with unity and the operations of language is made apparent throughout. For instance, the ship on which Desiderio, Lafleur/Albertina, and the Count sail from South America begins to suffer from slippages in consistency; although, because of the strength of the Count's will, it appears to be an early nineteenth-century vessel, the captain nevertheless has a radio. But Lafleur refers to these slippages as "puns," which refers us in turn to an expanded Freudian notion of parapraxis, whereby it is through these apparently unaccountable and accidental knots in time and space that we can glimpse the almost mechanical workings of consciousness and language as they go about their business of providing us with the necessary ground of consistency on which we can formulate our illusions of the integrated self. The parallel image is, again as in Flann O'Brien, the bicycle, the only means of transport which requires a continuous operation of will and thus the only one on which we can be sure of not falling prey to the Doctor's manipulations of the Real.[8] But it is, again, this inflexible will which is called into question in the shape of Desiderio, because it is his fate to will away pleasure for fear of the damage it might do to him and to others.

And the bicycle, again, connects with the view of social organization in the text, which is characteristically double. The Minister sees his society, and the city, as a neat and harmonious web of interlocking institutions; the Doctor, on the other hand, states that he has chosen the city as the site of his ambiguous liberationism precisely because of the weakness of those institutions, because of their hollowness. Presumably these manifestations of "advanced" society, like the more advanced forms of transport, suffer precisely because they do not require a continuous effort of will to keep them going, but thrive precisely on will-lessness, on the force of a custom whose origins have long been obscured. Thus again we come up against the ambiguity of the politics of the 1960s; is it that the apparent strength of conservatism has a real basis, in the forms of desire of a nation or of a subgroup within it, or is it a sham, will the walls crumble at the distant sound of surfacing desire? The Count himself shrinks and diminishes when his desires are thwarted, and the world he has imagined and thus brought into being consequently falls apart; but it is he who had "lived on closer terms with his own unconscious than we" (*Doctor Hoffman*, 239), and this is at least the guarantee of a temporary success in manifesting desire in the world around. What is also significant is that the Count may be seen in Carter's fiction as the last figure in connexion with whom this gift of living "close" to the unconscious can be asserted in a way free from the ultimate divisions of gender, the last figure in Carter's writings who escapes or transcends the gender distinction which she will now come to see as the major structuring principle in the organization of subjectivity.

The Passion of New Eve is dedicated to America, and as the novel unfolds the meaning of this inscription becomes clearer.

> It [New York] was . . . an alchemical city. It was chaos, dissolution, nigredo, night. Built on a grid like the harmonious cities of the Chinese Empire, planned, like those cities, in strict accord with the dictates of a doctrine of reason, the streets had been given numbers and not names out of a respect for pure function, had been designed in clean, abstract lines, discrete blocks, geometric intersections, to avoid just those vile repositories of the past, sewers of history, that poison the lives of European cities.[9]

New York has, of course, become precisely such a vile repository by the time Evelyn arrives there, although it could be said that the bizarre shapes of resistance which are haunting this city are less the relics of the past than the prefigurations of the future. But the point is nonetheless that there is a contradiction here, made actual in the decaying carcass of the city, between the neat lines of the skeleton and the grotesque abundance of flesh, between the grids of the streets and of electricity and the prowling lines on which the muggers, prostitutes, lunatics criss-cross those grids. It is not that one kind of order is disappearing below another: rather, that a moment is being recorded at which one fear gives way to another. That which is dying, encumbered by the weight of historicity, is itself a fantasy: if New York were projected along these lines, the product would be a vision of total order, total organization, Brave New World. What is happening is that such a fate is beginning to fade from consciousness and is being replaced with its dark twin, the evolution into chaos. From this conflict of fantasies spring the shapes of the landscapes through which Evelyn, and later Eve, passes; but also at root, of course, what is being represented is a conflict between the genders, although of a highly complex form and at such a level of psychoanalytic self-consciousness that its lines remain difficult to grasp.

Carter herself gives various explanations, through Leilah and other characters, of the internal connexions between different levels and stages of the narrative; in particular, what is emphasized is a struggle between symbolization and the forces of history, so that in the depths of the book we can see a political battle between symbolic action (writing, the formation of the new self, the representation of Woman within women) and historical action, guns blazing—although there is no question as to the materiality of both of these modes. Thus Eve herself becomes passé in the very moment of her new inception: while the finer points of the nature of the "new woman" are being explored by the technicians of Beulah, the world is collapsing and we are confronted with the fearful necessities enjoined by a power vacuum. And here we sense a problem: for the autodestruction of phallomorphic power is clearly not going to produce a situation in which new forms can simply flower in the desert. On the contrary, the women are doing military training with nuclear hand-weapons (!) just as the Blacks are sealing themselves into the armed fortress of Harlem, and although Leilah/Lilith's commando group are distinguished from the others by the fact that they wear no uniforms, in all other respects they adhere to the new conformities of guerilla warfare.

This brings us directly to the symbolic heart of *Passion of New Eve,* which has to do with mirroring.[10] We can list a number of crucial instances, crucial interchanges across the silvered boundary. Leilah's existence as whore is predicated on an everyday refraction of herself into the perceived Other, in which shape she figures male fantasies as she arrays herself in the form of the totally fleshly; her self slides away in a haze of narcotics and she reimplants herself nightly before the mirror, soulless, a self-creation of painted nipples and exotic furs. As Evelyn speeds away from her, having reduced her to the plight of grief which will provide the narrative dynamic for the rest of the book, he senses that by his contact with her he too has locked himself into Wonderland; although the fullness of this realization is long in coming. "I felt that I was in a great hurry but I did not know I was speeding toward the very enigma I had left behind—the dark room, the mirror, the woman" (*New Eve,* 39).

Later, Leilah redoubles herself: the existence which is predicated on the mirror is stripped and reincarnated in the form of Sophia, Evelyn's guardian through his time of transformation and rebirth.

> This girl had been my captress; I recognised the face she had revealed when she unmasked herself to drink from her water bottle, but now she wore civvies, a vest or tee-shirt with, silk-screened on the front, a design based on the motif of the broken phallus that had greeted me upon my arrival at the town, and a skimpy pair of blue denim shorts. She looked, however, entirely and comprehensively clothed, even though so much of her skin was showing; she looked like a woman who has never seen a mirror in all her life, not once exposed herself to those looking glasses that betray women into nakedness. (*New Eve,* 54)

Evelyn's brief attempts to convert Sophia into an object of male fantasy are entirely unsuccessful, and his bafflement serves to prefigure the moment when, transformed by the obsidian scalpel of Mother, he/she looks into the mirror for the first time and experiences the vertiginous doubleness which, it is implied, is parallel to the feminine impasse: "when I looked in the mirror, I saw Eve; I did not see myself. I saw a young woman who, though she was I, I could in no way acknowledge as myself, for this one was only lyrical arrangement of curved lines" (*New Eve*, 74). What, it seems, the new Eve does is experience, on behalf of the world, the wrench and dislocation which is at the heart of woman's relationship with herself in a world riddled with masculine power-structures: inner self forced apart from the subject of self-presentation, an awareness of hollowness, a disbelief that this self-on-view can be taken as a full representation of the person alongside the bitter knowledge that it will be, that at every point the woman is locked into the metaphysical insult of the masculine gaze.

At this point, of course, the structure of doubleness becomes too complex for narrative; we are not seriously invited, for instance, to explore the cohabitation of Eve's masculine and feminine selves within a female body, for instead we are to be offered the symbolic parallelism between Eve and Tristessa. The narrative of the mirror turns, for a time, into the narrative of glass. Tristessa's glass house (to which people come to throw stones) and her glass sculptures, shapes wrought from tears which achieve materiality by being dropped into the deep and scummy pool of the unconscious.[11] When the mirror reappears, it is in the caves which are the womb of Mother, to which Eve is (almost) finally returned.

> There was a mirror propped against the rugged wall, a fine mirror in a curly, gilt frame; but the glass was broken, cracked right across many times so it reflected nothing, was a bewilderment of splinters and I could not see myself nor any portion of myself in it. (*New Eve*, 181)

Eve, perhaps, has achieved freedom, although not through any particular actions of her own; it is rather as though, having proved useful in the incarnation of an idea, she may now be allowed to recede from the processes of history. In this respect she is rather like those Old Testament figures who, having had their all spent in one act of supernatural service to God—at God's own direction, and not their own—are permitted to short circuit the processes of life and death and to retire exhausted and, we may perhaps hypothesize, still only half-comprehending. From her part in the continuous cycle of the desert—it is the sand of the desert which is turned into glass, and the glass which is silvered into the mirror, in a process of alchemy which is constantly underlined, in Baroslav's production of gold, even in Zero's belief in sympathetic magic—Eve is allowed out to that other sand, to the far beach where there is the doubled blindness of Mother's caves and of the old woman with her vodka bottles, and where the absolute ocean forbids further development.

But the analysis of symbolism, of course, is inadequate in the absence of an analysis of narrative stance, and it is here that we sense the refractions of the mirror operating between reader and text. My own experience of the reading relations of the text, as a male reader, is bizarre, and makes me doubt—as it is designed to—the gendered structure of narrative. In one respect, the critique of male intellect is clear enough. Zero hates Tristessa—or, perhaps, he hates the sibilant (Sibylline) "name-of-Tristessa," as a bulwark against which, we may assume, he has resigned all naming, attempted to become the absolute zero, refused the lures of language—because she has destroyed his potency; and thus he accuses her of homosexuality:

> I think Zero must have picked up some distorted rumour about Beulah, unless there was some other women's commune in the desert he might have heard of, and speculated about; he fed his paranoia on rumours until his head was full of strange notions that cross-fertilised one another and ingeniously produced reams of fresh, false, self-contradictory but passionately believed information. He no longer needed news of the world, since he manufactured it himself to his own designs. (*New Eve*, 101)

I take it that this is a definition of the male psyche; not, presumably, a description of an eternal state of affairs, but a precise historical comment on the condition of paranoid suspicion to which the masculine has brought itself in a world where the feared rebirth of the feminine may be about to recur. It is the logical consequence of the historical systems of masculine competitive individualism, the bitter fruit of centuries of monadic metaphysics; out there in the desert, something real may be about to occur, a rough beast is indeed moving its (her) slow thighs, and Zero's response is to inoculate himself against female power by arranging around him a set of living symbols of female subjugation and then to construct his alternative, fantasized world in the hope that thus the forces of change can be repulsed.

But the harder question about narration, about the ways in which the sexes narrate the world, is both closer to the reader and simultaneously harder to grasp, because it has to do with the mirror through which we view the text. As a male reader, I find myself the victim of illusions. Although I am aware that Carter is a woman, and although that extratextual consciousness is incarnated within the text in her obvious proximity to Leilah/Lilith, I nonetheless find that the first-person narrative of Evelyn/Eve appears to me throughout, no matter what the overt sex at the time of the new Messiah, as a masculine narrative. When Evelyn becomes Eve, my experience is of viewing a masquerade; I read Eve still through the male consciousness (Evelyn's) of what he has become. It is as though Evelyn forms a barrier, a thin film which stretches between Carter and Eve at all points; and thus I too am forced to tread that line, to respond as a male to the residual male in Eve. Perhaps this is a recourse against humiliation, a refusal of the childed quality of masculinity which is postulated both in Evelyn's encounter with Mother and also, earlier on, in his fear when he is returned to the artificial womb of Beulah:

I was utterly helpless, in a strange land, in the strangest of places—buried deep in a blind room seamless as an egg deep in a nameless desert a long way from home. I broke down and I think I must have called for my mother because, when I did so, there was an explosion of soft, ironic laughter from the concealed loudspeakers so I knew that, however silent they were, they were always listening to me. At that, my shame became too much to bear and I buried my tear-stained face in my cold bed. Oh, that low, bubbling laughter! "Cry baby. Cry baby." No humiliation like a child's humiliation. (*New Eve*, 51)

And yet, of course, the real humiliation is not quite that; rather, it is the reemergence of the child at the inappropriate moment, the discovery that this solitude does not excite the enactment of male myths of heroism but is, instead, insupportable.

One of the many unlikely cities on which Marco Polo reports to Kubla Khan in Calvino's *Invisible Cities* (1972) is called Thekla, and it is perhaps worth recording the whole of the account he gives:

Those who arrive at Thekla can see little of the city, beyond the plank fences, the sackcloth screens, the scaffolding, the metal armatures, the wooden cat-walks hanging from ropes or supported by saw-horses, the ladders, the trestles. If you ask, "Why is Thekla's construction taking such a long time?" the inhabitants continue hoisting sacks, lowering leaded strings, moving long brushes up and down, as they answer, "So that its destruction cannot begin." And if asked whether they fear that, once the scaffolding is removed, the city may begin to crumble and fall to pieces, they add hastily, in a whisper, "not only the city."

If, dissatisfied with the answer, someone puts his eye to a crack in a fence, he sees cranes pulling up other cranes, scaffolding that embraces other scaffolding, beams that prop up other beams. "What meaning does your construction have?" he asks. "What is the aim of a city under construction unless it is a city? Where is the plan you are following, the blueprint?"

"We will show it to you as soon as the working day is over; we cannot interrupt our work now," they answer.

Work stops at sunset. Darkness falls over the building site. The sky is filled with stars. "There is the blueprint," they say.[12]

The "blueprint" of Beulah, Carter tells us, is also "a state of mind": "in Beulah, myth is a made thing, not a found thing" (*New Eve*, 49–56). Thus there is constant questioning of the limits of the "natural"; Blake used the term Beulah for his land of restfulness, stasis, a retreat from the hard labor of political and interpersonal progress, relapse into the pleasures of the flesh and the delights of wordless music. Carter ignores this, or rather on occasions she savagely parodies it; what she takes up from the Blakean myth is the connotation of Beulah as the land where extremes meet, and here what is at stake are the extremes of technology and magic. Mother is a surgeon and a prophetess; she wields a ritual scalpel but she wields also a hypodermic syringe. Magic, says Evelyn, there masquerades as surgery, but this is by no means the last word; rather, it is the voice of a man who cannot believe that the script of magical matriarchy has also a material validity in the real world, cannot believe that efficacy and power can be conjoined with incantation and rite.[13] Zero's one-eyed view is much the same:

> . . . Tristessa, Witch, bitch and Typhoid Mary of sterility. She'd blasted his seed because he was masculinity incarnate, you see. Utilising various cabbalistic devices, Tristessa had magicked away his reproductive capacity via the medium of the cinema screen. (*New Eve*, 104)

And it is here, of course, that the cinema and the star system become the most potent and ambivalent images of the union of technology and charisma. What is at stake in the hovering presence of Tristessa is the shaping of fluidity: as she drops her glass sculptures into the pool and sees them harden on the instant into the frozen forms of pain, so she/he, a living person, is dropped into the alchemical medium of the screen, which corresponds to the mirror as prerecorded tape to the blank cassette, and frozen into the perpetual form of female suffering, his "natural" sex, the referent, irrelevant in the system of significations of which he/she has become the linchpin, hidden under the weight of desire.

To this name-of-Tristessa, Zero counterposes the interdictions of the Father, and foremost among them is the prohibition of speech.[14] This is coupled with his intense fear of female homosexuality to produce a world where, on his isolated ranch, all the lines of power and communication pass through his own body, and thereby acquire the imprint of his own mutilation. His control is only partially effective: it leaves, again, the trace of the double image, the whispering in the shadows, just as the attempt of the children's crusade, the "Moral Majority," to practise self-control as a prelude to reactionary power leaves them whimpering in the night for mother. As a representation of the still point, the urge towards control and stasis, Zero is obviously endowed with a good deal more specificity than Desiderio had been in *Doctor Hoffman:* the struggle of Eros and Thanatos, recognized already in the earlier text to be shaped by specific histories, is now shaped also and predominantly by the societal processes of gendering.

And it is this area which Carter goes on to explore in greater detail in *The Sadeian Woman,* a text which takes to an extreme point the problems of the manifestation of desire encountered in *Doctor Hoffman.* As an empirical history, or indeed as a history with traces of the empirical, the stance of *Sadeian Woman* appears at first reading tangential to the feminism which it ostensibly espouses; but what is really at stake is not so much a history as a reading of the sign and of the processes of sign-formation. For *Sadeian Woman* is a history of representations, but with the added implicit claim that that is all the history there is: we do not have access to a neutral world of "facts," but are ourselves the constructs of desire, but particularly of those desires which are allowed approbation and material confirmation because they serve the interests of the social formation. It is pointless to say in response to *Sadeian Woman,* as has been said, that the claim that women are "impregnated" with a will to submission leads into a stance of political defeatism,[15] according to Carter there is no eventual, Platonic essence of femininity which is done disservice by this claim, for the concept and stereotype of feminity is itself constructed within the overarching web of ideological forces which shape the substance of subjectivity.[16] It is not even a question of collusion, for collusion implies choice; rather, we are required to move into a world where the symbols and signboards are our total environment, behind them lying nothing but vacuity, or perhaps the nameless, shapeless essence of sexuality which Doctor Hoffman seeks to free in the form of nebulous time.

But if there is no world beyond the hoardings, this does not mean that no activity is possible, for we remain face-to-face with the work of interpretation, forced up against it at every point: for if the process of signification is built on the interlocking of projections and introjections, all the questions about our relation to the stereotypes remain open, as do the questions about the picture of society which we can form from our investigations of the semiotic milieu.[17] For nothing here is accidental: the least curve of a thigh, the faintest hint of proffered pleasure, on the cinema screen or on the tube-train advertisement, constitute the geometry of the social formation and can be read as such. Therefore each and every action, and especially each manifestation of sexuality, becomes instantaneously inserted into a code becomes a fragment of text to be read. The endpoint of this self-consciousness, of this ceaseless plotting of event onto the structure of language, is the pronunciation of sex as impossible, and this motif is reiterated throughout Carter's fiction: from the rape of *Love* (1971) and the momentary encounter with the idiot boy in the earlier *Heroes and Villains* (1969), to the evasion of consummation in *Doctor Hoffman* and the lifeless mating of Eve and Tristessa in *New Eve,* the sexual act can be figured only as instant emission, an eruption of desire so small and so unsatisfactory that it serves only to confirm the boundary between the genders and the incompatibility of desires.

Eve's new body, equipped with an instantly pleasured clitoris but racked with unassuaged desire (for unity within the self, for unification with another) is the symbol for this promise which cannot be satisfied; and although *New Eve* and *Sadeian Woman* loftily, and even on occasion gloatingly, ironize this state of deferral, the suspicion remains that all ejaculation is premature, and that this truth applies also to narrative itself, insofar as the urge towards climax and ending is to be read only as the displaced version of an urge to return to the womb and obliterate self-differentiation: Insofar as we do not and cannot fulfil this urge, all else remains provisional, and to imagine it could be otherwise is to immerse ourselves in fantasy—just, again, as this immersion in fantasy remains the only route open to the writer who wishes to avoid the ideologically collusive techniques of realism. Through fictions, our interpretations of the social codes may be enhanced; but only in the direction of isolation, rejection, an accommodation with death as the circle within which provisional actions take place.

The notion of an alternative accommodation, between the genders, is no longer on the "agenda," and it is here that Sade, present throughout Carter's work, provides the bounding line, for in his life and works are figured a resolution which relies on a double movement: the adoption of the outward forms of violence and organization which typify society, accompanied by a withdrawal of the inward to a still point from which all is ironized, and everybody looks much the same.[18] The divided self which has been produced in women cannot be reunified; but it can be turned into a weapon and a sanctuary, worn on the sleeve as the simultaneous mark of threat and rejection, of the conjoined liberation and despair which are signified by the broken phallus which, in *New Eve,* gapes backward to reveal the unslakeable womb beneath the skin.

Notes

1. This essay follows on from my analysis of some of Carter's earlier work in *The Literature of Terror: A History of Gothic Fictions from 1765 to the Present Day* (London, 1980), pp. 396–400.

2. For the theory here, see Jacques Lacan, *The Four Fundamental Concepts of Psychoanalysis* ed. J.-A. Miller, trans. A. Sheridan (London, 1977), pp. 67–119.

3. See Rosalind Coward and John Ellis, *Language and Materialism: Developments in Semiology and the Theory of the Subject* (London, 1977), pp. 10, 112–20.

4. Carter, *The Infernal Desire Machines of Doctor Hoffman* (London, 1972), p. 190.

5. See Flann O'Brien, *The Third Policeman* (London, 1967).

6. See Gilles Deleuze and Felix Guattari, *Anti-Oedipus: Capitalism and Schizophrenia,* trans. R. Hurley et al. (New York, 1977).

7. I am assuming that Desiderio's foreign name and location are displacements of a type familiar in Gothic and neo-Gothic fiction.

8. See O'Brien, *Third Policeman,* e.g., pp. 74–79.

9. Carter, *The Passion of New Eve* (London, 1977), p. 16.

10. I am using, of course, Lacan's discoveries about the formation of the psyche, although in a way which, I hope, does not involve too many phallocentric assumptions: see Lacan, "The mirror stage as formative of the function of the I," in *Ecrits: a Selection,* trans. A. Sheridan (London, 1977), pp. 1–7.

11. See Jung on the "glass-house": see *The Practice of Psychotherapy: Essays on the Psychology of the Transference and Other Subjects,* in *The Collected Works of C.G. Jung,* ed. Sir Herbert Read et al. (20 vols., London, 1957–79), XVI, 241, 245.

12. Italo Calvino, *Invisible Cities,* trans. W. Weaver (London, 1974), p. 101.

13. See the Editorial Collective of *Questions feministes,* "Variations on Common Themes," in *New French Feminisms,* ed. E. Marks and I. de Courtivron (Amherst, Mass., 1980), p. 221.

14. I am aware that this formulation runs counter to Lacanian theory; that, indeed, is the point. See Lacan, "On a question preliminary to any possible treatment of psychosis," in *Ecrits,* pp. 179–225.

15. See Andrea Dworkin, *Pornography: Men Possessing Women* (New York, 1981), pp. 84–85.

16. See Carter, *The Sadeian Woman: An Exercise in Cultural History* (London, 1979), pp. 9–17.

17. This, it seems to me, is part of the answer which needs to be made to Terry Lovell's critique of "conventionalism": see Lovell, *Pictures of Reality: Aesthetics, Politics and Pleasure* (London, 1980), pp. 14–17, 79–84.

18. See *Sadeian Woman*, p. 146.

The Violence of Gendering:
Castration Images in Angela Carter's
The Magic Toyshop, The Passion of New Eve,
and "Peter and the Wolf"

JEAN WYATT

In an essay on life in the '60s, Angela Carter describes how she became committed to "demythologising" "the social fictions that regulate our lives": "I began to question . . . the nature of my reality as a woman. How that social fiction of my 'femininity' was created, by means outside my control, and palmed off on me as the real thing" ("Notes," 71; 70). Her novels and short stories take on some of the master narratives that continue to construct femininity in Western culture—giving us, for instance, in *The Bloody Chamber,* reconstructed fairy tales that transform the original tales' helpless virgins into active sexual subjects. The best defense against a social myth is, perhaps, another myth: by telling the old stories differently, Carter both points up the age-old patriarchal preference for certain kinds of heroines—passive, inert—and sets an alternative model of womanhood in place of the old. If fairy tales are among the "mind-forged manacles" that circumscribe female identity ("Notes," 70), so, to judge from Carter's essays and interviews, are Freud's tales. I argue that Carter rewrites Freud's story of a little boy's discovery of sexual difference in "Peter and the Wolf," explores the narrative possibilities of Freud's concept of woman as a castrated man in *The Passion of New Eve,* and rewrites Freud's account of a girl's oedipal transformation in *The Magic Toyshop,* exposing the power relations masked by Freud's emphasis on female anatomical lack.

The castrated female body, a pivotal image in Freud's narratives of sexual difference, strikes Carter as a powerful ideological tool for inscribing and so insuring women's inferiority. On the other hand, the image of woman's castration serves Carter's own polemical purposes as a metaphor for the painful curtailment of a woman's erotic potential and active impulses when she accepts the limitations of the feminine role. Carter returns to the image of

From *Women's Studies* 25 (1996): 549–70. © 1996 Overseas Publishers Association. Reprinted by permission.

castrated woman again and again, addressing it as ideological issue, as narrative device, as image.

The Sadeian Woman, Carter's essay on pornography, describes the cultural reverberations of the castration image:

> The social fiction of the female wound, the bleeding scar left by her castration . . . is a psychic fiction as deeply at the heart of Western culture as the myth of Oedipus, to which it is related in the complex dialectic of imagination and reality that produces culture. Female castration is an imaginary fact that pervades the whole of men's attitude towards women and our attitude to ourselves (23).

On the one hand, Carter emphasizes the force of the physical image: because it is present to our imaginations not as metaphor but as anatomical fact—as "bleeding wound"—the image of castrated woman provides a powerful physical correlative to the cultural assumption of women's inferiority. In an interview, Carter attributes the image to Freud: "he could only think of women as castrated men" (Sage, 56). And it is Freud who is Carter's target when she is working the physical register of culture. "Peter and the Wolf" challenges the story of Freud's generic little boy, who discovers with horror that a little girl's body has "nothing there," where the penis should be: when Carter's little boy, Peter, catches a glimpse of his girl cousin's body he sees what *is* there—and the text describes in precise detail the complex configuration of female genitalia.

On the other hand, the passage from *The Sadeian Woman* reveals Carter's interest in the way that the image of woman as castrate interacts with other mythic images "in the complex dialectic of imagination and reality" that sustains patriarchy. It is Lacan, rather than Freud, whose theories are most helpful in understanding Carter's reflections on the cultural uses of the castrated woman image. *The Magic Toyshop* not only describes what lures are offered, what pressures exerted, to seduce and coerce a girl into accepting the limitations of femininity. It also explores how woman as castrated, silenced object supports the ideal of masculinity as mastery, self-sufficiency, control. But it offers an alternative as well, a deviation that upsets the power balance of gender: a young man, refusing to aspire to the mastery his gender entitles him to, rejects the phallic legacy—most graphically by chopping off and throwing away a clear and obvious symbol of the phallus.

CARTER'S DIALOGUE WITH FREUD: "PETER AND THE WOLF" AND *THE PASSION OF NEW EVE*

In "Peter and the Wolf," as I read it, Carter challenges Freud's image of woman as castrate, attempting to displace it by entering into the cultural imaginary her own picture of an intact female body. In Freud's narrative of sexual discovery, a boy catches sight of a little girl's genitals, and seeing there no penis assumes she has been castrated; the idea that castration could be visited upon him, too, precipitates the boy's flight from his mother and his alignment with his father's authority, resolving the oedipal crisis and positioning him appropriately in the sex/gender system. Throughout Freud's many versions of this story, he endorses the small boy's "recognition that women are castrated" ("Passing," 179), referring in his own voice to the "discovery of her organic inferiority" ("Female Sexuality," 200), "the reality of castration" ("Infantile," 231; 275), "the fact of her castration" ("Inhibitions," 123; "Anatomical," 188; "Female Sexuality," 202).[1] Backed by Freud's authority, the fiction of female castration probably influences not only men's images of women, but, as Carter says in the passage quoted above, "our attitudes toward ourselves." That is, the material terms in which woman's inferiority has been encoded undermine the bodily basis of woman's self-esteem, giving her a foundational sense of inferiority.

"Peter and the Wolf" attempts to revise this founding narrative of sexual difference by articulating the female genitalia as material presence. The plot need concern us only insofar as it brings about an encounter between Peter, a seven-year-old boy, and his cousin of the same age, who has been raised by wolves. When the family traps her and brings her into their house, she sits on the hearth howling for her brethren wolves:

> Peter's heart gave a hop, a skip, so that he had a sensation of falling; . . . he could not take his eyes off the sight of the crevice of her girl-child's sex, that was perfectly visible to him as she sat there square on the base of her spine. . . . Her lips opened up as she howled so that she offered him, without her own intention or volition, a view of a set of Chinese boxes of whorled flesh that seemed to open one upon another into herself, drawing him into an inner, secret place in which destination perpetually receded before him, his first, devastating, vertiginous intimation of infinity. (83)

Carter answers Freud's "no thing" with a complex whorl of fleshly things, his "nothing" with a material "infinity." (Carter may be deliberately troping Freud here, her intact wolf girl playing off the figure of castrated wolf central to the "Wolf Man's" castration anxiety dream. ["Infantile," 213–234]).

Carter revises the male look crucial to the oedipal turn. Peter doesn't reduce female difference to a logic of the same (having/not having the penis): he sees his cousin's vagina in all its "puzzling otherness," its "unresolved materiality," its heterogeneity (Gallop, 61).[2] Freud's cognitive alliance with the little boy who sees only that the girl's body is penis-less leaves him open to the criticism (made most persuasively by Irigaray) that he himself refuses to see what *is* there: if the female genitalia were admitted "as the signifier of the possibility of an other libidinal economy" (*Speculum,* 48), the social and linguistic categories constructed along the axis presence/absence—in fact the whole system of phallocentric meanings—would collapse. Indeed, when Peter, years later, gets a second glimpse of his cousin's radically other sexuality he ceases to believe in the masculinist systems—Catholic theology and Latin language—he has lived by: "What would he do at the seminary, now? . . . He experienced the vertigo of freedom" (86). He enters a world unmapped by linguistic and doctrinal meanings, a world wide open to his discovery (87). Carter's story suggests that the vision of real difference, taken in without denial or defensive categorization, opens the mind to the previously unsignified, springing the subject free from established categories of thought.

"Peter and the Wolf" performs an important service for women by honoring the female body through representation. If representation governs what we believe in as real, the absence of representation has the effect of erasing reality. The occlusion of female sex organs from cultural representations, as well as their resurgence in pornography as a "desexed hole" (*Sadeian Woman*, 20), has doubtless diminished female sexual capacity and undermined female self-esteem. Michele Montrelay's "Inquiry into Femininity" implies that verbal articulation is a crucial dimension of sexuality itself. Claiming that women generally have a "blank" where a representation of their sexuality should be, she cites several cases recorded by Maria Torok in which a female patient, following a session in which the analyst provides a description of her sexuality, has a dream which includes orgasm. Apparently a dialectic between body and word is necessary to a full experience of physical sensation. "Pleasure is the effect of the word of the other" (Montrelay, 95): hence the pleasure that women readers (at least this reader) derive from Carter's description. By entering the female body into a structuring discourse, Carter supplies a missing dimension of female sexual identity.

The Passion of New Eve deals with a literal castration: Evelyn, a man, is surgically deprived of his penis, and a female anatomy is constructed on the basis of that castrated body: he becomes Eve. Carter seems to be giving body to Freud's myth of woman as a castrated man and so reinforcing it—till it becomes evident that Eve, "the perfect woman," is constructed according to the specifications of male desire. The relevant question then becomes, Why does man (including Freud) need to represent woman as castrated?

Feminist answers to this question begin with deBeauvoir's notion of woman as man's other: a man needs a defective other to reflect back to him his own full manly reality (xxiii). If woman's lack is integral to a male sense of sufficiency, then it is imperative to make a plausible case for her deficiency: what more convincing way to argue the inferiority of woman than to ground that inferiority in her body? It then seems to be a part of factual reality— irrefutable. Freud's insistent iteration of "the fact of her castration" then responds to a cultural imperative. (Thomas Laqueur's work shows that women's social subordination has always been encoded as genital inferiority. Before European science discovered her difference, it was her similarity to men that established her inferior status: pre-eighteenth century medical texts describe woman's uterus, ovaries, and vagina, as inverted and inferior imitations of, respectively, the male scrotum, testicles, and penis [4,25–62,236].)

Lacan carries the logic of the other one step further. In his lexicon everyone is "castrated"—but masculinity is founded on the denial of that fundamental lack. "Castration" is the founding term of subjectivity: when a child enters language and the social order it loses the direct and immediate relation to things (including the mother's body) that it had before signifiers intervened; and it is divided from itself, losing to the unconscious the part of the self split off from the socially determined narrow "I" of the linguistic register. The subject feels the loss of an originary wholeness, imagined retrospectively, from a site within the symbolic order, as a lost unity with the maternal body. "Through his relationship to the signifier, the subject is deprived of something of himself, of his very life" (Lacan, "Desire,"28). "Castration" in the Lacanian system represents the loss of that part one thought one had, the vital part that made one whole, "that pound of flesh which is mortgaged in [the subject's] relationship to the signifier" (Lacan, "Desire," 28). The relevant point here is that no one retains the "pound of flesh," no one has the missing link to completeness: "no one has the phallus—it is a signifier, the initial signifier of 'the lack-in-being that determines the subject's relation to the signifier'" (Lacan, *Ecrits,* 710; qt. in Heath, 52). But conventional masculinity is founded on a pretense of wholeness, and on a pretension to the phallus as the insignia of masculine power, authority, and invulnerability—founded, in other words, on a denial of the "castration" that is the unavoidable price of entering the symbolic order.[3] This affirmation of phallic intactness is both "central to our present symbolic order" and "precariously maintained," since it rests on "a negation of the lack installed by language" (Silverman, 135–6).

The fiction that a man can embody the phallic ideal can only be sustained through a series of props—and the first of these is woman. "The subject is constituted in lack and the woman represents lack" (Health, 52). In order to be "the woman men want," then, a woman must put on the masquerade of femininity: as "the Real is full and 'lacks' nothing" (Lacan, "La relation," 851–2), a woman has to disguise herself as "castrated" in order to appear desirable. In Lacanian symbology the veil constitutes the exemplary disguise: "Such is the woman behind her veil: it is the absence of the penis that makes her . . . object of desire" (Lacan, *Ecrits,* 322). *The Passion of New Eve* and *The Magic Toyshop* deploy veils as Lacan does—to signify the castrated female body whose lack confirms the value of what man has.[4]

In *The Passion of New Eve* the masquerade is literal: Tristessa, a Hollywood star who is every movie-goer's ideal of femininity, hides a male body beneath her veils. At the moment of her/his unveiling the narrator, Eve, understands that Tristessa has been "the most beautiful woman in the world" because "she" has been constructed by a man: "That was why he had been the

perfect man's woman! He had made himself the shrine of his own desires . . .
How could a real woman ever have been so much a woman as [he]?" (128–9).
And what are the characteristics of this quintessential woman, this archetype
of man's desire? Tristessa's attractiveness rests, the narrator says, on "your
beautiful lack of being, as if your essence were hung up in a closet . . . and
you were reduced to going out only in your appearance" (72). Here Carter
spells out the meaning of Tristessa's veils: she is costumed as "lack-of-being."
She is equal to "the secret aspirations of man" (128) because she can act out
man's lack—so he need not assume it. This Lacanian perspective focuses the
otherwise puzzling behaviors of Tristessa on screen: throughout her many
screen roles she weeps, seeming to "distill . . . the sorrows of the world"; her
"melancholy," her "ache of eternal longing" take on significance as elaborate
rituals of mourning over some loss too fundamental to name (121, 110, 72).

"The woman men want" is a castrated woman. As if to hammer in the
point, Carter doubles Tristessa's representation of lack with a literally castrated body: the narrator Eve, originally Evelyn, is (involuntarily) castrated,
then surgically reconstructed as the "ideal woman" (78). Modeled on a blueprint "drawn up from a protracted study of the media," including the Playboy centerfold, she is made to incarnate male fantasies of Woman (78, 75).
Eve and Tristessa thus literalize the notion of femininity as a male construct.
At their first encounter, the narrator Eve mentally addresses Tristessa in language that approaches the theoretical level of a Lacanian polemic on femininity:

> The abyss on which [Tristessa's] eyes open, ah! it is the abyss of myself, of
> emptiness, of inward void . . . With her glance like a beam of black light, she
> ordered me to negate myself with her (125).

It is as "emptiness," "void," "negation" that "Woman" exists, as the negative sign—"minus phallus, minus power" (Féral, 89)—that establishes the
man as the standard of positive value.[5]

BECOMING AN OBJECT: *THE MAGIC TOYSHOP* (I)

Beneath its patina of Gothic thrills, *The Magic Toyshop* presents a careful, if
parodic, inventory of the practices, cultural and familial, that rob a young girl
of agency—indeed, of subjectivity—reducing her to the position of feminine
object. The fifteen-year-old protagonist, Melanie, puts on the veils of femininity twice: once before her mirror, where she decks herself out in the gauzy
costumes pictured by various male artists, recreating herself as the object of
their gaze (1–2); and again when her uncle Philip forces her to play a chiffon-
draped Leda in a family theatrical.

Shortly after the novel opens, Melanie's parents are killed in an airplane crash, and she is placed in her Uncle Philip's household. Philip's only passion is making life-sized puppets and putting on puppet shows. Philip sees in Melanie the potential for embodying his idea of a naive young ingenue and casts her as Leda opposite his puppet swan in a production of "Leda and the Swan."

I read this episode as a parodic enactment of the violence implicit in father-daughter relations. For despite its touches of the fantastic and macabre, *The Magic Toyshop* is at bottom a family novel. In an extreme but recognizable schematic of the lines of power in a patriarchal nuclear family, Philip's family is structured by his paternal authority. He effectively controls the time and labor of his wife Margaret and his "children"—Finn and Francie, Margaret's two brothers—from whom he exacts unquestioning filial obedience. His wife Margaret is correspondingly passive, without will and without voice (struck dumb on her wedding day, she has remained mute ever since.) When Melanie goes to live with them, she slips into the position of daughter to Philip. Given the hyperbolic imbalance of voice and authority in Philip's family, it comes as no surprise that Carter dramatizes the "daughter's" oedipal crisis in a way that heightens the power dimension of father-daughter relations.

The play, "Leda and the Swan," fulfills the function of the oedipal stage: that is, it organizes Melanie's sexuality to accord with her gender role. And, as in the theories of feminist theorists like deBeauvoir, Chodorow, and Benjamin, it is the "father" who is the agent of Melanie's transformation from active girl to woman-as-object. As Leda, she goes on stage swathed in the white chiffon costume Philip has designed; and she is utterly dependent upon his voice-on-high for direction. "She halted, at a loss what to do next. . . . She prayed for a cue. Uncle Philip read out: 'Leda attempts to flee her heavenly visitant but his beauty and majesty bear her to the ground' " (166). Melanie sees approaching from the wings a grotesque puppet-swan: "It was nothing like the wild, phallic bird of her imaginings. It was dumpy and homely and eccentric. She nearly laughed aloud to see its lumbering progress" (165). Crude or not, Philip's fantasy (as well as, by implication, the male sexual fantasies dramatized in myths like Leda and the Swan) is effective, holding the woman to her role within the male imaginary:

All her laughter was snuffed out. She was hallucinated; she felt herself not herself, wrenched from her own personality, watching this whole fantasy from another place. . . . The swan towered over the black-haired girl who was Melanie and who was not. . . . The swan made a lumpish jump forward and settled on her loins. She thrust with all her force to get rid of it but the wings came down all around her. . . . The gilded beak dug deeply into the soft flesh. She screamed. . . . She was covered completely. . . . The obscene swan had mounted her. She screamed again. There were feathers in her mouth. . . . After a gap of consciousness, she . . . looked around for her swan. (166–7)

While the swan is, mercifully, not anatomically correct, the "act" of rape retains the psychological effect that theorists and survivors of rape report: that is, women experience rape not only as a physical violation but as a denial of their humanity, of their agency and self-determination: "the real crime is the annihilation by the man of the woman as a human being" (Griffin, 39). *The Sadeian Woman* makes clear that Carter shares this understanding of rape: "In a rape . . . all humanity departs from the sexed beings . . . Somewhere in the fear of rape is . . . a fear of psychic disintegration, . . . a fear of a loss or dismemberment of the self" (6). In *The Magic Toyshop,* then, Carter uses rape as a metaphor for the psychic "dismemberment" of a young girl. Like Gayle Rubin, Carter revises Freud's notion that it is the recognition of her anatomical lack, of her actual "castration," that persuades a girl at the oedipal juncture to acknowledge her "inferiority" ("Female Sexuality," 200); rather, oedipal socialization itself is shown as a castrating process that strips a girl of her active impulses, her agency, and indeed her subjectivity, reducing her to the feminine object required by a patriarchal social order.

For the play teaches Melanie to define herself as object: "The swan towered over the girl who was Melanie and who was not" (166). John Berger has given us the paradigm for this doubling: existing within a world defined by the male gaze and dependent upon male approval for her welfare, a woman learns to see herself as men see her, carrying "the surveyor and the surveyed within her" (46). But Carter's description suggests a still more radical self-division. "The black-haired girl who was Melanie" is the girl seen from outside, not from the position of "surveyor within her," not from a subjective (if colonized) center, but "wrenched from her own personality, watching this whole fantasy from another place"—from a place that approximates the site of the male gaze; and "the black-haired girl . . . who was not [Melanie]" is the void within. Rather than being split into an object which is seen and a subject who sees, Melanie is split into an object—viewed from a male perspective external to her—and, perceived from within, a nothing.

At tea after the play, Melanie retains the consciousness—paradoxically—of an object. Since she lacks a subjective center from which to organize the world, reality hemorrhages from the things she perceives, flowing toward the subject who now organizes *her* as an object in his world. "The cake seemed extremely unlikely, a figment of the imagination. She ate her slice but tasted nothing. The company round the tea-table was distorted and alien. . . . Everything was flattened to paper cut-outs by the personified gravity of Uncle Philip as he ate his tea" (169). There is only one subject now, and "his silence reached from here to the sky. It filled the room" (168). Since Philip is silent, giving Melanie no script (or rather, no voice-over) she is silent too.

The violence of gendering is usually masked by the dynamic of love that produces it: according to the feminist theorists cited by Nancy Chodorow, a father "bribes" his daughter with "love and tenderness" when she exhibits the passive feminine behaviors that please him and so gradually trains her to derive self-esteem from his praise rather than from her own actions—to become, in the familiar phrase, the apple of his eye, the submissive object of his affection (Deutsch, 251–2; Maccoby and Jacklin, 329; qt. in Chodorow, 139, 119). The idealization of the father as powerful subject in relation to a passive and dependent self "becomes the basis for future relationships of ideal love, the submission to a powerful other who seems to embody the agency and desire one lacks in oneself" (Benjamin, "Desire," 86). By stripping the oedipal conversion from subject to object of compensatory fatherly affection and condensing a process of adaptation that usually takes years into the space of a single scene, Carter dramatizes the violence of the father-daughter relations which force the identity of passive object on a girl—a violence already implicit, if unexplored, in deBeauvoir's description of a daughter's normal oedipal resolution: "It is a full abdication of the subject, consenting to become object in submission [to the father]" (287).

The oedipal stage which transforms an active girl into a passive object is always governed by the needs of a male-dominant social order,[6] but the social dimension is usually hidden by the family's enclosure within a seemingly private space. Carter emphasizes that the closed space of the family doubles as cultural space by superimposing the myth of Leda and the Swan on Melanie's oedipal initiation. At a founding moment of Western civilization—for the rape of Leda engendered Helen, hence the Trojan War, hence the master epic of the Western tradition, Homer's *Iliad*—as in every girl's oedipal experience, Carter implies, woman's subjectivity is erased as she is inserted into the patriarchal order. As the exaggerated conventionality of his patriarchal traits suggests, Philip's puppet workshop represents more than a family business: it doubles as a cultural site where the myths that sustain patriarchy are fabricated. (Philip's other puppet plays also dramatize a particular idea of womanhood: in "The Death of the Wood-Nymph," for instance, his chiffon-draped ballerina puppet is exquisitely graceful and then, in death, exquisitely graceful, silent, and quiescent.)[7]

If Philip's imagination is crude, incapable of reaching beyond the terms of brute power, so, Carter implies, is the patriarchal imaginary. Rape is a basic trope of our Western cultural heritage: by Amy Richlin's count, Leda's is one of fifty rapes in Ovid's *Metamorphoses* alone (158). And Yeats's modernist update of "Leda and the Swan" manages to celebrate rape as an act of power and beauty by eliding, again, the woman as subject. Leda is reduced to a body part, her sensations of pain and feelings of violation dead-ended in a synecdoche: "How can those terrified vague fingers push/The feathered glory from her loosening thighs?" Carter's clumsy swan is a joke on patriarchal mythmakers who dress up the principle of male domination in grandiose poetry—but it is a serious joke. Yeats mystifies rape as a moment of divine transcendence ("Did she put on his knowledge with his power?") Carter shows it to be an act of brute force.[8]

That Philip represents a cultural site for the production of social myths as well as a domestic tyrant, that the "rape" of Melanie's subjectivity is meant to represent not just the plight of one abused daughter but the structural alienation of woman in patriarchy—these larger meanings are reinforced by the parallel between Philip's ideal of a womanhood effaced behind white veils and the diaphanous white costumes that Melanie designs for herself at the beginning of the novel, before her parents' death and her move to Philip's house. Melanie is just coming into womanhood as the novel opens:

> The summer she was fifteen, Melanie discovered she was made of flesh and blood. O, my America, my new found land. She embarked on a tranced voyage, exploring the whole of herself, clambering her own mountain ranges, penetrating the most richness of her secret valleys, a physiological Cortez, daGama or Mungo Park.

The metaphors of exploration indicate that Melanie is discovering herself for herself—her body an uncharted territory for her delectation alone. But the text immediately suggests the impossibility of discovering anything new:

> For hours she stared at herself, naked, in the mirror of her wardrobe; . . . she posed in attitudes . . . Pre-Raphaelite, she combed out her long, black hair to stream straight down from a centre parting and thoughtfully regarded herself as she held a tiger-lily from the garden under her chin . . . She was too thin for a Titian or a Renoir but she contrived a pale, smug Cranach Venus with a bit of net curtain wound round her head . . . After she read *Lady Chatterley's Lover,* she secretly picked forget-me-nots and stuck them in her pubic hair. Further, she used the net curtain as raw material for a series of nightgowns suitable for her wedding-night which she designed upon herself. (1–2)

The sequence of artists' names draws the reader's attention to the male hand, the male gaze, that direct and define Melanie even in the apparently unmediated act of self-exploration. Melanie continues to think of herself as exuberant subject when she is already part of a system of representations that defines her as object. "A la Toulouse Lautrec, she dragged her hair sluttishly across her face and sat down in a chair with her legs apart and a bowl of water and a towel at her feet. She always felt particularly wicked when she posed for Lautrec" (1). Between taking on the man's image of woman and presenting that same image to his gaze ("posing for Lautrec"), there is no room for an autonomous female subject; such a closed circuit makes a mockery of self-discovery. Rather than ask; as Melanie does, "What am I?" (141), a woman might well ask, "What do I represent?" Limiting her analysis to the visual register of culture, Carter condenses the process of interpellation, dramatizing "the passage from cultural representations to self-representations" (deLauretis, 12.) Melanie accepts the culture's representation of woman as her own because she believes it will give her power—the sexual power to attract a romantic bridegroom who will carry her off to "honeymoon Cannes. Or Venice." But when she fancies her veiled self "gift-wrapped for a phantom lover" (2) she unwittingly acknowledges her subjection. As passive visual object offered to the man's gaze, she is utterly dependent on his desire to "invest her veils" with "charm," to quote Emily Dickinson. In fact (as Dickinson's poem goes on to suggest) the "charm" attaches not to the woman, but to the veil: the woman herself is meant to recede behind the identity of the veil, a screen onto which the male viewer can project his ideal of womanhood.[9]

Lacan's theory of the gaze, because it is also limited to the visual register, can help explain how Melanie "becomes" a representation—how she is interpellated into the symbolic order. According to Lacan's schema of the visual field (diagrammed in *The Four Fundamental Concepts*), when I look at an object an "image" comes between my gaze and the object: when I in turn become the object of the gaze, the gaze surveys me through an intervening "screen." What is this image through which I view an object? What is the screen through which the gaze fixes me? Lacan doesn't say; but Kaja Silverman treats both image and screen as cultural artifacts (145–52). The first proposition obviously fits Melanie's case: she cannot see her reflection directly, but only in a form dictated by the culture. The second part of Lacan's algorithm seems at first not to apply: the other looks at me through a cultural screen— or, more precisely (since, Lacan says, the screen is opaque), the gaze fits me into the configuration of the cultural screen it projects upon me. But Melanie is alone in her room: that is what gives her the illusion of creating her own image in an autonomous space. Lacan goes to great lengths, however, to distinguish the gaze from any specific eye. He repeatedly insists on our status as objects of the gaze, even if no one else is present: "That which makes us consciousness institutes us by the same token as *speculum mundi* . . . that gaze that circumscribes us . . . makes us beings who are looked at, but without showing this" (Lacan, *Four,* 75). The gaze is all around us, a function of our existence in a visual field; being the object of the gaze is an inalienable dimension of human being. Although she is alone Melanie is nevertheless subject to the world's gaze, and that gaze fits her into a screen of cultural images. To credit oneself as possessor of the gaze, as Melanie does in this scene of presumed visual power, is to be deluded: "In the scopic field, the gaze is outside, I am looked at, that is to say, I am a picture" (Lacan, *Four,* 106). Further, Lacan implies that being turned into a "picture," being mapped onto a background of pre-existing images, pressures us to adopt their forms. "If I am anything in the picture, it is always in the form of the screen" (Lacan, *Four,* 97). Carter literalizes "the process whereby the subject assumes the form of representation—becomes a picture" (Silverman, 148) by having Melanie mold herself to the shapes of the cultural screen, step into the canvases of Lautrec, Cranach, the Pre-Raphaelites.

Compared to his analysis of the gaze, Lacan's notion of the mirror stage is relatively straightforward: the child takes on, assumes as his own identity, the unified body image in the mirror. Carter gives the mirror stage a cultural edge as Melanie accepts the icon in the mirror as her own self-image. In a final veiling, decked out in her mother's wedding dress, Melanie jubilantly declares, "she *was* . . . the beautiful girl . . . in her mirror. Moonlight, white satin, roses. A bride" (italics mine; 16), and so embraces her function as a cultural sign in a symbolic system not of her own making.[10] Visually articulated into the cultural screen, Melanie leaves the prolonged mirror stage of the novel's opening pages not as agent, but as object of the gaze: to borrow Lacan's phrase, she defines herself as *speculum mundi,* offering her bridal-veiled self as spectacle to the world's gaze. " 'Look at me!' she cried to the apple tree . . . 'Look at me!' she cried passionately to the pumpkin moon" (16).

Melanie has already absorbed her cultural identity as object, then, well before she acts out Philip's script. Carter's idea of how "the social fiction of [her] femininity" is "palmed off" on a woman ("Notes," 70) is by no means simple. She complicates the psychoanalytic model of a femininity produced largely through father-daughter relations by connecting Philip's ideal of femininity as veiled impotence to the representations of women in Western art and myth.

Philip's brutal theater of gender does add some important information to the messages about womanhood that Melanie gets from the better known artisans of femininity whose images crowd her solitude. Throughout the mirror scene, Melanie is seduced by a hypocritical culture's promise that dressing provocatively gives a young woman sexual power. Philip's dramatization offers a more realistic assessment of the veils' power. The rape of Leda by a figure of omnipotent masculinity illustrates the power relations that patriarchal culture misrepresents as love relations. As in feminist accounts of rape as a political instrument of oppression that intimidates *all* women, Philip deploys rape to "teach the objective, innate, and unchanging subordination of women" (Brownmiller, 5; Mehrhof and Kearon, 80). Negated as subject, Melanie is forcibly instructed in what the veils mean in a masculine symbolic system: they represent the erasure of the female subject, her transformation into a place-marker signifying lack. As Lacan suggests, the veils' allure stems from their capacity to suggest an absence beneath—to suggest the nothing that supports the something of man. "Adornment *is* the woman, she exists veiled: only thus can she represent lack, be what is wanted" (Heath, 52).

"Dismembering" the Phallic Body: *The Magic Toyshop* (II)

The Magic Toyshop offers an alternative as well as a critique of patriarchal sexual relations. Melanie forms a romantic alliance with Finn, her counterpart in age, status, and subordination to the father—her "brother," in a word, in this family structure. Choosing the more egalitarian structure of the brother-sister bond defeats the aim of the father-daughter relation, which is meant to shape female desire to the passive responsiveness that sustains male dominance.[11] It is not that Melanie suddenly changes from the impressionable girl that I have been describing into an autonomous and self-defining heroine; rather, it is Finn who makes the revolutionary gesture of forfeiting the privileges of masculinity, opening up the possibility of a different relationship between man and woman.

During the night following the play, Finn comes to Melanie's bedside asking for comfort. He has destroyed the puppet swan, he says, and he is trembling with shock at his own audacity and with fear at the terrible vengeance that awaits him—for Philip loves all his puppets inordinately, especially the newly-created swan. Finn describes chopping up the swan and carrying the pieces to a park nearby to bury:

> "First of all, I dismembered [the swan] . . . with Maggie's little axe . . . the swan's neck refused to be chopped up; the axe bounced off it. It kept sticking itself out of my raincoat when I buttoned it up to hide it and it kept peering around while I was carrying it, along with all the bits of the swan . . . It must have looked, to a passer-by, as if I was indecently exposing myself, when the swan's neck stuck out. I was embarrassed with myself and kept feeling to see if my fly was done up . . . it seemed best . . . to bury it in the pleasure garden" (171–173).

It is from his own body that the false "phallus" pokes out, so in chopping it off Finn refuses the masquerade of masculinity: he acknowledges his own castration. In the family structure, Finn is in the position of son to Philip, "apprenticed" to him ostensibly to learn the art of toymaking, but implicitly to learn the art of male dominance. "He is a master," says Finn, referring to Philip's skills as dollmaker; but in the field of gender relations as in woodcraft Finn is meant to identify with the father figure, become "master" in relation to woman. (Before the play, for instance, Philip sent Finn to "rehearse" Melanie in the role of Leda—in other words, to play the part of the rapist swan; Finn initially complied, but bolted in the middle of the act). Severing and throwing away the paternal symbol is equivalent to refusing the phallic function. In Lacan's terms, Finn acknowledges the lack that is everyone's inevitable lot. He presents himself at Melanie's bedside as castrated—that is, as incomplete, insecure, in need of comfort: "Sick and sorry, he came creeping to her bed . . . 'Melanie . . . can I come in with you for a little while? I feel terrible' " (170). Finn not only derails the family agenda; by rejecting "the affirmation central to our present symbolic order that the exemplary male is adequate to the paternal function" (Silverman, 135) Finn subverts the power relations of patriarchy.

A remark dropped during an interview suggests what Carter was up to when she staged this male castration.

> "But you see, one of the things I love about Charlotte Bronte, about *Jane Eyre,* is that she won't look at Rochester until she's castrated him . . . [Then] she's

very nice to him, she can afford to be, this is where she can start behaving like a human being. Actually, in Freudian terms (not Freudian, Freud would be terribly upset) what she's done is to get him on an egalitarian and reciprocal basis, because in fact she hasn't castrated him at all, she's got rid of his troublesome *machismo*" (Sage, 56).

Carter's nod to Freud's discomfiture suggests that she is aware of the revolutionary potential of shifting castration from woman to man. Freud would be "terribly upset" because he inscribed his notion of gendered power relations across the genitals, with the active penis representing the triumphant male subject and the corresponding blank representing a necessarily passive female space. Fixing the sign of castration on the male body, dispensing with a "troublesome *machismo*," with the aspiration to invulnerable masculinity—with the phallus, not the penis—would shift the balance of power to which Freud subscribed, opening the way for an "egalitarian and reciprocal" relation between man and woman.

Indeed, Melanie responds to Finn's display of neediness with a new set of responses:

> He must have been through a great ordeal. . . . "I have been in that place, too," she thought. She could have cried for them both. . . . "You must have had a time of it, poor Finn." She felt that somehow their experience ran parallel. She understood his frenzy. "Poor Finn." (172–173)

Finn's refusal to disavow castration has started a general collapse of the fortifications that defend the system of sexual difference. Melanie's recognition that she and Finn are alike undermines gender hierarchy. A founding principle of the sex/gender system, Gayle Rubin shows, is "the idea that men and women are mutually exclusive categories"; that social fiction contradicts "nature," where "men and women are closer to each other than either is to anything else—for instance, mountains, kangaroos, or coconut palms. . . . Far from being an expression of natural differences, exclusive gender identity is the suppression of natural similarities" (179–80). Jessica Benjamin, analyzing the principles governing erotic dominance in "The Story of O," finds that each act of the master "signifies the male pronouncement of difference over sameness" ("Master," 288). Absolute mastery depends on absolute differentiation from the subjugated woman, especially on a denial of mutual dependency. In less extreme cases of male dominance as well, a man's fear of being demoted to the feminine position safeguards the system of sexual difference from an admission of similarity. "Psychological domination is ultimately the failure to recognize the other person as like, although separate from oneself" (Benjamin, "Master," 283).

Finn is released from the fear that he will be reduced to similarity; he is already there. And Finn's renunciation of all claim to phallic sufficiency necessarily releases Melanie from the task of patriarchy's good woman—seeing and desiring a man "only through the mediation of images of an unimpaired masculinity" (Silverman, 42). The dangers to gender hierarchy of admitting resemblance are immediately clear, as Melanie moves from empathy to a geometry of equality: "their experience ran parallel" (173). The image of lives lived along parallel lines implies the replacement of hierarchy by a lateral relationship, "egalitarian and reciprocal."

Angela Carter does not idealize the sibling model of erotic relations, either. A relationship with a vulnerable other who is needy like oneself entails giving up dreams of romantic love—and Melanie is reluctant to give up the fantasy bridegroom who would transport her to "honeymoon Cannes. Or Venice" (2). If the man doesn't have enormous power in relation to one's small self, then he doesn't have the power to sweep one off one's feet and carry one away to a new life. Melanie has to sacrifice transcendence in the passive mode.

> They were peaceful in bed as two married people who had lain in bed easily together all their lives. . . . She knew they would get married one day and live together all their lives and there would be . . . washing to be done and toast burning all the rest of her life. And never any glamour or romance or charm. Nothing fancy. (174)

If the other is not markedly different from oneself, there is no hope of a radical break between the humdrum present and a glamorous future—only an infinitely protracted dailiness.

In the light of Finn's "simple and honest" (170) declaration of vulnerability and request for comfort, Philip's conventional masculinity takes on the appearance of masquerade (or parade, Lacan's term for masculinity). The assumption of phallic identity—of a masterful, coherent and self-contained sufficiency—entails an impossible consistency: Philip is invariably overbearing, always brutal and insensitive, single-minded in his determination to control everyone—with no lapses, no gaps, no needs. His one-dimensional consistency makes the model of dominant masculinity look implausible.

Likewise, Finn's relationship with Melanie, based on a recognition of mutual need, throws a parodic light on the standard patriarchal couple represented by Philip and Margaret. Since Philip pretends to the phallic ideal, his wife must support the fiction by revering him as the phallic ideal: in Silverman's phrase, the "dominant fiction" requires that both the man and his attendant woman "deny all knowledge of male castration by believing in the commensurability of penis and phallus, actual and symbolic father" (42). Margaret attests to Philip's absolute power by applauding his omnipotence as puppet-master (128) and by maintaining a consistent show of shrinking, cowed obedience.

In other words, the parade of phallic sufficiency requires the masquerade of castrated woman. If the man is to deny castration, the woman must serve as the site where he can deposit his lack. Margaret's lack is indeed conspicuous: she has no voice. And every Sunday she puts on a rather literal masquerade of femininity, donning the necklace Philip has made for her. This silver necklace, reaching from shoulder to chin, is alternately described as a "choker"—it prevents any movement of the head—and a "collar," worn like other collars in the spirit of subjection (112–113). Finn says that Margaret and Philip make love every Sunday: to attract the man the woman ornaments herself; but the ornament itself signifies her subjection to the man; and it is adornment as a sign of submission that makes her desirable.

Silent, passive, and compliant, Margaret appears to be the perfect "castrated woman." But if such true womanliness is "a presentation for the man, . . . as he would have her" (Heath, 50), a question lingers: what hides behind the presentation? In particular, if "the masquerade . . . is what women do . . . in order to participate in man's desire, but at the cost of giving up their own" (Irigaray, *This Sex,* 133), what becomes of that displaced desire? Is there perhaps a hint of anxiety in Freud's question, "What does a woman want?"

In the concluding pages of the novel, the reader, Melanie, and Philip all find out what is behind the mask. Margaret and Francie (Margaret's other brother) are lovers: "They have always been lovers" (194). When Philip finds his wife in her brother's arms, he burns down the house. Given Carter's affection for *Jane Eyre,* the parallel with Bertha and her fire seems inescapable: female desire, forced into a patriarchal lock-up by a system of repressive gender roles, gains in intensity from its very suppression until it explodes from within, destroying the patriarchal family structure that confined and silenced it.

Finn and Melanie, escaping to the garden next door[12] while "everything" burns, "faced each other in a wild surmise" (200). This closing allusion to Cortez's discovery of the Pacific (in Keats's "On First Reading Chapman's Homer") encourages readers to hope that the destruction of Philip's factory of patriarchal fantasies opens up before Melanie and Finn an uncharted space free of the old gender demarcations. Or does it? The opening page's metaphors of global exploration have taught us to be skeptical about the possibility of brave new worlds.

Critics have objected that Carter's early novels (*The Magic Toyshop,* 1967, *Heroes and Villains,* 1969, and *The Passion of New Eve,* 1977) critique patriarchy without offering any positive alternatives: thus Paulina Palmer comments that "while presenting a brilliantly accurate analysis of the oppressive effects of patriarchal structures, [the novels run] the risk of making these structures appear even more closed and impenetrable than, in actual fact, they are" by discounting all possibilities for change (180–181).[13] I would argue that although Carter rewrites social myths in ways that bring out their hidden damages—the pain of Melanie's gendering, for instance, is not softened by parental tenderness—her revisions are liberatory not just because of their "demythologizing" effect: they also suggest alternative forms of masculinity—and therewith, since gender is a relational term, the possibility of revising notions of femininity as well. Both "Peter and the Wolf" and *The Magic Toyshop* picture what would happen if a male subject refused the privileges of masculinity. "Peter and the Wolf" revises the look central to male identity formation, substituting an active receptivity to female difference for Freud's defensive wrestling of difference into a familiar binary that separates those who have from those who don't. Finn's "castration" undoes the rigid structural opposition between man and woman, suggesting the possibility of distributing strength and weakness, need and comfort, more equably between the sexes. What Carter is unwilling to compromise or soften in these early novels is her depiction of woman's structural position within patriarchy: becoming a woman requires, in *The Passion of New Eve*, a literal castration and, in *The Magic Toyshop*, a "rape," an alienation of a woman's subjective agency that amounts to a mutilation.[14]

Notes

1.   Shortly after the publication of Freud's first essay on femininity in 1925, Karen Horney shrewdly observed that Freud's description of female development "differs in no case by a hair's breadth from the typical ideas that the boy has of the girl" (174). See also Luce Irigaray's analysis of Freud's "nothing there" (*Speculum,* 48) and Jane Gallop's commentary on Irigaray (58–9;65–6). Juliet Mitchell is more forgiving: she argues that Freud was consciously analyzing women's condition under patriarchal oppression; recognizing her "castration" meant recognizing her lack of phallic power (34).

2.   Peter's way of seeing problematizes the Freudian concept of "disavowal." As Freud defines it, "disavowal" is the boy's refusal to accept that the woman has no penis, to admit "the reality of castration" ("Infantile," 231–275); that denial of "reality" becomes the basis of fetishism and the psychoses. If looking (as Peter looks, without defenses) in fact yields a view of what is actually there, then the term "disavowal" would seem to fit the perception that Freud calls "normal," the perception that there is nothing there; and what Freud calls pathogenic "disavowal" would seem to be a refusal to deny what is there. (Admittedly, all this is complicated by the recessed position of the female genitals: nevertheless, Carter's story makes us question the pathogenic character of what Freud calls "disavowal," as well as what Freud means by the "reality" of castration.)

3.   A developmental perspective may serve to sort out some of the values attached to the phallus. The phallus signifies lack—the lack accompanying the accession to language and the symbolic order. But at the oedipal phase, the phallus also becomes implicated in sexual difference, with the father presumed to have it and the mother to lack it. So "having the phallus" would mean in the first instance possessing wholeness; secondarily, "having the phallus" would extend that sufficiency to include qualities attributed to the (idealized) father such as mastery and control (See Lapsley and Westlake, 72–3; Heath, 52–3). See also Rose, 38–9.

4.   This essay deals with the veil as signifier in Western cultural discourse only. For the complex relation of the veil to gender and politics in Muslim countries see Enloe, Odeh, and Wikan.

5.   Roberta Rubenstein makes the crucial point that Tristessa and Eve both suffer from the "recognition that each is an Other, an object constructed by others—as in a mirror or in another's gaze—and not a subject or self" (111). Rubenstein thinks that Carter's story remains

too bound by prevailing definitions of gender to provide a "re-gendered" vision of human possibility (116). Likewise, Carol Siegel comments that while the novel insists upon "the constructed, anti-natural quality of gender," it does not "release passion from determination by the concept of femininity as the binary opposite of masculinity or from the association of masochism with femininity" (12). Susan Suleiman, on the other hand, credits the novel with "expand[ing] our notions of what it is possible to dream in the domain of sexuality. . . . It is to the . . . dream of going beyond the old dichotomies, of imagining 'unguessable modes of humanity' that *The Passion of New Eve* succeeds in giving textual embodiment" (139–40).

6. As Irigaray says, "In the last analysis, the female Oedipus complex is woman's entry into a system of values that is not hers, and in which she can 'appear' and circulate only when enveloped in the needs/desires/fantasies of others, namely men" (*This Sex*, 134).

7. Bram Dijkstra documents the popularity of the dead beauty in nineteenth century paintings; the dead woman represents "the apotheosis of an ideal of feminine passivity and helplessness" (36). See also Bronfen, 59–64.

8. Lynn Higgins and Brenda Silver's anthology, *Rape and Representation,* shows that the simultaneous inscription and erasure of sexual violence against women that characterizes Yeats's poem occurs again and again in classical as well as modern texts. See especially the introduction by Higgins and Silver and the essays by Joplin and Silver.

9. The relevant stanza reads:

> "A Charm invests a face
> Imperfectly beheld—
> The Lady dare not lift her Veil
> For fear it be dispelled."

I am indebted to Cay Strode's analysis of the poem's visual power dynamic.

10. It is the underlying male structure, the exchange of women between men, that gives the wedding dress its meaning: while a woman may think her wedding dress celebrates her power—the beauty and virtue that have secured her a husband—the white of the wedding dress refers to male interests only, signifying that the woman is unexchanged, unused, and so keeps her full value as commodity, as the gift that ratifies the bond between the father who gives her and the husband who takes her. Perhaps because it thus suggests the alienation of woman into a symbol, the wedding dress is often an accoutrement of femininity in Carter's novels. In *Heroes and Villains* Marianne is forced to put on an ancient wedding dress for her arranged marriage, becoming a signifier in Donally's symbolic system, which incorporates Levi-Strauss's model of the exchange of women. In *Love* and "The Bloody Chamber" a wedding dress is likewise imposed upon the woman rather than self-chosen.

11. I have discussed the structural similarities (including power asymmetries) between father-daughter relations and romantic love relations in *Reconstructing Desire*, 26–31.

Elizabeth Abel analyzes the subversive potential of the brother-sister bond in Sophocles' *Antigone* and in Doris Lessing's work: by making the familiar, the familial, man the object of desire in place of a stranger, brother-sister incest challenges "the fundamental structure of partriarchy" by preventing the exchange of women.

12. Flora Alexander finds a parallel between Finn and Melanie's new beginning in the garden and Adam and Eve's: "They have quarreled with a patriarchal figure like God the Father and it has been their good fortune to escape" (65).

13. Robert Clark faults Carter for not always providing enough cues to produce a parodic reading of the patriarchal tropes she incorporates into her fiction. "The ideologic power of the form being infinitely greater than the power of the individual to overcome it," Carter risks reinscribing the ideology of erotic domination by presenting rape and other forms of sexual violence as thrilling, without the necessary "moral and historical context" (152–3) to provide a critical perspective. Elaine Jordan makes a spirited rejoinder to Clark's argument. She claims that "Angela Carter is offering experiments in overcoming ideas, images, representations, that have determined our options for thinking and feeling" (34).

14. In the later *Nights at the Circus* (1984) Carter offers a picture of female sexuality exuberant in its excesses rather than curbed of its potential. In that novel she rewrites "Leda and the Swan" to a woman's advantage, creating in the protagonist Fevvers her own mythic version of Leda's offspring. Because she is sprung from the egg laid by Leda, Fevvers has too many appendages rather than too few—and her wings are just one of the excesses that contribute, like her laughter and her verbal fluency, to stumping definitions of femininity (as spectacle, as sexual victim, and so on) that various male characters try to impose on her. See Robinson, 117–131.

Works Cited

Abel, Elizabeth. "Resisting Exchange: Brother-Sister Incest in Fiction by Doris Lessing." *Doris Lessing: The Alchemy of Survival.* Ed. Carey Kaplan and Elizabeth Cronan Rose. Athens: U of Ohio P, 1988:115–126.

Alexander, Flora. *Contemporary Women Novelists.* London: Edward Arnold, 1989.

Benjamin, Jessica, "A Desire of One's Own: Psychoanalytic Feminism and Intersubjective Space." *Feminist Studies/Critical Studies.* Ed. Teresa de Lauretis. Indiana UP, 1986: 78–101.

———. "Master and Slave: The Fantasy of Erotic Domination." *Powers of Desire: The Politics of Sexuality.* Ed. Ann Snitow, Christine Stansell, and Sharon Thompson. New York: Monthly Review Press, 1983: 280–299.

Berger, John. *Ways of Seeing.* New York: Viking, 1973.

Bronfen, Elizabeth. *Over Her Dead Body: Death, Femininity, and the Aesthetic.* New York: Routledge, 1992.

Brownmiller, Susan. *Against Our Will: Men, Women and Rape.* New York: Simon and Schuster, 1975.

Carter, Angela. *The Bloody Chamber and Other Stories.* London: Penguin, 1981.

———. *Heroes and Villains.* London: Penguin, 1981.

———. *Love.* London: Penguin, 1988.

———. *The Magic Toyshop.* London: Virago Press, 1981.

———. *Nights at the Circus.* New York: Viking Penguin, 1985.

———. "Notes from the Front Line." *On Gender and Writing.* Ed. Michelene Wandor. London: Pandora P, 1983: 69–77.

———. *The Passion of New Eve.* London: Virago, 1992.

———. "Peter and the Wolf." *Black Venus.* London: Pan Books, 1986: 77–87.

———. *The Sadeian Woman and the Ideology of Pornography.* New York: Pantheon, 1978.

Chodorow, Nancy. *The Reproduction of Mothering: Psychoanalysis and the Sociology of Gender.* Berkeley: U of California P, 1978.

Clark, Robert. "Angela Carter's Desire Machine." *Women's Studies* 14.2 (1987): 147–161.

de Beauvoir, Simone. *The Second Sex.* Trans. H.M. Parshley. New York: Random, 1989.

Deutsch, Helene. *Psychology of Women* (Vol. 1). New York: Grune and Stratton, 1944.

Dickinson, Emily. "A Charm Invests a Face." *The Complete Poems of Emily Dickinson.* Ed. Thomas Johnson. Boston: Little, Brown, 1958: Vol. 1, 421.

Dijkstra, Bram. *Idols of Perversity: Fantasies of Feminine Evil in Fin-de-Siècle Culture.* Oxford: Oxford U. Press, 1986.

Enloe, Cynthia. *Bananas, Beaches and Bases.* Berkeley: U of California Press, 1990.

Féral, Josette. "The Powers of Difference." *The Future of Difference.* Ed. Hester Eisenstein and Alice Jardine. New Brunswick: Rutgers UP, 1985: 88–94.

Freud, Sigmund. "Female Sexuality" (1931). *Women and Analysis.* Ed. Jean Strouse. Boston: G.K. Hall, 1985: 73–94.

————. "Femininity" (1933). *Women and Analysis*. Ed. Jean Strouse. Boston: G.K. Hall, 1985: 73–94.

————. "From the History of an Infantile Neurosis." (1918) ("Wolf Man" case history). *Three Case Histories*. Ed. Philip Rieff. New York: Macmillan, 1963: 187–316.

————. *Inhibitions, Symptoms, and Anxiety* (1926). Standard Edition, ed. James Strachey 20: 75–174.

————. "The Passing of the Oedipus-Complex" (1924). *Sexuality and the Psychology of Love*. Ed. Philip Rieff. New York: Macmillan, 1963: 176–82.

————. "Some Psychological Consequences of the Anatomical Distinction Between the Sexes" (1925). *Sexuality and the Psychology of Love*. Ed. Philip Rieff. New York: Macmillan, 1963: 183–93.

Gallop, Jane. *The Daughter's Seduction: Feminism and Psychoanalysis*. Ithaca: Cornell UP, 1982.

Griffin, Susan. *Rape: The Power of Consciousness*. San Francisco: Harper and Row, 1979.

Heath, Stephen. "Joan Riviere and the Masquerade." *Formations of Fantasy*. Ed. Victor Burgin, James Donald, and Cora Kaplan. London: Methuen, 1986: 45–61.

Higgins, Lynn and Brenda Silver. "Introduction: Rereading Rape." *Rape and Representation*. Ed. Lynn Higgins and Brenda Silver. New York: Columbia UP, 1991: 1–11.

Horney, Karen. "The Flight from Womanhood" (1926). *Women and Analysis*. Ed. Jean Strouse. Boston: G.K. Hall, 1985: 171–186.

Irigaray, Luce. *Speculum of the Other Woman*. Trans. Gillian Gill. Ithaca: Cornell UP, 1985.

————. *This Sex Which Is Not One*. Trans. Catherine Porter. Ithaca: Cornell UP, 1985.

Joplin, Patricia Kleindienst. "The Voice of the Shuttle is Ours." *Rape and Representation*. Ed. Lynn Higgins and Brenda Silver. New York: Columbia UP, 1991: 35–64.

Jordan, Elaine. "Enthralment: Angela Carter's Speculative Fictions." *Plotting Change: Contemporary Women's Fiction*. Ed. Linda Anderson. London: Edward Arnold. 1990: 19–40.

Lacan, Jacques. "Desire and the Interpretation of Desire in *Hamlet*." Trans. James Hulbert. *Literature and Psychoanalysis: The Question of Reading: Otherwise*. Ed. Shoshana Felman. Baltimore: Johns Hopkins UP, 1982: 11–52.

————. *Ecrits*. Paris: Seuil, 1966.

————. *Ecrits: A Selection*. Trans. Alan Sheridan. London: Tavistock, 1977.

————. *The Four Fundamental Concepts of Psycho-Analysis*. Trans. Alan Sheridan. New York: Norton, 1981.

————. Le Seminaire, Livre II, *Le moi dans la theorie de Freud et dans la technique de la psychanalyse*. Paris: Seuil, 1978.

————. "La Relation d'objet et les structures freudiennes." *Bulletin de Psychologie* 10.14 (June 1957): 851–854.

Lapsley, Robert, and Michael Westlake. *Film Theory: An Introduction*. Manchester: Manchester UP, 1988.

Laqueur, Thomas. *Making Sex: Body and Gender from the Greeks to Freud*. Cambridge, Mass: Harvard UP, 1990.

Maccoby, Eleanor, and Carol Jacklin. *The Psychology of Sex Differences*. Stanford: Stanford UP, 1974.

Mehrhof, Barbara, and Pamela Kearon. *Notes from the Third Year: Women's Liberation*. New York, 1971.

Mitchell, Juliet. "On Freud and the Distinction Between the Sexes." *Women and Analysis*. Ed Jean Strouse. Boston: G.K. Hall, 1985: 27–36.

Montrelay, Michele. "Inquiry into Femininity." Trans. Parveen Adams. *m/f* 1 (1978): 83–101.

Odeh, Lama Abu. "Post-Colonial Feminism and the Veil: Thinking the Difference." *Feminist Review* 43 (Spring 1993): 26–37.

Palmer, Paulina. "From 'Coded Mannequin' to Bird Woman: Angela Carter's Magic Flight." *Women Reading Women's Writing*. Ed. Sue Roe. New York: St. Martin's P, 1987: 179–205.

Richlin, Amy. "Reading Ovid's Rapes." *Pornography and Representation in Greece and Rome*. Ed. Amy Richlin. New York: Oxford UP, 1992: 158–179.

Robinson, Sally. *Engendering the Subject: Gender and Self-Representation in Contemporary Women's Fiction*. Albany: State U of New York P, 1991.

Rose, Jacqueline. Introduction II. *Feminine Sexuality: Jacques Lacan and the ecole freudienne*. Ed. Juliet Mitchell and Jacqueline Rose. New York: Norton, 1982: 27–57.

Rubenstein, Roberta. "Intersexions: Gender Metamorphosis in Angela Carter's *The Passion of New Eve* and Lois Gould's *A Sea-Change*." *Tulsa Studies in Women's Literature*, 12.1 (1993): 103–118.

Rubin, Gayle. "The Traffic in Women: Notes on the 'Political Economy' of Sex." *Toward an Anthropology of Women*. Ed. Rayna Reiter. New York: Monthly Review P, 1975: 157–210.

Sage, Lorna. "The Savage Sideshow: A Profile of Angela Carter." *New Review* 52.2 (1977): 51–57.

Siegel, Carol. "Postmodern Women Novelists Review Victorian Male Masochism." *Genders* 11 (1991): 1–16.

Silver, Brenda. "Periphrasis, Power, and Rape in *A Passage to India*." *Rape and Representation*. New York: Columbia UP, 1991: 115–137.

Silverman, Kaja. *Male Subjectivity at the Margins*. New York: Routledge, 1992.

Strode, Cay. "The Dynamics of Feminine Representation: A Feminist Reading of Emily Dickinson's 'A Charm Invests a Face'." Unpublished thesis submitted for English departmental honors. Eagle Rock, CA: Occidental College, 1987.

Suleiman, Susan Rubin. *Subversive Intent: Gender, Politics, and the Avant-Grade*. Cambridge, Mass: Harvard UP, 1990.

Wikan, Unni. *Behind the Veil in Arabia: Women in Oman*. Chicago: Chicago UP, 1982.

Wyatt, Jean. *Reconstructing Desire: The Role of the Unconscious in Women's Reading and Writing*. Chapel Hill: U of North Carolina P, 1990.

Yeats, William Butler. "Leda and the Swan." *Selected Poems and Three Plays of William Butler Yeats*. Ed. M.L. Rosenthal. New York: Macmillan, 1986: 121.

THE SHORT STORIES

♦

Re-Constructing Oedipus through "Beauty and the Beast"

Sylvia Bryant

Once upon a time, there lived a rich merchant who gave his three sons and his three daughters the best money could buy. . . . All the girls were very pretty, especially the youngest. When she was a baby, she was nick-named "Little Beauty," and the name stayed with her as she grew older. . . .

—"Beauty and the Beast"[1]

The traditional narrative framework of the fairy tale has generated an ideologically potent mythology of moral exempla produced, as Angela Carter explains in her recent translation of some classic tales, especially for children who as "apprentice adults . . . will benefit from advice on how to charm, whom to trust, how to grow rich."[2] For centuries, through oral and written narratives, these tenacious "parables of instruction" have inculcated into Western society absolute representative patterns for growing up which are both products and producers of a pervasive ideological system that is deceptively simple in its fantasy, for apparently "children need only be 'good' in order to deserve happy endings."[3]

Film-maker Jean Cocteau, a translator like Carter of the traditional fairy tale narrative into not the textual medium but the filmic, envisioned fairy tale characters as "archetypes or stereotypes" which may be allowed "no subtle nuances between black and white, good and evil."[4] And Cocteau's assessment is certainly historically accurate, for the narratives of these characters' lives have systematically codified socially acceptable parameters for individual behavior and experience, reinforcing essential sexual differences which are perpetuated by a cultural double standard of desire. Yet the seductively familiar, formulaic narrative repeatedly and successfully obscures the genre's inherent binarism of desire, glosses over the seemingly un-self-conscious gender bifurcation, and denies, in fact, the presence of any narrative—any personal,

From *Criticism* 31, no. 4 (Fall 1989): 439–53. © 1989 Wayne State University Press. Reprinted by permission.

individual story—to the characters at all. Both the moral of the tale and the fate of the girls and boys loom large—not just once, but upon every time.

This social scenario of reward based on essential goodness presents an essential problem, particularly for the "girls" seeking their own stories and experiences other than those which literature and history has proffered to them. There is a heavy-handed evaluative double standard operating in the fairy tale, on the general level of representation and in regard to the specific level of that "moral" which positions the female character, and hence the subject-seeking female reader, at the definitional mercy of the dominant culture's inscribing pen. The central female of "Beauty and the Beast" manifests a particular brand of this essential prescriptiveness; as Carter explains it, "Beauty's happiness is founded on her abstract quality of virtue": the moral "is all to do with something indefinable, not with 'doing well,' but with 'being good.' "[5] That "indefinable" quality of "virtue" is really quite clear, however, in the endless re-inscription of what has always already been: "The end of a fairy story is the end of a fairy story," as Cocteau explains the fate of his filmic heroine; "Beauty is docile."[6]

In *Alice Doesn't: Feminism, Semiotics, Cinema*, Teresa de Lauretis traces the "mapping of differences, and specifically, first and foremost, of sexual difference into each text" back to what has been a sort of Ur-story on which Western culture has built and bifurcated its society, and hence its fictions, of sexual differences—the myth of Oedipus.[7] She summarizes this basic narrative paradigm of Oedipus as "a passage, a transformation predicated on the figure of a hero, the mythic subject"[8]—"hero" being itself marked, in a sense, for gender and thus already excluding women from its central narrative position. Thus, the narrative fixity of women in fairy tales falls into peripheral positions which are either undesirable in their extremities or contradictory in their desirability. Or, as Ellen Cronan Rose has succinctly observed, the list of possible positionalities available to the female reader has been consolidated to only a select few: "madonnas and whores, saints and witches, good little girls and wicked queens."[9]

Since the controlling narrative paradigm maps difference and desire, as de Lauretis describes it, predominantly "from the point of view of Oedipus . . . that of masculine desire,"[10] traditional narrative has literally en-cultur-ated the sexual binary into restrictive, predetermined representations and positionalities of "acceptable" behavior and desire—for the female character/reader: goodness, purity, docility. And under the rubric of the Oedipal myth, woman's story is/can be only man's story—which is, after all, the same old story. In other words, no story. De Lauretis explains this woman's dilemma as Other in Oedipal narrative in, appropriately enough, a fairy tale frame of reference: "The end of the girl's journey, if successful, will bring her to the place where the boy will find her, like Sleeping Beauty, awaiting him, Prince Charming. . . . Thus the itinerary of the female's journey . . . so her story, like any other story, is a question of his desire."[11]

That the narrative grip of Oedipus is difficult to break free from is evinced, certainly, by the tenacity of those revered fairy tales which have hooked into our cultural ideology, and also by what in the past has been a marked absence of narratives which work to disrupt the status quo. Yet such resistant, cross-grain re-writing is precisely the task of Angela Carter, whose feminist revisionary rewriting of some of those classic fairy tales is, as Lorna Sage has described her work, more concerned with "myth-breaking" than "myth-making"—rewriting which "take[s] myths and turn[s] them inside out."[12]

In *The Bloody Chamber,* Carter proffers two versions of the classic tale "Beauty and the Beast." One version, "The Courtship of Mr. Lyon," a hip, contemporary '60s-style parody featuring a cigarette-smoking Beauty, is an overt expose of the contrived gender differences and positionalities that inform the original tale. In the companion piece, "The Tiger's Bride," Carter takes her re-visioning a crucial step further, subverting "that old story" by re-positioning and redefining woman's desire on her own terms. Carter's imaginative conceptions and formulations of what sorts of possibilities are available to women through cultural myths are a far cry, certainly, from those of Oedipus, which are, as de Lauretis explains, "honed by a centuries-long patriarchal tradition."[13] In fact, these iconoclastic, tradition-breaking tales—especially "The Tiger's Bride"—do precisely what de Lauretis argues feminist writing and re-writing must do to subvert the continued predominance of the pattern of the Oedipal narrative: Woman—Beauty—is imagined/imaged as "mythical and social subject" in her own right, providing her own referential frame of experience, writing her ending to her own story.[14]

"To a certain extent," Carter acknowledges regarding the fore-grounding of a political agenda in her work, "I'm making a conscious critique of the culture I was born to."[15] And to the extent that we read her narrative revisions as critiques of the dominant culture's inscriptions of sexual difference and desire, it is interesting and illuminating to read Carter's "Beauty" stories against Jean Cocteau's classic 1946 film text, *La Belle et La Bête,* which has always been studied as an experimental, avant-garde venture into the possibilities of cinematic production, yet which is nevertheless as familiar a rendering of the fairy story as Carter's versions are de-familiar ones. Cocteau's film text is, obviously, a product of a different era than Carter's texts; yet it can be and must be studied as an equally powerful and persuasive vehicle for the re-inscribing of the values of the dominant culture—those same gender positionalities represented in the original fairy tale. For, like written narrative, as de Lauretis has pointed out, (culturally) dominant cinema, too, "works for Oedipus."[16]

Of course, filmic narratives have a singular advantage and seductive appeal over written ones; as Seymour Chatman has reminded us, "Seeing is, after all, believing."[17] Laura Mulvey and other film critics have defined scopophilia as a primary cinematic technique for inscribing gender differences and mapping desire.[18] And *La Belle et La Bête* very much solicits looking, for it is replete with fantastic and unexpected magic: Beauty's tears materialize as diamonds, rugs unroll up stairs, the trees surrounding the Beast's castle keep watch as sentinels, candelabra are held and wine is poured by dis-embodied arms and hands. The most pervasive and compelling visual lure, of course, is Beauty herself, the female object of difference designed to the traditional specifications of masculine desire. Beautiful, blond, ethereal, she is typically a classic representation of the ways in which "woman is to be looked at" as well as her "to-be-looked-at-ness."[19] And by appropriating her beauty, both the traditional, moral "off-screen" attributes of the "good little girl" and the on-screen physical beauty of actress Josette Day, Cocteau shows us a cinematic projection of woman defined by masculine desire through means of conventional cinematic codes—the dominant social human nature of the on-screen interactions between Beauty and the Beast, the appropriation of the female body as the beast/male's possession—and extra-cinematic ones—the gender representations and narrative resolutions (the "happily-ever-after")—that the traditional reading of the fairy tale has instructed him to re-inscribe.

Cocteau in *La Belle et La Bête* works from the same original source as does Carter in her versions: Madame Marie Leprince de Beaumont's 1757 fairy tale.[20] The narrative in "Beauty and the Beast" is, essentially, the boy-meets-girl love story, a too-familiar story line which unfolds with striking parallels to de Lauretis' Oedipal paradigm. The opening lines introduce the Merchant and list his prized possessions, signaling immediately that, although Beauty is given top billing in the title, this tale is actually not even her story. And when all is decided and done, the Beast/Prince informs Beauty somewhat indifferently, "A bad fairy condemned me to the Beast's shape until I found *a* beautiful girl who would agree to marry me."[21] His desire has not really been for her as individual human at all but, rather, only as generic female.

From the beginning of the tale, Beauty is doomed to be female "other," running the gamut in assuming various traditional female roles yet really changing very little as a character. Beauty is indeed a character type—or, more accurately, several character types; she is inscribed, in de Lauretis' terms, as a "literary topos" through which "the hero and his story move to their destination and to accomplish meaning."[22] In order to satisfy the controlling male desire of the narrative, to facilitate his "happy ending," Beauty is variously, and often simultaneously, in the problematic but traditional situation of being: the ideal wife—she refuses suitors because "she could not possibly abandon her father in his misfortune" and thus must "console him and toil beside him" (p. 46); mother/care-giver—she "got up at four in the morning, cleaned the house and got their dinners ready" (p. 46); sibling—"she wished her sisters well although they hated her" (p. 50); and sacrifice—"If the Beast will take a daughter instead of the father, then I shall gladly go" (p. 50). She is both object of barter and plot device: "I would like to forgive you," the Beast negotiates with her father, "but only on this condition, that one of your daughters comes here of her own free will, to die in your place" (p. 49). And ultimately, expectedly, she is consummately guilty, somehow to blame for the fate both of her father—"Take your roses, Beauty. They cost your father very dearly" (p. 50)—and of the Beast: "You forgot your promise to me. When you did not come back to me, I could not eat, and now I am dying, Beauty" (p. 60).

The story's controlling male desire, implicit in that privileged point of view, is intensified in the film, for the omniscient look of the camera conspires with the voyeurism already inherent in the narrative itself to implicate even the viewer as silent, passive observer of the Beast's manipulations of Beauty's person and her will. The Beast's questioning of Beauty—"May I sit here and watch you eat your supper?"—is a moot one, for he is as undeniably "master" of his own house as she is mastered by the controlling desire of the film narrative. Repeatedly framed by the "look" of the camera, Beauty is presented as an object to be observed/looked at by the cinematic iconography with which Cocteau constructs the film. In the opening scenes, for instance, in attempting to seduce a kiss from the reluctant, uninterested Beauty, Avenant bends over her as she kneels to scrub the floor, pinning her between his body and the dis-embodied image of his face reflected in the waxed floor beneath her; when she stands to turn away, he pinions her body against his with an arrow. (She only successfully escapes from this "frame" due to the unexpected arrival of her father in the room below.)

Likewise, the Beast constantly captures Beauty in his gaze, for it is primarily through his eyes that her story is filmed. He stands behind her chair, peeping over her shoulder, seeing her—as the spectator sees her—while she sees nothing but the table before her; he peers at her from a hidden vantage point while she is in his garden; and his image over-fills the screen and becomes her waking vision as he leans over the unconscious Beauty in her bed. He "sees" her, even, when she is absent from the line of his vision, for as omnipotent master, his omniscient eye frames her to physical advantage in doorways and on staircases as she moves through his house.

This voyeuristic perspective insinuates itself most familiarly and climatically in that most personal and intimate of chambers, Beauty's bedroom, which becomes the scene of the most masterful bit of construction by the camera (and by the Beast). In a dramatic, tightly edited sequence of close-up shots, the camera literally cuts Beauty's body into sections as the Beast carries her from the anteroom into her bedroom after she faints at the sight of him. Through a series of alternating shots created by a spliced sequence of frames from anterior and interior vantage points, Beauty's metamorphosis from the father's daughter to the Beast's consort occurs with stark deliberation, foreshadowing the final shift in roles that will make her Prince Charming's wife: she is un-dressed of the coarse, modest garments that positioned her in her former role and re-dressed in the virginal, luxurious gown that marks her as well-kept possession of the Beast/master. Silently, rapidly, her body is appropriated by the camera as her will is appropriated by the Beast; and her new life as mistress of the Beast is spliced together for her, according to the controlling cinematic narrative masculine gaze.

The focus of all this looking is, of course, Beauty herself. Her name, acquired as a child because she was "very pretty," functions as metaphor for her worth as person in the narrative—Beauty/beauty is indeed somehow inextricably linked to goodness—and as metonym for her imaging in the film, reflecting the double standards of desire and expectations according to gender which operate explicitly in Cocteau's work. The Beauty of the written text comes to accept and love the Beast as he physically is: "A woman doesn't need a handsome face and a clever tongue in a husband. She needs strength of character, goodness, and kindness. And these the Beast has, all three" (p. 60). And, of course, in the film she comes similarly to this realization, although without even so many words to soften the blow. Yet in both texts/contexts, without her beauty, Beauty is, apparently, nothing. The camera presents little else of her as an individual being besides her physical appearance: virtually every shot fetishizes her wide-eyed, smooth-skinned face and the halo of "golden" hair. Her female form is indeed her essence, her totality, for when the Prince marries Beauty, they are magically granted that state of "happily ever after, in a contentment perfect because it was founded on goodness" (p. 60)—founded, in fact, on Beauty's beauty.

That trite, story-book ending is perhaps the most unsatisfying and unrealistic aspect of this, and any, fairy tale. And the ending series of images with which Cocteau closes his film is perhaps the most blatant, heavy-handed and thus disturbing sequence of construction in the entire work, for it is rendered as something of a joke at women's expense. Cocteau commented in the *Diary* of the film: the resurrected Prince Charming, who emerges as the Beast is shaken off, "looks extraordinarily like Avenant," Beauty's earlier aggressive suitor; and this Prince-Cum-Beast-Cum-Avenant "worries Beauty. She seems to miss the kind Beast a little, and to be a little afraid of this unexpected Avenant."[23] Yet after only a moment's hesitation, as the established filmic framework has led us to anticipate, Beauty melts into Prince Charming's arms and, with glowing face and eyes, tells him, "I'd like to be . . . with you." This trade-off, Beast for Prince, which is effected without her consent, is explicit in the "happy ending" it intends. Her desires are, in fact, doubly discounted, for despite her requisite self-sacrifice, Beauty doesn't get what/whom she bargained for. The "Prince with three faces"[24] with whom she flies away is a composite of the single, inescapable face of the patriarchal culture which has made her, inscribed her—Avenant, Beast, Prince Charming, father, lord. And even her physical presence as determinate of identity is compromised—indeed, revoked, for the last image the spectator sees is the Prince's smiling face; Beauty's back, encircled by the Prince's arms, is turned to face the camera. In *La Belle et La Bête,* her story once again turns into his story; the narrative ending has been prestaged, pre-determined by the Oedipal constructs of the genre and the media even before the narrative discourse begins.

In *La Belle et La Bête,* the narrative tradition which inscribed, and which subsequently is inscribed by, the classic fairy tale remains unaltered in the end and is seemingly to be preserved at all costs; no questions asked. Angela Carter, however, sets out to count those costs and to ask some of those questions in her perverse, satirical versions of the classic fairy tale. "The Courtship of Mr. Lyon," written from the same omniscient point of view as is her source, keeps the original plot more or less intact; hence, ostensibly Oedipus is still at work. But a principle deviation Carter makes from the original, and one which facilitates her breaking away from Oedipus, concerns the time frame of the story. The setting is twentieth-century England, and the tensions which Carter exposes as the modern Beauty confronts the archaic social systems still at work in her contemporary world construct a more overt critique of those systems—represented here more by the Beast even than by Beauty's father—than either traditional narrative or dominant cinematic versions have heretofore discovered.

In "The Courtship of Mr. Lyon," Beauty replays the typical patterning of female roles—daughter, mother, even wife (her father calls home to say he'll be late for dinner)—until finally she accepts her allotted place at Mr. Lyon's side, thereby balancing a social system initially disrupted when "her birth killed her mother."[25] As in the original version, male experience is privileged and the masculine domain is foregrounded; the title, in fact, is completely his, without the mention of her at all. The Beast's materialism bespeaks a certain luxury and camaraderie reserved, apparently, for the Masters of society; his estate, "a place of privilege," is "plainly that of an exceedingly wealthy man" (p. 42). And a certain duplicity exists between the Beast and Beauty's father, for both are indeed accustomed to being masters, possessors of beautiful and valuable things; the Beast, upon seeing Beauty framed in a photograph, recognizes and desires her because of a "certain look" that the camera had "captured" (p. 44). This proprietary conspiracy among masters is apparently nothing new to Beauty, and she acquiesces willingly yet ruefully, "with a pang of dread" but with little surprise that she is the token of barter offered to the Beast: "the price of her father's good fortune . . . on some magically reciprocal scale" (p. 45).

That the Beast and Beauty's father inhabit the same gender-privileged realm is reinforced throughout the narrative by the increasingly blurred lines of demarcation between animal and man. Mr. Lyon is distinguished perhaps most obviously from a mere animal by the socially stratifying title of "Sir" which precedes his name; and he is something of a gentleman's intellectual, able to converse with Beauty about "the nature of the moon . . . about the stars . . . about the variable transformation of the weather" (p. 47). Beauty's sense of obligation to this Beast is a familiar one: she is still passive, the virginal object of barter—a "young girl who looked as if she had been carved out of a single pearl" (p. 46)—who "stayed, and smiled, because her father wanted her to do so" (p. 45). And although she realizes her fate as "Miss Lamb, spotless, sacrificial" (p. 45), she herself expedites the process, offering herself to the Beast almost in desperation, as if she fears not being taken otherwise. Beauty returns to find this Beast dying not in nature but in his "modest bedroom" (which, with only "a nightlight on the mantlepiece, no curtains at the windows, no carpet on the floor" is, surely, in need of a woman's touch [p. 50]); the scene is replete with sexual overtones: "She flung herself upon him, so that the iron bedstead groaned, and covered his poor paws with kisses. 'Don't die, Beast! If you'll have me, I'll never leave you' " (p. 50–51). Carter ironically and explicitly implies that, sans Beast, this Beauty, too, is somehow not completely Beauty, for she is not possessed of that desirable goodness: left on her own in London, for instance, Beauty's "pearly skin . . . was plumping out, a little, with high living and compliments . . . her face was acquiring, instead of beauty, a lacquer of the invincible prettiness that characterized certain pampered exquisite, expensive cats" (p. 40).

Beauty's fate is indeed that of a "kept," pampered woman; but her keeper must be, it seems, only the Beast and not merely herself. Her constructed space at his estate is comfortable and opulent but well-defined and artificial, a bedroom with "precious books and pictures and the flowers grown by invisible gardeners in the Beast's hothouse" (p. 46). She has everything she could possibly need, the narrative implies—everything but a sense of her own identity and a story of her own. The pattern of Oedipus emerges most fully in the closing scene, for although she has made the sacrifice, it is his desires that are fulfilled. And under the "soft transformation" of her silent tears, the Beast comes into his proper, formerly hidden, manly self: "a man with an unkept mane of hair and, how strange, a broken nose, such as the noses of retired boxers, that gave him a distant, heroic resemblance to the handsomest of all the beasts" (p. 51). Ironically, Carter ascribes the last words of this text to Mr. Lyon, rapidly re-inscribing Beauty back into her womanly supporting role. The story ends, but the ideology of the narrative continues; and under the patronymic of the masterful Beast, "Mr. and Mrs. Lyon walk in the garden" (p. 51)—happily, ever after.

"My father lost me to The Beast at cards."[26] So begins "The Tiger's Bride," which follows thematically on the heels of "The Courtship of Mr. Lyon" yet is a striking departure from—indeed a cross-grain rereading of— "Mr. Lyon." By appropriating the personal voice, the girl in this second tale not only takes charge of telling the narrative of her life, and consequently of the narrative traditions of the fairy tale, but she also makes clear from the start that what blame there is to be assigned lies not with her but with the dominant systems to which she is only a bargaining chip. This Beauty has shaken both the name—she is referred to only as "the girl," "the young lady"—and the consequent sexually-specific images that are intertwined with it: she is not so delicate and feminine "a pearl" who easily capitulates but a darker, stronger, more resilient "woman of honor" (p. 59) who ably watches out after herself because no one else will. And in carving out her own life-story, in resisting the story which literary and cultural traditions have patterned for her, her narrative becomes an alternative model for the female subject's desire, constructing what de Lauretis says feminist cinematic and written narrative must: "the terms of reference of another measure of desire and the conditions of visibility for a different social subject."[27]

"The Tiger's Bride," like the original "Beauty and the Beast," is a narrative which is inherently voyeuristic; the terms of looking, however, are significantly altered, for the girl is subject of the [her] gaze as well as object of the [his, the tiger's] gaze. The girl's desires seem to hark back to a primal and natural state, literally and metaphorically—one that is pre-Oedipal, almost pre-ideological, prior to the time it became "not natural for humankind to go naked" (p. 66). And the tiger's request, "to see the pretty young lady unclothed nude without her dress" (p. 58), is so shocking and untenable to her because to comply she must throw off the familiar ideological constructs and patterns that have so comfortably clothed and covered over her own unexpressed sexual desires that she realizes not that she even possesses them: " 'Take off my clothes for you, like a ballet girl? Is that all you want of me?' . . . That he should want so little was the reason why I could not give it" (p. 61).

The transformation in "The Tiger's Bride" indeed centers on the girl, not The Beast, thus presenting a narrative challenge to the Oedipal myth that, as de Lauretis describes such re-patterning, "represent[s] not just the power of female desire, but its duplicity and ambivalence" (p. 154). This female subject is not so readily categorized as her fictional predecessors; she is, in fact, the antithesis of Mrs. Lyon who was "possessed of a sense of obligation" that subsumed her own will ("Lyon," p. 45). The girl knows, moreover, what she does not want—to be passively passed, like her mother before her, from one player to another in the hegemonic power game: "My mother did not blossom long; bartered for her dowry . . ." (p. 52). Precisely what it is that she does want, however, she does not know, for like the white rose The Beast gives to her, she is herself "unnatural, out of season" (p. 53). And her ripping apart of the rose "petal by petal" portends the un-layering to which she will subject herself in order to discover the potential of her heretofore unconsidered, unexplored sexual self. Actively initiating herself into the dominant discourse, she bargains with the status quo to redeem her story and her subjectivity on her own terms. This time it is she who picks the rose at her father's request, implicating his carelessness in her fate: "When I break off a stem, I prick my finger and so he gets his rose all smeared with blood" (p. 55).

Not only is this girl not your typical Beauty; neither does she face the typical Beast. Just as she is entrapped in an unfamiliar land—demographically, and also socially, sexually—so he is encased in an unfamiliar skin; and, ill-fitted for traditional roles, both are outsiders because of their differences. Unlike

his fictional predecessors, or the "tiger-man" of the old wives' tale who wore a
" 'big black travelling cloak lined with fur, just like your daddy's' " (p. 56), the
Beast of this story is indeed more animal than man, bearing "an odd air of self-
imposed restraint, as if fighting a battle with himself to remain upright when
he would far rather drop down on all fours" (p. 53), and searching not for personal luxury or social status in the "vast-man trap" of his palazzo—but "solitude" (p. 57). He never desires to alter his nature permanently, and his temporary attempts at a false disguise cause him to appear a garish parody of the
beast in humans that is so thinly and disingeniously covered: "I never saw a
man look so two-dimensional. . . . He wears a mask with a man's face painted
most beautifully on it. Oh, yes, a beautiful face; but one with too much formal
symmetry of feature to be entirely human: one profile of his mask is the mirror
image of the other, too perfect, uncanny" (p. 53). Never in complicity with the
dominant, oppressive ideology, The Beast in fact stands directly opposed to it,
taking issue against its double standards and short-sightedness and acquiring
the girl not out of a selfish desire to save (or serve) himself, but because she,
like he, is different, a rarity—to him, a thing unknown, a non-pearl of great
price: "If you are so careless of your treasures," he growls at her father, "you
should expect them to be taken from you" (p. 55).

The Beast's very otherness is what intrigues the girl in the first place.
Like her, beneath the constructed facade of his social appearance, he seems to
be seeking self-knowledge, self-fulfillment of some sort—a commonality she
senses she shares with The Beast yet cannot name: "it cannot be his face that
looks like mine" (p. 56). Her sympathy and inclination toward other than
what society has dictated must be signals her own difference and surfaces
explicitly in her natural affinity for the little black gelding, "the noblest of
creatures": "I lirruped and hurrumphed to my shining black companion and
he acknowledged my greeting with a kiss on the forehead from his soft lips"
(p. 62). And it is when she recognizes that she and The Beast are (in their
silence) "speaking" the same speech of difference—a relationship to which
there are no ideological strings of social /sexual expectation attached—that
she feels "at liberty for the first time in [her] life" (p. 64). In both bearing her
gaze and forcing her to look upon his natural nakedness, The Beast consequently brings her to a clear seeing of herself—or at least, a clear seeing of
her desire to better "see," to know, herself: "I felt my breast ripped apart as if
I suffered a marvellous wound" (p. 64).

The sacrifice in "The Tiger's Bride"—if indeed there is a sacrifice at all—
is his, for ultimately he asks her to do nothing for him that he has not done
for her. Because "nothing about him reminded [her] of humanity" (p. 64)—
physically, intellectually—she undresses for him, consummating the reciprocal relationship of desire and trust, not with words, but with the equal, non-
differentiating, illuminating gaze that makes her subject, not just object, and
makes a place for her desire—the multiple sexual subjectivity she has experienced and embraced: "[His tongue,] abrasive as sandpaper, ripped off skin

after skin, all the skins of a life in the world, and left behind a nascent patina of shining hairs. My earrings turned back to water and trickled down my shoulders; I shrugged the drops off my beautiful fur" (p. 67). And her final act, the sleight-of-hand substitution of the maid, the "marvellous machine," marks a significant break with the past in favor of her emerging personal, female desires; for with this simulacrum of woman, she effects both a deliberate completion of her own story on her own terms and handily interrupts the old story of female goodness and fidelity: "I will dress her in my own clothes, wind her up, send her back to perform the part of my father's daughter" (p. 65).

In "real life," the conflictive beast woman must confront is, of course, not a representative tiger but the literal social/sexual limitations society ideologically imposes. In "The Tiger's Bride," Carter does rethink social/sexual stereotypes and re-cast the direction fairy tales may take in our culture, but her heroine bucks a tremendous tradition of literary representation and cultural ideology—a tradition that does not lightly permit a ready escape, for Oedipus still looms large. Carter's re-routing of the same old narrative paradigm is remarkable in one sense, for if the trend of recent video productions is indicative, such tradition-breaking re-visioning of fairy tale myth is, to a large extent, apparently still culturally cross-grain, especially in media produced for popular audiences. Since *La Belle et La Bête,* for example, there have been several re-makes of "Beauty and the Beast," ranging from Disney cartoons to pornographic productions. All of these re-makes, however, have basically reiterated the traditional social/sexual patterns and representations, with only slight variations on the essential theme of female beauty = essential goodness. One, a 1987 Golan-Globus musical production directed by Eugene Marner, constructs a more matriarchal Beauty who sits opposite her father at the family dinner table, ordering and orchestrating her family members' lives: "What," they sing, "would we do without you?" Beauty has evolved little as a subject within this film or from previous versions, like Cocteau's: she is still most animated when the Beast joins her at dinner—"May I serve you, Beast?"—and again readily capitulates to his marriage proposal as a means of self-completion; her acceptance is based solely upon her romantic assessment of his situation; unlike her family, as she tells him, "You need me." And in this film the voyeuristic aspect of the narrative is even more pervasive than in Cocteau's, for the Beast knows always what Beauty is thinking; he is inside her mind, he peoples her dreams, granting her every wish, instructing her how to love him—"See with your heart," he sings to her—while constructing her as his ideal lover.

There is also the highly-rated television series "Beauty and the Beast," which features a sexually charged, although never physically consummated, fairy-tale romance. Here the Beast is incarnated as a handsome, selfless, multilingual "man" named Vincent who quotes Shakespeare in a soft-spoken yet wise and authoritative voice of experience. In contrast, "Beauty," an independent, gutsy, Lois-Lane-with-a-heart woman named Catharine, dauntlessly

spouts moral platitudes from beneath a halo of blond hair, yet always ultimately defers to Vincent's other-worldly wisdom in matters great and small.
Set in contemporary New York, this pair fights modern evils, always putting
others before themselves; consequently, their relationship never develops or
changes because they share "a bond of friendship stronger than love"—a self-
subsuming bond of almost slavish attraction which is mysterious yet insa-
tiable in its demands upon the other's attentions. It is unclear just who has
redeemed whom in this paradigm—much less what new positionalities it
could possibly be offering—for both Catharine and Vincent are pretty well
mired in the romantic scenarios and idealisms the production constructs
around them—a relationship too good to be true but, apparently, just right
for prime-time TV and the same old story it intends to convey.

Margaret Atwood has written in her *Circe/Mud Poems:* "It's the story that
counts. No use telling me this isn't a story or not the same story. . . . The
story is ruthless."[28] And the continuing production and passive acceptance of
the familiar stories in written and filmic narratives, especially through readily
accessible popular cultural media models based on the traditional standards
of sexual difference and masculine desire, are disturbing and motivating
reminders that those traditions must be subverted, those stories must be
retold. To tell a different story, to imagine and construct otherness as positive
not negative difference, and to offer positive positionalities for identification
within that otherness, to disrupt the ideological status quo enough to disturb
the heretofore complacent acceptance it has met among readers and viewers;
such is precisely the work of Carter's fairy tale narratives. For from the sim-
plistic level of the fairy tale to the material complexities of narrative cinema,
the story of Oedipus and the narratives of his standard-bearers must be
actively re-examined and openly challenged—as shown particularly both by
Cocteau, in his reinscriptions of them, and by Carter, in her shattering of
them. De Lauretis argues that the best work in and the acceptable agenda for
re-writing and re-making contemporary narrative is and can only be "narrative and Oedipal with a vengeance,"[29] an argument which we in our readings
and writings must extend, as Carter has done in her revisionary work, in
order to set the socio-cultural stage for new narrative traditions, granting
voice and place, subjectivity and desire to a different female social subject,
according to other than the same old story.

Notes

1.   Angela Carter (trans.), *Sleeping Beauty and Other Favorite Fairy Tales* (New York:
Schocken, 1989), p. 45.
2.   Carter, *Sleeping Beauty,* p. 125.
3.   Carter, *Sleeping Beauty,* p. 125.

4. Jean Cocteau, *"Beauty and the Beast": Diary of a Film* (1947; New York: Dover, 1972), p. iv.

5. Carter, *Sleeping Beauty,* p. 128.

6. Cocteau, p. 3.

7. Teresa de Lauretis, *Alice Doesn't: Feminism, Semiotics, Cinema* (Bloomington: Indiana, 1984), Univ. Press, p. 121.

8. De Lauretis, p. 113.

9. Ellen Cronan Rose, "Through the Looking Glass: When Women Tell Fairy Tales," in *The Voyage In: Fictions of Female Development,* eds. Elizabeth Abel, Marianne Hirsch, and Elizabeth Langland (Hanover: Univ. Press of New England, 1983), p. 211.

10. De Lauretis, p. 107.

11. De Lauretis, p. 133.

12. Lorna Sage, "The Savage Sideshow: A Profile of Angela Carter," *New Review,* 39/40 (1977), 56.

13. De Lauretis, p. 125.

14. De Lauretis, p. 131.

15. Sage, p. 56.

16. De Lauretis, p. 153.

17. Seymour Chapman, "What Novels Can Do That Films Can't (and Vice Versa)," *Critical Inquiry,* 7 (1980), 128.

18. Laura Mulvey, "Visual Pleasure and Narrative Cinema," *Screen,* 16 (1975), 19.

19. Mulvey, p. 17.

20. Carter's translation of de Beaumont's fairy tales appear in *Sleeping Beauty and Other Favorite Fairy Tales,* and it is her version of "Beauty and the Beast" to which I refer throughout this essay.

21. Carter, *Sleeping Beauty,* p. 61; emphasis mine. Subsequent quotations from "Sleeping Beauty" will be documented in the main text.

22. De Laurctis, p. 109.

23. Cocteau, p. 3.

24. Cocteau, p. 3.

25. Angela Carter, "The Courtship of Mr. Lyon," *The Bloody Chamber and Other Stories* (London: Penguin, 1979), p. 48. Subsequent quotations from "The Courtship of Mr. Lyon" will be documented in the main text.

26. Angela Carter, "The Tiger's Bride," *The Bloody Chamber and Other Stories* (London: Penguin, 1979), p. 51. Subsequent quotations from "The Tiger's Bride" will be documented in the main text.

27. De Lauretis, p. 155.

28. Margaret Atwood, *Circe/Mud Poems,* from *The Norton Anthology of Literature by Women,* eds. Sandra Gilbert and Susan Gubar (New York: Norton, 1985), p. 2298.

29. DeLauretis, p. 157.

Pornography, Fairy Tales, and Feminism: Angela Carter's "The Bloody Chamber"

ROBIN ANN SHEETS

British author Angela Carter holds a problematic place in the debates about pornography that have polarized Anglo-American feminists, originally over issues of sadomasochism and other sexual practices, and more recently over questions of artistic representation. In Carter's case, much of the controversy has come to center on *The Sadeian Woman and the Ideology of Pornography* (1978). Carter defends Sade because "he treats all sexual reality as a political reality" and he "declares himself unequivocally for the right of women to fuck" as aggressively, tyrannously, and cruelly as men.[1] In this essay, I propose to reassess Carter's stance on pornography by reading *The Sadeian Woman* in conjunction with "The Bloody Chamber" (1979), one of her most brilliant "adult tales," and by situating both works in relationship to the feminist debates on pornography that began during the mid-1970s and continue to the present. Such an approach makes two assumptions: (1) that fiction constitutes an important part of the contemporary discourse on sexuality; and (2) that an interdisciplinary approach is necessary for reading imaginative literature about sexuality. Recent works by feminist philosophers, psychologists, and film critics furnish new insights into the issues Carter explores in "The Bloody Chamber," such as the link between sexually violent imagery and male aggression, the meaning of masochism for women, and the relationship of pornography to other literary and artistic forms.

After providing a brief account of *The Sadeian Woman,* I will analyze the relevant issues in the feminist pornography debates, including the arguments about sadomasochism that were so divisive in the late 1970s and early 1980s and the discussions about representation that became increasingly prevalent during the 1980s. Because the written debate was earlier, more extensive, more explicit, and more theoretical in America than in Great Britain,[2] I rely primarily on American polemicists, such as Andrea Dworkin, Robin Morgan, Gayle Rubin, and Pat Califia, for matters of sexual practice. For issues of representation, I draw upon British and American film theorists and cultural

From *Journal of the History of Sexuality* 1, no. 4 (April 1991): 633–57. © 1991 University of Chicago Press. Reprinted by permission.

critics, such as Laura Mulvey, Annette Kuhn, Susan Kappeler, Mary Ann Doane, and Linda Williams. In offering a detailed study of one story, I am striving for the "fully realized feminist thematic reading" of pornography advocated by Susan Rubin Suleiman.[3]

I

In 1978 *The Sadeian Woman* seemed isolated and idiosyncratic. Sade existed as "a potent vacancy" in British literary circles because publication of his books had been curtailed in response to a highly publicized murder trial.[4] Public discussion of pornography was shaped by two opposing factions, neither of which was particularly helpful to feminists: (1) the liberal consensus represented by the Williams Committee on Obscenity and Film Censorship, which in its 1979 report allowed the circulation but not the display of pornographic materials; and (2) the religiously based, right-wing, pro-censorship lobby led by Mary Whitehouse and the National Festival of Light.[5] In the late 1970s, representatives of various women's groups testified before the Williams Committee, critiques of pornography appeared in magazines like *Spare Rib,* and "Reclaim the Night" marches began in London and other cities. Rejecting traditional definitions that emphasize content (the explicit representation of sexual organs or activities) and intention (to arouse the audience, generally assumed to be male), feminists sought to redefine pornography as a form of violence against women and to classify as pornographic those representations which eroticize male domination. Organized attacks on sex shops and "adult" bookstores would begin in 1980, and the 1981 publication of books by Andrea Dworkin and Susan Griffin, feminists active in the American antipornography movement, would bring new urgency to the discussions in Great Britain.[6]

Unlike literary critics in France and America, Carter was not interested in defending pornography in aesthetic terms. She did not follow traditional political approaches—liberal or conservative; nor did she pursue arguments being formulated by feminists active in the early phases of the antipornography movement. Yet in retrospect, publication of *The Sadeian Woman* marked the beginning edge of a controversy that would be at the center of feminist discourse for more than a decade.

Although Carter assumes that most pornography is reactionary because it serves "to reinforce the prevailing system of values and ideas in a given society," she envisions the possibility of a "moral pornographer" who would use the genre "as a critique of current relations between the sexes." As a critic, the moral pornographer would "penetrate to the heart of the contempt for women that distorts our culture." As a visionary hoping to transform society and human nature, such a person would create "a world of absolute sexual licence for all the genders" (*SW,* pp. 18–20). Carter acknowledges Sade's misogyny—his fantasies of "woman-monsters" and his "hatred of the mothering function"—but she commends Sade "for claiming rights of free sexuality for women, and in installing women as beings of power in his imaginary worlds" (*SW,* pp. 25, 36). Sade invented women who suffer, most notably the innocent and always abused Justine, but he also invented women who cause suffering, such as Justine's sexually aggressive, whip-wielding sister, Juliette. Sade believed "it would only be through the medium of sexual violence that women might heal themselves of their socially inflicted scars, in a praxis of destruction and sacrilege" (*SW,* p. 26). Asking that we "give the old monster his due," Carter asserts that Sade "put pornography in the service of women, or, perhaps, allowed it to be invaded by an ideology not inimical to women" (*SW,* p. 37). Initial reviews were positive, but as the feminist antipornography movement gained momentum in England and North America, *The Sadeian Woman* was denounced by Andrea Dworkin as "a pseudofeminist literary essay."[7]

II

When Robin Morgan characterized women who opposed the antipornography movement as "Sade's new Juliettes," she revealed how deeply the issue had divided feminists of the early 1980s. According to Morgan, writers like Ellen Willis, Gayle Rubin, and Pat Califia have no right to call themselves feminists. By supporting pornography, they have chosen a sexual practice based on domination, aligned themselves with Juliette, the power-mad protagonist of Sade's novels who enslaved others in pursuit of her own pleasure, and given up "all hope of connecting with *real* sexual energy."[8]

Morgan's scornful comment about other women writers is typical of the intensely acrimonious debate in its sense of rigid oppositions—"for" or "against," "feminist" or "antifeminist"—and in its reliance on unstated assumptions about woman's nature. No matter how the conflicting positions are labeled, each side perceives the other "as falling into the dominant view of women associated with the right or left: virgins or whores, prudes or sexual objects, victims or consenting participants."[9] Feminists who defend pornography, such as Willis, Califia, and Rubin, often present themselves as "bad girls," adventurous sexual outlaws daring to break restraints. They depict the antipornography essayists as "good girls"—sentimental, naive, and sexually repressed. These "new Juliettes" regard Morgan and other antipornography activists as the "new Justines": by their constant complaints against male brutality, they make themselves into perpetual victims.

Robin Morgan issued the rallying cry of the feminist antipornography movement during the mid-1970s: "Pornography is the theory, and rape the practice."[10] Some activists distinguished between "pornography," condemned as cause of women's oppression, and "erotica," celebrated by Gloria Steinem as "a mutually pleasurable, sexual expression between people who have enough power to be there by positive choice."[11] More radical feminists, such as Andrea Dworkin, opposed all heterosexual relationships, claiming that the violence and aggression of pornography are essential characteristics of male sexuality. According to antipornography feminists, pornography does not produce sexual pleasure; instead, it displays male power—"the power of the self, physical power over and against others, the power of terror, the power of naming, the power of owning, the power of money, and the power of sex."[12] Pornography is not simply a form of expression; rather, it is an action against women.

Although some critics have attempted to center discussion on a category called "violent pornography,"[13] many argue that *all* pornography is violent: in its content—which involves scenes of bondage, rape, mutilation and torture—and in its structures of representation, which silence, objectify, and fragment the female. In the pornographic scenario analyzed by Susanne Kappeler, "The woman object is twice objectified: once as object of the action of the scenario, and once as object of the representation, the object of viewing."[14] Drawing upon theories of the male gaze introduced by filmmaker Laura Mulvey and defining sadomasochism quite broadly "as any sexual practice that involves the eroticization of relations of domination and submission,"[15] these feminists maintain that pornography encourages sadomasochism by placing the male viewer/reader in the sadist's active position while assigning the masochist's passive role to the female viewer/reader.

Antipornography feminists decry the harm done to women in the production and circulation of pornographic materials: as performers whose bodies are exploited on stages and in film studios; as victims of men whose misogynistic attitudes and hostile actions have been encouraged by their consumption of pornography; and as readers/viewers whose autonomy and self-respect are threatened by exposure to the genre. Calling for personal and political reform, Dworkin insists that "freedom for women must begin in the repudiation of our own masochism."[16] She and Morgan urge women to rid society of pornographic images by participating in "Take Back the Night" marches, joining organizations such as Women against Violence in Pornography and Media (WAVPM), teaching, and lobbying in support of antipornography ordinances.[17]

In opposing the antipornography movement, the writers Morgan denounces—Ellen Willis, Pat Califia, and Gayle Rubin—claim that pornography, even sadomasochistic pornography, is a possible source of erotic pleasure; they deny the right of WAVPM or any other group to limit women's fantasies or proscribe their practices. Willis declared that women should be free to experience sex as "an expression of violent and unpretty emotion": "A woman who is raped is a victim; a woman who enjoys pornography (even if that means enjoying a rape fantasy) is in a sense a rebel, insisting on an aspect of her sexuality that has been defined as a male preserve. Insofar as pornography glorifies male supremacy and sexual alienation, it is deeply reactionary. But in rejecting sexual repression and hypocrisy—which have inflicted even more damage on women than on men—it expresses a radical impulse."[18] Advocates of pornography argue that the genre serves women's interests by offering them an escape from the repressions of bourgeois ideology: it counteracts romantic love, undermines heterosexual monogamy, and subverts procreative sex.

Morgan's reference to the "new Juliettes" reveals the extent to which the problem of sadomasochism has permeated the discussions. When the National Organization of Women (NOW) condemned pornography at its 1980 convention, the resolution appeared under the rubric of "Lesbian Rights." It appeared to be directed at specific sexual minorities, for it also condemned sadomasochism, public sex, and pederasty as "issues of exploitation and violence" rather than sexual or affectional preference.[19] The protests of Pat Califia, Gayle Rubin, and other members of Samois, a self-defined "group of feminist lesbians who share a positive interest in sadomasochism," helped shape arguments against the antipornography movement. Although proponents of sadomasochism insist that power is an integral part of sexual relationships, they deny that one person keeps the other in a state of submission. Emphasizing fantasy, theatricality—scripts, costumes, and props—and play, they present sadomasochism as "an eroticized exchange of power negotiated between two or more sexual partners."[20] Under the terms of this analysis, sadomasochism does not replicate the structures of oppression. Rather, it is "the quintessence of nonreproductive sex" and "the most radical attempt in the field of sexual politics to promote the fundamental purpose of sex as being simply pleasure."[21]

Although concerns about sexual practices dominated the early phases of the debates, by the mid-1980s questions about representation were becoming equally divisive, especially in artistic and academic communities. Using increasingly broad definitions of pornography, antipornography feminists challenged the lines between hard-core and soft-core, pornography and art, popular culture and high culture; they also cut across historical boundaries. For example, in her analysis of objectification—a key characteristic of pornography—Dworkin links the philosophy of Ernest Becker, "every soap and cosmetic commercial," the prose of Norman Mailer, and the poetry of John Keats.[22] Although such juxtapositions are often provocative, polemicists like Dworkin and Griffin tend to ignore variables of genre, audience, and context.

Moreover, when Catharine MacKinnon declares that pornography "*is* a form of forced sex," she identifies the representation of a rape with the rape itself.[23] There is no difference between image and act: "When a man looks at a pornographic picture—pornographic meaning that the woman is defined as to be acted upon, a sexual object, a sexual thing—the *viewing* is an *act,* an act of male supremacy? . . . Pornography is not imagery in some relation to a reality elsewhere constructed. It is not a distortion, reflection, projection, expression, fantasy, representation, or symbol either. It is sexual reality."[24] In *The Pornography of Representation,* Susanne Kappeler insists that the pornographer and the artist do the same thing "in terms of representation, and with respect to the objectification of the female gender. . . . What feminist analysis identifies as the pornographic structure of representation—not the presence of a variable quality of 'sex,' but the systematic objectification of women in the interest of the exclusive subjectification of men—is a common place of art and literature as well as of conventional pornography." Given current political conditions, Kappeler concludes that a committed feminist cannot be a committed artist.[25] The problem is clear. As Kathy Myers has argued, if feminists accept such "perceptual essentialism" and agree that all forms of representation are harmful to women, then they will lose the ability to communicate, relinquish the right to represent their own sexuality, and deny themselves pleasure.[26] "Good girls" will have neither voice nor vision; all the artists will be "bad girls."

Although scholars in several disciplines now express dissatisfaction with the generalized and ahistorical pronouncements of the feminist antipornography movement, the most promising recent work has come from film critics who also refute some of the traditional tenets of psychoanalytic theory while giving careful attention to economic and social contexts. Convinced that previous theories of representation and audience response have proved to be inadequate, Gaylyn Studlar, Tania Modleski, and Kaja Silverman call for a reconceptualization of the pleasures of masochism. Determined to understand what masochism means to women, Mary Ann Doane, Carol J. Clover, and Linda Williams propose careful distinctions among different types of materials and narrow their focus to a particular genre, such as the "paranoid woman's film" of the 1940s, the slasher film of the 1970s and 1980s, or the stag film; in analyzing audience response, they seek a theory of the spectator that has historical and sexual specificity. Like many other critics of the visual arts, they object to Mulvey's account of the male gaze because it reduces the woman to object and denies her pleasure. As an alternative theory, Doane suggests that viewers might identify with the female protagonists who exercise "an active investigating gaze" in gothic films.[27] Rejecting the concept of a fixed viewing position, Williams and Clover discover multiple and fluid cross-gender identifications. According to Williams, a female viewer of a torture scene might not identify with the character being beaten: "She may also, simultaneously, identify with the beater or with the less involved spectator who simply looks on. And even if she does identify only with the tortured woman, she might identify alternately or simultaneously with her pleasure and/or her pain." Williams urges feminists to recognize that male and female spectators "find both power and pleasure in identifying not only with a sadist's control but also with a masochist's abandon."[28] Sadomasochistic pornography can serve women's interests.

Williams turns from women spectators to women producers in her account of Femme Productions, a film company formed by Candida Royalle and other well-known female porn stars. The representation of mothers as sexual subjects in *Three Daughters* (Candida Royalle, 1986) and other Femme Production films is particularly important in suggesting ways that women might learn to express their desire. Working from psychoanalyst Jessica Benjamin's theories of female identity, Williams treats penis envy as a social problem. A young girl needs to identify "with a sexual agent—an agent who could just as well be the mother if the mother was also associated with the outside and articulated as a sexual subject of desire." Pornography for women can be an important arena for change, "especially if it is a pornography that can combine the holding and nurturing of motherhood with sexual representation."[29]

By demonstrating that representation need not encode structures of domination and by describing terms whereby women artists and audience members might pursue their own pleasures, feminist film critics can help the parties in the pornography debates move beyond their current oppositions; by offering new perspectives on such issues as masochism and motherhood, they also provide strategies for resolving some of the interpretive dilemmas in Angela Carter's work.

III

In her protests against the repression of women's sexual desire, her determination to break the ideological link between sex and romance, and her apparent willingness to accept sadomasochism as an eroticized exchange of power negotiated between partners, Carter anticipates many of the arguments made in support of pornography during the 1980s. Indeed, in *The Sadeian Woman,* Carter appears to be one of the new Juliettes, a "bad girl" promoting an aggressive, power-oriented sexuality. James Sloan Allen describes Carter as an "author of pornography"; Amanda Sebestyen calls her "the high priestess of post-graduate porn."[30] According to Avis Lewallen, Carter is caught in Sade's scheme of binary oppositions; according to Kappeler, she has fled to a "literary sanctuary" where she treats Sade as a cultural artifact beyond the reach of political criticism.[31]

In contrast, I will argue that Carter is practicing intensely political criticism. Her stance on pornography resists easy categorization. Indeed, the thematics of "The Bloody Chamber" align her with the antipornography feminists who have been among her most vehement critics. In this story, male sexuality is death-oriented: the male murders with his eye, his penis, his sword. Pornography becomes a display of male power, expression *and* cause of men's aggression against women. The pornography represented in the story does not offer the woman a way to be a sexual rebel; instead, it subjects her to harm. Has Carter become one of the "good girls," repudiating pornography, even at the risk of ending heterosexual relationships? Or does she seek to escape from dichotomies altogether, including the "good girl/bad girl" dichotomy that has divided feminists at both the practical and the theoretical levels?

In her collection, *The Bloody Chamber and Other Adult Tales* (1979), Carter retells such well-known fairy tales as "Bluebeard," "Beauty and the Beast," "Puss in Boots," and "Little Red Riding Hood." "I was using the latent content of those traditional stories," she told an interviewer. "And that latent content is violently sexual."[32] Carter associates traditional tales with the "subliterary forms of pornography, ballad and dream."[33] "The Bloody Chamber," the first story in the volume, continues—but also qualifies—the analysis of sexuality and culture that Carter had begun a year earlier in *The Sadeian Woman.* Drawing upon that study, I will read "The Bloody Chamber" against three kinds of fiction: (1) the fairy tale of "Bluebeard" and the interpretive traditions surrounding it during the nineteenth and twentieth centuries; (2) pornographic fiction, especially *Justine* (1791), the Sade novel Carter describes as "a black, inverted fairy tale" (*SW,* p. 39); and (3) Freud's theory of female development, which is, according to Carter, an account "of such extraordinary poetic force that . . . it retains a cultural importance analogous . . . to the myth of the crime of Eve" (*SW,* p. 125).

Carter takes the basic elements of her story from Charles Perrault's "La Barbe Bleue" (1697), which is the earliest written version of the Bluebeard tale. In Perrault's seventeenth-century *conte,* a young girl is revolted by her suitor's blue beard and suspicious about the mysterious disappearance of his previous wives. But she is so dazzled by his extravagant wealth and the seemingly endless pleasures of his parties that she soon marries him. Shortly after the marriage, Bluebeard subjects his wife to a test: he departs from the mansion, giving her the keys to all the rooms but warning her against entering a "little room . . . at the end of a dark little corridor." Consumed, almost immediately, with "the desire to open the door of the forbidden room," the wife finds corpses of his murdered wives strewn about the chamber. In her horror, she drops the key on the blood-clotted floor and is unable to remove the stain. When the husband discovers the bloody key, he immediately realizes what has happened. Enraged at his wife's transgression, Bluebeard orders her to prepare for death. But just as he lifts his cutlass to behead her, her brothers burst through the door and kill him. The wife inherits her husband's money, which she uses to help her sister and brothers and "to marry herself to an honest man who made her forget her sorrows as the wife of Bluebeard."[34]

According to folklorists, oral versions of this tale were widespread throughout Europe long before Perrault composed his *conte.* In one version, the maiden waits for her brothers to rescue her from the murderous ogre; in another, a clever young woman tricks the ogre, secures her own escape, and saves her sisters from his rage.[35] These oral tales, which are lacking in didacticism, provide little commentary on the characters' actions. When Perrault developed the first literary version of the Bluebeard tale, he chose the helpless heroine rather than the clever one. He also appended two sophisticated *moralités* in verse: the first, presumably addressed to his women readers, cautions against the dangers of curiosity; the second warns husbands against making impossible demands on their wives. Although the moral lesson of this prohibition/transgression tale is "somewhat ambiguous,"[36] it does seem that Perrault is as much concerned with the husband's jealousy as with the wife's curiosity.

However, by the early nineteenth century, "the rich ambiguities attending the curiosity of Bluebeard's wife in Perrault's tale are sorted out and funneled into two separate tale types by the Grimms. . . . By the time that the *Nursery and Household Tales* appeared [in 1812], 'Bluebeard' had branched off into two separate narratives: one a cautionary fairy tale about the hazards of curiosity [such as "Mary's Child"], the other a folk tale depicting the triumph of a clever young woman over a bloodthirsty villain [such as "Fowler's Fowl"]."[37] Tales of female triumph abound in the folk tradition,[38] but it was the other type—the didactic story warning against female curiosity—that gained popularity on the stages and in the bookstalls of nineteenth-century Europe. Maria Tatar has found that "nearly every nineteenth-century printed version of 'Bluebeard' singles out the heroine's curiosity as an especially undesirable trait."[39] Thus by the nineteenth century the wife's disobedience had become a much more serious issue than the husband's violence.

Twentieth-century sympathizers with the wife have sometimes recast her transgression as a heroic search for knowledge.[40] But in the most influential modern interpretation of the story, psychoanalyst Bruno Bettelheim emphasizes the wife's wrongdoing, which he defines in explicitly sexual terms. According to Bettelheim, the blood on the key "seems to symbolize that the woman had sexual relations" with the castle's guests. For Bettelheim, this is "a cautionary tale which warns: Women, don't give in to your sexual curiosity; men, don't permit yourself to be carried away by your anger at being sexually betrayed."[41]

Writing *against* the interpretive tradition that emphasizes the wife's illicit sexual curiosity, Angela Carter makes four important changes in the tale. First, she depicts the husband, whom she renames "the Marquis," as a patron of the arts and collector of pornography, thereby demonstrating a cultural foundation for his sadism and suggesting a relationship between art and aggression. Second, she grants moral complexity and narrative control to the wife, who tells the tale from her own point of view. Third, she develops the character of the second husband so that he stands as an alternative to the type of masculinity represented by the Marquis. Fourth, she restores to prominence a figure who is strikingly, ominously, absent from fairly tales, from pornographic fiction, and from the Freudian theory of female development: the strong, loving, and courageous mother.[42]

Although Carter follows her seventeenth-century source by making the husband wealthy, she moves beyond Perrault by depicting the husband as a devotee of opera, an admirer of Baudelaire, and a collector of books and paintings. Here she draws upon the popular French tradition of associating Bluebeard with Gilles de Rais (1404–40), companion-in-arms to Joan of Arc, Marshal of France under Charles VII, refined patron of the arts, *and* child-murderer.[43] Interest in Gilles de Rais had "suddenly revived" during the nineteenth century, exactly when it could be fitted into a new category of crime: sex-killing.[44] With his atrocious crimes *and* his aesthetic sensibilities, Gilles de Rais became an important figure in decadent literature, most especially in J. F. Huysman's *Là-bas* (1891), a copy of which is lavishly displayed in the Marquis's library. The Marquis's shimmering castle by the sea seems to come from an imaginary world. But by locating it in Brittany and by describing the villagers' fears of the bloodthirsty Marquis, Carter also evokes the brutal feudalism of the historical Gilles de Rais. Unfortunately, abuses of male power—social, economic, cultural, political, and sexual—are not confined to past societies. The Marquis's purchases, such as the wardrobe by Poirer, bring the story into "more democratic times,"[45] the early part of the twentieth century. References to the telephone, the stock market, and the international drug trade identify the Marquis as a modern businessman and establish the economic basis of his art collection.

With his wealth, the Marquis can offer the young woman tickets to *Tristan,* a Bechstein piano, an early Flemish primitive of Saint Cecelia. From courtship through consummation, he uses art to aid in seduction. Thus Carter situates the story in the tradition of "aesthetic sadomasochism": works that center on the "education of one person in the sexual fantasy of another through complex role playing cued to works of art and imagination."[46] As the bride is being undressed, she realizes that her husband has arranged their encounter to resemble an etching. "And when nothing but my scarlet, palpitating core remained, I saw, in the mirror, the living image of an etching by Rops from the collection he had shown me . . . the child with her sticklike limbs, naked but for her button boots, her gloves, shielding her face with her hand as though her face were the last repository of her modesty; and the old, monocled lecher who examined her, limb by limb" (*BC,* p. 12). The gentleman displays age, wealth, experience, and the power of the eye; the child-like female is reduced to an object of the male gaze. Perhaps the narrator calls this the "most pornographic of all confrontations" (*BC,* p. 12) because she realizes that by giving herself to be looked at, she has entered what Jonathan Elmer calls "the classic pornographic contract."[47]

Later that day, the young wife is shocked by illustrations in one of her husband's books: "I had not bargained for this, the girl with tears hanging on her cheeks like stuck pearls, her cunt a split fig below the great globes of her buttocks on which the knotted tails of the cat were about to descend, while a man in a black mask fingered with his free hand his prick, that curved upwards like the scimitar he held. The picture had a caption: 'Reproof of curiosity' " (*BC,* p. 14). Through the caption, Carter links the flagellation scene, a staple of nineteenth-century pornography, to the Bluebeard tale. Moreover, by representing the male as a Turkish sultan raising his scimitar, Carter acknowledges the orientalizing of the tale which occurred among dramatists and illustrators.[48] Another engraving, "Immolation of the wives of the Sultan," stimulates the groom to take his bride to bed in a mirror-lined room in broad daylight. "All the better to see you," he says (*BC,* p. 15).

In both episodes—the disrobing and the defloration—the contrast between the husband's action and the wife's immobility seems to support the theory of the male gaze articulated by film critic E. Ann Kaplan: "To begin with, men do not simply look; their gaze carries with it the power of action and possession that is lacking in the female gaze. Women receive and return a gaze, but cannot act on it. Second, the sexualization and objectification of women is not simply for the purposes of eroticism; from a psychoanalytic point of view, it is designed to annihilate the threat that woman (as castrated, and possessing a sinister genital organ) poses."[49] According to Laura Mulvey, "the woman as icon, displayed for the gaze and enjoyment of men, the active controllers of the look, always threatens to evoke anxiety." The male unconscious might escape from this castration anxiety by becoming preoccupied with "the re-enactment of the original trauma"; Mulvey calls this reaction, which involves investigating and demystifying the woman, "voyeurism": "Voyeurism . . . has associations with sadism: pleasure lies in ascertaining guilt (immediately associated with castration), asserting control and subjecting the guilty person through punishment or forgiveness. This sadistic side fits in well with narrative. Sadism demands a story, depends on making something happen, forcing a change in another person, a battle of will and strength, victory/defeat, all occurring in a linear time with a beginning and an end."[50] Carter's voyeuristic Marquis is indeed a sadist—in terms of his sexual practices and in terms of his control of narrative: he has arranged the setting, written the script, and set the plot in motion.

According to the bride, the initial sexual encounter taught her the truth of Baudelaire's statement: "There is a striking resemblance between the act of love and the ministrations of a torturer" (*BC,* p. 29). The husband's poetic allusions and his penchant for forcing his nude wife to wear a jeweled collar show his allegiance to Baudelaire, while his title, his sexual practices, and the furnishings in his forbidden room link him to Sade. The Marquis's bloody chamber recalls several rooms in *Justine,* such as the monks' pavilion, which is reached through a winding underground tunnel and filled with "scourges, ferules, withes, cords, and a thousand other instruments of torture,"[51] and Roland's subterranean cave, which is hung with skulls, skeletons, bundles of whips, and collections of sabers. Carter's Marquis bears a particularly close resemblance to the Comte de Gernande, the aristocrat in *Justine* who equips his apartment with straps to bind his wives and surgical devices to bleed them to death. Both the Marquis and Gernande have already killed three wives; both have a lust for blood. Unlike most libertines, they are committed to torturing women within marriage.

For these male characters, sex does not appear to be a pleasurable experience. According to Carter, the libertine's orgasm is "annihilating, appalling," marked by screams, blasphemies, and fits; it requires him "to die in pain and to painfully return from death" (*SW,* pp. 149–50). The bride of "The Bloody Chamber" gives a similar description of her husband: "I had heard him shriek and blaspheme at the orgasm." For this "one-sided struggle," the Marquis brought his bride to "the carved, gilded bed on which he had been conceived"—and presumably born (*BC,* p. 15). Immolating the woman upon his ancestral bed becomes an act of protest against his mother. In *The Sadeian Woman* Carter explains that the libertine feels "greed, envy and jealousy, a helpless rage at the organs of generation that bore us into a world of pain where the enjoyment of the senses is all that can alleviate the daily horror of living. . . . Sade's quarrel, therefore, is not only with the mother, who can deprive him of love and sustenance at will; it is the very fact of generation that he finds intolerable" (*SW,* p. 135). Perhaps the Marquis, like the Sadeian libertine, "cannot forgive the other, not for what she is, but for what she has done—for having thoughtlessly, needlessly inflicted life upon him" (*SW,* p. 135). This animosity toward the mother also helps account for the emphasis on the Marquis's gaze. According to Kaplan, "The domination of women by the male gaze is part of men's strategy to contain the threat that the mother embodies, and to control the positive and negative impulses the memory traces of being mothered have left in the male unconscious."[52]

While the husband is defeated, reduced even before death to one of "those clockwork tableaux of Bluebeard that you see in glass cases at fairs" (*BC,* p. 45), the wife survives to tell the story of her moral development. Unlike the women in the illustrations, she is not trapped in a visual representation. Because she has a voice, she can be heard without being seen. To be sure, the use of a female narrator does not in and of itself constitute a challenge to the conventions of pornography. As Kappeler has argued, the "assumption of the female point of view and narrative voice—the assumption of linguistic and narrative female 'subjectivity'—in no way lessens the pornographic structure, the fundamental elision of the woman as subject."[53] Sade's Juliette personifies "the whore as story-teller," using narrative to entertain her captors and evade death (*SW,* p. 81). Yet unlike the female narrators who have such a prominent place in the history of pornographic fiction, Carter's narrator is not using language to provide sexual entertainment for male readers.[54] Roland Barthes would see the protagonist's control of language as evidence of a shift in power: "The master is he who speaks, who disposes of the entirety of language; the object is he who is silent, who remains separate, by a mutilation more absolute than any erotic torture, from any access to discourse, because he does not even have any right to receive the master's word."[55]

Susan Griffin would see the female voice as constituting a challenge to pornography, a genre which assumes male control of language and "expresses an almost morbid fear of female speech."[56]

The young woman not only escapes from silence; she also avoids the dichotomized treatment of female characters in fairly tales and pornographic fiction. In *The Sadeian Woman,* Carter argued that Sade's "straitjacket psychology"—his belief that virtue and vice are innate—"relates his fiction directly to the black and white ethical world of fairy tale and fable" (*SW,* p. 82). Fairy tales, as Andrea Dworkin indicates, offer only "two definitions of woman": "There is the good woman. She is a victim. There is the bad woman. She must be destroyed. The good woman must be possessed. The bad woman must be killed, or punished. Both must be nullified."[57] The woman in "The Bloody Chamber" is not modeled after either of the protagonists in the traditional Bluebeard tales described by Maria Tatar: the victim who is rightly punished for her curiosity or the avenger, the triumphant heroine who single-handedly defeats the tyrant. Nor does she fit the Sadeian categories, for she is neither Juliette, the aggressor, nor Justine, the helpless martyr who aspires to be "the perfect woman." According to Carter, Justine defines virtue in passive terms of obedience and sexual abstinence. Unable to act, unchanged by experience, she is "the heroine of a black, inverted fairy-tale":

> To be the *object* of desire is to be defined in the passive case.
> To exist in the passive case is to die in the passive case—that is, to be killed.
> This is the moral of the fairy tale about the perfect woman. [*SW,* pp. 76–77]

In Carter's analysis, "Justine marks the start of a self-regarding female masochism"; *she,* not Sade, personifies the pornography of the female condition during the twentieth century (*SW,* p. 57). In contrast, the protagonist of "The Bloody Chamber" learns that she is not a perfect woman; she has the right to act, to experience the consequences of her decisions, to learn from error. Hence she achieves a much more complicated sense of morality than Bluebeard's wife or Sade's Justine.

That morality is, however, founded on her sense of "shame" (*BC,* p. 46).[58] In Sade's novel, the ever pure Justine was able to have the brand on her shoulder removed by a surgeon. In contrast, Carter's young bride must bear a permanent mark on her forehead: a "heart-shaped stain" from the bloody key (*BC,* p. 40).[59]

Reflecting on her experiences, the narrator feels ashamed of the materialism that drove her to marry the Marquis and of her complicity in sadomasochism. Carter casts her protagonist in genteel poverty to show "relationships between the sexes are determined by . . . the historical fact of the economic dependence of women upon men" (*SW,* pp. 6–7). Raised by a widowed mother who "beggared herself for love," the young woman wears "twice-darned underwear" and "faded gingham" so that she can continue her study of music (*BC,* pp. 2, 6). When the Marquis appears offering opera tickets and an opal ring, the protagonist willingly forsakes her mother's shabbiness for his extravagance: "This ring, the bloody bandage of rubies, the wardrobe of clothes from Poiret and Worth, his scent of Russian leather—all had conspired to seduce me" (*BC,* p. 8). She later realizes that she sold herself for "a handful of colored stones and the pelts of dead beasts" (*BC,* p. 16). At the end of Perrault's tale, the protagonist kept Bluebeard's money to further her happiness and that of her family; Carter's protagonist distributes her inheritance to charity, retaining only enough to start a small music school.

The narrator's understanding of sexuality also changes. Her mother had given her a legacy of romance and a bit of factual knowledge. "My mother, with all the precision of her eccentricity, had told me what it was that lovers did; I was innocent but not naive," she recalls (*BC,* p. 14). During the engagement, she discovers her "potentiality for corruption" when she attends the opera wearing the ruby choker given to her by the Marquis:

> I saw him watching me in the gilded mirrors with the assessing eye of a connoisseur inspecting horseflesh, or even of a housewife in the market, inspecting cuts on the slab. I'd never seen, or else had never acknowledged, that regard of his before, the sheer carnal avarice of it; and it was strangely magnified by the monocle lodged in his left eye. . . . And I saw myself, suddenly, as he saw me, my pale face, the way the muscles in my neck stuck out like thin wire. I saw how much that cruel necklace became me. And for the first time in my innocent and confined life, I sensed in myself a potentiality for corruption that took my breath away. [*BC,* p. 7]

Aspects of this scene are repeated later during the disrobing. Again, he is the purchaser; she, the commodity, the piece of meat, "bare as a lamb chop." He examines her through his monocle; she watches in the mirror. "And, as at the opera, when I had first seen my flesh in his eyes, I was aghast to feel myself stirring" (*BC,* p. 12).

To understand why she might take sexual pleasure in being objectified, it is helpful to turn to the psychoanalytic account of women's castration anxiety. According to Kaplan:

> The entry of the father as the third term disrupts the mother/child dyad, causing the child to understand the mother's castration and possession by the father. In the symbolic world the girl now enters, she learns not only subject/object positions but the sexed pronouns "he" and "she." Assigned the place of object (since she lacks the phallus, the symbol of the signifier), she is the recipient of male desire, the passive recipient of his gaze. If she is to have sexual pleasure, it can only be constructed around her objectification; it cannot be a pleasure that comes from desire for the other (a subject position). . . . Women . . . have learned to associate their sexuality with domination by the male gaze, a position involving a degree of masochism in finding their objectification erotic.[60]

Given that this position involves a "degree of masochism," it is not surprising to find the protagonist clinging to the man who impaled her, "as though only the one who had inflicted the pain could comfort [her] for suffering it" (*BC*, p. 16). The Marquis disgusts her, but she craves him like pregnant women crave "for the taste of coal or chalk or tainted food" (*BC*, p. 21).

In his absence, she searches the castle for "the evidence of his real life" (*BC*, p. 25). Like the heroines in the "paranoid Gothic films" of the 1940s—films like *Gaslight* and *Secret beyond the Door*, which are linked to the Bluebeard tale through Robertson Stevenson's version of *Jane Eyre* (1944)—the narrator becomes an active investigator, bringing light into the darkened corridors.[61] She approaches the forbidden room through a gallery hung with Venetian tapestries depicting "some grisly mythological subject," possibly the rape of the Sabine women (*BC*, p. 28). When she enters the bloody chamber, she finds "a little museum of his perversity," a collection of deathly artifacts—Etruscan funerary urns, a medieval rack and great wheel, an "ominous bier of Renaissance workmanship" (*BC*, p. 29). Here, within the bloody chamber, she discovers her ties to other women. Driven by her "mother's spirit . . . to know the very worst," she examines the physical remains of the Marquis's former wives: the embalmed corpse of the opera singer, the veiled skull of the artist's model, the still-bleeding body of the Romanian countess (*BC*, pp. 29–30).

Like the wife in a "paranoid Gothic film" who finds mutilated traces of other wives in her house, the narrator sees herself "slowly becoming another, duplicating an earlier identity as though history, particularly in the case of women, were bound to repeat itself."[62] She sobs with pity for "the fated sisterhood" of her husband's other victims and with anguish for her own lost innocence (*BC*, p. 30). As Philip Lewis says in his stimulating reading of Perrault, the bloody floor subsumes "the blood of consanguinity, the bloodshed of violence and death, and . . . the red blood of womanhood"; it is "the double agent of the dual perception the wife experiences in discovering herself, and that Bluebeard experiences in his turn when the blood appears to his eyes as a tarnish or a taint on the magic key."[63] The revelation that she, like the other women, has chosen death shocks the protagonist into life. Masochism may have served her interests during the courtship and the initial sexual encounter: perhaps she assumed a passive role as a way to disguise her curiosity about sex and her desire for wealth. But she did not contract for death. "My first thought," she says, "when I saw the ring for which I had sold myself to this fate, was how to escape it" (*BC*, p. 31). Unfortunately, with her husband's sudden reappearance, she seems to be trapped in his deadly plot.

Attired only in the ruby choker, her hair drawn back as it was for the sexual encounter, the bride anticipates her beheading. She is saved, not by her brothers but by her mother, who bursts through the gate, with one hand on the reins of a rearing horse, and the other clutching her husband's military revolver which she has removed from her reticule. The mother shoots the

Marquis, frees her daughter, and restores her to a life of emotional and moral integrity. Through this witty and flamboyantly triumphant ending, Carter rewrites Perrault's fairy tale, the Gernande section of *Justine,* and the Freudian account of female development. In Sade's novel, the Comtesse de Gernande, whose husband was trying to bleed her to death, asked Justine to carry a letter to her mother; she felt certain that her mother would "hasten with all expedition to sever her daughter's bonds."[64] But Gernande thwarted that plan; strong and loving mothers do not appear in Sade.

In Freud the mother is rendered powerless—to herself and to her daughter—by her lack of a penis. "The turning away from the mother is accompanied by hostility; the attachment to the mother ends in hate," hypothesizes Freud (*SW,* p. 125). According to Carter, the "psychic fiction" of women's castration does not just affect individual development; it pervades our culture and helps to account for the recurrence of sexual violence. "The whippings, the beatings, the gougings, the stabbings of erotic violence reawaken the memory of the social fiction of the female wound, the bleeding scar left by her castration, which is a psychic fiction as deeply at the heart of Western culture as the myth of Oedipus. . . . Female castration is an imaginary fact that pervades the whole of men's attitude towards women and our attitude to ourselves, that transforms women from human beings into wounded creatures who were born to bleed" (*SW,* p. 23). In "The Bloody Chamber," the mother certainly does not act like a wounded creature born to bleed. Indeed, her courage sustains the young bride who realizes that she has inherited her "nerves and a will from the mother who had defied the yellow outlaws of Indochina" (*BC,* p. 29). The mother has performed legendary feats of male and female heroism: "Her mother had outfaced a junkful of Chinese pirates, nursed a village through a visitation of the plague, [and] shot a man-eating tiger with her own hand" (*BC,* p. 2). Similarly, Carter equips the mother with male and female Freudian symbols, making several references to the father's gun kept in the mother's reticule. This parent is powerful enough to serve as father and mother to the young woman. Instead of rejecting her, the daughter and her new husband join the mother to form a new family.

Since the theories of individuation that permeate our culture stress the necessity of renouncing the bond with the mother—that dangerous, archaic force who would "pull us back to what Freud called the 'limitless narcissism' of infancy"[65]—some readers see the protagonist's reunion with her mother as a regression. But I think that Carter, like psychoanalyst Jessica Benjamin, is challenging the Oedipal models of development which privilege separation over dependence. Benjamin urges women "to reconceive the ideal" of motherhood, not by idealizing female nurturance but by acknowledging the mother as an independently existing subject, one who expresses her own desire.[66] The mother in "The Bloody Chamber" has experienced autonomy and adventure in the world; she has also acted according to her desires, having "gladly, scandalously, defiantly" married for love (*BC,* p. 2). Carter seems to anticipate the recent work of women filmmakers and critics who believe that "some part of Motherhood lies outside of patriarchal concerns . . . and eludes control"[67] and that recognizing the mother as sexual subject might provide a solution to the representation of desire, especially if she is also granted access to the outside world of freedom.

In addition to criticizing the position of the mother in pornography, popular literature, and psychoanalytic theory, Carter also challenges definitions of masculinity based on domination. In Perraults's "Bluebeard," the second husband seemed to be an afterthought, part of the reward accorded to the wife at the end of the story. In "The Bloody Chamber," he appears as the bride's humble friend and confidant. A poor piano tuner, Jean-Yves has neither the power of the Marquis nor the glamor of a fairy tale prince. Because of his blindness, he will never look at the materials in the Marquis's library; nor will he see the mark of shame on the narrator's forehead. Jean-Yves is not perfect: when he tells the bride that she, like Eve, should be punished for her disobedience, he reveals that his attitudes have been shaped by myths of feminine evil. Despite this limitation, he is a sympathetic listener, loyal, tender, and sensitive, as he offers to "be of some comfort . . . though not much use" to the despairing bride (BC, p.42). The Marquis treated the narrator's musical talent as a stylish accomplishment to be displayed in his mansion; Jean-Yves expresses reverence for her art. The Marquis took the young woman away from her mother; Jean-Yves helps open the courtyard gate so that the mother might return.

However, in a culture that eroticizes domination, it is not surprising that some readers are reluctant to accept Jean-Yves as the hero. His relationship with the narrator does not appear to have a sexual dimension. According to Patricia Duncker, "while blindness, as symbolic castration, may signal the end of male sexual aggression, it is also mutilation. As such it cannot be offered as the answer, the new male erotic identity."[68] In rejecting pornography, did Carter feel compelled to eliminate all signs of a physical attraction? Must women choose between a dangerous but exciting sexuality based on male dominance, or a sweet, safe, and utterly asexual relationship between equals? And does that "equality" demand that the male be disfigured?

Perhaps if Carter were to continue the story, she would develop a male sexuality centered on smell, touch, and sound; indeed, this is already implicit in Jean-Yves's extreme sensitivity to music. After the narrator relinquishes her position as object of the male gaze, she may eventually glimpse the "benign sexuality" that eluded Justine (SW, p. 49). But in assuming the subject's position, she has not yet found the language to express her desire. In other words, the new relationship may have erotic possibilities that the narrator does not know how to represent and that we do not know how to read. Perhaps Jackie Byars's argument pertains: we need to learn to recognize a tradition of mutual gazing that "expresses a 'different voice' and a different kind of gaze that we've not heard or seen before because our theories have discouraged such 'hearing' and 'seeing.' "[69] In the meantime, mother and daughter will be the only members of this household who can gaze lovingly at one another.

Has Angela Carter become a "moral pornographer" exposing the misogyny that distorts our culture and envisioning a new world of sexual freedom? Although "The Bloody Chamber" does, I think, use pornography as a critique of the current relations between the sexes, Carter's hopes for a world of "absolute sexual licence" seem subdued and her attitude toward Sade more critical than in *The Sadeian Woman*. Carter refuses to define pornography as the primary cause of women's oppression, for she believes that complicated economic, social, and psychological forces contribute to the objectification, fetishization, and violation of women. But in "The Bloody Chamber" Carter moves closer to the antipornography feminists: she assumes that pornography encourages violence against women and that the association of sex, power, and sadomasochism in pornography is part of society's common prescription for heterosexual relations. Like the feminists opposed to pornography, she urges women to challenge assumptions about female masochism and to define a sexuality outside of dominant-submissive power relations.

"The Bloody Chamber" ultimately fulfills Kappeler's definition of feminist critique: "It shows up and criticizes the folklore nature of the pornographic plot, the rearticulation of an unchanging archetype, reiterated in the patriarchal culture at large, which recites the same tale over and over again, convincing itself through these rearticulations of the impossibility of change."[70] Carter refuses to isolate pornography—as a genre or as a social problem. Instead of treating pornography as a specialized subgenre appealing to a small group of male consumers, Carter employs a complex series of allusions to link pornography to fairy tales, psychoanalysis, and other forms of fiction. With Catharine A. MacKinnon, she treats psychoanalysis and pornography as "epistemic sites in the same ontology," "mirrors of each other, male supremacist sexuality looking at itself looking at itself."[71] Thus Carter achieves Annette Kuhn's goal: to deconstruct, debunk, and demystify pornography. Such an approach "insists that pornography is not after all special, is not a privileged order of representation; that it shares many of its modes of address, many of its codes and conventions, with representations which are not looked upon as a 'problem' in the way pornography is. This has significant consequences for any feminist politics around pornography in particular and around representation in general."[72]

In a debate that has cast women in the very oppositions defined by Sade—I am thinking again of Robin Morgan's characterization of feminists who defend pornography as "Sade's new Juliettes"[73]—it is impossible to categorize Angela Carter as a good girl or a bad girl, for she, like her protagonist, has escaped from absolutes. She rejects the argument of feminists who defend the right to engage in sadomasochistic practices on the grounds of essentialism or psychological determinism. She also finds the claim that "feminists should not desire or be aroused by physical manifestations of dominance or submission" naive because "it too ignores the social and political realities in which our sexuality is constructed."[74] Carter insists that the young woman understand why she finds her objectification erotic. A recent critic of "The Bloody Chamber" complains, "We are asked to place ourselves imaginatively as masochistic victims in a pornographic scenario and to sympathise in some way with the ambivalent feelings this produces."[75] This is precisely Carter's point. We cannot achieve freedom, according to Angela Carter, until we understand our own historically determined involvement in sadomasochism. And if we are to move beyond the oppositions of male/female, dominant/submissive, sadist/masochist, then a reconceptualization of the mother's role might be the place to begin.

Notes

I would like to thank Michael Atkinson, Gisela Ecker, Tom LeClair, and Ellen Peel for their helpful suggestions. I would also like to express my appreciation to the Taft Foundation for a summer grant to support the initial research for this essay.

    1.   Angela Carter, *The Sadeian Woman and the Ideology of Pornography* (New York, 1978), p. 27; further references to this work, abbreviated *SW,* will be included in the text. The book was published a year later in London under the title of *The Sadeian Woman; An Exercise in Cultural History.*

    2.   Many British commentators base their theoretical analyses of pornography on American texts. For example, in their article about lesbian sadomasochism, Susan Ardell and Sue O'Sullivan decry the "almost complete absence of talking or writing about sex" in England ("Upsetting an Applecart: Difference, Desire and Lesbian Sadomasochism," *Feminist Review* 23 [June 1986]: 41). A. W. B. Simpson, a member of the Williams Committee, notes that "virtually everything which has been produced by the radical feminist movement on the subject is American" (*Pornography and Politics: A Look Back to the Williams Committee* [London, 1983], p. 67).

    3.   Susan Rubin Suleiman, "Pornography, Transgression, and the Avant-Garde: Bataille's *Story of the Eye,*" in *The Poetics of Gender,* ed. Nancy K. Miller (New York, 1986), p. 130.

    4.   *Justine* was first published in mass-market paperback in 1965 and quickly went through four editions. But when the press covering the Brady-Hindley trial revealed that the murderers had tortured their victims in imitation of particular scenes in Sade's novels, some politicians and editorial writers urged that respectable publishers refuse to handle Sade's works. According to John Sutherland, "Since 1966, no British publisher has been prepared to put his name to the Divine Marquis's more notorious books" (*Offensive Literature: Decensorship in Britain, 1960–1982* [London, 1982], p. 72).

    5.   For a feminist critique of the Williams Committee, see Susanne Kappeler, *The Pornography of Representation* (Minneapolis, 1986), pp. 19–34; for further information on Mary Whitehouse, see Rosemary Betterton, ed., *Looking On: Images of Femininity in the Visual Arts and Media* (London, 1987), p. 145; and especially Ruth Wallsgrove, "Between the Devil and the True Blue Whitehouse," in Betterton, ed., pp. 170–74.

    6.   Sutherland, p. 143.

    7.   Andrea Dworkin, *Pornography: Men Possessing Women* (New York, 1981), p. 84.

8. Robin Morgan, *Anatomy of Freedom: Feminism, Physics, and Global Politics* (New York, 1982), pp. 116–17, my emphasis.

9. Ann Russo, "Conflicts and Contradictions among Feminists over Issues of Pornography and Sexual Freedom," *Women's Studies International Forum* 10 (1987): 106. Critics have utilized a variety of terms to define the opposing positions in the feminist pornography debates: "anti-porn" versus "pro-porn" (Russo); "radical" versus "libertarian" (Cheryl H. Cohen, "The Feminist Sexuality Debate: Ethics and Politics," *Hypatia* I [1986]: 71–86); "cultural feminists" versus "radical feminists" (Alice Echols, "The Taming of the Id: Feminist Sexual Politics, 1968–83," in *Pleasure and Danger: Exploring Female Sexuality*, ed. Carole S. Vance [Boston, 1984], pp. 50–72); "puritans" versus "perverts" (Joanne Russ, *Magic Mommas, Trembling Sisters, Puritans and Perverts: Feminist Essays* [Trumansburg, NY, 1985]); "good girls" versus "bad girls" (Lisa Orlando, "Bad Girls and 'Good' Politics," *Voice Literary Supplement* [December 7, 1982], pp. 1, 16–19); "anti-pornography feminists" versus "social constructionists" (Linda Williams, *Hard Core: Power, Pleasure, and "The Frenzy of the Visible"* [Berkeley, 1989]).

10. Robin Morgan, *Going Too Far: The Personal Chronicle of a Feminist* (New York, 1977), p. 174.

11. Gloria Steinem, "Erotica and Pornography: A Clear and Present Difference," in *Take Back the Night: Women on Pornography,* ed. Laura Lederer (New York, 1980), p. 37.

12. Dworkin, *Pornography,* p. 24.

13. See, for example, the essays anthologized in *For Adults Users Only: The Dilemmas of Violent Pornography,* eds. Susan Gubar and Joan Hoff (Bloomington, IN, 1989).

14. Kappeler (n. 5 above), p. 52.

15. Sandra Lee Bartky, "Feminine Masochism and the Politics of Personal Transformation," *Women's Studies International Forum* 7 (1984): 323.

16. Andrea Dworkin, *Our Blood: Prophecies and Discourses on Sexual Politics* (London, 1982), p. 111.

17. The best known campaigns were those in support of the MacKinnon-Dworkin ordinances in Minneapolis (1983) and Indianapolis (1984). The legal complexities of the MacKinnon-Dworkin argument are beyond the scope of this article. Interested readers should see Donald Alexander Downs, *The New Politics of Pornography* (Chicago, 1989); and Catharine A. MacKinnon, *Feminism Unmodified: Discourses on Life and Law* (Cambridge, MA, 1987).

18. Ellen Willis, "Feminism, Moralism, and Pornography," in *Powers of Desire: The Politics of Sexuality,* eds. Ann Snitow, Christine Stansell, and Sharon Thompson (New York, 1983), p. 464.

19. Pat Califia, "A Personal View of the History of the Lesbian S/M Community and Movement in San Francisco," in *Coming to Power: Writings and Graphics on Lesbian S/M,* ed. Samois (Boston, 1982), p. 270. Many feminists who defend sadomasochism speak from a lesbian viewpoint.

20. Samois, ed., p. 288.

21. Jeffrey Weeks, *Sexuality and Its Discontents: Meanings, Myths and Modern Sexualities* (London, 1985), pp. 239–40.

22. Dworkin, *Pornography* (n. 7 above), p. 115.

23. MacKinnon, *Feminism Unmodified,* p. 148, my emphasis.

24. Ibid., pp. 130, 149.

25. Kappeler (n. 5 above), pp. 102–3. Kappeler does, however, encourage "the active participation of women (and other non-experts) in cultural practice." For the future, she envisions a feminist cultural practice that would arise "from a changed consciousness of what culture and its practices are" and "from a different social and economic organization" (pp. 221–22).

26. Kathy Myers, "Towards a Feminist Erotica," in Betterton, ed. (n. 5 above), p. 200.

27. Mary Ann Doane, "The 'Woman's Film': Possession and Address," in *Re-Vision: Feminist Essays in Film Criticism,* eds. Mary Ann Doane, Pat Mellencamp, and Linda Williams (Frederick, MD, 1984), p. 72.

28. Williams (n. 9 above), pp. 215, 217.

29. Ibid., p. 259.

30. James Sloan Allen, "Where Ego Was," *Nation* 229 (October 6, 1979): 312; Amanda Sebestyen, "The Mannerist Marketplace," *New Socialist* 47 (March 1987): 38.

31. Avis Lewallen, "Wayward Girls but Wicked Women? Female Sexuality in Angela Carter's *The Bloody Chamber*," in *Perspectives on Pornography: Sexuality in Film and Literature,* eds. Gary Day and Clive Bloom (New York, 1988), p. 146; Kappeler, p. 134.

32. Kerryn Goldsworthy, "Angela Carter," *Meanjin* 44 (March 1985): 6.

33. Angela Carter, "Afterword," in her *Fireworks: Nine Profane Pieces* (London, 1974), p. 122.

34. Charles Perrault, "Bluebeard," in *Sleeping Beauty and Other Favourite Fairy Tales,* trans. Angela Carter (New York, 1984), pp. 20, 34, 39.

35. Antti Aarne, *The Types of the Folktale,* trans. and enlarged by Stith Thompson (Helsinki, 1964), pp. 101–2.

36. Jeanne Morgan, *Perrault's Morals for Moderns* (New York, 1985), pp. 110–11.

37. Maria Tatar, *The Hard Facts of the Grimms' Fairy Tales* (Princeton, NJ, 1987), pp. 171, 178.

38. Tales of triumphant women include the English "Mr. Fox," where Lady Margaret outwits her wife-murdering suitor before the marriage; the Italian "Silver Nose," where a young girl recognizes the demonic male and rescues her sisters from the hellish fires of his forbidden chamber; and the Grimm brothers' "Fowler's Fowl," where the heroine finds the mutilated bodies of her sisters in the secret room, magically restores them to life, and tricks the blood-thirsty wizard into taking them home to their parents.

39. Tatar, p. 158.

40. See, for example, Maeterlinck's play *Ariadne et Barbe-Bleue,* in Maurice Maeterlinck, *"Sister Beatrice" and "Ariadne and Barbe Bleue,"* trans. Bernard Miall (New York, 1910) and Sylvia Townsend Warner's short story, "Bluebeard's Daughter" (in her *The Cat's Cradle Book* [New York, 1940]).

41. Bruno Bettelheim, *The Uses of Enchantment: The Meaning and Importance of Fairy Tales* (New York, 1977), pp. 301–2.

42. In some variants of the Bluebeard tale, the mother is the cause of the daughter's enslavement. The story begins when the mother is imprisoned and decides to give her daughter to the tyrant in order to save her own life.

43. According to Reginald Hyatte, Perrault did not base his characterization of Bluebeard on Gilles de Rais. Rather, it was the people of Brittany who traditionally associated the historical child-murderer with the fictional wife-murderer (*Laughter for the Devil: The Trials of Gilles de Rais, Companion-in-Arms of Joan of Arc* [Rutherford, NJ, 1984], p. 25). Comorre the Cursed (ca. 500), a Bretton chieftain who murdered his wives when they became pregnant, has also been suggested as a historical antecedent for Bluebeard.

44. Deborah Cameron and Elizabeth Frazer, *The Lust to Kill: A Feminist Investigation of Sexual Murder* (New York, 1987), p. 22.

45. Angela Carter, *The Bloody Chamber and Other Adult Tales* (New York, 1981), p. 36; subsequent references to this work, abbreviated *BC,* will be incorporated into the text.

46. Williams (n. 9 above), p. 224.

47. Jonathan Elmer, "The Exciting Conflict: The Rhetoric of Pornography and Anti-Pornography," *Cultural Critique* 8 (Winter 1987–88): 67.

48. As examples of the way the tale has been orientalized in England, Juliet McMaster discusses George Coleman's popular pantomime, *Blue-beard, or Female Curiosity.* (1798) and William Thackeray's illustrations to *The Awful History of Blue Beard* (1833) (see her "Bluebeard: A Tale of Matrimony," *A Room of One's Own* 2 [Summer/Fall 1976]: 10–19).

49. E. Ann Kaplan, "Is the Gaze Male?" in Snitow, Stansell, and Thompson, eds. (n. 18 above), p. 311. Some psychoanalytic critics such as Susan Lurie ("Pornography and the Dread

of Women: The Male Sexual Dilemma," in Lederer, ed. [n. 11 above], pp. 159, 73) question whether the boy is traumatized by the possibility of his mother's castration; as Linda Williams explains, a boy's real fear may be that his mother is *not* mutilated. Thus, the notion of woman as castrated man may be "a comforting, wishful fantasy intended to combat the child's imagined dread of what his mother's very real power could do to him" (Linda Williams, "When the Woman Looks," in Doane, Mellencamp, and Williams, eds. [n. 27 above], p. 89). The theory of the male gaze is being questioned, revised, and refuted, especially by feminist film critics trying to find a place for the female spectator. I emphasize Laura Mulvey ("Visual Pleasure and Narrative Cinema," *Screen* 16 [Autumn 1975]: 6–18) and Kaplan ("Is the Gaze Male?" and *Women and Film: Both Sides of the Camera* [New York, 1983]) because their theories have the most explanatory power for "The Bloody Chamber" and *The Sadeian Woman.*

50. Mulvey, pp. 13–14.

51. D. A. F. de Sade, *Three Complete Novels,* trans. Richard Seaver and Austryn Wainhouse (New York, 1965), p. 567.

52. Kaplan, "Is the Gaze Male?" p. 324.

53. Kappeler (n. 5 above), p. 90.

54. The narrator addresses the reader as "you" at seven points in the story. On two occasions, the narrator recognizes the reader's right to judge her and issues a modest plea for leniency (*BC,* pp. 9, 17). On two other occasions, she doubts her ability to convey the quality of her experience to the reader: she cannot transmit the intensity of horror she felt upon seeing her husband's car return (*BC,* p. 36); nor can she find anything in the reader's experience comparable to the strange sight of her mother riding to her rescue (*BC,* p. 45). In two places, she assumes that she and the reader have some common experiences: the reader has seen "clock work tableaux of Bluebeard" at fairs (p. 45); the reader might also share some knowledge of practices in the brothel. But the narrator does not want the reader to indulge in too much fantasy: in the next paragraph, she tells the reader not to imagine "much finesse" in her husband's ritualistic foreplay (*BC,* p. 12).

55. Roland Barthes, *Sade, Fourier, Loyola,* trans. Richard Miller (New York, 1976), p. 31.

56. Susan Griffin, *Pornography and Silence: Culture's Revenge against Nature* (New York, 1981), p. 89.

57. Andrea Dworkin, *Women Hating* (New York, 1974), p. 48.

58. Instead of recognizing a painful but ultimately human pattern of moral growth, Avis Lewallen (n. 31 above) argues that it is "unfair" for the woman to be "branded as guilty" (p. 152).

59. Kari E. Lokke, who interprets the story as a challenge to sadomasochism, argues that the heart is "also a badge of courage . . . evidence of the unconditional power of love, both the indomitable love of the mother and the total acceptance of the gentle male partner" ("*Bluebeard* and *The Bloody Chamber:* The Grotesque of Self-Parody and Self-Assertion," *Frontiers* 10 [1988]: 11).

60. Kaplan, "Is the Gaze Male?" (n. 49 above), pp. 315–16, 324.

61. Mary Ann Doane, *The Desire to Desire: The Woman's Film of the 1940's* (Bloomington, IN, 1987), pp. 123–54.

62. Ibid., p. 142.

63. Philip Lewis, "Bluebeard's Magic Key," in *Les Contes de Perrault; La contestation et ses limites; furetière,* ed. Michael Bareau et al. (Paris, 1987), p. 42.

64. Sade (n. 51 above), p. 651. Jane Gallop discusses Sade's treatment of mothers in *Thinking through the Body* (New York, 1988), pp. 55–71.

65. Jessica Benjamin, *The Bonds of Love: Psychoanalysis, Feminism, and the Problem of Domination* (New York, 1988), p. 135.

66. Ibid., p. 82.

67. Kaplan, *Women and Film* (n. 49 above), p. 206.

68.   Patricia Duncker, "Re-Imagining the Fairy Tale: Angela Carter's Bloody Chambers," *Literature and History* 10 (Spring 1984): 11.

69.   Jackie Byars, "Gazes/Voices/Power: Expanding Psychoanalysis for Feminist Film and Television Theory," in *Female Spectators: Looking at Film and Television,* ed. E. Deidre Pribram (London, 1988), p. 124.

70.   Kappeler (n. 5 above), p. 146.

71.   Catharine A. MacKinnon, "Sexuality, Pornography, and Method: 'Pleasure under Patriarchy,' " *Ethics* 99 (1989): 342.

72.   Annette Kuhn, *The Power of the Image: Essays on Representation and Sexuality* (London, 1985), p. 22.

73.   Morgan, *Anatomy of Freedom* (n. 8 above), p. 116.

74.   Karen Rian, "Sadomasochism and the Social Construction of Desire," in *Against Sademasochism: A Radical Feminist Analysis,* ed. Robin Ruth Linden et al. (East Palo Alto, CA, 1982), p. 46.

75.   Lewallen (n. 31 above), p. 151.

Isn't It Romantic?:
Angela Carter's Bloody Revision of the
Romantic Aesthetic in "The Erl-King"

How sweet I roam'd from field to field,
  And tasted all the summer's pride,
'Till I the prince of love beheld,
  Who in the sunny beams did glide!

He shew'd me lilies for my hair,
  And blushing roses for my brow;
He led me through his gardens fair,
  Where all his golden pleasures grow.

With sweet May dews my wings were wet,
  And Phoebus fir'd my vocal rage;
He caught me in his silken net,
  And shut me in his golden cage.

He loves to hear me sit and sing,
  Then, laughing, sports and plays with me;
Then stretches out my golden wing,
  And mocks my loss of liberty.

—William Blake, "Song"

How does a contemporary writer with her imagination as clearly immersed in the Romantic tradition as Angela Carter's is deflect the aesthetic that inscribes so many of her nineteenth-century predecessors as romanticized subjects? How does she mark a path out of the dark Romantic woods once made consonant with her being, having been transformed, like Daphne, from huntress-nymph to laurel tree as she fled Apollo's rapacious embrace, only to find herself worshiped by druidical poet-sons who crown their work with her leaves? How does she claim a voice that projects beyond the bars of idealized domesticity's golden cage, having been converted from wild bird to proper

From *Contemporary Literature* 35, no. 2 (Summer 1994): 305–23. © 1994 University of Wisconsin Press. Reprinted by permission.

119

lady, deified as the house-bound angel who economically husbands her song for the private pleasures of her spouse? As articulated by feminist critics, both high Romantic aesthetic theory and Victorian cultural ideology make the act of writing problematic for nineteenth-century women. They cannot partici-pate in the Bloomian oedipal conflict that enables young male poets to replace their fathers by wedding themselves to nature, because the female is nature.[1] Nor can they violate the strictures of that proper lady who estab-lishes the boundaries of the woman writer's separate sphere.[2] Published even as the feminist project began its critique, Carter's revisionary fairy tales in *The Bloody Chamber* (1979) venture through these woods and houses again and again, demarcating paths that may or may not lead to a new aesthetic theory more enabling to the woman writer. Among all these venturings, the most pronounced investigation of the Romantic heritage occurs in "The Erl-King," a literalization of William Wordsworth's "we murder to dissect" ("The Tables Turned" 28) that offers literary criticism through fiction by narrating the position of the Romantic subject.

Carter's reimagining of the subject's position in Romantic poetics and ideology offers a more complex analysis than the simple identification of bla-tant oppression; seeking a larger understanding of the many manifestations of desire in all her writings (to the palpable discomfort of quite a few critics and readers), Carter examines not only the ways in which male desire defines and confines the female, but also the ways in which female desire colludes in erecting the bars of the golden cage for the Romantic as well as the contem-porary writer.[3] Balancing desire with aesthetic empowerment is the ultimate feat her characters attempt to perform as they dance across the tightrope of cultural expectations; and the geometric variations that the conflation of desire, aesthetic theory, and cultural ideology produces shape the stories that compose *The Bloody Chamber.* Most critical discussion of *The Bloody Chamber* focuses on Carter's feminist rewriting of the patriarchal plots and perspectives that inscribe gendered roles in traditional tales, particularly noting her tech-nique of recentering consciousness in the minds of increasingly aware female participants and often criticizing the lack of "political correctness" in her ren-dition of human sexuality and her stance as self-styled "moral pornographer."[4] Almost no attention has been paid to the deliberateness with which Carter reshapes the Romantic myth of creation to restore speech to the subordinated or silenced female voice. As much about the act of storytelling as it is the sub-versive undoing of old stories and sexual politics, *The Bloody Chamber* ulti-mately recodes literary history to sanction the feminist writer who comes to embrace her own desire. In "The Erl-King," Carter tests the outlines of the Romantic ideology to see whether and how its contours might embody a female aesthetic form.

The narrative of "The Erl-King" is so conspicuously overlaid with echoes of canonical nineteenth-century lyric poetry that the leaved woods which house the erl-king might furnish an anthology of William Blake, Wordsworth,

Samuel Coleridge, John Keats, Percy Shelley, Robert Browning, and Christina Rossetti. Unlike other stories in *The Bloody Chamber* that stay relatively close to their antecedents in Charles Perrault's fairy tales, "The Erl-King" strays far afield of Perrault as well as the Goethe ballad of fathers and sons the title invokes. Carter's story turns on the protagonist's refusal to enact one of the constituent master plots of nineteenth-century masculinist poetry, which relegates women to the silence, containment, absence, or death awaiting such figures as Wordsworth's Lucy, Shelley's high-born maiden, Keats's Belle Dame, or Browning's Porphyria.[5] So often requiring a male interlocutor to transliterate their embodied language—like Keats's fairy child in "La Belle Dame Sans Merci," whose feckless knight translates her "language strange" as "I love thee true" (lines 27, 28) but reports the dire warnings of his spectral male precursors in plain English; or Wordsworth's "dearest Friend" Dorothy, in whose "voice I catch / The language of my former heart, and read / My former pleasures in the shooting lights / Of thy wild eyes" ("Tintern Abbey" lines 116–19)—the women whom the masculinist tradition represents are almost always encapsulated within the male, as if they can only be Blakean emanations whose separate existence in a public sphere so threatens the integrity of the male Zoa that it precipitates the collapse of Edenic civilization.

When the protagonist of "The Erl-King" describes how a walk through the woods leads her directly into the seductive arms of an erl-king, whose practice of caging his singing birds strikes her as ominous, the narrative foregrounds her generic danger: the plots of countless captivity or transformation tales warn that "Erl-King will do you grievous harm" (85), while the Romantic literary archetype invoked through the citation from Blake's "How sweet I roam'd" (88) conditions a belief that the erl-king plans to cage her, too: "I shall become so small you can keep me in one of your osier cages and mock my loss of liberty. I have seen the cage you are weaving for me; it is a very pretty one and I shall sit, hereafter, in my cage among the other singing birds" (90). Anticipating her entrapment in a cage of Romantic subjectivity that at best confines and at worst silences the female voice, the protagonist envisions, finally, an alternate ending to the murderous plot of "Porphyria's Lover" in which she strangles the erl-king with his own long hair before she loses her integral self to the image mirrored back in his mesmerizing eyes:

> The gelid green of your eyes fixes my reflective face. It is a preservative, like a green liquid amber; it catches me. I am afraid I will be trapped in it for ever. . . .
>   Your green eye is a reducing chamber. If I look into it long enough, I will becomes as small as my own reflection, I will diminish to a point and vanish. I will be drawn down into that black whirlpool and be consumed by you. (90)

Violently rejecting the standard feminine position of reflexive image, she plans not only to kill the erl-king but also to appropriate his knife and carve

off his great mane so that she may restring a broken fiddle with his hair, shaping her own kind of eolian harp to offer up "discordant music without a hand
touching it. The bow will dance over the new strings of its own accord and
they will cry out: 'Mother, mother, you have murdered me!' " (91). Rewriting
the text of nineteenth-century poetry by substituting female for male in the
family romance to ensure her passage into maternal voice, the protagonist of
"The Erl-King" imagines the fiercest of defenses against the devouring consummation the male canon inscribes.

Were it only a matter of escaping the erl-king's unequivocally "nefari-
ous" desire, the protagonist's role might be much simpler. Her own desire to
be desired, however, to be drawn "towards him on his magic lasso of inhuman
music" (89) as the fetishized beloved, alerts her to her susceptibility to the
cultural vertigo that invites the female to sacrifice ambition and serve as
seedbed for the male imaginative vision. Like Dorothy Wordsworth claiming
to write *The Grasmere Journals* "because I shall give Wm Pleasure by it" (May
14, 1800), the protagonist fears her all-too-willing complicity in succumbing
to an intensely erotic desire whose successive waves seem to break down the
walls of her selfhood and make her dependent on the erl-king's pleasure for
her existence: "I am not afraid of him; only, afraid of vertigo, of the vertigo
with which he seizes me. Afraid of falling down. . . . I fall down for him, and I
know it is only because he is kind to me that I do not fall still further"
(87–88). Rejecting the "self-same song" of Keats's nightingale, she tries to
conceive alternatives to the ingrained archetype of male singer and female
song: they might collaborate, or he might give birth to her as artist. But no
literary precedents strengthen her resolve.

If the men of Romanticism envision the women as silenced or dead, the
women writing during the nineteenth century represent themselves as pub-
licly silenced, transmuted into caged birds whose voices sing out for the private pleasures of their owners: Mary Shelley's Safie, who escapes the harem
her mother died in only to relocate herself in the confined domestic sphere of
the De Lacey family; Charlotte Brontë's Jane Eyre, consigned to the
unhealthy airs of Ferndean, where her artist's eyes serve to provide Rochester
with sight; George Eliot's Dorothea, firmly clasped in the arms of Will. Ultimately the protagonist of "The Erl-King" can only imagine exchanging the
female for the male in her solution: rather than die into emblematic nature or
turn into a reflection, she intends to kill him. Terrified of being caught in his
sensual music, she must go further than blinding and maiming the erl-king if
she would be more than his eyes and amusement; she must kill him, if she has
read it right, to find her own voice. In seizing on death as the answer, the protagonist writes herself out of one master plot only to place herself in another,
equally damning one. While several of Carter's other stories in *The Bloody
Chamber* intimate more inclusive possibilities for men and women, the protagonist of "The Erl-King" rejects the potential plenitude of commensal relations
to reinscribe the same old pattern: now the death of the father-son gives rise

to the voice of the daughter-mother. At the end of *The Sadeian Woman,* Carter writes: "In his diabolic solitude, only the possibility of love could awake the libertine to perfect, immaculate terror. It is in this holy terror of love that we find, in both men and women themselves, the source of all opposition to the emancipation of women" (150). For the protagonist in "The Erl-King," role reversal provides an empowering alternative to the subordinated Romantic subject; nevertheless, her solution to the problematic nature of desire is only a troubling return to the "delicious loneliness" of solitude that she experiences as her story begins (85).

There is a presumption of "girlish" innocence that readers seem expected to share as the temporal narrative unfolds a seduction story that concludes with premeditations of murder. But the narration of "The Erl-King" begins with the mediating presence of a highly sophisticated consciousness, who subtly implicates the reader as accessory through her initial use of a second-person narration that both heightens readerly identification and dispenses with psychological disengagement (making us experience, in some small way, the breakdown of ego boundaries that so frightens the protagonist). This consciousness sets up a contextual frame that subsequently casts doubt on the reliability of the narrative itself. As with Blake's guilty speakers in *Songs of Experience,* or Shelley's poet-narrator in *Alastor,* the extent of the narrator's self-knowledge or design is impossible to gauge, as is her relation to and distance from the protagonist. Despite the typical indeterminacy of the postmodernist narrative voice that modulates in this story from second to first to third person, the strength of the persona-protagonist's first-person voice, the explicit concern with the preservation of personal identity, and the positioning of intertextual references within the tale invite a nostalgic reading that suggestively equates the narrator and persona as one being who possesses a gothic history that the reader might unlock (similarly to several other personae in *The Bloody Chamber*). If the narrator is that presumed innocent persona-protagonist, a surprisingly strong hint of corruption underscores the first paragraph's conventionally Romantic description of autumnal nature in a series of carefully interspersed modifiers whose cumulative excess points to a potentially decadent perspective: the brass-colored light strikes the woods with "nicotine-stained fingers," withered blackberries dangle like "dour spooks on the discoloured brambles," the "russet slime of dead bracken" lies underfoot, the cold is "lancinating," the trees "have an anorexic look," and the weather suggests "a sickroom hush" (84).

Given this jaded representation of nature, the narrator's insistence that the wood functions as a pure sign signifying nothing beyond what the encoding human consciousness imposes seems surprising, but that, of course, is precisely the point; though stepping into the wood encloses one in an unchartable space that has "reverted to its original privacy," where there is "no clue to guide you through in perfect safety," where rabbits and foxes "make their own runs in the subtle labyrinth and nobody comes" (84), it is impossible for human beings to enter the wood without bringing their own sociocultural maps with them. Even as the narrator identifies the wood as an unmotivated sign, her cultural encoding functions as an interpretive screen through which she reads nature, already prefiguring one outcome of her protagonist's experience when she hears "The trees stir with a noise like taffeta skirts of women who have lost themselves in the woods and hunt round hopelessly for the way out" (84–85) and another when she reminds us how "A young girl would go as trustingly as Red Riding Hood to her granny's house" (85). While she knows that these images of endangered girls and abandoned women read as vacancy to the nonsignifying wood, that "she will be trapped in her own illusion because everything in the wood is exactly as it seems" (85), she cannot help modeling her own experience on these enculturated expectations; a smart semiotician, the narrator concludes her opening frame with a palimpsest that not only images the endless deferral of the signifier but also thoroughly destabilizes her narrative:

> The woods enclose and then enclose again, like a system of Chinese boxes opening one into another; the intimate perspective of the wood changed endlessly around the interloper, the imaginary traveller walking towards an invented distance that perpetually receded before me. It is easy to lose yourself in these woods. (85)

Pointing to the moral that Perrault would withhold until the end, even as the narration shifts from second person to first person, the narrator admits her own complicity in the story she is on the verge of telling. Doubly enclosed within the natural space of the wood by her perspective-bound and teleologically driven human consciousness, she responds to her reading with a series of interpretive efforts that continually recast the story she imagines herself as the protagonist enacting (as if her mind emulates some elegant computer game of perpetually shifting scenarios), the single constant being her habitual need to project a likely ending from whatever stage she inhabits.

The laying out of this metacommentary before the story begins establishes a narrative voice of infinite regression, in that the narrator-protagonist demonstrates that she can never stand outside her own cultural encoding to point to the way she is encoded; each attempt to stand outside merely places her within another of the Chinese boxes that contain human consciousness. As Blake's Urizen recognizes in *The Four Zoas,* there is no place outside human experience to provide such a foothold: "Where shall we take our stand to view the infinite & unbounded / Or where are human feet for Lo seek to explain her actions? As self-justifying murderer? As self-conscious architect of a new aesthetic theory? As disillusioned architect of an aesthetic theory that continues to operate within the patriarchal prototype in replacing the male with the female? Is this Carter herself, already preparing a response to the charge such critics as Andrea Dworkin and Susanne Kappeler will make, that her use of pornographic scenarios does not edify but rather perpetuates the patriarchal philosophy she seeks to undermine?[6]

With this inherently unstable perspective established, the narrative itself begins, language always contesting with or creating images of desire. Just as the narrator-protagonist tells us later that the erl-king "came alive from the desire of the woods" (86), the initiating incident of the narrative is her hearing the erl-king's song as the embodied sound of her desire: "The two notes of the song of a bird rose on the still air, as if my girlish and delicious loneliness had been made into a sound" (85). And the representation of nature that follows this articulation of desire demonstrates exactly how enclosed or encoded her consciousness is, as she richly alludes to nineteenth-century literary landscapes for images of sexual initiation that figure the female:

> There was a little tangled mist in the thickets, mimicking the tufts of old man's beard that flossed the lower branches of the trees and bushes; heavy bunches of red berries as ripe and delicious as goblin or enchanted fruit hung on the hawthorns. . . . The trees threaded a cat's cradle of half-stripped branches over me so that I felt I was in a house of nets. . . . Erl-King will do you grievous harm. (85)

Reminiscent of the virginal nook William Wordsworth's persona rapes and mutilates in "Nutting," of the natural landscapes Dorothy Wordsworth's solitary, abandoned women inhabit in *The Grasmere Journals,* of the goblin-tormented sisters who must resist tasting forbidden fruit in Christina Rossetti's "Goblin Market," and of the persona caught by the prince of love's nets in Blake's "How sweet I roam'd," the narrator-protagonist's allusive language reveals a knowledge of Romantic fictions that will write her role in the story she expects to enact, directing her walk "through the wood until all its perspectives converged upon a darkening clearing; as soon as I saw them, I knew at once that all its occupants had been waiting for me from the moment I first stepped into the wood" (85). She knows it because she has read it, just as she already "knows" the warning she repeats from her fairy tale books: the erl-king—or the Romantic male poet—will do her grievous harm.

That foregrounded repetition of the warning not only reminds the narrator-protagonist to be wary of the generically predictable outcome of her walk but also instills the same narrative expectations in her reader. When the story does reach conclusion we must return to this place and wonder whether she is innocently reporting the thinking that in some ways institutes the tragedy to follow, or whether she is experienced enough to lay the groundwork that might later exculpate her actions as a kind of self-defense. Of course, it is a defense of self; but the larger question that the story poses (as do others in *The Bloody Chamber*) is, What kind of self should women preserve? Trusting young girl, taffeta-skirted woman, or someone else entirely, who comes into existence, like the protagonist of Carter's "The Tiger's Bride," when the civilized veneer of skin is licked away to reveal an authentic human animal beneath? The proper lady or the demonic tiger—while the narrator-protagonist of "The Erl-King" wisely fears the typical Romantic plot that transforms women into caged birds or mythical trees, she also seems to fear the way her transformation from virginal girl to sexually gratified woman makes her subject to desire. Because the first image she offers of the erl-king places him at the center of a peaceable (though unmistakably salacious) king-dom, as if he is simply a gentle pied piper of some voluptuous wood, she needs another perspective-binding, foregrounded warning that juxtaposes a subtle evocation of the prototypical Romantic nature poet and fairy tale knowledge to strengthen her position as reader/writer:

> His eyes are quite green, as if from too much looking at the wood. There are some eyes can eat you. (86)

Afraid of being consumed by the gazer upon the wood/woman, she supplants his role by using language to shield herself from the desire language creates, transforming the erl-king into the big bad wolf before "his irrevocable hand" can transform her.

The protective shield the narrator-protagonist devises is essential to her reading, because if everything in the wood is exactly as it seems, the erl-king is an intriguingly androgynous being. Despite the nineteenth-century read-ing of nature as female, the male spirit she confronts in the wood performs an astonishing number of domestic tasks for so threatening a creature: living off the bounty of the woodland, he not only gathers mushrooms and grasses, prepares salads, collects and dries herbs, cooks soups and stews, even makes a "soft cheese that has a unique, rank, amniotic taste" (86), but also threads mats, weaves baskets, and functions in all as "an excellent housewife. His rus-tic home is spick and span. He puts his well-scoured saucepan and skillet neatly on the hearth side by side, like a pair of polished shoes" (87). But lest we begin to think him ideal, the narrator-protagonist tells us about his caged birds to contextualize these signs of domesticity as entrapment:

> He showed me how to thread mats from reeds and weave osier twigs into bas-kets and into the little cages in which he keeps his singing birds.
> His kitchen shakes and shivers with birdsong from cage upon cage of singing birds, larks and linnets, which he piles up one on another against the wall, a wall of trapped birds. (87)

As she goes to him more and more to be laid "at the mercy of his huge hands . . . the tender butcher who showed me how the price of flesh is love" (87), her continually increasing desire threatens to overwhelm her sense of self-direction until it fulfills the prophetic statement "It is easy to lose yourself in these woods" (85). Where once she freely roamed, "Now, when I go for walks

. . . I always go to the Erl-King" (87). It is then that she insistently seizes upon his caged birds as a means of distancing her self from her desire for him. Unlike Romantic women, the narrator-protagonist suggests, the erl-king emulates a tree only when he wants to trick the birds into coming to him, "those silly, fat, trusting woodies with the pretty wedding rings round their necks. He makes his whistles out of an elder twig and that is what he uses to call the birds out of the air—all the birds come; and the sweetest singers he will keep in cages" (87).

Not yet wed to the image of her desire, the narrator-protagonist self-consciously disparages the "trusting woodies" that do not stay clear of the cage she fears her own desire to be desired creates. Psychologically unable to conceive a manner of preserving identity intact while merging with the erl-king, lacking a cultural model that offers a means of matching his androgyny or constructing a complementary self, she fears her own complicity in falling subject to his enthralling gaze, to "the black vortex of his eye, the omission of light at the centre, there, that exerts on me such a tremendous pressure, it draws me inwards" (89). Expressing her fear of dependence as a fear of vertigo, she formulates a connection between romantic love and Romantic aesthetic theory by casting the erl-king as a Shelleyan persona whose ode to the west wind prophetically harnesses the wind's power to colonize the female:

> The wind stirs the dark wood; it blows through the bushes. . . . it crisps the hairs on the back of my neck but I am not afraid of him; only, afraid of vertigo. . . .
> Falling as a bird would fall through the air if the Erl-King tied up the winds in his handkerchief and knotted the ends together so they could not get out. Then the moving currents of the air would no longer sustain them and all the birds would fall. . . . The earth with its fragile fleece of last summer's dying leaves and grasses supports me only out of complicity with him. . . .
> He could thrust me into the seed-bed of next year's generation and I would have to wait until he whistled me up from my darkness. . . .
> Yet, when he shakes out those two clear notes from his bird call, I come, like any other trusting thing. (87–88)

Even as she articulates the master plot that her readings teach her to expect—this romantic subjugation of the female to the male—she acknowledges her susceptibility to his seductive song; she does not trust him, but she does not yet know how to resist his call.

Setting out this formulaic exposition of their relationship at the exact center of her narrative, the narrator-protagonist finally arrives at the darkening clearing she has anticipated from the beginning of her story, the place where the perspectives of the wood converge to reveal what seems to be the logical conclusion of her experience: captivity in the cage that feeds the male Romantic poet's vision. Having unraveled this plot, seen the invented distance that perpetually recedes, located a model that seems to account for the experience, and viewed their pairing through the prism of Romanticism, she determines to retell her story as empowered subject. Starting out all over again, she compactly renarrates her initial meeting with the erl-king as well as several key events already reported in the first half of the narrative, rewriting the rest of her story from this turning point to reach an alternate convergence, a darkening clearing that changes the conclusion she assumes Romanticism requires. Once again we hear how the fox plants his muzzle on the erl-king's knee, how the erl-king cages birds, of the erl-king's domesticity; but in this revisionist history she introduces a rationale that might later serve to justify her surprising willingness to enter the erl-king's cottage (given her depiction of herself as the blameless "perfect child of the meadows of summer" [89]): "The first drops of rain fall. In the wood, no shelter but his cottage" (88). And in this telling she deliberately supplants the erl-king's role by casting him as the spirit of the woods, transforming the male into the wooded tree: "His skin is the tint and texture of sour cream, he has stiff, russet nipples ripe as berries. Like a tree that bears bloom and fruit on the same bough together, how pleasing, how lovely" (88). In the struggle for control, in her efforts to overcome feared vertigo, she turns him into an image of nature, encasing him in her language just as she believes he would have entrapped her.

Invoking the light of the conventionally Romantic "white moon" to "illuminate the still tableaux of our embracements" (90), the narrator-protagonist encodes her text with increasingly frequent sampling of the nineteenth-century lyrics whose plot she consciously rejects, as if she has determined not to be seedbed to his desiring gaze but to make him the seedbed for hers, using language to perform a sort of verbal exorcism. The quotations assembled below extract only some of the echoes that compose her pastiche of nineteenth-century poetry and poetics:

> How sweet I roamed, or, rather, used to roam. . . . And shakes over me dead leaves as if into a stream I have become. . . . Eat me, drink me; thirsty, cankered, goblin-ridden, I go back and back to him. . . . He spreads out a goblin feast of fruit for me, such appalling succulence; I lie above him and see the light from the fire sucked into the black vortex of his eye. . . . I shall become so small you can keep me in one of your osier cages and mock my loss of liberty. . . . now I know the birds don't sing. (88–90)

Blake's "How sweet I roam'd," Rossetti's "Goblin Market," Keats's "The Eve of St. Agnes" and "La Belle Dame Sans Merci," Shelley's "Ode to the West Wind," the vortex image that pervades Romantic thought—these are the texts that shape her text, whose messages she recites as she carves a path to another ending where the female is no longer sacrificed for the male poetic vision.

Even as these citations strengthen her resolve to subvert the master plot that inscribes the strangulation of the female voice, by plotting, instead, to strangle the erl-king, the narrator-protagonist briefly contemplates three alternate outcomes as "the imaginary traveller walking towards an invented distance" (85) before she settles on the violent path the conclusion suggests. First she imagines their collaborative production of a music that would enable them to dance together rather than struggle for power: "If I strung that old fiddle with your hair, we could waltz together . . . we should have better music than the shrill prothalamions of the larks stacked in their pretty cages" (89). Then she recasts his phallic description of the grass snakes in an almost wistful imaging of the erl-king as nurturer of her vision; whereas "He told me about the grass snakes, how the old ones open their mouths wide when they smell danger and the thin little ones disappear down the old ones' throats until the fright is over and out they come again, to run around as usual" (86), she "should like to grow enormously small, so that you could swallow me, like those queens in fairy tales who conceive when they swallow a grain of corn or a sesame seed. Then I could lodge inside your body and you would bear me" (89). But always the repressive reminders of Romantic poetry cloud these possibilities, so that the third outcome is already a movement toward rebellion, through her considering a spiteful silence: "I have seen the cage you are weaving for me; it is a very pretty one and I shall sit, hereafter, in my cage among the other singing birds but I—I shall be dumb, from spite" (90).

Perhaps because this is the path many nineteenth-century women historically walked, the narrator-protagonist rejects it to arrive at what she presents as her recognition of the illusion-shattering truth:

> When I realized what the Erl-King meant to do to me, I was shaken with a terrible fear and I did not know what to do for I loved him with all my heart and yet I had no wish to join the whistling congregation he kept in his cages although he looked after them very affectionately, gave them fresh water every day and fed them well. His embraces were his enticements and yet, oh yet! they were the branches of which the trap itself was woven. But in his innocence he never knew he might be the death of me, although I knew from the first moment I saw him how Erl-King would do me grievous harm (90).

Having inscribed her imagination—and ours—with all the literary precedents that represent the erl-king as male Romantic poet and the protagonist as subjugated female, she baldly states the case: while male Romantic poets intend no harm, the trap is the trap of Romantic aesthetic theory for females, ensnared by images that bind with affection as they transform women into nature; the trap is the cultural ideology of separate spheres that enshrines such nineteenth-century women as Catherine Blake, the angelic helpmate taught to read and write and paint only to enact her husband's visions. Despite the narrator-protagonist's desire, she is not going to become one of the anorexic trees the opening paragraph describes, so hungry for affection that she would starve herself into the image of *his* desire. An increasingly resistant reader, she writes herself into the fourth and final possibility: if there is to be no collaboration and no nurturing, she will not inhabit a resentful silence but will gain her own voice by silencing his.

The feminist reader of this feminist reader cries, "Good!" But the discomforting repetition of the foregrounded phrase "I knew from the first moment I saw him how Erl-King would do me grievous harm" suggests another level of entrapment: while the narrator-protagonist's reading of Romantic poetics alerts her to the danger she is in, it also shapes her expectations of the erl-king to induce a self-fulfilling prophecy. Yes, the Romantic poet's aesthetic theory subjugates the female, yet the erl-king she encounters neither indicates he will harm her nor hints that the caged birds she repeatedly marks are former narrators enchanted by a transforming spell. Instead we learn that the birds flock to him for refuge and the succor of the food he offers them in a harsh winter: "the Erl-King gives them corn and when he whistles to them, a moment later you cannot see him for the birds that have covered him like a soft fall of feathered snow" (89). Nevertheless, her astute analysis of nineteenth-century literature so codes her understanding that she cannot see the erl-king in any other framework, despite his potentiality for plenitude; once she recognizes how the sociocultural map of Romanticism configures her experience, she offers a different order of Bloomian misreading to authenticate or at least preserve her voice, but she is still "trapped in her own illusion because everything in the wood is exactly as it seems" (85).

Still locked into the dictates of high Romantic aesthetic theory, the narrator-protagonist's projected conclusion only substitutes female for male in the constituent master plot of nineteenth-century lyric poetry, as she rescripts the murderous story Browning chronicles in "Porphyria's Lover" (offering a curiously self-reflexive mirroring of Carter's own revisionary approach to folktales in The Bloody Chamber): "I shall take two huge handfuls of his rustling hair as he lies half dreaming, half waking, and wind them into ropes, very softly, so he will not wake up, and, softly, with hands as gentle as rain, I shall strangle him with them" (91). Reinventing her position in these literary precedents to become the empowered subject, even as she shifts narrative voice from first person to third person, the narrator-protagonist envisions herself as a great liberator who frees the erl-king's caged birds before she produces her own eolian music out of elements appropriated from his dead body:

> She will carve off his great mane with the knife he uses to skin the rabbits; she will string the old fiddle with five single strings of ashbrown hair.
> Then it will play discordant music without a hand touching it. The bow will dance over the new strings of its own accord and they will cry out: "Mother, mother, you have murdered me!" (91)

Reconstituting the aesthetic theory that enables Coleridge to liken the sound of his lute to "some coy maid half yielding to her lover,/It pours such sweet upbraiding, as must needs/Tempt to repeat the wrong" (lines 15–17), the narrator-protagonist's version of "The Eolian Harp" rewrites the family romance to show the daughter become mother by murdering the father-son. She claims her public voice (signaled by her assumption of that most conventional of writerly signatures, the third-person narration) by recasting the scenario she feared would silence it, turning from victim to victimizer in true Sadeian fashion, failing to envision male and female roles in any new way. Enclosed within the system of Chinese boxes her psychological and literary education produces, she continues to adhere to a model of development that privileges separation over dependence (Sheets 654) and an epistemology that insists on the culturally gendered dualism of subject/object or presence/absence distinctions. To preserve her "self" intact, she simply repositions the erl-king as object without imagining any way out of the binary opposition of gender that shapes the entire feminist project, beginning with Simone de Beauvoir's essential recognition of the female as "other."

The path the narrator-protagonist delineates through the dark Romantic wood leads to a dead end for both herself and the erl-king. She carefully deflects his enticing but threatening gaze by refusing to look into his eyes just before she anticipates strangling him:

> Eyes green as apples. Green as dead sea fruit. . . .
> . . . He winds me into the circle of his eye on a reel of birdsong. There is a black hole in the middle of both your eyes; it is their still centre, looking there makes me giddy, as if I might fall into it. . . .
> . . . Lay your head on my knee so that I can't see the greenish, inward-turning suns of your eyes any more (89–91).

Her understandable fear of being trapped in his gaze forever makes her reject the potentially exhilarating giddiness that looking into his eyes produces; but that fearful rejection dooms her to loneliness, to the embittered sensibility of the mediating voice that utters the opening frame and the fragmentation of identity that Carter makes iconic through the use of three narrative persons. As the narrative itself strategically shifts from second person to first person to third person, the chronological sequence for the narrator-protagonist would be first to third to second, as if her unraveling narrative voice points to a diminishing sense of self that diminishes in spite of her extreme efforts to preserve it intact. Her method of gaining a voice as the speaking subject exacts a heavy price; whereas the erl-king "showed me how the price of flesh is love" (87), she destroys her possibilities for love to flesh out the Romantic model of the poet in her substitution fantasy. While other stories in *The Bloody Chamber* suggest alternate solutions to the problematic nature of desire, even directing us to a place where men and women might function as independent yet interdependent creators, none offers so self-conscious an analysis of the problematics of high Romantic aesthetic theory and nineteenth-century culture ideology for both men and women; in "The Erl-King," Carter demonstrates the larger failure of a Romantic aesthetics whose master plot requires the subjugation of the other.

Notes

1. Both of Margaret Homans's discussions of Romanticism as well as Sandra Gilbert's and Susan Gubar's analysis of nineteenth-century women writers point to the psychological problems the anxiety of influence holds for women.

2. Several feminist critics, including Ellen Moers, Elaine Showalter, Nina Auerbach, and Mary Poovey, have pointed to the doctrine of separate spheres and its implications for British (and American) nineteenth-century women writers.

3. I number myself among those critics and readers made uncomfortable; it is hard not to cringe before some of Carter's more baroque descriptions of the real or fantasied excesses of human sexual experience, such as the rape of Desiderio by the nine Moroccan acrobats of desire in *The Infernal Desire Machines of Doctor Hoffman*. Despite its parodic and deconstructive elements, the scene still horrifies.

4. For discussion of Carter's feminist revisions of patriarchal plots, see Rose, Lokke, Wilson, and Bryant. Readers who focus on Carter's stylistic technique of recentering consciousness in female protagonists include Lewallen, Duncker, and Sheets. See Duncker, Clark, Lewallen, and Palmer for interrogations of Carter as "Pornographer."

5. These are among the mothers, daughters, beloveds, muses, and *femmes fatales* that Diane Long Hoeveler catalogues.

6. Elaine Jordan's recent discussion "The Dangers of Angela Carter" defends Carter from her critics by pointing out how "Repeating and departing from the inheritance . . . list the strongest answer to the charge that she merely reinscribes patriarchy. Where else can you start from, if not from where you actually are?" (125).

Works Cited

Auerbach, Nina. *Woman and the Demon: The Life of a Victorian Myth*. Cambridge: Harvard UP, 1982.

Blake, William. *The Complete Poetry and Prose of William Blake*. Ed. David V. Erdman. Rev. ed. Berkeley: U of California P, 1982.

Bryant, Sylvia. "Re-Constructing Oedipus through 'Beauty and the Beast.'" *Criticism* 31 (1989): 439–53.

Carter, Angela. *The Bloody Chamber and Other Stories*. London: Penguin, 1979.

———. "The Erl-King." *The Bloody Chamber and Other Stories*. 84–91.

———. *The Infernal Desire Machines of Doctor Hoffman*. London: Penguin, 1972.

———. *The Sadeian Woman*. London: Virago, 1979.

———. "The Tiger's Bride." *The Bloody Chamber and Other Stories*. 51–67.

Clark, Robert. "Angela Carter's Desire Machine." *Women's Studies* 14 (1987): 147–61.

Coleridge, Samuel Taylor. *Coleridge: Complete Poetical Works*. Ed. Ernest H. Coleridge. 2 vols. London: Oxford UP, 1912.

Duncker, Patricia. "Re-Imagining the Fairy Tales: Angela Carter's Bloody Chambers." *Literature and History* 10 (1988): 3–14.

Dworkin, Andrea. *Pornography: Men Possessing Women*. New York: Putnam, 1981.

Gilbert, Sandra, and Susan Gubar. *The Madwoman in the Attic: The Woman Writer and the Nineteenth-Century Literary Imagination.* New Haven: Yale UP, 1979.

Hoeveler, Diane Long. *Romantic Androgyny: The Women Within.* University Park: Pennsylvania State UP, 1990.

Homans, Margaret. *Bearing the Word: Language and Female Experience in Nineteenth-Century Women's Writing.* Chicago: U of Chicago P, 1986.

———. *Women Writers and Poetic Identity: Dorothy Wordsworth, Emily Brontë, and Emily Dickinson.* Princeton: Princeton UP, 1980.

Jordan, Elaine. "The Dangers of Angela Carter." *New Feminist Discourses: Critical Essays on Theories and Texts.* Ed. Isobel Armstrong. New York: Routledge, 1992. 119–31.

Kappeler, Susanne. *The Pornography of Representation.* Minneapolis: U of Minnesota P, 1986.

Keats, John. *Complete Poems.* Ed. Jack Stillinger. Cambridge: Harvard UP, 1978.

Lewallen, Avis. "Wayward Girls but Wicked Women? Female Sexuality in Angela Carter's *The Bloody Chamber.*" *Perspectives on Pornography: Sexuality in Film and Literature.* Ed. Gary Day and Clive Bloom. New York: St. Martin's, 1988. 144–58.

Lokke, Kari E. "*Bluebeard* and *The Bloody Chamber:* The Grotesque of Self-Parody and Self-Assertion." *Frontiers* 10 (1988): 7–12.

Moers, Ellen. *Literary Women.* New York: Oxford, 1976.

Palmer, Paulina. "From 'Coded Mannequin' to Bird Woman: Angela Carter's Magic Flight." *Women Reading Women's Writing.* Ed. Sue Roe. Brighton, Eng.: Harvester, 1987. 177–205.

Poovey, Mary. *The Proper Lady and the Woman Writer: Ideology as Style in the Works of Mary Wollstonecraft, Mary Shelley, and Jane Austen.* Chicago: U of Chicago P, 1984.

Rose, Ellen Cronan. "Through the Looking Glass: When Women Tell Fairy Tales." *The Voyage In: Fictions of Female Development.* Ed. Elizabeth Abel, Marianne Hirsch, and Elizabeth Langland. Hanover, NH: UP of New England, 1983. 209–27.

Sheets, Robin Ann. "Pornography, Fairy Tales, and Feminism: Angela Carter's 'The Bloody Chamber.'" *Journal of the History of Sexuality* 1 (1991): 633–57.

Showalter, Elaine. *A Literature of Their Own: British Women Novelists from Brontë to Lessing.* Princeton: Princeton UP, 1977.

Wilson, Robert Rawdon. "SLIP PAGE: Angela Carter, In/Out/In the Postmodern Nexus." *Ariel: A Review of International English Literature* 20 (1989): 96–114.

Wordsworth, Dorothy. *The Grasmere Journals, 1800–1803. Journals of Dorothy Wordsworth.* Ed. Mary Moorman. 2nd ed. London: Oxford UP, 1971. 15–16.

Wordsworth, William. *William Wordsworth.* Ed. Stephen Gill. New York: Oxford UP, 1984.

Blonde, Black and Hottentot Venus: Context and Critique in Angela Carter's "Black Venus"

JILL MATUS

Angela Carter's "Black Venus" takes Jeanne Duval, the Eurafrican mistress of Charles Baudelaire, as the subject of its subversive narrative. Baudelaire's letters and poems, as well as the accounts of Jeanne Duval offered by his biographers, provide Carter with material for this short narrative fiction. Engaging the "Black Venus" cycle of poems from *Les Fleurs du Mal* in a series of ironic allusions, Carter's text alternates imaginative, dramatic scenes of Jeanne and Baudelaire (and the cat) in his gloomy apartment with speculative commentary on such diverse matters as Jeanne's native land, the state of the colonies under Napoleon, Manet's representation of female nudity, and the evidence provided by Nadar (alias Felix Tournachon, photographer and friend of Baudelaire) about the fate of Jeanne as an old woman. Does Carter's story claim to be a substituting or superseding version, presenting a new and improved Jeanne Duval? The concerns raised in this question are perhaps allayed by the narrator's awareness of the problem, for the narrative voice continually dissolves the illusions it creates and disputes its own authority (along with that of Baudelaire, Nadar or anyone else) to tell the real story about this woman.

Yet even as it disclaims the truth of its own representations, and teases out the racist and colonialist assumptions that inform traditional versions of Jeanne Duval, Carter's fiction appropriates and reconstructs Jeanne in its own politically-interested image. "Black Venus" is engaged and interested in challenging the politics of assumptions about the sexualized woman as dark, diseased and corrupting. The title of the story refers, therefore, not only to a cluster of poems Baudelaire wrote, and to the woman who inspired them, but to a wider context—the ironized discourse of Venus in nineteenth-century constructions of female sexuality. What informs and underscores Carter's story is a network of associations from nineteenth-century comparative anthropology, physiology and anatomy, as well as from art and literature, in which blackness, primitive

From *Studies in Short Fiction* 28 (1991): 467–76. © 1991, Newberry College. Reprinted by permission.

sexuality, prostitution and disease are closely linked. This essay approaches the contexts in which such associations develop by considering, for example, how Baudelaire's poem on the anthropologist Cuvier relates to Cuvier's verdict on the Hottentot Venus; what derogatory connotations the term "steatopygia" has in nineteenth-century constructions of female sexuality, and how Angela Carter uses this term in celebratory description; what connection the Hottentot Venus may have with Zola's Nana and Manet's painting "Nana"; and what Carter's Jeanne has to do with Manet's portrait of Jeanne Duval or, strangely, Courbet's effacement of her from his painting "L'Atelier du Peintre."

Venus, goddess of love, has a long history as the signifier of feminine beauty and purity. Mythology, visual representation and literature show, however, that the figure of Venus has also been used to suggest whorish seductiveness and voluptuousness, narcissistic female self-absorption, and a variety of other denigrating versions of woman. The context for the label "Black Venus" is frequently colonial, where it reveals much about colonial perceptions of race and gender. Its range of associations is wide, from the virulence of Jef Geeraert's *Gangrene*, subtitled *Black Venus,* to the benign paternalism of Stephen Gray's poem "Black Venus," in which the speaker implores an island beauty not to yearn for the white man's world, sure to spoil her charms (Gray, *World* 56). Both idealization and denigration may be suggested by the term "Black Venus"—Baudelaire's friend Banville captures its quality when he describes Jeanne as both bestial and divine (qtd. in Starkie 87). But like "Hottentot Venus," the term is often employed in a bitterly ironic or oxymoronic way—as if to say, "How can what is black also be Venus-like?"

In a discussion of Zola's *Nana,* Roland Barthes uses the term "Hottentot Venus" in this way when he suggests that it would be ludicrous to imagine a woman like the Hottentot Venus possessing seductive power. Writing of Zola's capacity to objectify, he points out how the men and women of the Second Empire become a "piece of anthropology as strange as the life of the Papuans" (92). Barthes likens Zola to an ethnologist studying a Kwakiutl tribe, so awesome is his detachment. We have an overwhelming sense of difference between ourselves and the people of whom he writes—we may even find it "difficult to understand the wholesale devastation that Nana brings about; affectively, it seems to us almost as improbable as the seductive power of the Venus of the Hottentots." Barthes's implication is that, as unbelievable as the seductive power of the Hottentot Venus may be, so improbable seems Nana's capacity for devastation. Just as Papuans and the Kwakiutl tribe are other, so are the Hottentot Venus as a seductive power, and Nana as maneater. (*Manageuses d'hommes* is a common term for prostitutes in nineteenth-century France [Bernheimer 96]). But what Barthes's analogy does not make clear is that "the historically particular version of the eternal Man-eater," the Hottentot Venus, and a remote "primitive" tribe, have a specific kind of sexual otherness in common. To explore this further, we need to know more about the historically particular version of the Hottentot Venus.

In the second decade of the nineteenth century, a young African woman called Saartjie Baartman was exhibited in London and then Paris to show the peculiar and "typical" physiognomy of the African woman. She was known as the Hottentot Venus.[1] About five years later she died in Paris and the renowned Georges Cuvier wrote up his observations on her cadaver (see Gilman 76–108). Cuvier's paper drew attention to the similarity of woman and ape and noted the distortions and anomalies of her "organ of generation." According to Cuvier, the highest form of ape—the orangutan—was comparable to the lowest form of man/woman, and more particularly, black woman. The Hottentot Venus was exhibited not as an incidental freak in a cheap circus, but as a type—the essence of woman's low position on the evolutionary ladder and the irrefutable evidence of her bestial and degenerate associations.

Sander Gilman's detailed study of the Hottentot Venus suggests that Cuvier was responsible for constituting the Hottentot Venus as the major signifier for the image of the Hottentot as sexual primitive in the nineteenth century (83–89). According to Gilman, the idea of primitive sexuality is also signified in images of size and grossness, particularly the steatopygia of the Hottentot woman. So, for example, Gilman argues that in a painting like Manet's "Nana," the line of the exaggerated buttocks in the prostitute associates her with the Hottentot Venus and signifies her internal blackness and atavistic sexuality. (In nineteenth-century iconographies of the prostitute, steatopygia is a recurrent characteristic.) But the nineteenth-century association of the prostitute with the black was most readily compounded by the belief that prostitutes differed physiologically from ordinary women, that they were sexually primitive, even degenerate. Since the prostitute was also associated with disease, the link between blackness, primitive sexuality and corruption was further determined. In a complex variety of combinations, these characteristics could signal the grotesque and degenerate, as well as the exotic, forbidden and exciting. So, for example, Carter has Baudelaire, poet of decadence, look with fascination upon his dark mistress as "an ambulant fetish, savage, obscene, terrifying" (20).

Baudelaire wrote a poem called "Cuvier's Verdict," in which Cuvier, questioned about where he would situate the Belgian on the chain of being, replies that this is indeed a problem since there is quite a gap between ape and mollusk. Another Belgian poem deals with the unsanitary habits of Belgian women, who surely use black soap since they always appear to be dirty. (Carter's Jeanne complains that Baudelaire will not pay for hot water for her bath and adds caustically that he probably thinks she does not need to bathe because her dark skin doesn't show the dirt.) Baudelaire's disparagement of Belgians, especially Belgian women, draws on the two categories that inform Cuvier's remarks about the Hottentot Venus—degeneration and blackness. Although Baudelaire did not write a poem about Cuvier's verdict on the Hottentot Venus, Carter's implication is that he nevertheless inscribed that verdict in the "Black Venus" poems.

Degeneration and blackness also define the white prostitute, such as Zola's Nana, celebrated in the novel as "la Blonde Vénus." In the opening scenes of *Nana* she takes part in an operetta called *La Blonde Vénus* at the Théâtre des Variétés. Although she is not able to move members of the audience with her artistic talents, she can certainly move its male members with the sight of her naked body. Zola describes her as a Venus in the true sense of the word, and as a force of nature. Although at first sight, La Blonde Vénus and the Hottentot Venus do not appear to have much in common, their association is closer and more complex than Barthes's analogy suggests. Though the former may arouse and seduce while the latter provokes curiosity and derision, they are both versions of female sexuality characterized as primitive and other, black and degenerate. It is, however, only when Zola's Blonde Vénus is dying, having contracted smallpox from her son, that her concealed inner blackness and rot are revealed. Smallpox, in this sense, is not so much small as it is merely pox—syphilis. Nana's demise is instructive in that her putrefaction is described as the rotting and decomposition of Venus. Since her son's contagion is the cause of her death, the text suggests that it is, of course, the produce of her thighs that eventually contaminates her. Those "snowy thighs" that corrupted Paris mock the association of snow and whiteness with purity, demonstrating that white as they are, hers are no different from the black ones overtly associated with corruption and disease. Nana reminds us of Nanahuatzin, the Aztec goddess, whom Carter mentions in "Black Venus" as the one blamed by Europeans for sending venereal disease from the New World to the Old—an erotic vengeance for imperialist plunder. Carter, however, mines the irony that Baudelaire's "black-thighed witch" (as his poem "Sed Non Satiata" styles her) may have contracted syphilis from him.

Carter's "Black Venus" situates itself squarely within the contexts of Venus mythology that I have been discussing, and confronts stereotypes with iconoclastic wit. The story displays qualities of much of Carter's work, which has been described by various critics as shocking, intoxicating, revisionist, abrasive. A characteristic procedure of Carter's is to seize upon some image, icon or bit of mythology and draw out its implications, making gorgeous what is denigrated or scorned, blaspheming against what is held sacred, and exposing what is usually kept covert. Carter's fiction relishes the so-called freaks excluded from the Western pantheon of Venuses and relegated to circuses and sideshows. Carter is interested in women larger than life, the giantesses of myth and history and fiction—Helen, Venus, Josephine Baker, Jeanne Duval and Sophia Fevvers, the birdwoman in *Nights at the Circus,* in whom the association of gross size, deformity and sexual licentiousness, for example, are brought gloriously together. A poster advertises the attractions of the bewinged aerialiste Fevvers thus:

> The artist had chosen to depict her ascent from behind—bums aloft, you might say; up she goes, in a steatopygous perspective, shaking out about her those tremendous . . . pinions . . . powerful enough to bear up such a big girl as she. (Carter, *Nights* 7)

Celebratory emphasis on the rear of this "Cockney Venus" seems to mock the association of grossness with female sexuality.

Although not specific about Jeanne in the way that she is about the "Cockney Venus," Carter emphasizes Jeanne's size, describes her as a "woman of immense height," and imagines Jeanne thinking of herself as a "great gawk of an ignorant black girl, good for nothing" (18). In opposition to Jeanne's self-deprecation, Carter regards her as one of "those beautiful giantesses who, a hundred years later, would grace the stages of the Crazy Horse or the Casino de Paris in sequin cache-sexe and tinsel pasties, divinely tall, the color and texture of suede. Josephine Baker!" (12). In contrast to the Hottentot Venus, exhibited in Paris as the butt of racist and misogynist humor, Josephine Baker exhibited herself at the Revue Nègre, commanding awe and capitalizing on her "savage" and "primitive" blackness. A recent biography, *Jazz Cleopatra,* describes how the dancer marketed herself in Paris by emphasizing her black animality, symbolized by the extraordinary life and power of her undulating buttocks. "The rear end exists," said Baker. "I see no reason to be ashamed of it. It's true that there are rear ends so stupid, so pretentious, so insignificant, that they're only good for sitting on" (qtd. in Rose 24).

Biographers of Baudelaire who write about Jeanne Duval concede her beauty, but in such a way as to suggest that she is an aesthetic object rather than a beautiful woman. She had that "enigmatic stylized black beauty which combines line and patina to produce an aesthetic effect, like a work of art in bronze or dark stone" writes Baudelaire's biographer, A. E. Carter (37). But he also says she was "a common slut, totally uncultivated and extremely stupid; and like most whores she lied with a deliberate compulsive mendacity which is close to paranoia" (37). Rather than an exotic and fetishized *objet d'art,* she is, for Carter, a means to unsettle and parody canonical Western art. Carter asks us to imagine "The Birth of Black Venus," describing her (in terms of Botticelli's painting) aloft her scallop-shell, "clutching an enormous handful of dreadlocks to her pubic mound" while "wee black cherubs" blow her across the Atlantic (18). Artistic representations of Jeanne Duval by Manet and Courbet provide an interesting gloss on Carter's representation of Duval in the story. Courbet originally painted her next to Baudelaire himself in the "Atelier" but later removed her at Baudelaire's request.[2] A close scrutiny of the painting reveals the ghostly traces of her effacement, which underscores Carter's suggestion in the story that Jeanne exists for Baudelaire as something on which he may feast his eyes, or that he may remove from sight, according to his whim. Carter mentions Manet's "Le Déjeuner sur l'Herbe" in relation to a scene where Baudelaire sits impeccably dressed while Jeanne must be naked, clothed only in her skin, but she does not mention Manet's portrait of Jeanne (1862) in which she is positioned half-reclining, but very much clothed in full crinoline. Like Zola's Nana, Jeanne was reputed to be a bad actress and a good courtesan; however, Manet paints her very differently from the young and seductive Nana, in whom signs of degeneration are covert (see Gilman 102). In Manet's portrait of Duval, such signs are (at least in the eyes of some critics) more obvious. She is described as suffering the wages of her pathological sexuality: "stiff and half-paralysed, and her face . . . stupid and bestial from alcoholism and vice" (Perruchot 98).

In "Black Venus" one of the problems confronting Carter is how to represent Jeanne without presuming to speak for her or know her mind. Bakhtin's notion of dialogic interchange may help to explain Carter's sense of Jeanne, since Bakhtin emphasizes how the word in language is always half someone else's, "exists in other people's mouths." It becomes one's own only when the speaker populates it with intention and "expropriates" the word, adapting it to his or her own semantic and expressive needs (294). Jeanne's words, Carter suggests, have been more than half someone else's. A Francophone whose Creole patois made her feel in France as if "her tongue had been cut out and another one sewn in that did not fit well," Carter's Jeanne is without words, without country, without history (18). Noting that Baudelaire's eloquence has denied Jeanne her language, the narrator is concerned to make the silences of Jeanne's own narrative speak. Since her sugar daddy does not hear her, we should. As she dances for her "Daddy," Jeanne hums "a Creole melody . . . but Daddy paid no attention to what song his siren sang" (12). As she does with other mythic ideas, Carter uses the notion of the irresistible song of the sirens to ironic effect. Baudelaire may call his mistress his siren, pose her as a seductress, but he is far too self-absorbed to hear any song but his own as irresistible.

Though Jeanne has been, in effect, silenced by Baudelaire's words and eclipsed by his shadow, Carter does not presume to appropriate Jeanne's story by knowing her mind; rather, she draws attention to other possible representations of her than those we already have by persistently imagining her as an ordinary down-to-earth woman concerned with her own immediate material conditions. Her language cannot speak for Jeanne, but it can compete with and challenge the languages that have sought to possess and exploit her. She attempts to formulate an alternative vocabulary to Baudelaire's and to expose the contingencies of his vocabulary. Carter's habit of unsettling ascriptions and projections manifests itself in making the reader scrutinize language closely and attend to the nuances of apparent tautology and the connotations that make a crucial difference. A good example hinges on how we understand "promiscuous": "Her lover assumed she was promiscuous because she *was* promiscuous" (13). But Jeanne has her own code of honor. To her

> prostitution was a question of number; of being paid by more than one person at a time. That was bad. She was not a bad girl. When she slept with anyone else but Daddy, she never let them pay. It was a matter of honour. It was a question of fidelity. (12)

The passage draws attention to the misconstruction of Jeanne's actions from the point of view of the onlooker. Because she was promiscuous—took many sexual partners—does not mean in her terms that she was promiscuous (unable to discriminate among them).

One way in which Carter questions distorting versions of Jeanne is by challenging the poet's metaphoric power: "My monkey, my pussy-cat, my pet" he croons as he imagines taking her back to the island where the "jewelled parrot rocks on the enamel branch" and where she can crunch sugar-cane between her teeth (10). "But, on these days," the narrator counters, "no pet nor pussy she; she looks more like an old crow with rusty feathers in a miserable huddle by the smoky fire" (10). Nor is there any romanticizing of her as the dispossessed child of the islands, yearning for her heritage: she doesn't know that she has a heritage, let alone that she has been deprived of it. Since the colony—white and imperious—fathered her, she is a child without history. The narrative suggests that traditional poetic tropes are inadequate and appropriating when they underscore Western constructions of motivation and desire.

As the poet's "agonised romanticism" transforms the homely Caribbean smell of coconut oil into the perfume of the air of tropical islands, his imagination performs an "alchemical alteration on the healthy tang of her sweat" (19). "He thinks her sweat smells of cinnamon because she has spices in her pores." In place of the poet's "weird goddess, dusky as the night," "vase of darkness,"—a "black Helen" to his tortured Faust—the narrative shows us a woman who lights the smelly cheroots she smokes with his manuscripts, who tells him to let the cat out before it craps on the Bokhara, and who fears the syphilis she has contracted from her "first white protector"—Baudelaire.

Another strategy Carter uses is to challenge the mythical constructs that allow Jeanne to be represented as the exotic Eve, black temptress and queen of sin. The poet might like to believe she has come from an island paradise, but the narrator describes it as a "stinking Eden." Her fall, after she bites "a custard apple," is presented as a fall into the European—civilized—world. Later, however, the narrator offers another interpretation: if Jeanne is to occupy any position in the Genesis story, she would have to be the forbidden fruit—and Baudelaire has consumed her. (Felix Nadar once described her as a special dish for the ultrarefined palate.)

Baudelaire's biographers agree that Jeanne was a "mulatto" from the French Caribbean.[3] Angela Carter writes:

> Where she came from is a problem; books suggest Mauritius, in the Indian ocean, or Santo Domingo, in the Caribbean, take your pick of two different sides of the world. (Her *pays d'origine* of less importance than it would have been had she been a wine). (16)

What is important to Carter's story, whose ending envisages Jeanne's return to Martinique, is that her origins are colonial. Insofar as Jeanne's story is ever told it usually ends with Nadar's description of her hobbling on crutches, her teeth and hair gone. Carter, however, constructs a possible resurrection for her in the last pages of the story: "You can buy teeth, you know; you can buy hair." While Carter's narrator points out that the poet near death is so estranged from himself he is said to have bowed politely to his reflection in the mirror, Jeanne is pictured as having found herself. "She had come down to earth, and, with the aid of her cane, she walked perfectly well on it" (23). A number of sources mention Duval's brother—a man she claimed was her brother—who lived off her and absconded with her possessions while she was in hospital (see Starkie 404; Hemmings 184). In Carter's closure this "high-yellow, demi-sibling" takes over her finances and, "a born entrepreneur," sets her back on her feet. She makes for Martinique and starts up a brothel.

The inclusion of this putative brother figure in the story preserves a bit of the biographical data, but what is the significance of this managing male? A self-directed female avenger might be thought more appropriate to the text's feminist politics, but Carter's text, besides challenging Western sexual stereotypes, is also a fable from a post-colonial perspective. Carter uses the brother figure to make a point about pimping, capitalist enterprise and colonial trade. Earlier the narrator tells us: "Seller and commodity in one, a whore is her own investment in the world and so she must take care of herself" (20). Jeanne has not taken care of herself in this way, but under the management of this possibly demonic brother (we are told that for all Jeanne cares he could be Mephistopheles), who seems to be out for a cut of the profits, she gets a new lease on life dispensing pleasure and death to the colonial administrators of her native land. The last sentence of the story imagines her keeping in circulation the "gift" that Baudelaire had given her:

> Until at last, in extreme old age, she succumbs to the ache in her bones and a cortege of grieving girls takes her to the churchyard, she will continue to dispense, to the most privileged of the colonial administration, at a not excessive price, the veritable, the authentic, the true Baudelairean syphilis. (23)

What goes around comes around. If Baudelaire's poems about Jeanne are often called the "Black Venus cycle," the name is apt, not least because they recycle a cluster of attitudes that govern the representation of sexualized woman, be she a Blonde, Black or Hottentot Venus. Angela Carter has, however, given that cycle a new turn.

Notes

1. Stephen Gray's poem "Hottento Venus" (1979) begins:

   > My name is Saartjie Baartman and I come from Kat River
   >   they call me the Hottentot Venus
   > they rang up the curtains on a classy peepshow two pennies
   >   two pennies in the slot and I'd wind up

> shift a fan and roll my rolypoly burn
> and rock the capitals of Europe into mirth.

2.   I am grateful to my student Mary Kavoukis for bringing this painting to my attention.

3.   See Hemmings, who suggests that her grandmother was a black woman shipped to Nantes to become a prostitute there, her mother was most probably a mulatto, and Jeanne herself was a quadroon (50).

Works Cited

Bakhtin, M. M. *The Dialogic Imagination: Four Essays*. Trans. Caryl Emerson and Michael Holquist. Ed. Michael Holquist. Austin: U of Texas P, 1981.

Barthes, Roland. "Man-Eater." *Critical Essays on Émile Zola*. Ed. David Baguley. Boston: Hall, 1986. 90–93.

Baudelaire, Charles. *Correspondence*. Ed. Claude Pichois and Jean Ziegler. Paris: Bibliotèque de la Pléiade, 1973.

———. *Flowers of Evil*. Trans. George Dillon and Edna St. Vincent Millay. New York: Harper, 1936.

———. *Oeuvres Complètes*. 2 vols. Ed. Claude Pichois. Paris: Bibliotèque de la Pléiade, 1975–76.

Bernheimer, Charles. *Figures of Ill Repute: Representing Prostitution in Nineteenth-Century France*. Cambridge: Harvard UP, 1989.

Carter, Angela. *Nights at the Circus,* London: Viking, 1984.

———. "Black Venus." *Black Venus*. London: Chatto & Windus, 1985. 9–24.

Carter, A. E. *Charles Baudelaire*. Boston: Twayne, 1977.

Geeraerts, Jef. *Gangrene*. Trans. Jon Swan. New York: Viking, 1975.

Gilman, Sander. *Difference and Pathology: Stereotypes of Sexuality, Race and Madness*. Ithaca: Cornell UP, 1985.

Gray, Stephen, ed. *A World of Their Own: Southern African Poets of the Seventies*. Johannesburg: Donker, 1976.

———. *Hottentot Venus and Other Poems*. Cape Town: David Philip, 1979.

Hemmings. F. W. J. *Baudelaire the Damned: A Biography*. London: Hamish Hamilton, 1982.

Knapp, Bettina L. *Émile Zola*. New York: Ungar, 1980.

Nadar. *Charles Baudelaire Intime: Le Poète Vierge*. Paris, 1911.

Perruchot, Henri. *Manet*. Trans. Humphrey Hare. Ed. Jean Ellsmoor. London: Perpetua, 1962.

Rose, Phyllis, *Jazz Cleopatra*. New York: Doubleday, 1989.

Starkie, Enid. *Baudelaire*. London: Faber, 1957.

THE NOVELS
◆

Written on the Body:
The Materiality of Myth in Angela Carter's
Heroes and Villains

JOANNE GASS

When Virginia Woolf dedicated *Orlando* to Vita Sackville-West, she paid tribute not only to her friend, but also to her friend's historic family name and, above all, to Vita's family home, Knole. In fact, she made Knole the central image of the novel, for the great house, given to Thomas Sackville by Queen Elizabeth for service to the crown, emblematizes the edifice of British history as perhaps no other image could. Knole epitomizes the English country house, and the English country house epitomizes England. Mark Girouard, in *A Country House Companion,* makes very clear the importance of the English country house to British mythology:

> The English upper-classes, unlike their continental counterparts, have always been firmly rooted in their estates. They know the land, and enjoy its ways and its sports. They look after their tenantry and their servants, and have an easy and natural relationship with working-class people. At the same time they have a sense of duty, which leads them to devote much of their lives to public service, with no thought of personal gain. Their lives are a happy mean between country sports and pastimes, public service, and the cultivation of the mind. Their houses are filled with beautiful pictures and fine furniture. Their libraries are well stocked with books bound in vellum or tooled leather; temples and classical monuments dot their parks. They share their life with their friends, in a free hospitality which results in one of the most enviable ways of life ever devised. (8)

What could be more genteel, more to be desired, than access to such an edifice?[1] Vita herself attested to the historic significance of her family house when she wrote its history in 1922. In *Knole & the Sackvilles,* she associates the house with essential Englishness, with legend, myth and history. She tells us that Knole's origins are lost in the mists of history, that "it is suggested that a Roman building once occupied the site" (20); hence, the history of England

From *Arkansas Review* 4, no. 1 (Spring 1995): 12–30. Reprinted by permission.

and of Knole parallel one another. Vita also repeats the legend, which she her-self has not verified, that the house contains seven courtyards, a number which "is supposed to correspond to the days in the week and in pursuance of this conceit there are in the house fifty-two staircases, corresponding to the weeks in the year, and three hundred and sixty-five rooms, corresponding to the days" (19). Knole, therefore, represents time, the eternal and perpetual continuity found in the house. Finally, Vita points out the symbiotic relation-ship between Knole and England:

> It is, above all, an English house. It has the tone of England; it melts into the green of the garden turf, into the tawnier green of the park beyond, into the blue of the pale English sky; it settles down into its hollow amongst the cush-ioned tops of the trees; the brown-red of those roofs is the brown-red of the roofs of humble farms and pointed oast-houses, such as stain over a wide land-scape of England the quilt-like pattern of the fields. I make bold to say that it stoops to nothing either pretentious or meretricious. (18)

Vita, and I dare say, Virginia, both subscribed whole-heartedly to the myth of the English country house. They both accepted that symbiotic relationship between the country house and history and both longed for legitimate access into the venerable halls of both the country house estate and of English his-tory, for that is the point of *Orlando:* it is about one English woman's loss because she cannot legitimately keep what she inherited (and therefore, her estate must be given to the state) and about another woman's desire to write herself into English literature and history.

What has that to do with Angela Carter, myth, rhetoric, materiality, and woman's body? Maybe everything. For the myth of the country house and the desire it creates in both Virginia Woolf and Vita Sackville-West is a func-tion of rhetoric. It ceases to be a material object and becomes a metaphor—a representation—of an ideal which then exerts discursive power upon those who become the subjects of such discourse. The country house metaphor is an ideal, a metaphysic, which exerts its power over all British subjects, women especially. It embodies everything that is "civilized" about England. One might say that it is the physical representation of what Joseph Conrad called "the idea" in *Heart of Darkness:*

> The conquest of the earth, which mostly means the taking it away from those who have a different complexion or slightly flatter noses than ourselves, is not a pretty thing when you look into it too much. What redeems it is the idea only. An idea at the back of it; not a sentimental pretence but an idea; and an unselfish belief in the idea—something you can set up, and bow down before, and offer a sacrifice to. . . .(7)

This idea of civilization redeems Marlow (and maybe even Kurtz) in *Heart of Darkness,* and this same idea permeates Conrad's other novel of colonialism,

Lord Jim, for Jim's "ideal" Englishness, in the end, saves him in Marlow's eyes.[2] It is the "rightness" of England, despite its obvious and lamentable flaws, which makes Conrad, and even Virginia Woolf and Vita Sackville-West, assert the value of "the idea," England, and civilization. And it is just this metaphysics which Angela Carter spent her writing career debunking.

Angela Carter spent her entire creative life exposing the material conditions which determined women's and men's lives. For Carter, having taken Simone de Beauvoir's injunction to women "to know the economic and social structure" of the world in order to become themselves (*The Second Sex* 52), myth's power lies not in its metaphysical, universal potency but in its material potency by which the economic and social power is and has been invested in patriarchal oppression. One of her most frequent targets was myth and its claim to metaphysical truth and power. Her project appears to have been to expose myth for what it is: an aspect of rhetoric. Nearly all of her works—fiction, essays, and criticism—explore the rhetoric employed by those in power as a means of preserving their power. From *The Bloody Chamber,* to *The Sadeian Woman,* to *Nights at the Circus* and *Wise Children,* she probes the discourses we use to define and identify human beings, particularly women. "Myth deals in false universals, to dull the pain of particular circumstances," she says in one of her most-often cited remarks about myth in the "Polemical Preface" to *The Sadeian Woman.* She goes on to say:

> All the mythic versions of women, from the myth of the redeeming purity of the virgin to that of the healing, reconciling mother, are consolatory nonsense; and consolatory nonsense seems to me a fair definition of myth, anyway. Mother goddesses are just as silly a notion as father gods. If a revival of the myths of these cults gives women emotional satisfaction, it does so at the price of obscuring the real conditions of life. This is why they were invented in the first place. (5)

Her work, however, was not aimed at debunking only Father gods and Mother goddesses; as her works amply illustrate, Angela Carter set out to undermine and eventually to overthrow the rhetorical power of myth, and the instrument she used to effect such a revolution was parody. Nearly all of her novels and short stories parody an accepted literary form in order to expose the rhetoric of myth and its claim to metaphysical truth and power. Carter, like many writers and thinkers we label as "post-moderns," viewed languages as a material aspect of our existence; therefore, if myth was an aspect of language, it could not have pretensions to absolutes—ideals, truth, eternal verities—instead, the language which defines subjects could be changed; definitions of femininity, masculinity, truth, might, progress; they might even liberate humans rather than enslave them. If language could be used as a tool of repression, it could also be a tool of liberation, and she used it as such a tool.

Heroes and Villains, first published in 1969, exemplifies Carter's use of parody as a means of dismantling the rhetoric of the myth of the "idea" of civilization. One of the four epigraphs to the novel, which comes from Leslie Fiedler's *Love and Death in the American Novel,* provides a clue to Carter's intent in *Heroes and Villains.* Of the Gothic novel, Carter quotes Fiedler as having written: "The Gothic mode is essentially a form of parody, a way of assailing clichés by exaggerating them to the limit of grotesqueness." According to Fiedler, the Gothic tradition, especially as it was developed by Edgar Allan Poe, parodied its contemporaries in order to expose the grotesqueness of their own premises. In other words, in Poe's hands the novel of heroic western expansion became *The Narrative of Arthur Gordon Pym,* a grotesque parody of its genre. In precisely the same way, Carter uses the Gothic mode in *Heroes and Villains* to expose the clichés inherent in the West's use of myth as a means of colonizing its subjects and to demythologize myth by exposing its material, rhetorical base.[3]

The novel's plot goes something as follows: Marianne, a young, intelligent, and resourceful woman, lives in post-apocalyptic England in an enclave of civilization surrounded by Barbarians and Out People. The enclave is populated by Professors who preserve the values of Western Civilization while warding off the raids of the Barbarians—savage nomads who raid the enclaves for women and food. Marianne's world also includes the Out People, who are sub-human mutants as a result of atomic radiation from the war (presumably fought by the civilized nations). Marianne, bored with life in the enclave, decides to run away. She runs into the arms of a wild, handsome Barbarian named Jewel (the very Barbarian who, a few years before, she had witnessed killing her brother in one of their raids). Jewel promptly rapes her then takes her back to his tribe, which is spending the winter in the ruins of an English country house. The tribe is controlled by a renegade Professor named Donally, who rules the tribe through superstition, using the myths and assumptions of western civilization as means of repression, and who has educated Jewel but not taught him to read. Marianne is forced to marry Jewel, and they live together in a state of sexual excitement and mutual resentment until the tribe, at the end of the winter, moves on to search for food. When the tribe sets out, Jewel and Marianne expel Donally from the tribe; Jewel is killed attempting to rescue Donally, and Marianne becomes the Queen, "the tiger lady [who] will rule them with a rod of iron" (150).

To put it perhaps too crudely, *Heroes and Villains* parodies Joseph Conrad's *Heart of Darkness* and *Lord Jim.* It holds up to ridicule the patriarchal, imperialistic, and colonialist myths of the Western world, making us see that these discourses are not natural, immutable, inherent, or necessarily true, but that they are, as Carter herself says, "false universals, to dull the pain of particular circumstances" (*The Sadeian Woman* 5). Conrad's defense of imperialism and colonialism has been thoroughly analyzed and documented by a number of contemporary culture critics, most notably and persuasively by

Edward Said, so I don't think that I have to reiterate the argument here. Suffice it to say that Conrad, in both *Heart of Darkness* and *Lord Jim*, while ostensibly critiquing the "horrors" perpetrated by colonial cultures from the Romans to the English, nevertheless upholds the essential "virtues" which these same cultures carry with them on their colonial missions. Although Carter herself does not evoke Conrad's name in her novel, she nevertheless embeds so many obvious references to both Conrad novels that one cannot avoid the conclusion that she has, in *Heroes and Villains*, made Conrad's name the unspoken yet ever-present presence in the novel. She has, in making Conrad's presence the unspoken "horror" that parodies and parallels Kurtz's unheard "the horror" at the end of *Heart of Darkness*, created a feminist, gothic tale which grossly parodies the ideas that Conrad, and Virginia Woolf and Vita Sackville-West, so obviously cherished.

Donally, the renegade professor who escapes the civilized stronghold of the Professors, parallels Conrad's Kurtz in many ways, but most of all in his use of rhetoric as a means of control. Donally employs the rituals and myths of the West in order to control the illiterate and superstitious Barbarians, deliberately keeping his vassals ignorant. Donally, like Kurtz, sets up his "kingdom" in the midst of the wilderness, only Donally's kingdom is in the ruins of an English country house. There, he reenacts the rituals common to our culture before a baffled group of illiterate Barbarians. He rules, he says, by fear, "the ruling passion"; and he brags that he "can provoke an ecstasy of dread by raising [his] little finger" (51). He employs the rituals and symbols of Christianity because "religion [is] a social necessity" (51). In order to reinforce his power and frighten the tribe, he keeps a snake in a cage which he uses during ceremonies. In the end, we discover that the snake is a stuffed animal; merely a sign which, as Jewel points out, "signifies nothing." Just as Kurtz recited poetry in the midst of the "heart of darkness" and in doing so "enlarged [the] mind" of the company manager (HD 65), Donally likes to post slogans on the walls of the crumbling house—slogans like "ONENESS WITH DESTINY GIVES STYLE AND DISTINCTION" (59); "MISTRUST APPEARANCES, THEY NEVER CONCEAL ANYTHING" (60); "AS I AM, SO YE SHALL BE" (63), and "MEMORY IS DEATH" (87). Since no one but Donally can read the slogans, they mean nothing, but they *do* signify to the Barbarians; they signify the mystery which Donally has "worked hard and bided [his] time" in establishing (51). Donally parodies the mad, egomaniacal Kurtz, in that he truly does have nothing to say; he has no devoted Marlow who will faithfully report his words in the dark on the deck of a ship, and say of him: "Better his cry—much better. It was an affirmation, a moral victory paid for by innumerable defeats, by abominable terrors, by abominable satisfactions. But it was a victory!" (HD 72). Marlow affirms Kurtz's "magnificent eloquence" which comes from a "soul as translucently pure as a cliff of crystal" (HD 72), and testifies to the essential truth of Kurtz's horror. Donally's slogans, his fake symbols, his crass and deliberate use of the trappings of civilization, underline their materiality, their transience, their insignificance.

In the ruins of the country house, there is a library, and Donally has his collection of books which include "Teilhard de Chardin, Levi-Strauss, Weber, Durkheim and so on, all marked by fire and flood. He had been reading some books about society" (62). Of course, he's been reading anthropology, the social science which tries to define culture and civilization. Just as his slogans mean nothing in this post-atomic wilderness, neither do the pompous postulations of science in its attempts to quantify human beings mean anything. They will soon be burned along with the remains of the English country house and all that it metaphorically represents.

The library and its store of books (and not just anthropology books) play a role in Donally's imposition of rhetoric upon his vassals. For example, he forces Marianne to marry Jewel "by the book"—the *Book of Common Prayer*. Marianne wears an ancient wedding dress of white tulle which exhibits its anachronistic "virtue" by disintegrating into a cloud of brittle shards both when she puts it on and during the wedding ceremony. Marianne describes the wedding ceremony itself as an "ordeal of imagery" (81). The ritual euphemizes the brutality which lies at the heart of the wedding ceremony. The bride, who is essentially Donally's captive, has been forced into marriage; she partakes in the blood sacrifice which lies at the heart of Judeo-Christian myth—she and Jewel cut their arms and mingle their blood. Even though Jewel has raped her, Marianne, as do all brides, stands for their "little holy image," their "lady of the wilderness," their "virgin of the swamp" (50). Each of the elements of the wedding ceremony is made literal, and in making them literal their rhetoricity is exposed. As they stand before Donally to be wed, Marianne reflects upon their significance:

> He was like a work of art, as if created, not begotten, a fantastic dandy of the void whose true nature had been entirely subsumed to the alien and terrible beauty of a rhetorical gesture. His appearance was abstracted from his body, and he was willfully reduced to sign language. He had become the sign of an idea of a hero: and she herself had been forced to impersonate the sign of a memory of a bride. But though she knew quite well she herself was only impersonating this sign, she could not tell whether Jewel was impersonating that other sign or had, indeed, become it, for every line of his outlandish figure expressed the most arrogant contempt and it was impossible to tell whether or not this contempt was in his script. (71–72)

In the parody that is their wedding ceremony, they expose the materiality of the rhetoric that persists in our patriarchal culture.

Jewel, Donally's son and his cleverest "creation," is both a parody of Jewel, Lord Jim's "creation," and of western rhetoric as well. First, Jim's Jewel, that savage girl whose unquestioning devotion to Jim leads her, after Jim's death, to leave her native village and to take up residence with the

European traders, becomes, as Conrad describes her, the paragon of English courage, devotion, and steadfastness. In fact, Jewel is thoroughly colonized and civilized by Jim. Conrad's Jewel imbibes Englishness and, filling up the hollow of self that Conrad seems to postulate for the uncivilized, becomes essentially English. Donally's Jewel has his civilization on his back. On their wedding night, Marianne discovers that Donally has tattooed upon Jewel's back the myth that informs nearly all of Judeo-Christian civilization:

> She parted the black curtain of his mane and drew her hands incredulously down the ornamented length of his back. He wore the figure of a man on the right side, a woman on the left and, tattooed the length of his spine, a tree with a snake curled round and round the trunk. This elaborate design was executed in blue, red, black and green. The woman offered the man a red apple and more red apples grew among green leaves at the top of the tree, spreading across his shoulders, and the black roots of the tree twisted and ended at the top of his buttocks. The figures were both stiff and lifelike; Eve wore a perfidious smile. The lines of colour were etched with obsessive precision on the shining, close-pored skin which rose and fell with Jewel's breathing, so it seemed the snake's forked tongue darted in and out and the leaves on the tree moved in a small wind, an effect the designer must have foreseen and allowed for. (85)

Jewel, it seems, is the visual, material representation of The Fall; he, however, does not let it fill him and define him in the way that Jim's Jewel has taken in Western discourse. Marianne observes, rather dryly, that Jewel can never "be properly by [himself], with Adam and Eve there all the time" (85). An observation which we should take very seriously, because, in fact, none of us is "by ourselves" with that myth perpetually tattooed upon our backs. Jewel replies that Donally "wanted to do the Last Judgement on [his] chest, but [he] didn't want nothing [he] could see all the time" (86). Jewel, who can see the "signs" but cannot read, never becomes civilized by the myth he carries, and yet he reenacts it as he moves. In a particularly graphic scene, Jewel exacts justice upon his brother, Precious, whose failure to guard the wall has caused three deaths. Marianne, who witnesses Precious' whipping, realizes that Jewel

> was nothing but the idea of that power which men fear to offend; his back flexed and his arm rose and fell. The snake on his back flicked its tongue in and out with the play of muscle beneath the skin and the tattooed Adam appeared to flinch again and again from the apple which Eve again and again leaned forward to offer him until it seemed that the moving picture of an endless temptation was projecting on Jewel's surfaces, an uncompleted series of actions with no conclusion, caught in a groove of time. And Jewel was also caught in this groove of time; frozen in the act of punishment. (113)

Before her, Marianne sees the graphic reenactment of the Temptation and Fall, and God's punishment and "justice" repeated again and again—"caught in a groove of time" with "no conclusion." Jewel, like Conrad's Jewel, is a victim of the Professors—Donally being only a representative of the genre—who preserve and perpetuate these humanistic, civilizing myths which we carry upon our backs and reenact again and again without conclusion, and who never consider or recognize their true human cost. Donally, speaking for all Professors, says, "I am an intellectual; . . . we are accustomed to examine things and scarcely bother ourselves about the hurt feelings of the things we examine, why should we?" (124) In the end, Jewel must die; he is, as he realizes, "doomed to be nothing but an exhibit" (124).

Marianne, on the other hand, is destined to live. She, it seems, is to become the "savior" of the Barbarians, if not then Donally who will rule them through fear. But before she can take her place as the Tiger Lady, she must recognize the true value of rhetoric—its value as appearance. In her role as parodic heroine on a quest for meaning, Marianne, like the mythic hero who returns to his society with a message which reveals an eternal truth, becomes the Tiger Lady because she recognizes that there is no *truth*. Having learned that she is pregnant, she enters a brief period of kitten-like dependence upon Jewel, a period that she will soon discard, but during this phase in which she clings to Jewel, she reflects:

> But I think that, in the long run, I shall be forced to trust appearances. When I was a little girl, we played at heroes and villains but now I don't know which is which any more, nor who is who, and what can I trust if not appearances? Because nobody can teach me which is which nor who is who because my father is dead. (124–5).

Jewel, wiser at this point than she, replies, "You'll have to learn for yourself, then. . . . Don't we all" (125). Marianne, then, becomes the post-modern heroine (or should I say post-Saussurian heroine?) who suspects that appearance is all there is, that language is the material by which discourse creates power. Marianne's transformation occurs near the end of the book and begins when she and Jewel expel Donally. From this point on, Marianne consciously weights the advantages of rhetoric against the possibilities of "truth." In the process, Donally, Jewel, and even civilization, shrink from the mythic proportions they have heretofore occupied to more human proportions, and patriarchal power is reduced to whining impotence. Her father, the Professor, is dead; patriarchal civilization and its myths have been reduced to entropic chaos. She and her child will have to forge a way for themselves.

The process of transformation begins with temptation: Donally offers her power. Trying to save himself, he pleads, "Marianne, come with me by yourself. Consider your researches into the *moeurs* of savage tribes completed." Marianne thinks, "So that is what I've been doing!" (132). Having rejected Donally's offer, Marianne "falls" into a different kind of temptation—the temptation to co-opt Donally's rhetoric. She begins to use the Donally's slogans: she tells Jewel, when Donally's son runs after him, "Blood is thicker than water" (132). Marianne's "fall," like Eve's, leads to knowledge, for Marianne's use of cliché becomes a conscious one:

> when she perceived she and her Jewel were, in some way, related to one another she was filled with pain for her idea of her own autonomy might, in fact, be not the truth but a passionately held conviction. However, might not such a conviction serve her as well as a proven certainty? When she realized she had begun to think in such circuitous slogans as Donally might paint on his wall, she was abashed and fixed her eyes on the carpet of weeds in the roadway. (132–33)

Realization—fall, if you will—leads to deployment of power. In the end, Marianne will *know* that she can use rhetoric to her own advantage. Unconsciously mouthing clichés is not the same thing as intentionally using them to control others; her embarrassment and even shame at this realization does not preclude her knowledge of its potential power. In the meantime, she must first destroy Jewel, the last vestige of Donally's power, and witness the fall of civilization. After she and Jewel dispose of Donally's material presence, she will strip Jewel of his rhetorical power and see the sunken city.

Jewel, unlike Marianne, cannot "see" beyond the image and the symbol; therefore, he is vulnerable to Marianne's growing knowledge. When he notices that Marianne no longer wears her wedding ring, he says, "In that case, how can you expect me to trust you?" Jewel "reconstruct[s] the world solely in terms of imagery" (133); if Marianne does not wear the symbol of marriage (read fidelity), she cannot *be* married; therefore she will betray him. Her betrayal lies in her relentless critique of Jewel's symbolic meaning. When Jewel paints his face and body, he believes he takes on a material presence he does not have when he is unpainted; he says, "Fetch my jars of paint, watch me turn into a nightmare. . . . [which is] true as long as one or the other of us wants to believe it" (145). Marianne replies, "You're not a human being at all, you're a metaphysical proposition" (145). Under the relentless attack of her critique, Jewel bungles this final putting on of the paint: "A heavy slowness affected all his movements; he smeared black colour in clumsy patches round his eyes" causing "dream and reality to merge" and Marianne to taunt, "You aren't yourself this morning, you aren't yourself this morning, you aren't yourself this morning. . . . You are no longer the perfect savage, you are not paying sufficient attention to detail. You aren't in the least impressive; what will become of you?" (146).[4] When Jewel leaves, Marianne thinks,

> "I have destroyed him" and [feels] a warm sense of satisfaction, for quite dissolved was the marvellous [sic], defiant construction of textures and colours she first glimpsed marauding her tranquil village; it had vanished as if an illusion which could not sustain itself in the white beams of the lighthouse. (147)

Marianne's victory (if we can call it that) comes after she has visited the sunken city with Jewel and saved him from drowning.

Angela Carter's parody ends with revelation, for Marianne learns from her trip to the sea that history's rhetorical, metaphysical, "truth-bearing" power is itself subject to a more implacable power, not historical power but entropic power. In *Heroes and Villains* history and time are reduced to artifacts which entropy, like erosion, will eventually reduce to sand. Marianne's confrontation with the sea, which heretofore she has never seen but only "known" intellectually, exposes her to human fragility in the face of physics and the laws of nature. Man's first rhetorical power, the act of naming and hence taming, ordering, and thus creating the world around him, is exposed as dependent upon man's ability to remember and to record; when those abilities are lost, so is order. Marianne follows Jewel to the edge of the shore, and she sees, "all the wonders of the seashore, to which Marianne could scarcely put a single name, though everything had once been scrupulously named" (136). To Marianne is revealed the truth that

> Losing their names, these things underwent a process of uncreation and reverted to chaos, existing only to themselves in an unstructured world where they were not formally acknowledged, becoming an ever-widening margin of undifferentiated and nameless matter surrounding the outposts of man, who no longer made himself familiar with these things or rendered them authentic in his experience by the gift of naming. (136–37)

Marianne now recognizes that she is faced with a choice: begin again and "begin a new subspecies. . . . [a] fearless and rational breed [which] would eschew such mysteries as the one now forcing her to walk behind the figure on the shore," or submit to the mystery which forces her to walk behind Jewel (137). Those mysteries, which I take to mean the metaphysics of patriarchal dominance, and Marianne's choice, present themselves again in the figures of the woman holding the clock in the submerged city and the lighthouse on the cliffs above.

The clock is held in the giant embrace of a scantily clad woman whose colossal figure juts out of the sea (one is tempted to make the parodic comparison to the Colossus of Rhodes) in what is surely a parody of the Botticelli Venus and of all other idealized versions of woman.

> It was the figure of a luxuriously endowed woman scantily clad in a one-piece bathing costume which, at the top, scarcely contained the rising swell of mountainous breasts in the shadowy cleft. . . . In daylight, this woman's garment still retained streaks of the cheerful blue with which it had been painted, just as the flesh was still stained here and there a vivid pink. . . . The head, equipped with exuberant, shoulder-length curls, was thrown back in erotic ecstasy and, though partially worn away by the salty winds, the face clearly displayed a gigantic pair of lips twisted in a wide, joyous smile revealing a fine

set of plaster teeth. The eyes used to shine since blue electric light bulbs had been set in the sockets and bulbs of different colours had also surrounded the clock. . . .(138)

She is a parody of the epitome of male desire—erotic, voluptuous, ageless, virginal (she wears blue, the Virgin's colors), and silent. Marianne recognizes that it is "lewd," but she does not recognize herself in the image; "it [does] not occur to her that her companion might regard her as more representative of the culture of the carrier of the defunct clock nor [can] she have understood how this was possible . . ."(139). That Marianne fails to "see" herself in this image indicates her growing self-consciousness and her growing power.

Marianne identifies instead with the lighthouse. It stands on a cliff which in time will be eroded away and destroyed by the force of the water; it is no longer useful since there are no more sailors to look for its warning light; besides, its light has been put out,

> yet, functionless as it was, it was intransigent. To Marianne, it looked the twin of the white tower in which she had been born and she was very much moved for, though neither tower any longer cast a useful light, both still served to warn and inform of surrounding dangers. Thus this tower glimpsed in darkness symbolized and clarified her resolution; abhor shipwreck, said the lighthouse, go in fear of unreason. Use your wits, said the lighthouse. She fell in love with the integrity of the lighthouse. (139)

Unlike the lewd clock-bearing figure of the woman with which Marianne cannot identify, she does see herself in the "integrity of the lighthouse" and its admonishment to use her wits. Thus Marianne rejects history, but not reason, and chooses in favor of the sub-species which will "eschew unreason and the mysteries" of the past. The lighthouse, perhaps a tribute to Virginia Woolf and a reminder that she used her wits and opted for reason in an attempt to create a room of her own in the history of English letters, symbolizes Marianne's choice and creates a rhetoric of its own. She has learned its value.

Which returns me, I suppose, to the matter of a house. For in what discursive structure will Marianne house herself? It isn't a matter of whether she will situate herself and her child within a discourse; it's a matter of what discourse. Her father is both symbolically and literally dead (he was, after all, a Professor of History (1)); when he was murdered by the old nurse, Marianne had burned his history books and drowned his clock in the swamp (15); now, she has completed her Oedipal revolution by burning the house, that "crumbling anachronism" (69), expelling Donally, burning his books, and witnessing yet another drowning of a clock. She leaves them behind, as she did her father's home, without the slightest trace of sentimentality or remorse. It is not for her the sentimentality, the bowing down before and offering a sacrifice to an idea, the cheerful optimism which is the timelessness of English historical progress. Compare Vita Sackville-West's encomium to Knole as she signs it over to the National Trust:

Does it breathe, does it live, does it hold a spirit of its own even as every ship has her own temper? Bacon made the subtle and profound remark that there was "no excellent beauty that hath not some strangeness in the proportion," but this is not true of Knole, which in every sobriety of proportion proclaims that straightfor-wardness of design and colour may also compose into a perfection, homogenous though diversified, without oddity, as continuous as history itself. History indeed is implicit here, for behind the roughest earliest portion which served as a tithe-barn in the days of Magna Carta, has grown up the vast structure which after soaring to its peak of pomp as a palace of the Archbishop of Canterbury and a palace of the Crown, then became for many generations the home of an English family and now in the days of democracy is about to pass into the possession of the nation for enjoyment of the people. (*Knole & the Sackvilles* 216)

Vita's rhetoric places her comfortably within the discourse of the country house. Angela Carter's description of the country house emphasizes its tran-sience; unlike Vita, she recognizes the materiality of the edifice; it isn't an immutable idea; it is a "crumbling anachronism"; the very structures which Vita identifies with history and permanence, Carter shows us to be not only mutable but subject to a more implacable force—entropy:

The house was a gigantic memory of rotten stone, a compilation of innumerable forgotten styles now given some green unity by the devouring web of creeper, fur of moss and fungoid growth of rot. Wholly abandoned to decay, baroque stonework of the late Jacobean period, Gothic turrets murmurous with birds and pathetic elegance of Palladian pillared façades weathered indiscriminately together towards irreducible rubble. The forest perched upon the tumbled roofs in the shapes of yellow and purple weeds rooted in the gapped tiles, besides a few small trees and bushes. The windows gaped or sprouted internal foliage, as if the forest were as well already camped inside, there gathering strength for a green eruption which would one day burst the walls sky high back to nature. A horse or two grazed upon a terrace built in some kind of florid English Renais-sance style. Upon the balustrade of this terrace were many pocked and armless statues in robes, or nude and garlanded. These looked like the petrified sur-vivors of a malign *fête-champêtre* ended long ago, in catastrophe. (31–32)

Carter's description of the country house is a gothic parody of Vita Sackville-West's hymn to Knole. What Carter exposes in her parody is the rhetoric of the idea. What remains problematic, however, is whether or not Marianne, herself a parody of the damsel-in-distress heroine who leads a revolution (like Marianne, the symbol of the French Revolution), truly does create her own discourse, her own house, her own freedom. Any too optimistic conclusion is tempered by Marianne's vision at the end as she awaits news of Jewel's death. Jewel has found he cannot live without his "father," Donally, and he has set out to rescue him from the Soldiers. As she stirs the pot and plans her escape, if she needs it, Marianne "encounter[s] her father, who merge[s] impercepti-bly with the image of the blind lighthouse and then disappear[s] in the slowly rising bubbles" (149). If Marianne has incorporated her father's rhetoric, she has done so with a rational and independent mind, and she chooses to exercise her own power in the end. Whether this choice is truly a revolution remains to be seen. However, Angela Carter's later novels, especially *Nights at the Circus* and even *Wise Children,* her last, seem to suggest that Marianne's revolution is certainly possible.

Notes

1. Girouard has written at length about the English country house in at least three works: *A Country House Companion, Life in the English Country House,* and *The Victorian Country House.* Virginia Kenny, in *The Country House Ethos in English Literature 1688–1750,* traces the image of the house and the rhetoric which accompanies it in her excellent analysis.

2. See my article, forthcoming in *Conradiana,* " 'The Significant Fact of an Unforgotten Grave': Encrypting the Feminine in Conrad's *Lord Jim,*" in which I explore Marlow's rhetoric of colonialism.

3. Fiedler also says of the "gothic fable":

> The gothic fable . . . though it may (in its more genteel examples) permit the happy ending, is committed to portraying the power of darkness. Perhaps another way to say this is that the fully developed gothic centers not in the heroine (the persecuted principle of salvation) but in the villain (the persecuting principle of damnation). The villain-hero is, indeed, an invention of the gothic form, while his temptation and suffering, the beauty and terror of his bondage to evil, are among its major themes. (128)

It is not outside the realm of possibilities to imagine that Angela Carter, in *Heroes and Villains,* parodies, in the process of writing a gothic novel, the gothic form itself by reversing the roles of hero and villain. Marianne's role at the end of the novel is certainly ambiguous enough to make her the parodic villain-hero, and the ending has sufficient dark overtones to support such a conclusion. We cannot be sure that she is *not* in bondage to evil at the end.

4. John Demos, in *The Unredeemed Captive,* points out the rhetorical power of face painting. In his fine study of captives of North American Indians in the eighteenth century, he says that captives were not only forced to learn the language of their captors but also to "adopt a native appearance."

> Titus King, captured by Canadian Abenakis in the 1750s, was made to exchange his "shurt . . . and Sleve buttons" for "an old shurt of theres that stand with Indian Sweet [sweat]"; at the same time his captors "put wonpon in my neck [and] painted my Face." As a result, "I began to think I was an Indian." If the captive themselves were thus persuaded, so also were other Europeans who might subsequently encounter them. (New York: Knopf, 1994) 174.

Works Consulted

Carter, Angela. *Heroes and Villains.* London: Penguin, 1969.
———. *The Sadeian Woman: An Exercise in Cultural History.* London: Virago, 1979.

Conrad, Joseph. *Heart of Darkness*. Ed. Robert Kinbrough. New York: Norton, 1971.

de Beauvoir, Simone. *The Second Sex*. Trans. and ed. H. M. Parshley. New York: Modern Library, 1968.

Demos, John. *The Unredeemed Captive*. New York: Knopf, 1994.

Fiedler, Leslie A. *Love and Death in the American Novel*. New York: Dell, 1960.

Girouard, Mark. *A Country House Companion*. New Haven: Yale UP, 1987.

———. *Life in the English Country House*. New Haven: Yale UP, 1978.

Kenny, Virginia. *The Country House Ethos in English Literature 1688–1750*. New York: St. Martin's, 1984.

Sackville-West, Vita. *Knole & the Sackvilles*. Tonbridge, Kent: Ernest Benn, Ltd., 1984.

Woolf, Virginia. *Orlando*. San Diego: Harcourt Brace, 1956.

The Anti-Hero as Oedipus:
Gender and the Postmodern Narrative
[in *The Infernal Desire Machines of Dr. Hoffman*]

SALLY ROBINSON

Angela Carter's novels employ a doubled feminist perspective by performing a movement between the "inside" and the "outside" of normative gender constructions, including the construction of Woman as Other to Man's self—whether that Other be denigrated or celebrated. For Carter, denigration and celebration of Woman as Other are both masculinist strategies within patriarchal cultures, whereby Man secures his hegemony over the places of enunciation. Woman, whether revered or reviled, is spoken through dominant representational practices, whereas women are prohibited from speaking. To speak, or write, as a woman means to enact the double relation of women to dominant representational practices. For Carter, this entails practicing the double strategies of mimicry, parody, and masquerade. Each of these performative strategies negotiates between the terms of a series of oppositions: construction/deconstruction of "natural" sexual difference; compliance/resistance to the ideologies of gender difference as offered through hegemonic discursive systems; and, inscription/subversion of the fit between Woman and women, between metaphorical figures constructed according to the logics of a desire encoded as masculine and social subjects who position themselves through processes of self-representation. Like Luce Irigaray's strategy of mimicry, Carter's parodies and masquerades point to an "elsewhere" of discourse, what Teresa de Lauretis refers to as the "chinks and cracks" in dominant representational practices. That elsewhere is the space of radical critique that exceeds the performance of mimicry or parody, and gets the text, and its readers, off the fence of what Linda Hutcheon calls the "political ambidexterity" of postmodernist parody.[1]

The Infernal Desire Machines of Doctor Hoffman chronicles a revolution in the relationship between reason and unreason in which Dr. Hoffman—a renegade philosopher, whose theoretical framework echoes Nietzsche, Der-

From *Engendering the Subject: Gender and Self-Representation in Contemporary Women's Fiction* (New York: State University of New York Press, 1991), 98–117. © 1991 State University of New York Press. Reprinted by permission.

rida, and others—has declared a war on reality, in order to liberate desire; he is intent on exploring and materializing the "obscure and controversial borderline between the thinkable and the unthinkable" (22). Eschewing binary and linear logic, Hoffman attempts to find the "loopholes in metaphysics" (212), rewriting the *cogito* to read: "I DESIRE, THEREFORE I EXIST" (211). Against the law of the city fathers—represented by the Minister of Determination who "is not a man but a theorem, clear, hard, unified and harmonious" (13)—Hoffman is "disseminating" "lawless images" (12). The Doctor is attractive in his ability to think beyond binary oppositions, to read the world in ways not wholly dependent on a logic which would repress the unconscious in a hegemony of logocentrism. But, early in the novel, something, sinister enters into the textual mapping of the Doctor's effects. In an absurd confrontation between Hoffman's Ambassador and the Minister, the former speaks for seduction and the latter for coercion; however, the two figures come closer together as the Ambassador describes the Doctor's terms for capitulation: he wants "absolute authority to establish a regime of total liberation" (38). The language here foregrounds the idea that the Doctor's liberatory schema is complicit in the same will to power that the Minister clings to.[2] The Minister, a representative of "logical positivism" (194) speaks for a humanist epistemology that cannot countenance contradiction in its systems. The Doctor speaks for a posthumanist epistemology where contradiction rules and where rationality has been put radically into question. Yet, the two systems are quickly seen to be complicit in the same ideological agenda: they both position Man as an imperialist subject whose desire gives free reign to exploitation and domination.

Desiderio, a postmodern Oedipus, is sent to destroy the doctor; but his quest is complicated by the fact that everything he sees and experiences turns out to be an emanation of his desires. The world across which Desiderio moves is literally a construction: the Doctor's desire machines have disrupted "reality" to the extent that any epistemological certainty has become impossible. Objects, people, landscapes, and even time are subject to the whims of the desire machines which are generating "eroto-energy" as a force in opposition to rational knowledge. This eroto-energy causes each subject to perceive and experience the world according to the logic—or, illogic—of his/her desires. Since we see everything through Desiderio's eyes, we are immersed in his desires and forced to experience them along with him. All of Desiderio's "experiences," thus, are constructions of his desire. In reading this text, we are constantly aware that desire is, indeed, the "motor force" of narrative, as Peter Brooks would have it; and, further, that the "engine" behind the narrative, like the male "eroto-energy" Dr. Hoffman's revolution unleashes, is hostile to women.[3] Desiderio's desire participates in the fantasy of colonization that, simultaneously, marks the Doctor's and the Minister's projects for "liberation"—this despite his ambiguously claimed membership in a colonized group, due to his being "of Indian extraction" (16). Desiderio's discursive self-positioning throughout the narrative is dependent on his negation of the various exotic and erotic "others" his desire invokes. Against these others, he claims the "unique allure of the norm" (101).

Despite the fact that Desiderio's narrative is anything but a traditional quest story, its structure follows pretty closely the form of that story: sent to seek and destroy the diabolical Doctor, Desiderio gets sidetracked and, in fact, seduced to the Doctor's side through the mediation of his daughter, Albertina. While his pursuit of the elusive woman disrupts his primary quest—a quest that originates through the imperative of a stern father figure—he nevertheless finally finds the Doctor, and it appears that he will get a bonus for his trouble: possession of Albertina. Finding himself duped, however, by Albertina—who turns out to be even more diabolical than her father—and his "physicality thwarted by metaphysics" (204), he kills them both, and returns to his city of origin, a hero. Like Oedipus, he has rid the city of its pollution and, also like Oedipus, must pay the price of his new knowledge: "I knew I was condemned to disillusionment in perpetuity," he reminisces. "My punishment had been my crime" (220). While culture's master narratives are losing their authority in this deconstructing textual world, the power relations embedded within white capitalist patriarchy remain intact. Desiderio begins his quest from the "thickly, obtusely masculine" city that "settled serge-clad buttocks at vulgar ease as if in a leather armchair" (15)—a city whose "smug, impenetrable, bourgeois affluence" is achieved at the expense of "indigenous" peoples whose names have now become "unmentionable" (16). At the end of his journey, instead of finding the disruption he expects through the Doctor's liberatory projects, Desiderio finds a "chaste, masculine room . . . with a narrow bed and a black leather armchair . . . and a magazine rack containing current numbers of *Playboy, The New Yorker, Time,* and *Newsweek*" (199). Woman, in Desiderio's narrative, as in the classical quest story, occupies a range of traditional object positions: she is a fetish, a foil, the exotic/erotic object awaiting the hero at the end of his quest, but never a subject. She is, like Derrida's "affirmative woman," an object put into circulation according to the logic of male desire. As object of the male gaze, she is subject to regulation, exploitation and violence.

Desiderio's narrative is, then, an exaggerated form of the mythical quest plot that de Lauretis identifies with the prevalence of Oedipus as paradigm in patriarchal culture. It is exaggerated in that Carter brings to the surface what often remains underground in male-centered fictions: the trajectories of desire whereby Woman becomes merely a foil or a "prize" in the stories of male subjectivity. For her part, Carter sees the primacy of the Oedipus story in culture's master narratives and would seem to agree with Laura Mulvey's observation that "sadism demands a story," and perhaps vice versa.[4] Speaking to the prevalence of erotic violence in representation and other social practices, Carter invokes Oedipus. Acts of violence, she writes,

> . . . reawaken the memory of the social fiction of the female wound, the bleed-
> ing scar left by her castration, which is a psychic fiction as deeply at the heart of
> Western culture as the myth of Oedipus, to which it is related in the complex
> dialectic of imagination and reality that produces culture. Female castration is
> an imaginary fact that pervades the whole of men's attitude towards women
> and our attitude to ourselves, that transforms women from human beings into
> wounded creatures who were born to bleed. (*The Sadeian Woman,* 23)

The Infernal Desire Machines of Doctor Hoffman reinscribes this transformation,
complete with erotic violence unleashed. Oedipal narrative not only keeps
woman "in her place," but does so in order to safeguard male subjectivity
from the "bleeding wound" of difference she represents. This text brings to
the surface the violent excesses of the transformation of women into Woman
by exaggerating the complicities between desire and domination in Western
culture's master narratives.

 The Infernal Desire Machines of Doctor Hoffman mimics male-centered fictions in a particularly ingenious and telling way. In this text, Carter assumes
the mask of maleness, using Desiderio as the only locus of narrative voice and
desire—a gendering of the "I" that the reader cannot forget for one moment.
Desiderio is the architect, or author, of a narrative of sexual exploitation and
violence—a quasi-pornographic writer who enlists an array of misogynist
sentiment and fantasy. In this novel, Carter is playing with a tradition of
pornographic fiction she describes in *The Sadeian Woman,* a tradition marked
by the appropriation of a woman's voice to speak for male sexuality:

> Many pornographic novels are written in the first person as if by a woman, or
> use a woman as the focus of the narrative; but this device only reinforces the
> male orientation of the fiction. John Cleland's *Fanny Hill* and the anonymous
> *The Story of O,* both classics of the genre, appear to describe a woman's mind
> through the fiction of her sexuality. This technique ensures that the gap left in
> the text is of just the right size for the reader to insert his prick into, the exact
> dimensions, in fact, of Fanny's vagina or O's anus. Pornography engages the
> reader in a most intimate fashion before it leaves him to his own resources.
> (15–16)[5]

In *The Infernal Desire Machines of Doctor Hoffman,* Carter appropriates a man's
subjectivity to describe the fictions of his sexuality, but does so self-consciously;
that is, the text foregrounds the problematics of gendered address by deliberately framing the female figures within the text, as well as the woman
reader, as figments of a masculine imaginary. In containing women within a
figure of Woman, Carter demonstrates how Woman is trapped *inside* gender. But, her strategic engagement with fictions of male subjectivity simultaneously demonstrates what it means to be *outside* hegemonic representations of gender, dismantling them from the margins. This text does, in fact,
inscribe a "hole" or gap; but it signifies an absence, rather than a presence.

While Woman is everywhere present in this novel, women are conspicuously absent.

How, then, does a text that seems so violently to foreclose on female subjectivity be read as a feminist critique of narrative structures? Or, to put it in slightly different terms, if Carter's text details the dangerous economies of male desire lurking behind narrative and representation, does it simply reinforce the power of these economies, thus closing off the possibility of changing them? How can one tell the difference between construction and deconstruction?[6] Linda Hutcheon, for one, wonders if it is possible to tell the difference at all. She claims that postmodernist artistic practices both use and abuse history, tradition, representation, humanist ideology, and so on. Through parody, the texts of postmodernism *inscribe* in order to *subvert* the master narratives of Western culture, a practice that results in what she calls the "political ambidexterity" of postmodernism. She writes: "Postmodernism knows it cannot escape implication in the economic (late capitalist) and ideological (liberal humanist) dominants of its time. There is no outside. All it can do is question from within" (*Poetics,* xiii). However, Hutcheon notes that perhaps women have more to win, than to lose, from critique of the politics of representation; and, further, that feminist postmodern practice would have little to gain through a "legitimation" of that which it critiques.[7] In other words, feminist postmodernist parody has a political stake in disrupting representations of woman, and such disruptions are marked by the desire to change these representations. The feminist postmodernist text

> . . . parodically inscribes the conventions of feminine representation, provokes our conditioned response and then subverts that response, making us aware of how it was induced in us. To work it must be complicitous with the values in challenges; we have to feel the seduction in order to question it and then to theorize the site of that contradiction. Such feminist use of postmodern tactics *politicize desire* in their play with the revealed and the hidden, the offered and the deferred. (*Politics,* 154, my emphasis)

Carter's text does, indeed, politicize desire, and does so by playing with the conventions of pornographic address, a strategy that Hutcheon notes in other feminist texts. Carter foregrounds the text's enunciative apparatus by making explicit the complicities between desire and domination. Throughout all of Desiderio's adventures, his subjectivity is guaranteed by his objectification of women—of all races, classes, and sexual orientations—who are never, in this text, "fully human" (73). They are "erotic toys," mutilated bodies, phallic mothers, castrating Amazons who are all punished for the crime of being female. Except, that is, for Albertina, the Doctor's daughter, who is punished, to be sure—in a gang rape by a group of Centaurs; but she is also the supreme object of desire, the "inexpressible woman" (13) who takes different shapes according to the logic of Desiderio's desire. Because of the mechanisms of identification built into a first-person quest narrative, this text seems to address its readers as male: as subjects who can enjoy, along with Desiderio, the triumphs of his desire. As feminist theorists of narrative film have suggested, when a woman reader approaches such a text, she may well find herself engaged in a split identification: the narrative positions her to identify with the (male) protagonist by various mechanisms, such as first-person narration as the locus of desire; while, by virtue of her gender, she may also feel identification with the female or feminine forces in the narrative.[8] The overt masculinization of the narrative in Carter's text, however, serves to subvert the mechanisms of identification that support the successful narrativization of violence against women. Carter's mimicry of pornographic narrative—an exaggerated form of all narratives mobilized by male desire—confronts the issue of gendered address head-on by placing the woman reader in an impossible position. There is, quite simply, *no place* for a woman reader in this text; and that no place foregrounds the hom(m)osexual economy Carter is mimicking in it.

The text, then, paradoxically addresses its reader as *feminist* by de-naturalizing the processes by which narrative constructs differences—sexual, racial, class, national—according to the twin logics of desire and domination; that is, it invites the reader to occupy a position not sanctioned by Desiderio's narrative itself but, rather, a position on the outside of that narrative. Carter's text offers this outsider position through a disruption of identification in a number of ways. First, and most obvious, is the fact that, because Desiderio is so clearly complicit in his adventures—which include a number of rapes and female mutilations—a reader who identifies with him will uncomfortably share in his complicity. Second, because the text makes explicit the economies of male desire behind representations of women, the reader does not so easily get seduced into identification—either with Desiderio, or with the female figures he encounters (constructs) on his journey. In other words, there is no illusion of "reality" in this text which might mask the fact that Desiderio's desire is the motor force of the narrative, and we are, thus, constantly aware that none of his constructions of women are "natural." The text demonstrates how Woman is *produced,* rather than simply represented, in narratives of male desire and subjectivity. Finally, Carter makes explicit the "underside" of narrative and history through the use and abuse of pornographic narrative conventions. This "underside"—the mechanics of desire and pleasure as they function beneath the violent and de-humanizing fictions of masculinist pornographic narrative—is brought to the surface and, thus, problematizes the identification that is necessary in order for pornography to do its "work."[9]

The text contains a number of explicit references to pornographic representation, including a couple of scenes straight out of the pages of the Marquis de Sade, and a "Peep Show," where very familiar representations are defamiliarized by being framed with ironic titles. If the text is pornographic, it is what Carter calls "pornography in the service of women." She speculates, in

The Sadeian Woman, that a political "pornographer would not be the enemy of women, perhaps because he might begin to penetrate to the heart of the contempt for women that distorts our culture even as he entered the realms of true obscenity as he describes it" (20). The use of the masculine pronoun here, always gendered in Carter's work, foregrounds, I think, the reasons behind her appropriation of male subjectivity in her novel. Because, according to Carter, pornography is representation by and for men, her intervention into the politics of representation must be, as Linda Hutcheon puts it, from the inside. Yet something of the "outside" of this representation remains in the novel, a critical perspective akin to the one Luce Irigaray claims as that which remains through women's mimicry. The text refuses to guarantee a voyeuristic or narcissistic position for its readers—male and female—because its metafictional strategies continuously disrupt the "pleasure" such positions traditionally afford. Take, for example, this description of the female figures who people the Sadeian "House of Anonymity" that Desiderio visits:

> Each was as circumscribed as a figure in rhetoric and you could not imagine they had names, for they had been reduced by the rigorous discipline of their vocation to the undifferentiated essence of the idea of the female. This ideational femaleness took amazingly different shapes though its nature was not that of Woman; when I examined them closely, I saw that none of them were any longer, or might never have been, woman. All, without exception, passed beyond or did not enter the realm of simple humanity. They were sinister, abominable, inverted mutations, part clockwork, part vegetable and part brute. (132)

Desiderio's confusion here marks the contradictions Carter sees in the construction of Woman through pornographic narrative. Are these figures women or Woman? Both and neither, it would seem, as Desiderio is forced to confront his complicity in the de-humanization of the objects of his desire. This passage is more like literary criticism than it is like pornography: here, Carter deconstructs representations of women as the machines of male pleasure, bringing to its logical conclusion the ideology of pornography that reduces agents to mere functions. Such a reduction removes sexuality and erotic domination from the social world and makes the "pursuit of pleasure" into "a metaphysical quest" (*The Sadeian Woman,* 16). Carter aims in *The Infernal Desire Machines* to show how "sexual relations between men and women always render explicit the nature of social relations in the society in which they take place" and how, "if described explicitly, will form a critique of those relations" (*The Sadeian Woman,* 20).

Carter's critique of desire as domination works through a literalization—or de-metaphorization—of the structures of male fantasy underlying traditional, and not so traditional, quest narratives. The notion of woman as "ideational femaleness" that "can take amazingly different shapes" in Carter's text resonates thematically with the philosophical trend chronicled by Jardine in *Gynesis*. Hoffman is a figure intent on liberating the repressed of culture, on exploring the margins of philosophy and reason—precisely, the "feminine" disorder that complements masculine order. At the end of the novel, we learn that the Doctor believes in the "inherent symmetry of divergent asymmetry" modeled on the "intercommunication of seed between male and female all things produced" (213), and represented, predictably, by his daughter Albertina. This woman-figure, like Irigaray's Athena, speaks the word of the father and makes that word flesh. The "divergent asymmetry" to which the Doctor refers is gender difference and Albertina's gender fluidity throughout the novel serves, not to blur the boundaries of sexual difference in order to liberate us from the tyranny of absolute division by gender, but to perpetuate the whole metaphysical apparatus as it works around the question of sexual difference. The fact that Hoffman's metaphysics are *openly* based on sexual difference does not significantly differentiate them from the old system against which he is working; as in Derrida's appropriation of the feminine in a new narrative of sexual difference, here we see a female object put into circulation according to a male desire to control representation. The "inherent symmetry" turns out not to be a symmetry at all; the male figures in the text retain power over the female, and put this power into play as Hoffman's "liberation of desire" results in increased objectification of, and sexual violence against, women. As Alice Jardine suggests, there tends to be a congruence between valorizations of the "feminine" as the repressed or "unnameable," and increased narrativization of violence against women in male-authored fictions.[10]

That Albertina Hoffman is as malleable as an ideational femaleness makes of her a fetish object. The blurring of "reality" and "fantasy" in this text, in fact, works by a fetishistic logic that makes of woman a tool of man's pleasure and self-representation. The mechanism of fetishism in classic Hollywood narrative is what leads Laura Mulvey to claim that "sadism demands a story," and to argue that that story entails the disavowal of the threat of castration represented by the woman in the narrative. Carter's novel actively engages with the fetishistic economy that Mulvey identifies in order to show how the "bleeding wound" of female castration sets off the trajectories of male desire for domination. A brief digression back into Derrida, via Freud, is in order here in that it will allow me to suggest how fetishism, like Oedipal narrative, places woman in the middle of male crises as a space across which the subject must travel in order to safeguard his subjectivity and self-representation. For, in spite of Alice Jardine's claim that "the crisis in the discursive itineraries of Western philosophy . . . involves first and foremost a problematization of the boundaries and spaces necessary to their existence, and this, in turn, involves a disruption of the male and female connotations upon which the latter depend" (71), a metaphorical version of this ideological representation of gender still obtains in the privileging of woman as a solution to that discursive crisis. As Mary Ann Doane points out, investigations of woman always mask a more pressing question for male subjectivity, "What signifies man?": "The claim to investigate an otherness is a pretense, haunted by the mirror-effect by means of which the question of the woman reflects only the man's own ontological doubts" ("Film and the Masquerade," 74–75).

Jardine suggests a causal logic behind Derrida's, and others', move toward the "feminine," and that logic has more than a slightly Freudian ring to it: "in the search for new kinds of legitimation, in the absence of Truth, in *anxiety* over the decline of paternal authority, and in the midst of spiraling diagnoses of Paranoia, the End of Man and History, "woman" has been set in motion both rhetorically and ideologically" (36, my emphasis). I highlight *anxiety* in her comment in order to suggest that the inscription of woman in modernity's texts can be read as a paranoid reaction which reproduces a certain castration scenario in relation to the death of the paternal metaphor, or the crisis in culture's master narratives. Because that crisis explicitly has to do with the loss of phallic privilege, it seems almost inevitable, given the fact that our cultural imaginations are dominated by Freudian problematics, that a certain anxiety would follow in its wake. The "solution" to this crisis is metaphorically akin to what Freud describes as the fetishist's solution to the problem of sexual difference.[11] The rhetoric of *Spurs,* with its emphasis on a simultaneous veiling/unveiling as the woman's operation, replicates Freud's discourse on the fetish.[12] Woman is a metaphor constructed according to a male desire reminiscent of the fetishist's desire to simultaneously affirm and disavow the threat to his narcissism that the woman represents, a threat evoked in the absence of paternal authority and the privilege of the phallus. In *Spurs,* the feminine is thus what Judith Roof calls a decoy, in that she functions to mask the text's hom(m)osexuality by representing a sexual difference which, ultimately, serves only to facilitate an exchange between men.[13] Derrida's text inscribes *"women's role as fetish-objects,* inasmuch as, in exchanges, they are the manifestation and the circulation of a power of the Phallus, establishing relationships of men with each other" (Irigaray, *This Sex,* 183). She is also a decoy in the sense that this figure draws attention away from what I am reading as the male philosopher's desire to retain the phallic privilege, including the privilege of subjectivity. As Shoshana Felman observes in another context, "ironically enough, femininity itself turns out to be metaphor of the phallus" (24–25).

In explaining fetishism, Freud highlights its status as an operation of undecidability: the construction of the fetish represents "both the disavowal and the affirmation of . . . castration" ("Fetishism," 156). The both/and logic of the fetish would undermine the notion of castration as truth-effect in that a fetishist can have it both ways: by constructing a fetish, he maintains that woman is both castrated and not castrated, and thus alleviates his own castration anxiety while retaining his belief in woman's lack. Fetishism, in Freud, serves to maintain the subject's belief in a sexual difference based on presence/absence; and, since the fetish "is a substitute for the woman's (the mother's) penis" (152), what is at stake in the fetishist's desire is the priority (or transcendence) of the phallic value. For any reader familiar with Derrida's discourse, it will come as no surprise that the fetishist's logic seems particularly appropriate to describe the deconstructive enterprise. What is attractive for Derrida in the fetish is that its construction "rests *at once* on the denial and on the affirmation, the assertion or the assumption of castration. This at-once, the in-the-same-stroke, the *du-même-coup* of the two contraries, of the two opposite operations, prohibits cutting through to a decision within the undecidable" (*Glas,* 210ai).[14] The fetish joins other privileged Derridean figures of oscillation and undecidability in having the power to undo oppositional thinking and the dialectic. In his reading of Freud's "Fetishism," Derrida foregrounds "the double bond and the undecidable mobility of the fetish, its power of excess in relation to the opposition (true/nontrue, substitute/nonsubstitute, denial/affirmation, and so on)" (*Glas,* 211ai).

What Derrida elides in his reading of Freud's text is the male narcissism at stake in fetishism. Freud writes:

> What happened, therefore, was that the boy refused to take cognizance of the fact of his having perceived that a woman does not possess a penis. No, that could not be true: for if a woman had been castrated, then his own possession of a penis was in danger; and against that there rose in rebellion the portion of his narcissism which Nature has, as a precaution, attached to that particular organ. [The same Nature, one presumes, that has been "less kind to women."[15]] In later life a grown man may perhaps experience a similar panic when the cry goes up that Throne and Altar are in danger, and similar illogical consequences will ensue. ("Fetishism," 153)

Clearly, Throne and Altar, as paternal signifiers, are in danger in contemporary critical discourse—even if deliberately so. It is my contention that the crisis in masculine subjectivity within these discourses has led to a fetishization of woman as a substitute for the missing phallus. Indeed, in *Spurs,* we can see the narcissistic investment at stake in privileging a woman-fetish; this figure allows the male philosopher to disavow his participation in phallogocentric systems while simultaneously saving himself from the fear of castration. The woman, as woman, remains a threatening figure in *Spurs;* it is only when she is constructed as a fetish—that is, as a substitute for the phallus—that she is "affirmative." Woman, as woman, is outside this economy; or, rather, she/we is/are trapped within its narrative, "framed" by its male-centered construction of sexual difference.

In Carter's text, Oedipus/Desiderio creates a fetish object, in the person of Albertina, a figure marked by undecidability. Like Derrida's woman-figure, Albertina is nearly impossible to pin down; she assumes numerous different identities, experiences gender fluidity, and takes any form that Desiderio's desire imposes on her. He seeks her as his "Platonic other, [his] necessary extinction, [his] dream made flesh" (215) and, as such, she can take any form;

she is an idea, not a woman—or, more precisely, she is Woman, rather than *a* woman. As our protagonist himself comes to realize, she "was inextricably mingled with [his] idea of her and her substance was so flexible she could have worn a left glove on her right hand" (142). This woman-object serves as a decoy to mask the real object of desire—the father cum-phallus-cum "Master." What actually circulates in hom(m)osexual economies, then, is not the woman, but the phallus represented by the woman. As Gayle Rubin observes in her analysis of Freud and Levi-Strauss, the interfamily exchange of women coincides with another, intrafamily, exchange: "in the cycle of exchange manifested by the Oedipal complex, the phallus passes through the medium of women from one man to another. . . . In this family *Kula* ring, women go one way, the phallus goes another. . . . It is an expression of the transmission of male dominance. It passes through women and settles upon men" (192). Desiderio himself eventually realizes that "perhaps the whole history of my adventure could be titled 'Desiderio in Search of a Master.' But I only wanted to find a master . . . so that I could lean on him at first and then, after a while, jeer" (190). Albertina's role here is to mediate between Desiderio and Hoffman, just as the affirmative woman's role in *Spurs* is to mediate between Derrida and Nietzsche.

Desiderio is literally fatherless: his mother, a prostitute, conceived him through her work in the Indian slums of the city. Thus, not only has his mother deprived him of a present father, but also, forced him to carry the "genetic imprint" of this lost father "on his face" (16). And, while he disclaims his Indian heritage in his life before Hoffman's revolution, this repressed material gets released once the desire machines start their work. Thus it is that Desiderio finds himself "adopted" by a family of "River people" in an adventure that plays out his ambivalence toward his mother's actions and his father's race. During his time with the river people, Desiderio's colonialist imagination is given full scope, as he constructs this isolated society as "excentric": primitive, naive, living with "a complex, hesitant but absolute immediacy" (71).[16] Not surprisingly, this way of life is encoded as "feminine": the River People don't "think in straight lines," but in "subtle and intricate interlocking circles"; concepts are relational, rather than absolute, opposites existing in "a locked tension"; the written form of their language is "beautiful," but "utterly lacking in signification" (75); and so on. Their society is "theoretically matrilinear though in practice all decisions devolved upon the father" (80). Because everything that happens to Desiderio is an emanation of his desires, we can read in this episode a nostalgic return to the "feminine," to his (absent) mother and the threat that this return evokes.

That threat, of course, is castration, and Desiderio's adventure with the river family replays the Freudian family romance in a new, although still recognizable, way. It is assumed that he will become the husband of one of the clan's daughter, Aoi, whom Desiderio consistently refers to as an "erotic toy" (86). In preparation for her marriage, Aoi's grandmother has manipulated her clitoris over the years, until it approximates a penis. Desiderio cannot help approving this practice: "[I]t was the custom for mothers of young girls to manipulate their daughters' private parts for a regulation hour a day from babyhood upwards, coaxing the sensitive little projection until it attained lengths the river people considered both aesthetically and sexually desirable" (84). What is important here is not so much this practice itself, but Desiderio's interpretation of it; from his male-centered frame of reference, the women are aspiring to masculinity.[17] His desire to masculinize the women amounts to a fetishistic desire to endow his "erotic toy" with a penis. He leaves the river people, reluctantly, after it becomes clear that the father is about to make good on the threat of castration—but not, however, until he succeeds in sleeping with the mother. It is this experience which prompts Desiderio to remark, "Indeed, I was growing almost reconciled to mothers" (85).

Desiderio's desire constructs women as phallic in order to alleviate his anxieties over his own masculinity, evoked by the absence of his father. We have Mamie Buckskin, a "freak" in a circus who is trapped within a conventional narrative from classical Hollywood Westerns. Mamie, Desiderio tells us, "was a paradox—a fully phallic female with the bosom of a nursing mother and a gun, death-dealing erectile tissue, perpetually at her thigh" (108). We have the tribe of Amazons on the coast of Africa who are much more threatening, the destructive mother of male fantasy, with a vengeance. The massive black cheiftain who presides over this tribe, a figure of racist fantasy, tells Desiderio and his companions about why he has chosen women to be his warriors—that is, after all "capacity for feeling" has been excised from them through clitorodectomy:

> Why, you may ask, have I built my army out of women since they are often held to be the gentler sex? Gentleman, if you rid your hearts of prejudice and examine the bases of the traditional notions of the figure of the female, you will find you have founded them all on the remote figure you thought you glimpsed, once, in your earliest childhood, bending over you with an offering of warm, sugared milk. . . . Tear this notion of the mother from your hearts. Vengeful as nature herself, she loves her children only in order to devour them better and if she herself rips her own veils of self-deceit, Mother perceives in herself untold abysses of cruelty as subtle as it is refined. (160)

Like the female figures in the House of Anonymity, these women "have passed far beyond all human feeling" (160), which is, of course, where both the cheiftain and Desiderio want them. They are not "human" because they have been dehumanized and it is the logic of Desiderio's desire that evokes these destructive, cannibalizing women. While the cheiftain, and Desiderio, thus, debunk one myth of femininity, they replace it with another: the all-good mother gives way to her opposite, both of whom are constructions of cultures where motherhood, whether revered or reviled, is the a priori condition of femaleness.

This adventure, like the episode with the River People, clearly shows how desire and domination are complicit and points to what I am reading as the text's inscription and subversion of a colonialist mentality. From here, Desiderio and Albertina move on to visit a tribe of centaurs who are evoked through a Western fantasy of "primitive" cultures. The complex religious mythology that governs the centaurs' lives is merely a translation of Christian mythology, complete with a genesis story, a Christ figure, resurrection, and salvation. As Brian McHale points out, Carter "has constructed an Africa wholly derived from European fantasy. She populates its coast with cannibal tribesmen straight out of party jokes, comic-strips, and slapstick comedy; while in the interior she places centaurs, in effect suppressing indigenous mythology in favor of an imported European myth. This is imperialism of the imagination, and Carter knows it; indeed, her purpose is to foreground it and expose it for what it is" (55). McHale further notes that these African figures are all "reifications of European desire"—especially since they are the figments of Desiderio's imaginary. But what McHale does not note is the continuity of violent misogyny we can discern throughout all of these adventures, a misogyny that is as much a part of an imperialist imagination. The centaurs, for example, "believed that women were only born to suffer" (172), and, thus, "the females were ritually degraded and reviled" (176). Desiderio, while not exactly applauding this orientation to sexual difference, respects this culture for elevating the "virile principle" to such a degree. He watches, "indifferently," while Albertina suffers a gang rape by the centaurs, later observing that "even the rape had had elements of the kind of punishment said to hurt the giver more than the receiver though I do not know what they were punishing her for, unless it was for being female to a degree unprecedented among them" (181). Later, when the centaurs understand that Albertina is Desiderio's mate, "and therefore [his] property" (182), they apologize to him for their "punishment" of Albertina's "crime." To put the finishing touches on this construction of femininity, Carter has Albertina suggest that the centaurs were an emanation of her desire, not Desiderio's, and that the gang rape was "dredged up and objectively reified from the dark abysses of [her] unconscious" (186).

The quest plot that structures *The Infernal Desire Machines of Doctor Hoffman* is a contorted version of Oedipal narrative that Carter uses to foreground the ideological stakes in this kind of story. Because Desiderio's adventures represent a direct expression of his desire—both conscious and unconscious—the text serves as a commentary on the gendering of that desire as masculine. This novel is an in-depth exploration of male subjectivity in narrative, and the construction of sexual difference along binary and often violent lines; as such, it foregrounds the problematics in reading as a woman. Yet Carter systematically disrupts the pleasure of the text by foregrounding the enunciative apparatus behind its inscriptions of desire. If the pleasure of the text is dependent on identification with Desiderio who, after all, has been produced as a "war hero" by History, that pleasure is continuously disrupted by Carter's insistence on what that official History leaves unspoken: the complicities between desire and domination. Desire, in this text, ultimately destroys both its subject and its object. For, although Desiderio emerges intact from his adventures, Carter deprives him at the last minute, of his "climax": he fails, after all, to find either a worthy master-father, since Hoffman turns out to be a "hypocrite," a "totalitarian of the unconscious"; or the object of desire, since Albertina must be killed in order for Desiderio to fulfill his mission and become a "hero." Desiderio, in turn, deprives his imagined reader of that climax, as well, breaking the pattern of narrative dénouement which would ensure the pleasure of the text through the release of tension, modeled, as Peter Brooks and others seem to assume, on male sexuality: "See, I have ruined all the suspense. I have quite spoiled my climax. But why do you deserve a climax, anyway?" (208). But the pleasure of this text resides elsewhere, an "alternative thrill," as Laura Mulvey would say, "that comes from leaving the past behind without rejecting it . . . or daring to break with normal pleasurable expectations in order to conceive a new language of desire" ("Visual Pleasure," 8). That thrill, in Carter's text, comes from the negotiation of seduction by and resistance to narrative forms and their production of gender.

In Linda Hutcheon's terms, the text "seduces" its readers into certain constructions of Woman, through its use of traditional conventions of first-person quest narrative. These conventions ensure that Man's self-representation is achieved through his objectification, appropriation, and exploitation of feminine figures: Self can only be realized in opposition to others. But Carter's exaggeration and literalization of these conventions serves to deconstruct the processes by which narrative engenders the subject as male through a violent negation of female subjectivity. Unlike Hutcheon, who implies that construction and deconstruction cancel each other out, and thus, leaves postmodern parody floundering in "political ambidexterity," I have argued that this double strategy in Carter's text carries a sharp ideological critique that is not neutralized by the fact that the text does, in fact, represent Woman in all too traditional ways.[18] On the contrary, it is through Carter's strategic engagement with various master narratives of Western culture that her critique of the politics of representation emerges. While this text presents many difficulties for a feminist reading, those difficulties foreground the stakes in pursuing such a reading. Carter is no idealist, not one to take a utopian leap beyond normative representations of Woman to some uncontaminated representation of women; rather, her text inscribes, in order to subvert, representations that produce women as Woman.

Notes

1. In both of Hutcheon's books, *A Poetics of Postmodernism* and *The Politics of Postmodernism,* she insists, repetitively that postmodernism's "complicitous critique" can only question; it paradoxically "both legitimizes and subverts that which it parodies" (*Politics,* 101). I will

question Hutcheon's certainty about the political ambidexterity of postmodernism later in this chapter.

2. Brian McHale, in *Postmodernist Fiction,* points to the text's Manichean opposition between the Apollonian Minister of Justice and the Dionysian Hoffman. But, in describing Hoffman as the "agent of fantasy and pleasure" (143), he banishes gender from this scene, and elides the question that is central to the text: *Whose* fantasy, and *whose* pleasure?

3. See Brooks, *Reading for the Plot* for an analysis of desire as the (phallic) "piston" of narrative, its "motor force."

4. Mulvey, "Visual Pleasure" (15–17). de Lauretis, in *Alice Doesn't,* explores the reversal of Mulvey's claim. See, particularly, 103 and 109.

5. For other, interesting, feminist discussions of *The Story of O,* see Kaja Silverman, *"Histoire d'O:* The Construction of a Female Subject," and Nancy K. Miller, "The Text's Heroine."

6. I wish to thank the students in my seminar on "Gender, Desire and Contemporary Fiction" at Case Western Reserve University for prompting me to consider these difficult questions.

7. Interestingly, when Hutcheon focuses explicitly on feminist postmodernist practice, her certainty about postmodernism's operations breaks down, particularly in her reading of Hannah Wilke's nude self-portrait. Wilke offers her image to the spectator between two slogans—"Marxism and Art" and "Beware of Fascist Feminism"—and Hutcheon is troubled by what she senses as the text's legitimation of masculinist images of female desire, as well as its seemingly anti-feminist ideology. Hutcheon's response to this photograph deserves quotation in its entirety: "If 'fascist feminism' meant prudish feminism, then the commodification of the female body in male art . . . might be what such feminism underwrites by refusing woman the use of her own body and its pleasures. But what about the position of the addressed viewer: is it voyeuristic, narcissistic, critical? Can we even tell? Does the work problematize or confirm the maleness of the gaze? I really cannot tell. In the face of the manifest contradictions of this work, it is tempting to say that, while Wilke is clearly playing with the conventions of pornographic address (her eyes meet and engage the viewer's) she is also juxtaposing this with the discourse of feminist protest—but turned against itself in some way. She does not make her own position clear and thus risks reinforcing what she might well be intending to contest, that is, patriarchal notions of female sexuality and male desire" (*Politics,* 159). This reading of the photograph, if we took out the questions and uncertainties, would qualify Wilke's work as postmodernist in the terms Hutcheon has set up and developed throughout both her books. That is, postmodernist art both "problematizes and confirms"—or legitimizes and subverts—the politics of representation. But the questions she asks here, it is worth noting, do not inform her readings of the texts of postmodernism produced by men. Nowhere else in her study does Hutcheon ask about the position of the viewer or reader, nor does she seem to think it problematic that postmodernist art does not "make its own position clear." There are two possible conclusions we could reach here: one, that feminist art doesn't really "qualify" as postmodernist; and, two, that feminist artists might have a slightly different stake in their articulations of "complicitous critique."

8. See Mulvey, "Afterthoughts" and Doane, "Film and the Masquerade."

9. According to Carter, pornography is "art with work to do"—its chief function being the arousal of sexual desire (*The Sadeian Woman,* 12). Carter disdains the opposition between pornography and erotica on the grounds of a class analysis, noting that erotica is "the pornography of the elite" (17).

10. Jardine never explicitly makes this point, but implies it in her discussions of fictional fantasies of (female) dismemberments and the like.

11. See my "Misappropriations of the Feminine" for a much more detailed analysis of fetishism in Derrida/Freud.

12. See Mary Ann Doane, "Veiling Over Desire: Close-ups of the Woman," for a fascinating and theoretically broad reading of the trope of the veil in Nietzsche, Derrida, Lacan, Irigaray, and various films which feature veiled women.

13. Roof's notion of the decoy is elaborated in her discussion of Diane Kurys' film *Entre Nous*, in her forthcoming book, *A Lure of Knowledge*. At one point, in reference to Lacan, Roof makes a suggestive connection between the fetish and the decoy: "the decoy, like the fetish, represents something which is essentially absent and its reassuring presence hides the threat of castration that lurks behind its production." Briefly, Roof argues that the film creates a series of decoys through its subversive use of conventional cinematic narrative techniques, such as a narrative economy which raises in the spectator both the expectation of and desire for what Roof calls "a traditional male narrative climax"—that is, a desire for the visual "revelation and representation of female *jouissance* in a lesbian confrontation between the two protagonists." What is subversive in the film is that the spectator is, in effect, "seduced" by this series of decoys—which chart the illusory trajectory of male desire—only to find that the decoys stand in for what is not there. Because the sexual encounters between the two women all take place off screen, Roof suggests that the film not only subverts the spectator's identification with a controlling male gaze—in the camera—but also, in effect, decenters the conventional cinematic apparatus and the scopophilic and fetishistic economies supported by that apparatus. Although I don't to it here, it would be possible to read the woman and the fetish as decoys in Roof's particular sense of the term to argue that Derrida attempts to seduce a (possibly feminist) reader. In this case, however, the "subversion" would fall to the reader.

14. Page references to *Glas* cite page number and column. The "i" indicates an insert in the column.

15. This comment can be found in "Femininity," 116, and relates to woman's "inferior" genital apparatus.

16. Linda Hutcheon notes that this episode "reveals the extreme of . . . ex-centric ethnicity" and that Carter "uses this society to ironic and satiric ends" (*Poetics*, 71).

17. Carter here is mimicking a scene from Sade, in which a woman sports her "flexible clitoris-cum-prick" (*The Sadeian Woman*, 112).

18. Robert Clark comes to an opposite conclusion in his reading of "Angela Carter's Desire Machine." For Clark, Carter's work, in general, fails to include "within its own critical representation an understanding of the complicity of that representation with the social forces it appears to reject" (154). Further, according to Clark, "Carter's insight into the patriarchal construction of feminity has a way of being her blindness: her writing is often a feminism in a male chauvinist drag, a transvestite style, and this may be because her primary allegience is to a postmodern aesthetics that emphasizes the non-referential emptiness of definitions. Such a commitment precludes an affirmative feminism founded in referential commitment to women's historical and organic being. Only in patriarchal eyes is femininity an empty category, the negation of masculinity" (158). Apart from the fact that the second statement seems to contradict the first, underlying these comments is an assumption of an essential femininity—an "organic being"—that Carter's "transvestite" style, in fact, works to deconstruct. Clark would have Carter leave behind what I am reading as her radical critique and focus, instead, on some affirmation that would place women *outside* patriarchal eyes.

Works Cited

Brooks, Peter. *Reading for the Plot: Design and Intention in Narrative.* New York: Alfred A. Knopf, 1984.

Carter, Angela. *The Infernal Desire Machines of Doctor Hoffman.* 1972. Rpt. New York: Penguin Books, 1985.

———. *The Sadeian Woman and the Ideology of Pornography.* 1978. Rpt. New York: Pantheon Books, 1988.

Clark, Robert. "Angela Carter's Desire Machine." *Women's Studies* 14, No. 2 (1987): 147–61.

Culler, Jonathan. *On Deconstruction: Theory and Criticism after Structuralism.* Ithaca: Cornell University Press, 1982.

de Lauretis, Teresa. *Alice Doesn't: Feminism, Semiotics, Cinema.* Bloomington: Indiana University Press, 1984.

————., ed. *Feminist Studies/Critical Studies.* Bloomington: Indiana University Press, 1987.

————. *Technologies of Gender: Essays on Theory, Film, and Fiction.* Bloomington: Indiana University Press, 1987.

Derrida, Jacques. *Dissemination.* Trans. Barbara Johnson. Chicago: University of Chicago Press, 1981.

————. *Glas.* 1974. Trans. John P. Leavey, Jr. Lincoln: University of Nebraska Press, 1986.

————. *Spurs/Eperons.* 1976. Trans. Barbara Harlow. Chicago: University of Chicago Press, 1979.

Doane, Mary Ann. "Film and the Masquerade: Theorising the Female Spectator." *Screen* 23 (Sept./Oct. 1982): 74–87.

————. "Veiling Over Desire: Close-ups of the Woman." Richard Feldstein and Judith Roof, eds. *Feminism and Psychoanalysis.* Ithaca: Cornell University Press, 1989, 105–41.

Freud, Sigmund. "Femininity." In *New Introductory Lectures on Psychoanalysis.* 1933. Trans. James Strachey. New York: W.W. Norton, 1965, 99–119.

————. "Fetishism." 1927. *The Standard Edition of the Complete Psychological Works.* 24 Vols. Trans. James Strachey. London: Hogarth, 1955. 21:152–57.

Fuss, Diana. *Essentially Speaking: Feminism, Nature and Difference.* New York and London: Routledge, 1989.

Hutcheon, Linda. *A Poetics of Postmodernism: History, Theory, Fiction.* New York and London: Routledge, 1988.

————. *The Politics of Postmodernism.* New York and London: Routledge, 1989.

Jardine, Alice. *Gynesis: Configurations of Woman and Modernity.* Ithaca: Cornell University Press, 1985.

McHale, Brian. *Postmodernist Fiction.* New York and London: Methuen, 1987.

Miller, Nancy K. "The Text's Heroine: A Feminist Critic and Her Fictions." *Diacritics* 12 (1982): 48–53.

Modleski, Tania. "Feminism and the Power of Interpretation: Some Critical Readings." de Lauretis, ed., 121–38.

Mulvey, Laura. "Afterthoughts on 'Visual Pleasure and Narrative Cinema' Inspired by 'Duel in the Sun' (King Vidor, 1946)." *Framework* Nos. 15, 16, 17 (1981): 12–15.

————. "Visual Pleasure and Narrative Cinema." *Screen* 16, No. 3 (1975): 6–18.

Robinson, Sally. "Misappropriations of the Feminine." *Substance* 59 (Fall 1989): 48–70.

Roof, Judith. *A Lure of Knowledge: Lesbian Sexuality and Theory.* New York: Columbia University Press, forthcoming, 1991.

Rubin, Gayle. "The Traffic in Women: Notes on the 'Political Economy' of Sex." Reiter Raynor, ed. *Toward an Anthropology of Women.* New York: Monthly Review Press, 1978, 157–210.

Silverman, Kaja. "*Histoire de'O:* The Construction of a Female Subject." Carole Vance, ed. *Pleasure and Danger: Exploring Female Sexuality.* Boston: Routledge & Kegan Paul, 1984, 320–49.

The Body of the City:
Angela Carter's *The Passion of New Eve*

NICOLETTA VALLORANI

"that shadowy land between the thinkable and the thing thought of"
—Angela Carter, *The Infernal Desire Machines of Dr. Hoffmann.*

1. **Building the body of the city.** The following is an essay on the representation of utopian cities in feminist science fiction, particularly the way it is exploited, interpreted, reversed, and reflected in Angela Carter's *PNE*. The main character of the story, a young Englishman called Evelyn, reports his journey through a dark and decayed New York, his escape to the desert, his arrival in a female community—where he is to be transformed into the New Eve—and his experiences as a woman in Zero's town. Three different urban spaces are described as complex metaphors of the interior space. For the purposes of this discussion, we will consider both the urban reality that provides the underlying structure of any utopian city and the fictional shape of utopia that, being fictional, is bracketed off from the world it represent.[1]

As an operational strategy, let us simplify and begin with the assumption that the passage from reality to the imagination implies a transcoding process: i.e., the symbols of what can be empirically perceived are to be translated into the complex web of metaphors that define the literary imagination. Understandably, the message becomes ambiguous, because ambiguity is inherent in the polysemy of signs. Cognition, therefore, becomes a complex process because it flows through fabulation and consequently is filtered through the perception of reality as a labyrinth, a tangible enigma of imaginative bricks and mortar which leads towards several conflicting solutions.

In the process of giving a definite—but never conclusive—shape to our vision of utopian cities, we may posit an analogy and a sort of contiguity between the physical body of a person and the urban body of a city. Thus we may read the signs in the urban space as we read wrinkles on the skin.[2]

From *Science-Fiction Studies* 21 (1994): 365–79. © 1994 DePauw University. Reprinted by permission.

The fictional city, in other words, is created through a process of doubling, with the literary purpose of articulating the psychological and physical bodies of the people living within its boundaries. An urban dimension conceived in this way augments the semantic load of the individual body and organizes it into a new pattern. The signifying system is amplified and gains imaginative and analogic veracity. An even further and deeper articulation, however, may obtain when the field of reference is no longer and not only utopia as such, but sexed utopia, that is, utopia as a genre which is given a definite gender. This gender is, in our case, female.

"As a woman," writes Marge Piercy, "I experience a city as a minefield. I am always a potential quarry, or target, or victim" (210). This perception of the city is a first stab towards correctly approaching Angela Carter's *PNE*. In Piercy's words, real cities are defined as dangerous places for women who end up being almost unavoidably isolated and marginalized however hard they try to react to this process. To a certain extent, the vision is similar when our reference is no longer the city defined in gendered terms, but the urban stereotype in modern fiction.

Burton Pike describes this stereotype: "During the nineteenth century, the literary city came more and more to express the isolation or exclusion of the individual from a community, and in the twentieth century to express the fragmentation of the very concept of community" (Pike, xii). *Civitas,* therefore, is felt to oppose *communitas;* the two terms, which used to pertain to the same semantic field, are now definitely divorced. Human solidarity as a vital link is dissolved and individuals are connected only through their incidental sharing of the same space. The feminist imagination, while appropriating this vision, problematizes the issue by redoubling urban isolation through the depiction of female marginalization in the city. A gendered space results.

Wendy Martin, quoting Julia Kristeva, Hélène Cixous and Luce Irigaray, and referring to the female perspective they adopt in their criticism, writes: "Women need to think with their bodies and, if possible, to return to the preoedipal experience, before the patriarchal grid imposed the bifurcation of mind and body, self and other" (258). In blunt terms, what is suggested here is that for women the process of rebuilding their original identity is to be filtered through a female space which is no longer defined as external to the body, but rather as its offshoot, a spreading of the female self in the physical world.

Urban spaces created by women to host female, feminist, and gynocratic societies are often symbolically loaded. Mizora (Mary Bradley Lane, *Mizora,* 1890), Herland (Charlotte Perkins Gilman, *Herland,* 1915), Whileaway (Joanna Russ, *The Female Man,* 1975), Mattapoiset (Marge Piercy, *Woman on the Edge of Time,* 1976) are different figures springing from the same female mind. All of these writers give their cities the shape of a female body which has been excised from history, disfigured, and sacrificed to the persisting use by and reference to, in concrete reality, patriarchal codes and signs. Femininity, while excluded from human history, returns to the surface in utopia and cannibalizes the urban space, absorbing it into a female body.

The utopian future is thus conceived not merely as a possible time, but as a new space that allows the process of re-tracing female history and tradition. The city becomes its favorite metaphor: an object which is a living body expanding and replacing the self of individuals—male and female—living within its boundaries.

> The city remains an alembic of human time, perhaps of human nature—an alembic, to be sure, employed less often by master alchemists than sorcerer's apprentices. Still, as a frame of choices and possibilities, the city enacts our sense of the future; not merely abstract, not mutable only, it fulfills time in utopic and dystopic images. (Hassan, 96)

This is Angela Carter's urban dimension: an alchemical space mapping out human nature, both male and female, not only squeezed into a narrow present reality, but projected towards a possible future, either utopian or dystopian. As a metaphor, therefore, the city occupies a crucial juncture in Carter's imagination and tends to become, as in *Nights at the Circus,* "a city built of hybris, imagination and desire, as we are ourselves, as we ought to be" (12). Within its *limina* any human being, man or woman, can see his/her own reflection in an urban structure imitating the architecture of desire. Its source is not an act, but a wish, a dream of invisible cities.[3]

In *PNE,* Carter goes one step further. Having posited the space/body identity, she proceeds by systematically inverting the traditional signifying process. The semantics of the body is appropriated by the object world of space. The latter, therefore, becomes the site of language, that is, of a code suitable to the city and consequently incomprehensible.

"The City cannot be comprehended," writes Joyce Carol Oates (30). While subscribing to this assumption, Angela Carter gives definite fictional plausibility to McLuhan's description of postmodern urban space, of the "city as a total field of inclusive awareness" (166). Since the city endlessly echoes and reflects the self, the typical processes of the body are coherently transferred to the objects inhabiting the city's space. And then the process is reversed. The body becomes a thing, *res* in reality, the most suitable *object* for literature, fictional space, myth. Ontologically, that is, the body and the city are identical in that they undergo the same fictionalizing process.[4] Understandably, "The vertiginous nature of {the City's} threat can be translated into language—a language necessarily oblique and circumspect" (Oates 30).

The resulting female writing will necessarily be sufficiently complex, polysemic, multivocal, and ambiguous in order to reproduce the hybrid grammar of the urban landscape.

2. Writing the Body of Evidence. The underlying structure of *PNE* is deeply postmodernist in that it exploits the basic procedure of adding up heterogeneous structural and functional elements without pretending to synthe-size them. The main thematic units of the novel lead to a human body—the protagonist's body—which undergoes a metamorphosis through the addi-tion/subtraction of sexual genders. Evelyn, a man given a woman's name, uses and abuses Leilah's female body while living in New York, the postmod-ern metropolis.[5] Within the borders of the city, he is a male, and behaves like one. After leaving the city, Evelyn becomes Eve. The metamorphosis is not the result of a choice, but of a surgical experiment planned and performed by the women of Beulah against the protagonist's will. In blunt terms, the experiment is described as an arithmetic operation: male attributes are sub-tracted from the protagonist's body, while female shapes are added. Eventu-ally, Evelyn/Eve will succeed in running away only to come back to a male world. His position in society is now deeply changed: he is a man with a female body of which he is not yet fully aware. Awareness will spring out of sorrow and humiliation when Eve/lyn experiences sexual violation and sexual abuse on his/her own body.

Through the whole process, Eve/lyn shows a double, ambiguous nature. The surgical operation has been compulsory and therefore no new awareness is implied in it. A female body has been simply added to a male identity. The two genders exhibit a contiguity which does not—and could never—become continuity. No integration is possible. Eve/lyn's body and mind diverge but, paradoxically, the resulting chaotic disposition triggers the process of compre-hension.[6]

Literally, Eve/lyn's body is carnivalized, made grotesque because it is seen in the process of becoming something else.[7] Carter shows a precise awareness of the disruptive power implied in carnivalization. The use she makes of this literary device is a function of a systematic analysis of feminin-ity, which eventually results in the complete deconstruction of both genders. What emerges from the whole process is simply the admission that the con-flict between genders can by no means be settled. Male and female as expo-nents of an irreducible dichotomy may be put side by side, summed up, deconstructed, agglutinated., but never fused nor composed in a complex fig-ure including both genders. In other words, sexes could be combined in androgyny, which is not—and never will be—a stable combination of gen-ders. Hybridization is the only possible operation and at its best it results in an enigma that cannot be unraveled.

Carnivalization, particularly when referring to genders, is semantically overloaded. In its complexity it makes for a dialogic novel, reflecting the fea-tures of a highly flexible and multivocal artistic vision (cf Bakhtin, 12ff). As it mixes up incompatible elements which are never to be fused in a monologic vision, it produces multiplicity in representation and multivocality in dis-course. The resulting picture is often disturbing because it is contrary to com-mon sense, disruptive, defamiliarizing, and defamiliarized. Whatever the pur-poses of using carnivalization in the artistic creation, the operations implied tend to be the same: deconstruction, accumulation, metamorphosis, fragmented and unnatural growth.

Once more, the core and structuring principle emerging in the urban landscape as well as in the description of the human body is a summing up procedure, producing a carnivalized space. It is not really an alchemical operation, since it does not result in a compound of different elements, but rather a mixture in which every ingredient maintains its own characteristics even while becoming part of a new whole. This is Angela Carter's city: the secular celebration of chaos, the weird place overlooking the impossible experiment of Baroslav, a Czechoslovak deserter persecuted for political reasons. Once in New York, he has found a new identity and a new life: he is a beggar and a magician, an alchemist who, before creating gold from steel before Evelyn's eyes, gives a short and very effective description of New York's urban space:

> Chaos, the primordial substance. . . . Chaos, the earliest state of disorganized creation, blindly impelled toward the creation of a new order of phenomena of hidden meanings. The *fructifying chaos of anteriority, the state before the beginning of the beginning* (14; italics mine).

In a way, this is also a definition of Carter's fictional space: a primordial chaos, whose elements are not melted into a rational and logical system, but merely summed up in a sequence with no understandable links. The resulting organism is complex in the etymological sense of the term, i.e., in that its constituents stick to their singularity even when combined. Metropolis, just like personality, is deconstructed. Disassembled units are then recombined according to principles contradicting any understandable logical process: a paradigmatic negation of common sense (cf Deleuze, 70ff). Paradox is the artistic form most suitable for representing this subversive attitude. And it is disturbing in that it translates, in fiction, into a deliberate rejection of any conceivable position.

The founding concept of Angela Carter's artistic vision is the "female gothic" as defined by Ellen Moers (90 ff). While appropriating the tools offered by paradox and satire, she provides a feminine perspective, and by doing so she discovers in SF an unprecedented potential for rupture. A wholly new order of things is prospected, and it is highly disturbing because it is not built according to men's needs. Systematic deconstruction affecting all the items making up the urban landscape produces what Barbara Ward defines as the "unintended city" (29): a city with no memories and no future, a cunning figure of life accepted on its surface, because it is exactly what it seems—a labyrinth with no exit. Urban space is therefore conceived, in *PNE*, as a closed system. Entropy affects not only the physical and social universe, but also its linguistic translation. The favored metaphor maintaining this vision is the postmodern city, an ambiguous "paradigm of self-reflexiveness," in Maria del

Sapio's words, which "synthesizes contemporary codes' potential for change obtained through an endless mirroring process" (26).

In depicting Eve/lyn's journey through gender stereotypes, *PNE* therefore combines a postmodernist selection and accumulation of themes and landscapes with a poststructuralist interpretation of language. In a multidimensional space conceived in this way, different writings are interwoven through a combinatorial rule which is incomprehensible and indescribable because it is always undergoing an endless, everlasting metamorphosis.

Angela Carter does not simply write fiction. She also works on the body of writing, on the linguistic and semantic formations we conceive to be the basic background to our human lives. Through an orderly process of deconstruction and recombination, she defines the issues of urban landscape and codes in gendered terms. *PNE* is therefore, literally, a gender novel, in that gender is the still center of a circular journey through three sexed utopian spaces that alternately host and reject the protagonist and determine his/her physical and psychological metamorphosis.

3. New York. Basically, Evelyn is a traveller. In the first pages of the novel, he moves from London to New York. His personal experience as a man, therefore, is deeply marked by the awareness of the body of a European metropolis that, as a literary *topos,* has always been considered male.[8]

When moving overseas, however, Evelyn finds an urban landscape which he perceives as unfamiliar and about which he says: "Nothing in my experience had prepared me for the city" (24). In terms of gender, New York is clearly male, but, when compared to London, it gives the impression of a further evolution in urban structure. The rational project underlying the city, while still evident in London, here seems blurred in New York by a progressive deterioration and decay that affects architecture as well as the social and individual way of life.

If London is the romantic style of nostalgia fading in the irony of memory, New York is grotesque, a hybrid, a postmodern and self-reflective metropolis forever hiding the ancient rational project instead of revealing it. Its true identity consists of being able to absorb a whirling semiotic universe with no logic and no meaning.[9]

Significantly, New York displays all the colors of decay. When describing the city, Evelyn's chromatic vocabulary seems limited to a few adjectival expressions, all of them with negative connotations: "black," "acid yellow," "mineral green." Organic and inorganic deterioration is mirrored everywhere and produces a totally defamiliarized image of the technological metropolis. The landscape's colors reflect the impossibility of any effective cognitive process. Chromatic contrasts are missing simply because they are unthinkable in an urban space conceived in this way. The landscape's tendency toward monochromatism wraps everything in a dark shade which is physical as well as psychological. Only a few sequences are perceived in the morning light, livid and defamiliarizing, that levels all contrasts and complicates comprehension.

To some extent the topography of the city is also incomprehensible: it is a fragmented, labyrinthine text that is largely unreadable.[10] Urban sites are located according to no apparent criterion. Seemingly they do not communicate, or meld. The city as a whole has no center and no depth: it is a web of symbols often with no meaning. The sign stands and acts for the idea. Knowledge is impossible because it has no object. Literally there is nothing to know.

In a way, Evelyn can perceive, or rather imagine, the original project: "a city of visible reason—that had been the intention" (16). However, the intention has apparently been lost in the urban space the protagonist describes: a place of liminality, an endless sequence of lurid suburbs which are the only tangible reality for the protagonist. In Evelyn's words, "it was then an alchemical city. It was chaos, dissolution, nigredo, night" (16).

The chromatic preference for darkness is functional for the representation of an urban kaleidoscope devoid of any rational plan/design. Having been built apparently with no planning, Carter's city may be disassembled and reassembled without running the risk of being unable to trace the original design. New York is, therefore, pure image, the slide of a city, endlessly reproducing itself like a modern work of art.[11] "Around us, as if cut out of dark paper and stuck against the sky," says Evelyn, "were the negative perspectives of the skyscrapers" (30): a paper city, therefore, the infinitely reproducible, reprintable silhouette of an urban space. The silhouette, far from showing a simple two-dimensional profile, proves capable of rendering once more the shape of an entropic universe that results from the senseless accumulation of disparate objects translating the accumulation and compression of personal and collective history.

The deconstructive model identifying the *disjecta membra* of the city requires that there be a code capable of writing an unwritable text. The description of the postmodern metropolis is given through syntagmatic oppositions which trigger conflicting semantic references: "Instead of hard edges and clean colours, a lurid, Gothic darkness that closed over my head entirely and became my world" (*PNE*, 10).

Manhattan resembles a medieval city, a place of disorder and darkness which Evelyn alternately loves and hates, as is often the case with things that are not understood but whose fascination is undeniable.

Only later will Evelyn realize the impossibility of fully accepting the "dying city" (37) and consequently leave it.

While looking for freedom, he finally gets to the city of Beulah.

4. Beulah. Beulah is a gynocratic society. Carter's decision to include a utopian space like this in *PNE* partly reflects the prophetic tendency that Wendy Martin acknowledges in many women writers:

> The utopian community of sisters . . . is a profoundly political phenomenon
> which results from an evolution in consciousness from acceptance of traditional
> values, or at least the effort to adjust them, to questioning of these values, to
> rebellion and finally separation from the dominant culture to form a new social
> order. (250)

Therefore Beulah is planned on the prototype of feminist separatist communities which are the underlying structures of some already mentioned novels.
Mizora (Lane), *Herland* (Perkins Gilman), *The Female Man* (Russ) or *Woman on
the Edge of Time* (Piercy) all exploit the same structural paradigm, each focus-
ing on different problematic issues. *PNE* offers a slightly diverging model, a
peculiar semantic and thematic shade so unusual in feminist fiction that it has
in some cases led to misunderstandings in the critical response to the novel.

Robert Clark, in particular, when referring to Beulah, maintains that the
city is planned and built as "an image of feminine society which exists only in
male chauvinist nightmares" (148). This claim presumes that Carter wishes to
proffer a serious operational model of the perfect female community. Such a
perfect model, according to Clark, can be discerned in Beulah.

I believe Clark's interpretation is not sufficiently grounded in an unprej-
udiced and objective critical analysis of Carter's novel. The general structure
of *PNE* seems to me to support Jane Palmer's less contradictory theory, that
the creation of Beulah is plausibly the result of Carter's typical approach in
writing fiction, an approach that could correctly be defined as "satirical on
the whole" (22). From this perspective, Beulah should be perceived and interpreted as a satirical model, an attempt to reverse the pattern of a rigid, traditional patriarchal tradition, and at the same time the corresponding feminist
utopian responses to it, which in some cases prove equally rigid. This sort of
double satire, which is rather unusual in feminist fiction, may be the source of
Clark's misreading. Obviously, Angela Carter does not—and does not mean
to—create an ideal city. Rather, she selects and then adds up some recurring
models in order to produce in the reader the sort of defamiliarizing effect frequently leading to cognition. In other words, Carter shows a precise awareness of the city as an artistic topos, an "adapted stereotype" (Gombrich, 68)
giving fictional reality and plausibility to the intention of reversing and/or
confirming a traditional paradigm.

Accordingly, in Carter's novel highly heterogeneous influences interweave
in the paradigm of the female community and they result in a contradictory and
sometimes paradoxical model of the city of women. In *PNE,* even the name of
the gynocratic community defines a specific satiric intention. As a literary topos,
Beulah appears for the first time in John Bunyan's *Pilgrim's Progress* and is
defined as a place "upon the border of Heaven" through which "pilgrims pass on
to eternal life" (155). The "daughters of Beulah" in William Blake's works are
the Muses inspiring the poet (420). Both Bunyan and Blake, moreover, seem to
suggest that Beulah is the ideal place for the perfect patriarchal marriage.

In my view, Carter revises the traditional stereotype, adapting it for her own purposes. When giving her gynocratic community a name borrowed from a patriarchal tradition, the author of *PNE* relocates meanings; in doing so she establishes a semantic contradiction and multiplies the symbolic associations. Again, what we have here is a reversed stereotype triggering a cognitive process.

The whole topography of the landscape which Carter describes apparently supports this critical view. First of all, Beulah can only be reached by crossing the desert, the traditional metaphor for wilderness and sterility, with all the associated symbolism.[12]

Analysis of the shape of the feminist community and recognition of its main structure reveal that its basic architecture is defined in gendered terms. Beulah is a rigidly homosexual and separatist female community, and consequently built on analogy to a womb.[13] "Beulah," says Evelyn, "lies in the interior, in the inward part of the earth" (47). Both from the psychological and the physical point of view, Beulah is the ideal place for Evelyn's re-birth. "It will become," says the protagonist, "the place where I was born" (47). It becomes the belly of the whale where the rite of death and re-birth will be performed.

Chromatically, Beulah displays the colors of a woman's womb. The symbolism of darkness is only superficially similar to the absence of light we identified in the urban landscape of the metropolis. Semantically, the "lurid darkness" of New York is diametrically opposed to the damp absence of light in the female womb, a symbol exemplifying the rejection of the male rational and monological ethics (cf Deleuze, 12 ff). In other words, New York still maps out an urban project, however decrepit, while Beulah is primarily the architectural figure of a womb.

Beulah's typical atmosphere is not pure darkness, but rather shadow, the kind of twilight which allows shapes to be seen in outlines, as in dreams. Evelyn's frequent reference to the idea of a nightmare when describing Beulah sets up a criterion according to which the gynocratic community is to be interpreted. In a place such as this, reality gradually fades away, together with the patriarchal logic of the male metropolis.

By the same token, the main female figure in this part of the novel, Mother, is defined as the "focus of darkness" (58). She is perceived by Evelyn as a nightmarish figure leading him—and compelling him—towards a new female identity in a voyage *au bout de la nuit,* a journey from the old, crumbling city into the dark womb of a new mother.

Besides echoing a tradition supported by other female utopias, the underground location of Beulah morphologically reproduces the symbolic meaning of the place for the protagonist. Before the surgical operation, he is kept there and protected from the dangers of the outside world just like an unborn child in the womb of its mother. The first phase of his journey towards female identity is performed inside the body of Beulah mapping out the topography built on the body of a pregnant woman.

Understandably, this topography shows a complex physical and psychological pattern and is therefore far from being linear. Beulah is a labyrinth, fragmentary, complex, self-reflexive, and multivocal like the city but built on the basis of diverging principles. In the same way as New York, the gynocratic community offers Evelyn interweaving routes. However, Beulah differs from the labyrinthine metropolis in that the former has been built on the basis of a project. The structuring principle of the gynocratic community, however meaningless it may be to Evelyn, functions throughout the part of the novel dedicated to Beulah. Rationality, in the male sense of the word, is not its guiding thread: indeed the project of Beulah is conceived to be a radical reversal not only of the structure but also of the meaning of patriarchy. Significantly, an ambiguous relationship to technology as a mainly male concept emerges in the definition of what Mother is: "Beneath this stone sits the Mother in a *complicated mix of mythology and technology*" (48; italics mine). Beulah, therefore, is not anti-technological but perceives technology differently, by considering it similar to mythology.

Once more the striking collusion of conflicting elements is revealed as the most suitable key for interpreting *PNE*. In New York, contradiction is a consequence of the deterioration of rationality, while in Beulah it is the structuring principle of the utopian space: "There is a place where contrarieties are equally true. This place is called Beulah" (48).

Juxtaposition is confirmed as a method of disrupting and subverting traditional semantic borders and the conflict is made more evident by the intrinsic nature of the terms placed side by side: technology and mythology stand for male and female, respectively. The assumed compatibility, the truth, of both dichotomic terms is actually an illusion because it is based on a vague and undefined principle of no-contradiction: series of phenomena belonging to two different orders can not be compared. Myth is neither more nor less reliable than technology. The two terms can however be placed side by side to produce a defamiliarizing effect.

In the structure of Beulah, this procedure produces an extremely heterogeneous dramatic configuration complicating the rules of mimesis. It is thus that the grammar of landscape is obtained through a combination of myth and technology. On the other hand, while the protagonist approaches the throbbing heart of darkness—and his own metamorphosis—the mythic and symbolic element tends to dominate and to be intensely reflected in the novel's landscape. Technology is not forgotten as a reference, but it becomes more and more similar to a sort of magic.

Metaphors of the body and of human physical processes define an urban space that is openly gendered. Referring to the ritual of cannibalism, the female principle has swallowed male reality in the bowels of the Earth to suggest the image of a female body as large as the city itself. And from this body, Eve, physically a woman and psychologically a man, will make a clean start on another journey.

5. **Zero's town.** When leaving Beulah, the protagonist is perfectly aware that his/her body has undergone an impossible change. The women of the female community have relocated its gender through a sort of mythical vengeance, a nemesis reproducing the modalities of the slaughter of Dionysus, the greedy child who, cut into seven pieces, boiled and roasted, is to become the main course in the Titans' banquet. His heart is spared, however just like Orpheus's head in a similar cannibalistic myth.

Evelyn's sacrifice, though similar to its mythical references, tends to respond to a more complex configuration. Evelyn's body is not literally gobbled up after having been cooked. The object of the women's ritual meal is not the protagonist's flesh and blood, but his male identity which is deprived of its anatomical support. His gender no longer coincides with his sex. Eve/lyn perceives him/herself—and is perceived by people belonging to the opposite sex—as an empty body promising endless pleasures. "I have not yet become a woman, though I possess a woman's shape," says the narrating voice. "Eve remains willfully in the state of innocence that precedes the fall" (83). The awareness of a terminally decentered life leads the protagonist towards a new ritual death perceived as the only possible way to recover a lost sexual identity.

In his/her frantic quest for a true self, Eve/lyn returns to the desert. Once more, wilderness and the absence of any possible fertility serves as a metaphor for the protagonist's condition of being a hybrid creature with no memories and no shared experiences: "a tabula erasa, a blank sheet of paper" (83). Lost, deeply unable to identify herself/himself in a paradoxical anatomic disguise which does not overlap with a corresponding psychological change, Evelyn is no longer a man but not yet a woman. Being a hybrid, he/she does not belong to any community: he/she has no history, no tradition, no shared life and finally no gender.

In other words, the protagonist is literally outside the *polis,* in the realm where, as Aristotle says, you cannot be truly human, but either a god or a beast. Therefore the new Eve, in his/her search for identity, will have to become integrated in a new urban reality and undergo a third, painful ritual.

The ideal site for this new change appears to be Zero's town. Both physically and psychologically, the place is built to reproduce the symbolic meaning of a patriarchal autocratic community. All the features of the landscape are borrowed from De Sade's novels and exacerbated with the obvious aim of producing a strong grotesque effect. The final result has an unprecedented potential for rupture: while maintaining some of the features of a model that Clark defines as "a patriarchal type not infrequent in history" (148), Carter appropriates the paradigm and deconstructs it for feminist use. The minimal units are reassembled through a clearly ironic stylistic procedure. The assumed rigidity of the patriarchal model is purposefully highlighted in order to provide a highly concentrated version of a woman's life in a harem.

By the same token, Zero, the father and owner of all the women living in the town, assembles all the negative features of patriarchal power. Poet and magician, master of words and dissipation, he is the uxoricidal tyrant forever performing the role of a wicked fool celebrating any form of perversion. His wives seem affected by what Joanna Russ defines as "idiocy," that is "what happens to those who have been told that it is their godgiven mission to mend socks, clean toilets and work in the fields; and nobody will let you make the real decision anyway" (225).

Decisions, actually, are up to Zero. His behavior is entirely defined by a precise theocratic will, determined not by rational design but by the wish to preserve a dogmatic attitude, made clear by the tendency to reproduce the masculine perception of linearity and univocality.

Significantly, Zero is a figure of totalitarian sexuality, opposite but similar to Mother. And just like Mother, he projects onto the urban landscape the dominant features of his *Weltanschauung*. Beulah is built on analogy to a womb and is, literally and figuratively, Mother's body. It shows the disquieting darkness and the incomprehensible but irresistible fascination of a female pregnant body. Similarly, the town in the desert is plunged in dazzling sunlight. The topological pattern underlying this choice is evident: the unfading brightness of the desert does not allow for any shadow in the same way as the rigidity of male rationality does not allow for any doubt. Once more, this makes a case for Deleuze's theory that dazzling light is a metaphor for what is obvious, self-evident, monologic, and linear: in short, what is male (cf Deleuze, 14ff).

The landscape is therefore used with the precise purpose of exposing the contradictory nature of male ethics. Dogmatism is the structuring principle and the still center of both the physical and the psychological scene. Urban and imaginative space show their mutual solidarity and prove to be deeply interwoven, producing a topographical pattern where no object occupies a neutral position: the semantic area covered by each element of the landscape tends to be modified according to the nature of the light that strikes it. The unrelenting sunlight typical of the desert should consequently shine upon the realm of absolute, unbending rationality.

Which is obviously not the case in Zero's town. While appropriating the stereotype, Carter succeeds in subverting it. In depicting the patriarchal community, she undermines the founding principles of male ethics not through an overtly feminist discourse, but by polarizing contradictions in the reproduction of the model which is inherently irrational, illogical, self-contradictory. This amounts to the creation of a city whose textual identity is programmatically reversed. The desert sun shines on an urban topography that is anything but rational. Far from giving a more concrete shape to the city, the dazzling light flooding the whole landscape seems to add a ghostlike shade to the old, rotting village: "The miner's town . . . looked, in the analytic light of the desert, far older than the rocks on which it was built" (*PNE*, 93).

Zero's town, therefore, proves to be a mere juxtaposition of crumbling houses, a built-up area with no center and no history, a town which is old without being ancient. Appropriately, Zero lives in a "ranch house in the ghost town" (85), a building reflecting the psychological identity of the person inhabiting it. A figure of an *essential* evil whose ideological reason has been lost, the ghost town disclaims and betrays the rational intention of its planner.

Semantically, an urban space conceived in this way reveals an underlying texture built on analogy with dream imagery. The frequent repetition of reference to nightmare marks the ultimate breakdown of borders between reality and imagination, which are placed side by side and given exactly the same sort of fictional existence. Reality is neither deeper nor more superficial than imagination. The two terms belong to the same level of perception. Words and their meanings are divorced, and the logical link between them is disrupted. Signs are legitimized as existing in their own right, apart from any connections with the objects normally designated by them. Language itself is rewritten in order to make it suitable for narrating the endless instability of representation: "Yet Zero's rhetoric transformed this world. The ranch house was Solomon's temple; the ghost town was the New Jerusalem" (100).

Reality and imagination are posed as conflicting—and yet coexisting—terms. Their mutual opposition is overtly re-enacted through a language that emphasizes syntagmatic oppositions rather than paradigmatic references. Through this specific choice of style Carter's novel displays a strong postmodernist inclination: multiplicity and multivocality seem to be expressed through a web of apparent semantic contradictions which are in fact subtle shifts through the usual semantic borders of the verbal signs. The attempt to rebuild the connection between signifier and signified, and therefore to defamiliarize language, is the principle guiding the novel as a whole, but it becomes openly disturbing and disruptive in the description of Zero's town.

"In the ruins of an old chapel," says the narrator, "under a sagging roof of corrugated iron, Zero kept his pigs" (95). The two key-words of this quotation cover semantically opposite fields: the term "chapel" conjures up the image of a holy space, which is however inhabited by "pigs": not ministers of religion, that is, but filthy beasts. The contiguity of the two terms makes the whole text subversive in that it displaces the presumed sacrality of the chapel, depicting it through a globally blasphemous perspective. The resulting linguistic and stylistic structure is a highly complex one, which focuses on multivocality as a strategy for resistance against the male univocality in language and ethics. Interestingly, the word as a unit is not deconstructed in Carter's novel: disintegration does not affect the syntax of the form; rather, it works on semantics as a field of meanings no longer permanently connected to specific signs.

Meanings are assembled through the same process of juxtaposition which is the structuring principle both of landscapes and the condensed universe of characters. The city as a multivocal, self-reflexive, and unwritable text is ultimately duplicated in the figure of Tristessa. A former movie star pinned to the fixity of his/her own beautiful but unreal image, s/he is the narrative focus of all contradiction. Anatomically, her/his body shows both male and female features. Tristessa therefore articulates Eve/lyn's deep dissociation, while making it more tangible. The split no longer affects the gender of the character, as in the case of the narrator, but it is duplicated and reflected in two sexes coexisting in the same body, assembling in order what is male and what is female. As a character, Tristessa demonstrates the contradiction inherent in the physical contiguity of two sexes that, when put side by side, are strongly focused as conflicting terms. "Tristessa. Enigma. Illusion. Woman? Ah" (6).

Just like the urban spaces of *PNE,* Tristessa can neither be understood nor explained, because she is "an illusion in a void" (110). Ontologically, she does not exist. Or better yet, she is given the same level of existence as New York, Beulah, and Zero's town: all of them are icons of themselves, images whose elements have been deconstructed and then re-assembled, enacting an impossible transition, the metaphor of a journey which can have no end because it is circular. "We start from our conclusions" says the narrator, defining the claustrophobic space that is overcrowded with objects and meanings. The landscape of the city, within the *limina* of this space, is shaped into a diluted body which resembles ultimately a sexed body.

Notes

1. For the concept of a "bracketed off world," see Iser 236–246.

2. To a certain extent this concept is implied in the utopian city as a literary *topos* which determines an analogy between the urban architecture and the shape of the human soul. The ideal city is a mainly psychological model representing the perfect organization of an idea. Therefore, a so-conceived urban space becomes literally a "disembodied city," a place which is real though not tangible, just like Calvino's *Invisible Cities.*

3. See Italo Calvino, *Le Città Invisibili.* Torino, 1985.

4. For the concept of fictionalizing act or process, see Iser 236.

5. The contiguity between postmodernism and women's science fiction is by no means limited to Carter's novels. As Robin Roberts says, "Feminist science fiction of the 1980s can be discussed most usefully in terms of post-structuralism and post modernism. Post-structuralist feminist SF problematizes language acquisition and the gendered hierarchical structures embedded in language" ("Post-Modernism and Feminist Science Fiction," SFS, 17:138, #51, July 1990).

6. The most obvious reference is Virginia Woolf's *Orlando.*

7. See M. Bakhtin. *Dostojevskij: Poetica e Stilistica* (Torino, 1968), 122–132.

8. "If a city may be said to have a sex," writes Jane Marcus, "London was, and is, unmistakably male" (Marcus, 139).

9. Carter refers to a literary topos which is to be considered as typical and recurring: "New York—that most mythical of cities—tends to emerge in recent literature as hellish, or at any rate murderous" (Oates, 30).

10. As Burton Pike writes, "The absence of shape in the form of orienting landmarks is a major problem for a person trying to define a real city or navigate within it. If shapes make

individual cities recognizable, urban shapelessness is a form of disorder, expressing anxiety and loss of coherence, and symbolizing the anonymous randomness of contemporary life" (129).

11.   See Walter Benjamin. *L'opera d'arte nell'epoca della sua riproducibilità tecnica* (Torino, 1980).

12.   Particularly clarifying are Jane Marcus's words on the subject: "Central to the concept of female wilderness is the rejection of heterosexuality. In the dream of freedom, one's womb is one's own only in the wilderness" (Marcus, 136).

13.   With reference to a possible continuity between the female womb and space in women's SF, some basic considerations are to be found in Oriana Palusci, "Judith Merrill e il grembo dell'astronave [Judith Merrill and the Spaceship Womb]," in her *Terra di lei* (Pescara, 1990), 59ff.

Works Cited

Blake, William. "Milton." *The Complete Writings of William Blake.* Ed. G. Keynes, London and New York, 1952.

Bunyan, John. *Pilgrim's Progress.* Oxford, 1960.

Carter, Angela. *Nights at the Circus.* London, 1984.

———. *The Passion of New Eve.* London, 1982.

Clark, Robert. "Angela Carter's Desire Machine," *Women's Studies,* 14:147–61, 1987.

Deleuze, Gilles. *La logica del senso.* Milano, 1979.

Del Sapio, Maria. *Alice nella cinà.* Pescara, 1988.

Gombrich, Ernst. *Art and Illusion. A Study in the Psychology of Pictorial Expression.* Princeton, NJ, 1961.

Hassan, Ihab. "City of Mind, Urban Words: the Dematerialization of Metropolis in Contemporary American Fiction." Jaye, 93–112.

Iser, W. *Prospecting: From Reader Response to Literary Anthropology.* Baltimore, 1989.

Jaye, Michael, and Ann Chalmers Watt, eds. *Literature and the Urban Experience: Essays on the City and Literature.* New Brunswick, NJ, 1981.

McLuhan, Marshall. *Understanding Media.* New York, 1965.

Marcus, Jane. "A Wilderness of One's Own: Feminist Fantasy Novels in the Twenties." Squier, 134–60.

Martin, Wendy. "A View of the *City Upon a Hill:* The Prophetic Vision of A. Rich." Squier, 249–65.

Moers, Ellen. *Literary Women.* London, 1978.

Oates, Joyce Carol. "Imaginary Cities: America," Jaye, 11–34.

Palmer, Jane. "From Coded Mannequin to Bird Woman: Angela Carter's Magic Flight," *Women Reading Women's Writing.* Ed. S.N. Roe. Brighton, Sussex, 1987. 179–205.

Piercy, Marge. "The City as Battleground." Jaye, 209–18.

Pike, Burton. *The Image of the City in Modern Literature.* Princeton, NJ, 1981.

Russ, Joanna. "Science Fiction and Technology as Mystification." SFS 16:250–60, #16, November 1978.

Squier, S. Merrill, ed. *Women Writers and the City: Essays in Feminist Literary Criticism.* Knoxville, TN, 1989.

Ward, Barbara. *The Home of Man.* New York, 1976.

Feminist Metafiction and Androcentric Reading Strategies: Angela Carter's Reconstructed Reader in *Nights at the Circus*

Beth A. Boehm

In his review of Robert Coover's *Gerald's Party,* Robert Christgau claims that writers of metafiction such as John Barth, Thomas Pynchon, John Hawkes, and Coover are "a significant subculture with a unique perspective on the world today. If we can speak of black fiction and women's fiction, surely we can speak of fiction by pretentious white American men" (7). As this comment indicates, metafiction—fiction that self-consciously reflects upon its fictional status and comments upon its own use of narrative conventions—is most often identified with male postmodernists, even though metafiction's potential to subvert the conventions of literary discourse would seem to make it an attractive genre for feminist writers. Gayle Greene, for instance, argues that metafiction "is a powerful tool of feminist critique, for to draw attention to the structures of fiction is also to draw attention to the conventionality of the codes that govern human behavior, to reveal how such codes have been constructed and how they can therefore be changed" (1–2). But the feminist writer who employs metafictional techniques to challenge the structures of literary discourse and patriarchy will necessarily find herself in a paradoxical position, not only because metafiction is associated with a group of "pretentious white American men," but also because the more an author attempts to undermine traditional literary conventions, the more she must hope her reader understands and expects those conventions to begin with. Metafiction, like other forms of parody, is therefore what Linda Hutcheon has called a doubly coded genre, for it "both legitimizes and subverts that which it parodies" (101); and as with other forms of parody, the double coding of metafiction— particularly feminist metafiction—offers the potential for misreadings.

Doris Lessing's account of the critical reception of *The Golden Notebook,* one of the first contemporary feminist metafictions and, in Greene's assessment, "the most influential novel written by a woman in this century" (26),

From *Critique* 37, no. 1 (Fall 1995): 35–49. Heldref Publications. © 1995 Helen Dwight Reid Educational Foundation. Reprinted by permission.

illustrates the paradox facing the feminist author of metafiction. Almost ten years after its publication in 1962, Lessing bitterly complained about the many "misreadings" produced by critics of her novel and about the fact that no one noticed that her major aim was indeed metafictional. After outlining the wide range of misreadings, some of which she calls "too silly to be true," Lessing both describes the reader she longs for and explains why such a reader is so difficult to find: "[The problem] is that writers are looking in the critics for an *alter ego,* that other self more intelligent than oneself who has seen what one is reaching for, and who judges you only by whether you have matched up to your aim or not" (xv). And although Lessing concedes that this desire is "impossible," she immediately undermines that concession by saying that "critics are not educated" to be the type of reader she desires:

> Children are taught submission to authority, how to search for other people's opinions and decisions, and how to quote and comply. . . . These children who have spent years inside the training system become critics and reviewers, and cannot give what the author, the artist, so foolishly looks for—imaginative and original judgment. What they can do, and what they do very well, is to tell the writer how the book or play accords with current patterns of feeling and thinking—the climate of opinion. (xv–xvi)

These remarks suggest that Lessing desires an "authorial reader," the term Peter Rabinowitz coined to describe the hypothetical audience for whom an author fashions her rhetorical effects. According to Rabinowitz, an author actually does not want the reader to search for her private psyche, but instead wants the reader to join the interpretive community she has imagined for her novel—an interpretive community that would "notice," in Lessing's case, her metafictional aim: "to shape a book which would make its own comment, a wordless statement: to talk through the way it was shaped" (xiv). As her discussion of the training system suggests, Lessing understands that critics read in socially constituted, *conventional* ways, and her complaint that readers were not original in their responses to *The Golden Notebook* reveals her disappointment that readers had not joined the authorial audience for her innovative text. Instead of reading the structure of her novel—its fragmented and "incoherent" form—as a commentary on the failings of the conventions of the realistic novel, her early critics submitted to the authority of the New Criticism and saw such fragmentation and disunity as flaws of *The Golden Notebook.*

Ironically, the publication of Lessing's introduction to *The Golden Notebook* in 1971 prompted a decade of criticism that did "notice" the form of her novel and focus on her metafictional intentions, but as Greene notes, "the political implications of Lessing [sic] critique of "the forms" have still not been much noticed, which is why the novel's feminism continues to be misunderstood" (115). To understand why critics have not noticed the feminist implications of Lessing's metafiction, we need to consider the implications of our tendency to view contemporary metafiction as a genre employed by "pretentious white American men." In his recent discussion of the canon of contemporary American fiction, Raymond Mazurek suggests that women have been excluded from the contemporary canon because they "have avoided the self-referential 'experimental' styles favored by critics but have tended to write more direct and even didactic fiction" (153). Although Mazurek writes specifically about American literature, his representation of "self-referential 'experimental' fiction" as indirect, non-didactic, formally complex, intellectually elitist, and encyclopedic accurately describes critical assumptions regarding contemporary metafiction written on both sides of the Atlantic. From different perspectives, critics like John Gardner and Gerald Graff have complained that self-conscious fiction, by questioning the ontological status of fictional worlds, makes a mere game of the literary transaction and undermines the potential for writers of fiction to make ethical statements about the world. As Graff suggests, self-reflexive fiction only "holds up the mirror to unreality" (179). For many readers of self-conscious works like Barth's *Lost in the Funhouse* or *Chimera*, metafiction raises expectations that the storyteller's task is not to help us understand or protest the ideological structures of our culture, but rather to simply entertain us with a virtuoso performance. That Lessing's readers began to ignore the feminist politics of her novel at the same time that they began to notice its metafictional intentions is thus in keeping with this critical assumption about the apolitical nature of self-conscious literature; the writer with an explicitly revisionist political agenda like feminism must undermine not only the conventions of the realistic novel and New Critical reading strategies, but this readerly assumption as well.

The following discussion of Angela Carter's *Nights at the Circus*, a complex metafictional feminist novel, is based on several premises. First, along with Rabinowitz (and Lessing), I assume that most readers, including professional reviewers and critics, desire to read as the authorial audience, at least as a first step toward understanding a text, and that many "misreadings" (failures to employ the interpretive strategies the author has imagined to be available to the reader) have their "origins, not in the readers as individuals, but in the culture that has taught them to read" (193).[1] Thus we can, as Rabinowitz suggests, "read" misreadings and view "misinterpretations produced by actual readers in particular cultural contexts as useful material for cultural analysis" (174). Second, in choosing to read "misreadings" of Carter's novel produced by critics for two influential literary periodicals—*The New York Times Book Review* and the *Times Literary Supplement*, I am relying upon Richard Ohmann's discussion of the prominent role of such periodicals in the success and eventual "canonization" of any particular novel. Because such literary reviews influence both a novel's popular (and thus economic) success and its success vis-à-vis the canon, misreadings by reviewers for these journals can be particularly devastating; further, because the reviewers for such journals are well-educated and culturally literate, their misreadings might reveal what

Rabinowitz calls the "masculinist bias in the normalized techniques of reading most academics have been trained to use" (215). Finally, an understanding of that bias might help us explain why we have constructed the canon of postmodernism around mostly male writers and why women who have used metafictional techniques have remained, in Mazurek's words, "less well-known" than their male counterparts.

> A great deal of my life has been spent reading, and it's been spent reflecting upon what I've read, and it's been spent responding to it and reacting to it in various ways. . . . For about ten years, between being twenty-nine and thirty-nine, I thought that writing, all fiction, really, was about other fiction. That there was no way out, really, of this solipsism; that books were about other books. And I would have regarded my own writing as a kind of elaborate form of literary criticism, and in some respects I still do. (Goldsworthy 4)

As this comment from Angela Carter suggests, much of the work of this extraordinarily prolitic writer has been metafictional, and much of her metafiction has been geared toward exposing the male bias behind both literary and cultural constructions. Her best known work in America, for instance, is *The Bloody Chamber,* a collection of revisionary fairy tales quite similar to an important American postmodern text, *Pricksongs and Descants.* But whereas Robert Coover implies the necessity of such mythic tales for revealing the dark and violent secrets of male sexuality, Carter explores the ways traditional folk and fairy tales have constructed femininity quite apart from the reality of female sexuality, a reality represented by the resonant bloody chamber. In her most overt act of literary criticism, a Foucauldian study of pornography called *The Sadeian Woman,* Carter further explores the culturally determined nature of "woman," arguing that "Pornographers are the enemies of women only because our contemporary ideology of pornography does not encompass the possibility of change, as if we were the slaves of history and not its makers, as if sexual relations were not necessarily an expression of social relations" (3). Carter's texts constantly seek not only to investigate the social and sexual fictions that regulate human lives, but also to provide new fictions, for by revealing the conventions that rule both human behavior and literature, Carter posits the possibility of change.

Nights at the Circus, like many carnivalized works, defies standard generic categories, but it resembles a picaresque with the intention of transforming the representation of women from Homer on. The female picaro, the "most famous aerialiste" of 1899, is first seen as she rejects the name she has been dubbed by the popular press—the Cockney Venus—for the self-given and more appropriate "Helen of the Highwire." "Just like Helen of Troy," she tells us, she was "hatched"; and the narrator adds that "evidently this Helen took after her putative father, the swan, around the shoulder parts" (7), which explains why her surrogate mother christened her "Fevvers." Raised in a respectable brothel run by a one-eyed metaphysical madame named Nelson before doing a stint as the Angel of Death in Madame Schreck's house of female freaks, this winged woman is a decidedly deromanticized Helen, one who has determined that if she is doomed to be the object of the male gaze, she will at least be so on her own terms:

> "Fevvermania." Everywhere you saw her picture; the shops were crammed with "Fevvers" garters, stockings, fans, cigars, shaving soap . . . She even lent it to a brand of baking powder; if you added a spoonful of the stuff, up in the air went your sponge cake, just as she did. Heroine of the hour, object of learned discussion and profane surmise, this Helen launched a thousand quips, mostly on the lewd side. (8)

As with most picaros, part of the appeal of this champagne-guzzling, bawdy entrepreneur is her ability to survive cruel economic and social conditions; indeed, Fevvers has much in common with the prostitute who earns Carter's respect in *The Sadeian Woman:* "At least the girl who sells herself with her eyes open is not a hypocrite and, in a world with a cash-sale ideology, that is a positive, even a heroic virtue" (55).

More important for this discussion is the metafictional question on everyone's lips about this winged woman, the question that motivates the narrative action and the reader's interest, the question asked by Fevvers' slogan: "Is she fact or is she fiction?" For the first third of the book, Fevvers, in a "voice that clanged like dustbin lids" (7), narrates her own story (with a few intrusions from her surrogate mother, Lizzie, a Marxist revolutionary ex-prostitute) to a skeptical American reporter named Jack Walser, who initially hopes to expose the winged woman as a hoax. Unable to prove her fictionality, Walser is nevertheless "lassooed" by her fantastic narrative style and by "the infinite plurality of worlds" (30) represented by her anachronistically postmodern tale. Disguised as a clown, he joins the circus on its tour to pre-revolutionary St. Petersburg and Siberia in pursuit of his mythic Helen.

Adam Mars-Jones and Carolyn See, Carter's two reviewers, agree that the first third of her novel—Fevvers's seduction of Walser (and Carter's seduction of the reader)—is delightfully entertaining. Their appreciation is based, I would argue, on the way Carter combines fantasy with comfortable narrative conventions. With Big Ben magically striking midnight three times during the course of her narration, Fevvers's story cleverly pushes the boundaries of realistic narrative, sometimes placing "actual" people in questionable but "unverifiable" situations. We are told, for instance, that Carlyle was a client of the brothel where Fevvers was raised and that an adoring Toulouse-Lautree painted the poster that advertises her circus act. And sometimes, her narrative lingers on the other female prodigies of nature who are employed by Madame Schreck (a "real" sleeping beauty, a woman with mamillary eyes, a bipartite, and a dwarf not three foot tall), making their lives seem all *too* real, as if these female "freaks" hold up, not a mirror to unreality, but rather a magnifying glass to reality.

Although the content of Fevvers's tale exists on the margins between the fantastic and the real, the factual and the fictional, the relationship between Fevvers and Walser is the entirely conventional relationship between teller and told, writer and reader. Walser, the skeptical American verifier of facts, is pulled into the narrative at the same time that he resists it, both believing and not believing her story; he must both suspend his disbelief to listen to Fevvers's tale and be duly attentive to (and skeptical of) the magic she employs to spin it. Walser's position as reader, though sometimes "discomposing" to him, is a mostly comfortable one, and readers of Carter's novel readily assume his position and point-of-view. But when Fevvers ceases her narration and the point of view is no longer Walser as reader of Fevvers but instead alternates between a third-person account of the sometimes separate wanderings of Walser and Fevvers, Walser's journalistic writings, and Fevvers's interior monologue, the novel becomes difficult to decode according to comfortable readerly conventions. And it is precisely at this point that both Mars-Jones and See begin to "misread."

See's review for the *New York Times Book Review* is the shorter and more dismissive. Reading the relationship between Walser and Fevvers sentimentally and literally rather than metafictionally, See applies the conventions of romance to the novel. In other words, instead of classifying Carter's novel as a metafiction that seeks to reveal the connections between literary structures and social structures and instead of reading the relationship between Fevvers and Walser as that of writer and reader, See reads as though they were characters in a romance, and the plot details she discusses are those most inducive to a romance. That her interpretive decision clearly denigrates the novel according to androcentric standards, rendering *Nights at the Circus* a "non-serious" work of fiction, is made clear by her description of the novel as "delicious, a sweet for the mind," which, after a while, makes one "a little queasy."

But more interesting than this derogatory judgment that the novel makes a better dessert than main course is the misreading that results from incorrectly classifying the novel as a romance. See focuses her attention on the romantic heroine, Fevvers, and completely ignores what happens to her love object, Walser: "We're not surprised to find, however, that when Fevvers loses Walser she droops like the proverbial bird in the gilded cage (which persona is also a part of her act); that she lets her hair grow in brown at the roots and that she even breaks a wing. You can't fly without love; well, that's a laudable sentiment, but not exactly a new one." Although it is true that the wreck of the circus train in the middle of Siberia results in Fevvers's broken wing and her separation from Walser, See must overlook a great many details to come to her conclusion. The narrator, for instance, explicitly tells us that Fevvers's "misery was exacerbated by the knowledge that the young American to whom she'd taken such a fancy was so near to her and yet so far away":

Exacerbated, but not caused. Her gloom had other causes. Did the speed with which she was losing her looks dismay her? Was it that? She was ashamed to admit it. . . . But there was more to it than that. She knew she had truly mislaid some vital something of herself along the road that brought her to this place. When she lost her weapon to the Grand Duke in his frozen palace, she had lost some of that sense of her own magnificence which had previously sustained her trajectory. . . . Now she was a crippled wonder. . . . Helen, formerly of the High-wire, now permanently grounded" (272–273 emphasis mine).

It is not "romantic" love that Fevvers needs to fly, but rather a mended wing. Her loss of confidence in her own power to protect herself and her inability to fly deny that vital something: the sense of her own magnificence, of her virtuosity as a performing subject. Like any virtuoso, what she needs most is an audience, and she longs for Walser as authorial reader more than as romantic lover: "The young American it was who kept the whole story of the old Fevvers in his notebooks; she longed for him to tell her she was true" (273).

Further, by employing interpretive strategies appropriate to the romantic quest, See completely overlooks the parodic, metafictional, *and* feminist conclusion of *Nights at the Circus,* a conclusion that revises the masculine bias of the heroic quest. Broken-winged and kidnapped by a band of peasant outlaws exiled to Siberia, Fevvers temporarily longs for a knight in shining armor. When both Walser and a rescue party have been sighted, she cries out: " 'My young man will come and save us.' " But Lizzie, always the pragmatist, provides the necessary corrective: " 'Hold hard, you sentimental booby, sounds like he's in no fit state to save himself. . . . I like the sound of the rescue party better!' " (241). With conventional romantic expectations for masculine heroic intervention dashed, Fevvers finally remembers her role as "female Quixote," as wily picaro, claiming, "We shall set boldly forth and rescue ourselves" (244).

Even more revisionary is Carter's metafictional treatment of the love plot. In *Writing beyond the Ending,* Rachel Blau DuPlessis reminds us that in nineteenth-century narratives with female heroes, "quest and love plots were intertwined, simultaneous discourses, but at the resolution of the work, the energies of the *Bildung* were incompatible with the closure in successful courtship or marriage. Quest for women was thus finite; we learn that any plot of self-realization was at the service of the marriage plot and was subordinate to, or covered within, the magnetic power of that ending" (6). The magnetic power of marriage as *the* fitting conclusion for both novels and women's lives is the subject of a discussion near the end of *Nights at the Circus,* just as the twentieth-century woman and the twentieth-century novel are about to emerge. Although Fevvers has earlier refused to debate the "significance" of an event by saying "I'm not in the mood for literary criticism" (244), Lizzie forces her to contemplate the power of literary conventions that seek to end women's stories, even those in which they are their own heroes, with marriage:

> "And, when you *do* find the young American, what the 'ell will you do, then? Don't you know the customary endings of the old comedies of separated lovers, misfortune overcome, adventures among outlaws and savage tribes? True lovers' reunions always end in a marriage. . . . Orlando takes his Rosalind. She says: 'To you I give myself, for I am yours.' And that," she added, a low thrust, "goes for a girl's bank account, too." (280)

Fevvers, appalled by the thought that marriage might tie her to the ground and empty her bank account, attempts to offer other "endings," all of which Lizzie rejects: " 'The Prince who rescues the princess from the dragon's lair is always forced to marry her, whether they've taken a liking to one another or not. That's the custom. And I don't doubt that custom will apply to the trapeze artiste who rescues the clown. The name of this custom is a "happy ending" (281). Although Carter's "happy ending" does reunite the lovers (but not in marriage), it does so in a self-conscious, metafictional way by drawing explicit connections between marriage as a literary device and marriage as a social convention. Ironically, See's description of the novel as an old-fashioned romance does prove Lizzie's point about the power of social custom and literary convention, and about the difficulty of providing new endings and new fictions to structure the human need for love.

See misreads as a result of misclassifying Carter's novel as a romance; however, Mars-Jones's misreading is in many ways more sophisticated and perhaps more threatening to feminist writers who would employ metafictional techniques to investigate the literary and social fictions that govern human behavior. Mars-Jones sees *Nights at the Circus* as an entree—no gooey dessert metaphors denigrate the text. But Mars-Jones clearly finds the novel difficult to "read" and make "coherent" according to the reading strategies most serious readers have been trained to use. His complaints about the novel's "false notes" reveal his attempts to read in such a way that Carter's metafiction will legitimize rather than subvert dominant ideological and literary structures. When, for instance, Mars-Jones places Carter's text on an intertextual grid, he compares it to "serious" works that are part of the academic tradition; thus he does not mention Carter's references to the romance tradition or complain about her anachronistic use of television jingles. Instead, he oversignifies what are small references to Carlyle and Toulouse-Lautrec, spending a long paragraph of his review trying to explain why Carter treats these figures differently.

Odder yet is Mars-Jones's decision to focus on Fevvers's references to poems by Yeats, references that must defy conventional point of view and/or literary history:

When Fevvers describes Madame Schreck's museum of female freaks as "this lumber room of femininity, this rag-and-bone shop of the heart," what should the reader make of the quotation from late Yeats? It must be deliberate, since the sentence can do quite well without it; the second phrase, in fact, rather blurs the first. The poem in question . . . is called "The Circus Animals' Desertion," which is clearly in some way relevant; but is the reference Fevvers's, or Angela Carter's? If it is Fevvers's then she is more than a marvel, she is literary prophet, and the possibility of her fraudulence (important for the balance of the section) must disappear; but if it is Angela, Carter's, then why is she interrupting her creature to invoke (in a novel about a winged woman) a poem about the renunciation of the imaginary? (1083).

On the one hand, Mars-Jones's desire for a consistently realistic point of view and non-anachronistic allusions seem entirely beside the point in "a novel about a winged woman," but on the other hand, his angst-filled discussion of his inability to interpret the references to Yeats reveals the power of androcentric interpretive strategies. There is a kind of intellectual gamesplaying underlying this discussion ("I recognize the allusions"), but Mars-Jones, trained to track and interpret such intertextuality as a sign of "literature," seems unable to imagine that Carter might refer to the canon irreverently or parodically. Instead of using literary allusions to shore up the male tradition of great literature, Carter often alludes to works of the past parodically, thereby challenging the unacknowledged politics of aesthetic representation, particularly the representations of femininity. Significantly, Hutcheon, in the only short paragraph she devotes to *Nights at the Circus* in *The Politics of Postmodernism*, also "notices" the reference to Yeats, but she reads it quite differently, as both feminist and parodic: "The novel's parodic echoes of *Pericles, Hamlet,* and *Gulliver's Travels* all function as do those of Yeats's poetry when describing a whorehouse full of bizarre women as 'this lumber room of femininity, this rag-and-bone shop of the heart': they are all ironic feminizations of traditional or canonic male representations of the so-called generic human—'Man.' This is the kind of politics of representation that parody calls to our attention" (98).

Mars-Jones's complaints about the fragmented point of view likewise reveal more about the ideological biases of his reading strategies than they do about the "flaws" in Carter's technique: "At one point, when Fevvers with reluctant good nature is giving succour to the abused Mignon, whom she assumes to be Walser's lover, the reader gets not only Mignon's past from childhood up, but also several paragraphs on the life of her first employers. . . . These compulsively elaborated histories are likely to baffle the reader, and weaken the focus of the book"(1082). Just as Lessing's early reviewers were baffled by "the flaws" of her "incoherently" structured novel, Mars-Jones is baffled by Carter's "incoherent" point of view, a point of view that makes perfect sense, however, if one reads both metafictionally and as a feminist. Mignon's history is the history of women without voices to speak themselves; she is entirely an object, to be used by the various men who mistreat her, and it would be impossible for her to tell her own story to Walser or Fevvers: "She had the febrile gaiety of a being without a past, without a present, yet she existed thus, without memory or history, only because her past was too bleak to think of and her future too terrible to contemplate"(139–40). The narrator tells Mignon's history along with the "compulsively elaborated" histories of other circus performers, husband murderers imprisoned in a panopticon, and a Shaman who "adopts" Walser after the train wreck—to give voice to eccentrics, those who exist on the margins of dominant culture and dominant literary structures. The elaborately detailed and embedded narratives center these characters, and the authorial reader, like Jack Walser, must step across the threshold to the unknown: "Walser felt the strangest sensation, as if these eyes of the *aerialiste* were a pair of sets of Chinese boxes, as if each one opened into a world into a world into a world, an infinite plurality of worlds, and these unguessable depths exercised the strongest possible attraction, so that he felt himself trembling as if he, too, stood on an unknown threshold" (30).

Both Mars Jones and See fail to cross that threshold, fail to enter the authorial audience for Carter's texts, and fail to understand the parodic, metafictional, and feminist intentions of *Nights at the Circus,* and they thus reveal the paradox confronting the feminist writer of metafiction. To deconstruct a particular ideology and a particular set of conventions, it is necessary to invoke those very ideologies and conventions one hopes to subvert, but as these misreadings suggest, the double coding of metafiction makes this a risky business for the feminist writer who hopes to show the connections between literary constructions and social constructions. Although Mars-Jones notices the many literary echoes of Carter's novel, he dismisses the book's "wistful ambition to say something about a real 1889. . . . *Nights at the Circus* at its best is quite resonant enough to need no relevance imposed on it." Mars-Jones, signifying the literary rather than the social resonancies, seems to want the novel to participate in that "apolitical" metafictional tradition that holds up a mirror flatteringly to literature. Interestingly, he attributes his inability to read Carter's text as a coherent novel to her "extravagance," a word Nancy Miller suggests is a code word for the feminine:

> The attack on female plots and plausibilities assume that women writers cannot or will not obey the rules of fiction. It also assumes that the truth devolving from *veri*similitude is male. For sensibility, sensitivity, "extravagance"—so many code words for feminine in our culture that the attack is in fact tautological—are taken to be not merely inferior modalities of production but deviations from some obvious truth. The blind spot here is both political (or philosophical) and literary. It does not see, nor does it want to, that the fictions of desire behind the disiderata of fiction are masculine and not universal constructs. It does not see that the maxims that pass for the truth of human expe-

rience and the encoding of that experience, in literature, are organizations, when they are not fantasies, of the dominant culture. (44)

The misreadings provided by See and Mars-Jones result from their attempts to decode the novel using the very androcentric reading strategies that it attempts to undermine. No wonder *Nights at the Circus* seems "extravagant" to Mars-Jones and makes See queasy.

Greene claims that Lessing's readers failed to notice the metafictional quality of *The Golden Notebook* because it was "ahead of its time, and, like other innovative works, it had to teach us how to read it" (114), and, as I suggested earlier, Lessing's extratextual introduction did outline the interpretive strategies by which her readers could enter the authorial audience. Carter, however, attempts to teach us how to read a feminist virtuoso performance within her text, through the example of Jack Walser. For while Fevvers is foregrounded as the Helen of the new myth of the free, confident, creative woman, the more interesting transformation actually occurs to her male reader. The American journalist, the skeptical verifier of fact, must learn the case with which fiction becomes fact, imaginative representations become reality: after suffering a broken arm in a fight with a circus tiger, Walser is deprived of his profession and realizes that "for the moment, his disguise disguises—nothing. He is no longer a journalist masquerading as a clown; willy-nilly, force of circumstance has turned him into a *real* clown" (145). Identity, Walser comes to understand, is constructed through both the fictions we are told and the fictions we tell.

The blow to the head that Walser suffers in the train wreck thus has far more significant implications than Fevvers's broken wing, for while she momentarily forgets her own magnificence, and her role as performing subject, Walser loses all memory, all cultural and historical contexts that might allow him to read his environment: "Walser no longer knew enough to ask: 'Where am I?' Like the landscape, he was a perfect blank" (222). Both Sally Robinson and Pauline Palmer have persuasively argued that Walser becomes a blank in order that his masculinity might be reconstructed to match Fevvers's femininity: however, more important is Carter's self-conscious reconstruction of Walser as a reader capable of appreciating Fevvers's performance. Now an amnesiac, who even as he recovers his wits has no interpretive strategies to make sense of his memories, Walser is tutored in the arts of magic by a Shaman. Like Fevvers, who says "I'm not the right one to ask questions of when it comes to what is real and what is not, because, like the duck-billed platypus, half the people who clap eyes on me don't believe what they see and the other half thinks they're seeing things" (244), the Shaman "made no categorical distinction between seeing and believing. It could be said that, for all the people of this region, there existed no difference between fact and fiction; instead, a sort of magic realism" (260). It is in the context of this world of "hard, if illusory, facts" that the ex-journalist struggles to interpret his memories and dreams, unable to determine whether the odd image of a six-foot woman with wings that haunts him is fact or fiction, memory or desire, and finally, he comes to understand that he has been asking the wrong questions all along.

Thus, when he is reunited with Fevvers at the end of the novel, Walser is a reconstructed reader, one who demands not "are you fact or are you fiction," but rather, "What is your name? Have you a soul? Can you love?" (291). And Fevvers, delighted at discovering "whom this reconstructed Walser . . . turn[s]out to be," cries out "That's the way to start the interview! . . . Get out your pencil and we'll begin!" (291). As they reenact the opening narration, they also prepare to make love for the first time, and Walser attempts to construct his interpretation of his life's story, both past and future:

> I am Jack Walser, an American citizen. I joined the circus of Colonel Kearney in order to delight my reading public with accounts of a few nights at the circus and, as a clown, performed before the Tsar of All the Russians, to great applause. (What a story!) I was derailed by brigands in Trans-baikalia and lived as a wizard among the natives for a while (God, what a story!) Let me introduce my wife, Mrs Sophie Walser, who formerly had a successful career on the music-hall stage under the name of—. (293–94)

This story, however, is a product of nineteenth-century patriarchal narrative forms and social conventions, and the marriage that robs Fevvers of both name and career is not to end *her* story. As the clock strikes midnight of the first day of the new century, Walser "took himself apart and put himself together again" as the new reader:

> Jack, ever an adventurous boy, ran away with the circus for the sake of a bottle blonde in whose hands he was putty since the first moment he saw her. . . . And now, hatched out of the shell of unknowing by a combination of a blow on the head and a sharp spasm of erotic ecstasy, I shall have to start all over again. (294)

The new relations between Fevvers as performing artist and Walser as appreciative reader are mirrored by the sexual position necessitated by Fevvers's wings. The novel ends with Fevvers on top of her newly constructed reader, laughing marvelously at her ability to "fool" Walser into believing that she had been the "only fully-feathered intacta in the history of the world" (294), and Walser laughs too, "not quite sure whether or not he might be the butt of the joke" (295).

Brain McHale has suggested that self-conscious fiction is not merely "about" itself, but that many postmodern works are also "about" love, not only because postmodern fiction often represents love between characters or explores the "theme" of love, but primarily because it models "erotic relations through fore-grounded violations of ontological boundaries" (227). Thus, authors "love" their characters and texts "seduce" their readers; "factual" worlds embrace "fictional" worlds. According to McHale, "Love, then, is less an object of representation than a *meta*object, less a theme than a *meta*theme. It characterizes not the fictional interactions *in* the text's world, but rather the interactions *between* the text and its world on the one hand, and the reader and his or her world on the other" (227). But the erotic paradigm offered by most of the male postmodern writers McHale discusses is that offered by John Barth in *Chimera,* where the teller's role "was essentially masculine, the listener's or reader's feminine" (34). *Nights at the Circus* offers a new model of erotic relationship between teller and told, one that literally turns Barth's male-biased paradigm on its back; Carter's "masculine" reader must abandon the androcentric world view and learn to interpret the feminist text anew. Lizzie tells Fevvers, the author of this new paradigm, "You never existed before. . . . You haven't any history and there are no expectations of you except the ones you yourself create" (198); and although she rejects the romantic ending that befell Rosalind, Fevvers believes that she need not reject readerly love altogether: "think of his malleable look. As if a girl could mould him any way she wanted. . . . I'll *sit* on him, I'll hatch him out, I'll make a new man of him" (281). But Fevvers's reader requires both the erotic spasm *and* the blow to the head, as do, it seems, Carter's reviewers. For despite what I believe are well-executed feminist metafictional strategies, the reviewers' androcentric interpretive strategies keep them from becoming authorial read-ers of Carter's novel. Lizzie's skeptical response to Fevvers's "I'll make a new man [ie., reader] of him" thus seems to anticipate the failure of Carter's reviewers to be as malleable as Walser: " 'Perhaps so, perhaps not,' she said, putting a damper on things. 'Perhaps safer not to plan ahead' " (281).

In the April 23, 1992 issue of *The New York Review of Books,* John Bayley reviewed eight of Carter's texts (excluding, curiously, *Nights at the Circus*) in an essay that unfortunately served as both a kind of "introduction" for Amer-ican readers and an obituary, because Carter died of cancer in February at the age of 51. Bayley claims that the novels she published in the sixties "were hailed in England as an enterprising native version of the kind of thing that was being done in North America by Thomas Pynchon and in South America by Gabriel Garcia Marquez" (9). Yet Carter has, for the most part, failed to gain either the popular American audience of writers like Marquez and Fowles or the critical attention afforded most postmodern authors we could name. The lack of the "right kinds of critical attention" is particularly baf-fling, as Carter is an exceptional writer who tells good stories in very funny ways and at the same time, she is a writer often on the cutting edge of post-modern theory.

Carter has blamed her failure to gain an American audience in part on American publishers: "None of them, of course, have been able to do any-thing with my work in the States anyway. They can make a best-seller if they want. . . . You know—'We love the book, but it's not going to sell.' Why don't they come right out and say they can't stand the book? 'We can't stand the book, that's why we think nobody will buy it, because we think that everybody's like us' " (Goldsworthy 11). "Everybody's like us." As Ohmann suggests, both the publication and success of a book depend upon "a small group of relatively homogeneous readers," a "nearly closed circle of marketing and consumption" (380). And Carter's texts, read "authorially," are extraordinarily subversive of what Rabinowitz calls the "masculinist bias in the normalized techniques of reading" that editors and publishers, professional critics and reviewers, academics and university educated readers have been trained to use. Carter's feminist metafictions demand that we constantly interrogate the conventions that regulate literature and human behavior, and transforming ourselves into Carter's authorial readers requires that we cross the threshold to the unknown, suspending not our disbelief but rather our attachment to androcentric interpretive strategies."Reading is just as creative an activity as writing and most intellectual development depends upon new readings of old texts," Carter wrote in "Notes from the Front Line." "I am all for putting new wine in old bottles, especially if the pressure of the new wine makes the old bottles explode" (69). Reconstructing old readers so that they might interpret in new ways might shatter those old androcentric bottles— and that, of course, is the desire of most feminist writers of metafiction.

Note

1. In defining the term "misreading," Rabinowitz makes an important distinction between interpretive practices that ignore authorial intention and those in which the reader tries, but fails, to enter the authorial audience. Both reviewers of Carter's novel, for instance, seem to try to understand "what Carter was doing," to enter her authorial audience, and what I call their "misreadings" are not their failures to "judge" the texts as I would, but rather, their failures to employ the appropriate interpretive strategies to "decode" the text. One might very well succeed in entering the authorial audience of *Nights at the Circus* and still judge the novel to be uninteresting, unworthy, or trivial.

Works Cited

Barth, John. *Chimera*. Greenwich, CT: Fawcett, 1972.
Bayley, John. "Fighting for the Crown." *The New York Review* (April 23, 1992): 9–11.
Carter, Angela. *The Bloody Chamber and Other Stories*. London: Gollancz, 1980; New York: Penguin, 1987.
———. *Nights at the Circus*. London: Chatto, 1984; New York: Penguin, 1986.
———. "Notes from the Front Line." *On Gender and Writing*. Ed. Michelle Wandor. London: Pandor Press, 1983, 69–77.
———. *The Sadeian Woman and the Ideology of Pornography*. New York: Pantheon, 1979, 1988.
Christgau Robert. "What Pretentious White Men Are Good For," *Voice Literary Supplement* (April 1986): 7–8.

DuPlessis, Rachel Blau. *Writing beyond the Ending*. Bloomington: Indiana UP, 1985.

Goldsworthy, Kerryn. "Angela Carter: An Interview," *Meanjin* (1985 March); 4–13.

Graff, Gerald. *Literature Against Itself*. Chicago: U of Chicago P, 1979.

Greene, Gayle. *Changing the Story: Feminist Fiction and the Tradition*. Bloomington: Indiana UP, 1991.

Hutcheon, Linda. *The Politics of Postmodernism*. London: Routledge, 1989.

Lessing, Doris. "Introduction" to *The Golden Notebook*, New York: Bantam Press, 1973.

Mars-Jones, Adam, "From Wonders to Prodigies." *Times Literary Supplement* (September 28, 1984): 1083.

Mazurek, Raymond. "Courses and Canons: The Post-1945 U.S. Novel." *Critique* (Spring 1990): 143–156.

McHule, Brian. *Postmodern Fiction*. London and New York: Routledge, 1991.

Miller, Nancy K. "Emphasis Added: Plots and plausibilities in Women's Fiction." *Subject to Change; Reading Feminist Writing*. New York: Columbia UP, 1988.

Ohmann, Richard. "The Shaping of a Canon: U.S. Fiction, 1960–1975." *Canons*. Ed. Robert von Hallberg. Chicago: U of Chicago P, 1984, 377–401.

Palmer, Paulina. "From 'Coded Mannequin' to Bird Woman: Angela Carter's Magic Flight," *Women Reading Women's Writing*. Ed. Sue Roe. New York: St. Martin's, 1987.

Rabinowitz, Peter. *Before Reading; Narrative Conventions and the Politics of Interpretation*. Ithaca, NY: Cornell UP, 1987.

Robinson, Sally. *Gender and Self-Representation in Contemporary Women's Fiction*. New York: State U of New York P. 1991.

See, Carolyn. "Come on and See the Winged Lady." *The New York Times Book Review* (February 24, 1985): 7.

Angela Carter's Nights at the Circus: An Engaged Feminism via Subversive Postmodern Strategies

MAGALI CORNIER MICHAEL

With extravagant playfulness, Angela Carter's *Nights at the Circus* (1984) weaves together elements of the carnivalesque and fantastic with those of harsh material realism as vehicles for feminist aims. Set in 1899, *Nights at the Circus* purports to usher in the twentieth century. Carter's depiction of the past is strikingly familiar, however, which suggests that the present is effectively her target and that 1899 and the 1980s are not worlds apart. The novel is set not only in the past but also in places that are out of the ordinary—a whorehouse, a museum for women monsters, a circus, and Siberia—which enables Carter to engage in flights of imagination that do not directly contradict the immediate context of the contemporary reader.

The feminism of *Nights at the Circus* is complex in that it brings together more than one strand of feminism, an engaged Marxist feminism and a subversive utopian feminism.[1] Lizzie and her adopted daughter Fevvers serve, respectively, as mouthpieces for each of these two feminisms, although there is an overlap as the two characters influence each other. The novel's omniscient narrative voice strives to conjoin these two strands of feminism in order to posit a feminism that would be liberating while retaining a sociohistorical grounding—a feminism that would free human beings from the hierarchical relations in which Western culture, with its binary logic, has entrapped them, without becoming disengaged from the material situation. In order to both analyze the status of women and of existing relationships between women and men within Western culture and, more radically, propose possible avenues for change, Carter pits a Marxist feminist realism against postmodern forms of tall tales or autobiographies, inverted norms, carnivalization, and fantasy. While disruptive strategies usually associated with postmodernism pervade *Nights at the Circus,* it uses these strategies specifically to strengthen and further its feminist aims. Even as she appropriates extraordinary and fan-

From *Contemporary Literature* 35, no. 3 (Fall 1994): 492–521. © 1994 University of Wisconsin Press. Reprinted by permission.

tastic elements, Carter retains certain conventions of realism and a firm connection to the historical material situation as means of securing her novel's feminist political edge and ensuring that her novel remains accessible to most readers.[2]

To accomplish its aims, the novel engages and attempts to resolve the tensions that have characterized the uneasy relationship between Marxist feminism and postmodernism. Marxist feminism has generally rejected postmodernism on the grounds that its tendency toward abstractions gives way to a disconnection from the material world and from history, that it rejects metanarratives (such as Marxism and gender theory), and that it dissolves the subject. In contrast, Marxist feminists emphasize the material world in which women are daily oppressed as women and situate their analyses of women's oppression within specific political, cultural, historical, economic, and ideological contexts. As Toril Moi explains, "patriarchy itself persists in oppressing women *as women*" (36), so that "as feminists we need to *situate* our deconstructive gestures in specific political contexts" (43). Materialist feminism thus takes as its point of departure "the oppression of women" and asserts "the social origins" of that oppression, employing both micro- and macro-analyses. Furthermore, as "a social movement," a "revolutionary movement" actively seeking to change the world (Delphy 215, 211), Marxist feminism requires active agents/subjects. Nancy Hartsock argues that "rather than getting rid of subjectivity or notions of the subject, as Foucault does ... we need to engage in the historical, political, and theoretical process of constituting ourselves as subjects as well as objects of history" ("Foucault" 170).[3]

Postmodernism, however, is a slippery area of contention that cannot be reduced to any oversimplified characterization. Indeed, many critics argue that postmodernism is not inherently antithetical to feminism and Marxism and is very much tied to the material world. Fredric Jameson, for example, views postmodernism as a "cultural dominant" linked to "a whole new type of society" (3), a "new social formation," "multinational capitalism" ("Postmodernism" 4), and Andreas Huyssen explains postmodernism as a cultural and historical phenomena, as "a slowly emerging cultural transformation in Western societies" (181). Critics like Linda Hutcheon argue that rather than being ahistorical, postmodernism "reinstalls historical contexts as significant and even determining" at the same time that "it problematizes the entire notion of historical knowledge" (*Poetics* 89). In addition, some critics assert that postmodernism does not necessarily invalidate all metanarratives. Jameson suggests that, as a cultural dominant, postmodernism is inherently political and that "Politics has to operate on the micro- and the macro-levels simultaneously" ("Afterword" 386). Likewise, Nancy Fraser and Linda Nicholson argue that "postmodern critique need forswear neither large historical narratives nor analyses of societal macrostructures," so that "postmodern feminists need not abandon the large theoretical tools needed to address large political problems" as long as their theory remains "explicitly historical" (34). Furthermore, critics like Huyssen assert that postmodernism seeks to reconsturct and reconceptualize rather than negate the subject by challenging "the *ideology of the subject* (as male, white, and middle class) by developing alternative and different notions of subjectivity," "working toward new theories and practices of speaking, writing, and acting subjects," and questioning "how codes, texts, images, and other cultural artifacts constitute subjectivity" (213). Similarly, Carter's novel aesthetically engages and conjoins Marxist feminism and postmodernism in an effort to construct an engaged feminism with liberatory potential.

Carter's novel highlights its own textuality with its three labeled parts and its presentation of a metafictional narrative in which so many other narratives are embedded that notions of authorship and single-leveled reality are undermined. One of the novel's central preoccupations is its challenge to the traditional Western opposition between reality and fiction. The novel's rejection of any neat demarcation between reality and fiction functions as the pivotal strategy for undermining the Western conception of the subject and of traditional gender categories and for offering forms of liberating power. This liberating power carries with it possibilities for change in the realms of subjecthood and the relations between the sexes and also anticipates potential new forms for feminist fiction.

Nights at the Circus is divided into three parts labeled in terms of geographical location: "London," "Petersburg," and "Siberia." The movement toward increasingly foreign and remote places is accompanied by a movement away from any stable ground of reality and toward the ever more fantastic. The narrative is fragmented by various embedded stories, told by and about women, that further destabilize conventional notions of reality, truth, and authorship. Although the omniscient narrator purports to concentrate on the central male character's point of view, the narrative's perspective continually shifts as it is appropriated by women characters telling their stories-histories in long monologues that often include vivid dialogue.

The novel's focus and central character is Fevvers, a huge female *"aerialiste."* with wings, whose fame rests on her indeterminate identity and origins: her slogan reads "Is she fact or is she fiction?" (7). Lizzie, a staunch Marxist feminist, is Fevvers's adopted mother and companion who took her in as a foundling. The "London" segment of the novel consists of an interview of Fevvers, in Lizzie's presence, by a young American journalist, Jack Walser. Walser's initial purpose is to expose Fevvers as "a hoax," as one of the "Great Humbugs of the World" (11). Although Walser is the interviewer, Fevvers and Lizzie control the session by telling Fevvers's life story and challenging his disbelief and skepticism. Walser's curiosity is only awakened by the women's "performance" (90) during the interview, and he decides to join the circus in order to follow up on this story.

The second part, "Petersburg," focuses on Walser's transformation into a clown as he becomes subsumed within the magical circus world and recognizes that he has fallen in love with Fevvers. This segment relies more heavily on authorial narration, although it also includes segments of dialogue as well as embedded stories of the abused female circus performers befriended by Fevvers. By the novel's last section, "Siberia," the fantastic has taken over. The train carrying the circus crashes and the various characters wander around Siberia in various groups, meeting extraordinary people and situations. Walser and Fevvers are separated, and the novel ends when they are reunited. In this segment the narrative shifts among Fevvers's and Walser's stream of consciousness, dialogue, embedded stories, and authorial narration.

Feminist and postmodern elements are so enmeshed in *Nights at the Circus* that any discussion of either necessarily overlaps with the other. It is, nevertheless, useful to begin with the more overt feminist currents. From its first page, Carter's novel begins to undermine conventional notions of gender construction and sexual hierarchy.[4] Fevvers asserts authority over her own story-history and evades attempts by Walser to fix an identity upon her. Although Walser is intent upon naming and thus objectifying Fevvers, the fact that his quest begins rather than ends the novel announces from the start the subversion of his attempts to appropriate her. Carter in this way begins to call into question accepted notions of identity and the binary logic on which they depend, as she attempts to create a new female subject that seeks to satisfy feminist aims.

Fevvers defies Walser's attempt to prove her a fake not by refusing to answer his questions but by taking command of her own self-definition as she tells him her story and thus assumes a position of authority. As Teresa de Lauretis asserts, "strategies of writing *and* reading are forms of cultural resistance" (7), and this argument surely can be extended to oral storytelling.[5] By having Fevvers read her own life and write, or rather tell, her own story-history as she chooses, the novel challenges the traditional appropriation of women's lives and histories endemic in Western, male-centered culture. Furthermore, Fevvers deliberately flirts with the boundary between truth and nontruth. Her story is both an autobiography and a tall tale and, as such, destabilizes both male definitions of women and notions of identity, truth, and reality.

The novel opens with Fevvers's assertion that she "never docked via what you might call the *normal channels,* sir, oh, dear me, no; but, just like Helen of Troy, was *hatched*"; and the narrative specifies that she accompanies her statement with direct eye contact "as if to dare him: 'Believe it or not!' " The reference to the mythical Helen, engendered by Zeus in the form of a swan and Leda, ironically links Fevvers's self-definition to the history of Western culture, as it raises her to mythic or at least fantastic proportions. The narrative normalizes the comparison, however, by playfully debasing it to the level of ordinary family resemblances: "Evidently this Helen took after her putative father, the swan, around the shoulder parts" (7). Moreover, Fevvers's claim that she was hatched suggests that she "fantasizes a beginning for her-

self outside the Oedipal triangle" associated with the nuclear family and subject formation (Schmidt 67).[6] To more thoroughly mystify her biological origins, Fevvers further asserts that she was a foundling. As a half-woman, half-
swan orphan, Fevvers challenges prevailing notions of identity that are
grounded in verifiable origins and binary logic.

By allowing her origins to remain a mystery and encouraging speculation about them, Fevvers maintains her status as "Heroine of the hour" (8).
Her fame depends precisely on her being suspect, whether or not her wings
are real. Although Walser is skeptical of Fevvers's claim that she is a "genuine
bird-woman," he "contemplate[s] the unimaginable" while watching her perform on the trapeze and recognizes the "paradox" that "in a secular age, an
authentic miracle" would have to "purport to be a hoax, in order to gain
credit in the world" (17). Walser's reflection highlights the precarious nature
of the opposition between reality and fiction by suggesting that the concepts
are intertwined. Fevvers's indeterminate identity and her insistence on preserving its mystery threaten the dichotomy between reality and fiction.

"At six feet two in her stockings" (12), Fevvers disrupts the conventions
of female characters. She asserts her authority by simply taking up space:
"Fevvers yawned with prodigious energy, opening up a crimson maw the size
of that of a basking shark, taking in enough air to lift a Montgolfier, and then
she stretched herself suddenly and hugely, extending every muscle as a cat
does, until it seemed she intended to fill up all the mirror, all the room with
her bulk." Walser is threatened by her appropriation of space and attempts to
escape the room so that "he might recover his sense of proportion" (52),
which is clearly male-defined. The novel's simultaneous insistence on
Fevvers's bodily presence and on her self-construction frustrates the traditional Western dichotomy between soul-self and body in which the body—
and in turn the material world—is relegated to irrelevance and inferiority.[7]
Fevvers significantly fills the mirror before she fills the room, highlighting the
postmodern notion that nothing exists outside of representation or a specific
context; yet she nevertheless fills the room as well, fulfilling the feminist
insistence that representation retain a firm link to the material situation.[8]

Fevvers's "raucous" voice and her "grand, vulgar" gestures (12, 13) indicate that she is comfortable with herself and has chosen her own codes of
behavior. She takes up a traditionally masculine role by asserting herself as
the author of her own actions and words. Having internalized conventional
categories, Walser describes Fevvers as having a "strong, firm, masculine
grip" (89) when she shakes his hand. The narrative also stresses her femininity, however, by describing her dressing room as "a mistresspiece of exquisitely feminine squalor" (9), using deliberately feminized language. Moreover,
the depiction of one of her feminine flirtatious gestures, when "she batted her
eyelashes at Walser in the mirror" (40), again presents Fevvers via the mediation of a mirror. Fevvers is altogether an ambivalent figure who threatens traditional binary categories: she possesses both masculine strength and author-

ity as well as feminine charms and wiles.[9] The interview reduces Walser rather than Fevvers to a passive state: "It was as if Walser had become a prisoner of her voice" (43). Carter's novel thus challenges the traditional association of female with femininity and of male with masculinity through the depiction of characters who confound accepted gender norms and polarity. As Sally Robinson suggests, "For Carter, gender is a relation of power, whereby the weak become 'feminine' and the strong become 'masculine.' And, because relations of power can change, this construction is always open to deconstruction" (77). Indeed, the novel does deconstruct the masculine/feminine hierarchical opposition itself by presenting Fevvers as co-opting both masculine and feminine characteristics to establish her power over Walser.

Fevvers and Lizzie assume control of the narrative in the novel's "London" section as they unfold Fevvers's life story-history through long dynamic monologues, interrupted by dialogues between the two women. The customary association of authorship and activeness with the male is here reversed: Fevvers and Lizzie are the active speakers-writers and Walser is the passive spectator-reader. Fevvers is able to "challenge and attack" (54) Walser's attempt to fix her identity, and thus objectify her, by controlling and thus constructing her own self and story-history. Fevvers exhibits herself as object for an audience's gaze; yet, as the author of herself as object, she is also a subject and thus has control over how much she will allow herself to be consumed by her viewers: "Look at me! With a grand, proud, ironic grace, she exhibited herself before the eyes of the audience as if she were a marvellous present too good to be played with. Look, not touch" (15).[10] Fevvers begins her working career by posing as a *"tableau vivant,"* thus actively constructing herself as an object to be seen but not touched: as a child she is "Cupid" (23), and as she matures she becomes "Winged Victory" (25) and then "Angel of Death" (70). Although Fevvers objectifies herself, she remains a subject by constructing her own objectified image. By destabilizing and yet retaining the conventional opposition between subject and object, the novel moves toward a nonhierarchical and nonbinary notion of subjectivity while simultaneously engaging and highlighting issues of power relations. Although feminists such as Hartsock have criticized postmodernism for "getting rid of subjectivity or notions of the subject," *Nights at the Circus* illustrates ways in which postmodern notions of subjectivity can be tapped for feminist purposes without disintegrating subjectivity to the point where it no longer exists. Carter's novel never loses touch with the material oppression of women even while it attempts to offer new forms of subjectivity that are not based in the binary thought system that has helped to oppress women in Western culture. The novel thus does precisely what Hartsock claims is necessary for feminism to move forward: "we need to engage in the historical, political, and theoretical process of constituting ourselves as subjects as well as objects of history," and "we need not only to critique the dominant culture but also to create alternatives" ("Foucault" 170, 172).

Carter's novel differentiates among those who are performing the objectification of women and for what purposes. Fevvers's existence as both subject and object challenges the type of objectification by which "male-subjectivity creates its Other precisely to designate itself as its superior, its creator-spectator-owner-judge" (Finn 91). Fevvers vehemently rejects her own objectification by men: "I did *not* await the kiss of a magic prince, sir! With my two eyes, I nightly saw how such a kiss would seal me up in my *appearance* for ever!" (39). The threat of being forced into the position of static object to be viewed and dominated is all too tangible for Fevvers, who is again and again faced with attempts to fix the ambivalent figure she presents to the world.

The novel contains two separate instances in which men literally attempt to objectify Fevvers. In both cases, the men seek to dominate her by depriving her of control over her own life. Their attempts to transform her into a corpse in one instance and into a toy in the other support the notion that "you can only objectify the living by taking away its life; by killing it either in fact or fantasy" (Finn 89). In the first episode, a wealthy gentleman purchases Fevvers from the museum of women monsters and attempts to kill her with a blade. Viewing her as a "reconciler of opposing states" and as his "rejuvenatrix" (81, 82), he tries to sacrifice her on May Day to ensure his own life and power. But Fevvers rejects the role of passive victim and of male-constructed object and pulls out her own sword to save her life. She thus asserts her authority and subject-hood by matching his phallic power—located in his weapon rather than in his penis—sword for sword. The novel in this way emphasizes the violence that is part of male domination and that is tried to the realm of sexuality. As Michele Barrett argues, "sexual relationships are political because they are socially constructed and therefore could be different" and because of "the unequal power of those involved in sexual relationships" (42, 43). After all, sexuality is "one of the fields of confrontation" or "struggle" between "social men and social women," so that oppression within the realm of sexuality is just "as material as economic oppression" (Delphy 217, 166).

Later in the novel, a Russian grand duke attempts to cage Fevvers among his collection of exotic toys, but again she fights against objectification. After the Grand Duke breaks her sword and thus deprives her of phallic power, Fevvers resorts to feminine wiles to distract him: "a deep instinct of self-preservation made her let his rooster out of the hen-coop for him and ruffle up its feathers." She masturbates him and makes her escape at the moment "the Grand Duke ejaculated" (191–92). The novel does not jettison the conventions of realism, even if it does push toward the postmodern, since it ultimately grounds seemingly extraordinary incidents—such as her narrow escapes from the wealthy gentleman and the Russian grand duke—in the daily victimization of women and thus challenges accepted notions of women as naturally and inevitably passive objects.[11]

Although Fevvers is presented as a fantastic being whose experiences encompass the extraordinary, the novel never severs the connection between her exploits and the material situation: Fevvers is fantastic but recogniz-able.[12] Her relationship with Lizzie is in this respect crucial, since Lizzie functions as the novel's didactic feminist voice. As a staunch Marxist feminist and former prostitute, Lizzie keeps the novel's focus from diverging too far from the economic aspects of material existence. In Hartsock's terms, Lizzie provides the novel with a "feminist standpoint [which] can allow us to descend further into materiality to an epistemological level at which we can better understand both why patriarchal institutions and ideologies take such perverse and deadly forms and how both theory and practice can be redirected in more liberatory directions" (*Money* 231). Fevvers's story also indicates that Lizzie's politics have influenced her adopted daughter, particularly in the depiction of the whorehouse in which Fevvers was raised as "the common daughter of half-a-dozen mothers" (21) and which disrupts the nuclear family developed under capitalism. Since "the family" is at present "itself the site of economic exploitation: that of women" (Delphy 59) and since "it is within the family that masculine and feminine people are constructed . . . [and] that the categories of gender are reproduced" (Barrett 77), the production of new forms of subjectivity requires new family structures and ideologies.[13]

Indeed, one of the means by which the novel begins to call into question the status quo and construct new notions of the subject is through its inversion of accepted norms in its treatment of prostitution and marriage. When Fevvers challenges Walser to print in his newspaper that she was raised by "women of the *worst class* and *defiled*," Walser's reply reveals his firm entrenchment in Western binary thought: "And, I myself have known some pretty decent whores, some damn' fine women, indeed, whom any man might have been proud to marry." Walser retains and even re-emphasizes the dichotomy between good women and bad women, wives and whores, by asserting that some whores are good enough to become wives. The novel rejects these oppositions through the voice of Lizzie, who asserts that wives and whores have more in common than not and, thereby, undermines the Western ideology of marriage: "What is marriage but prostitution to one man instead of many?" (21).

Lizzie's words echo not only Friedrich Engels's discussion of bourgeois marriage in *The Origin of the Family* but also Carter's own discussion of the subject in her book-length essay *The Sadeian Woman* (1978). *The Sadeian Woman* proposes that "sexual relations" are "necessarily an expression of social relations" and that, like prostitutes, "all wives of necessity fuck by contract" (9). Carter undermines the conventional hierarchical opposition between wives and whores by stressing that "Prostitutes are at least decently paid on the nail and boast fewer illusions about a hireling status that has no veneer of social acceptability" (9). *Nights at the Circus* fictionalizes this criticism of the bourgeois notion of marriage and of the traditional dichotomy between wife and whore by using prostitutes as its positive female characters, thus reducing marriage to nothing more than an unquestioned custom grounded in a false ideology of happiness: "The name of this custom is a 'happy ending' " (281).

Lizzie cynically defines marriage as forcing a woman to give to a man both herself and her "bank account" (280), thus highlighting the economic exploitation of women within the institution of marriage that is covered over by fictions of romance.

The novel's Marxist feminism and its stress on the economic as well as ideological oppression of women surface in the descriptions of prostitutes as "working women doing it for money," as "poor girls earning a living" (38, 39). Fevvers challenges the myths of whores as degenerates or nymphomaniacs by asserting that economics rather than pleasure informs the prostitute's work: "though some of the customers would swear that whores do it for pleasure, that is only to ease their own consciences, so that they will feel less foolish when they fork out hard cash for pleasure that has no real existence unless given freely—oh, indeed! we knew we only sold the *simulacra*. No woman would turn her belly to the trade unless pricked by economic necessity, sir" (39).[14] In addition, the assumption that sexual favors can be both "real" and "*simulacra*" of themselves calls into question the opposition between reality and fiction. Fevvers's words undermine the conventional association of sex with pleasure or desire by highlighting the contractual nature of all sexual relations. Sex is designated as a business transaction rather than a moral category. Carter suggests that both the prostitute and the wife engage in sex as an economic exchange; the only difference lies in the prostitute's explicit acknowledgment of the contract. The prostitute comes out ahead in the novel, precisely because she is depicted as more aware of her position within an economic system in which all women necessarily participate.

Carter transforms the whorehouse into a "wholly female world," a "sisterhood" of active, ambitious women, whose lives are "governed by a sweet and loving reason." The prostitutes are "all suffragists" (38–39)—not "suffragettes"—and professional women. They engage in "intellectual, artistic or political" (40) pursuits before the whorehouse opens each evening and are thus active subjects as well as sexual objects. By making the prostitute its version of the feminist, the novel disrupts accepted norms and dualisms—including conventionalized notions of feminists. The term "whore" becomes ambivalent as it is dislocated from its position as polar opposite of wife, good woman, and even feminist. Furthermore, although her use of the term "honour" to denote selfhood is conventional, Fevvers's explicit questioning of the common reduction of women to their bodily orifices challenges traditional stereotypes: "Wherein does a woman's honour reside, old chap? In her vagina or in her spirit?" (230). Fevvers's words also emphasize the ways in which the biological body has been co-opted in the service of those in power.[15]

Although some of the ideas Carter espouses in *The Sadeian Woman* find a voice within *Nights at the Circus,* the latter shapes Carter's ideas into a web of creative and overtly fictionalized narratives. In *Nights at the Circus,* Carter strengthens her feminist position through the use of various destabilizing aesthetic strategies. The novel's subversion of the notion of prostitution, for example, goes far beyond its overt analysis through the voices of Fevvers and Lizzie; it is reinforced by a thorough carnivalization of the whorehouse itself. Indeed, Carter's use of carnivalization and her creation of carnival spheres strengthen the novel's more subversive feminism.

Mikhail Bakhtin describes the process of "carnivalization" as the "transposition of carnival into the language of literature" (122) that brings to literary works the "carnival sense of the world [which] possesses a mighty life-creating and transforming power, an indestructible vivacity" (107). The carnival attitude challenges the status quo by sanctioning unofficial behavior and by celebrating the "joyful relativity" of everything (107), so that the "behavior, gesture and discourse of a person are freed from the authority" of "the all-powerful socio-hierarchical relationships of non-carnival life" (123). Bakhtin argues that this carnival attitude has been transmitted through the ages via various carnivalized genres, and in particular through Menippean satire (157–58).

Critics engaging postmodernism have been quick to point out a connection between the carnivalization implicit in Menippean satire and postmodern literature. Brian McHale, for example, argues that "Postmodernist fiction is the heir of Menippean satire" and demonstrates ways in which postmodern literature appropriates processes of carnivalization. McHale maintains that postmodern fiction compensates for the loss of "the carnival context by incorporating carnival, or some surrogate for carnival, at the level of its projected world," so that "In the absence of a *real* carnival context, it constructs fictional carnivals" (174). An examination of the basic characteristics of Menippean satire as delineated by Bakhtin further suggests that carnivalization has overt political implications and might, therefore, be adopted as a feminist strategy. *Nights at the Circus,* for example, utilizes a postmodern version of carnivalization as a vehicle for its more subversive feminist aims.

The political potential of Menippean and postmodern forms of carnivalization lies in what Bakhtin describes as its *"experimental fantasticality"* (116), its "creation of *extraordinary situations* for the provoking and testing of a philosophical idea" (114). Carnivalized scenes of "scandal," "eccentric behavior," and other "violations" of "established norms" are used to create "a breach in the stable, normal ('seemly') course of human affairs and events" so as to "free human behavior from the norms and motivations that predetermine it" (117). Bakhtin's further characterization of Menippean satire as having a "concern with current and topical issues" and as being "full of overt and hidden polemics" also points to the inherently political nature of this form of carnivalization (118). Carter's *Nights at the Circus* is a prime example of a carnivalized novel, whose ultimate aim is to expose current feminist concerns and offer possibilities for change.[16] The novel's use of extraordinary and fantastic characters and situations and its creation of actual and surrogate carnivals begin to destabilize existing norms as well as the binary logic which undergirds Western culture.

By constructing the whorehouse, the museum for women monsters, the circus, and Siberia as versions of carnival, the novel disrupts and challenges traditional Western notions of reality and provides an aesthetic vocabulary for delineating possibilities of change. Since the carnival is a space within which the dominant hierarchical system and its laws and prohibitions are suspended, the carnival allows for ambivalence and relativity as well as for new forms of interrelationships—a primary feminist aim. The whorehouse in the "London" section of *Nights at the Circus,* for example, functions as a surrogate carnival and, as such, reinforces the novel's disruption of the accepted notion of prostitution and of the binary logic on which it depends.

The novel's presentation of prostitutes in a positive light and of prostitution in nonmoral terms as well as its use of an extraordinary heroine with wings are carnivalesque disruptions of established norms. The physical description of the whorehouse itself further establishes its carnival status. The house's "staircase that went up with a flourish like, pardon me, a whore's bum" and its "drawing room [that] was snug as a groin" are comic touches that transform conventional imagery by inserting a whorehouse world view within a traditional descriptive style. Fevvers's outrageous depiction of the house as having an "air of rectitude and propriety" and as being "a place of privilege" in which "rational desires might be rationally gratified" (26) further challenges the status quo by deploying adjectives generally reserved for officially sanctioned institutions. The novel thus brings together high and low culture, destabilizing the distinction between them. The whorehouse of the novel's "London" section is a carnival sphere, in the sense that it defies established conventions and codes; it becomes other than what it is generally thought to be and thus challenges the ruling order.

Fevvers is herself an ambivalent figure of carnival stature, disrupting established conventions of female characters. Not only are her identity and origins nebulous, but her reputation as "Virgin Whore" (55) defies the highly charged opposition between virgin and whore used by Western culture to name, objectify, categorize, and marginalize women. By claiming that she is the "only fully-feathered intacta in the history of the world" (294), Fevvers participates in her own social definition. Her admission at the end of the novel that she is after all not an "intacta" demonstrates that, in the absence of an essential self or soul, the possibility of self-construction exists alongside construction by others; Fevvers is able to create the being that others see her to be. The outrageous nature of Fevvers as a character thus heightens the novel's challenge to Western culture's version of women as passive objects.[17]

The novel uses Lizzie's voice to reinforce didactically and theoretically the claim that selves are constructed rather than essential. Lizzie rejects the notion of "*soul*" as "a thing that don't exist" and asserts that it is history "that forged the institutions which create the human nature of the present in the first place." In line with her staunch Marxism, Lizzie argues that the possibility of change rests on a thorough dismantling and restructuring of society: "It's not the human 'soul' that must be forged on the anvil of history but the anvil itself must be changed in order to change humanity" (239–40). Lizzie's declaration lends a Marxist tinge to the novel's feminism, with its implication that women's oppression will not end until social structures are radically altered. Carter uses the novel's two central female characters, Lizzie and Fevvers, to conjoin a material analysis of existing means of subject construction and a carnivalized version of female self-construction, as a way of exploring the possibility of a new female subject.

As a fantastic and indeterminate being, Fevvers can never be pinned down as a subject; her status is always in the process of becoming other than itself.[18] Her identity is unstable, since she is a site of apparent contradictions: woman and bird, virgin and whore, fact and fiction, subject and object. Fevvers begins to lose her power and her subjecthood, however, when she questions her own status—"Am I what I know I am? Or am I what he thinks I am?"—and regains it only when she reasserts her indeterminate identity by spreading her wings and recognizing herself through "the eyes that told her who she was" (290). Once again, she creates herself as the object of her spectators' desires and is thus both subject and object of desire.[19] Fevvers's subjectivity pushes toward the postmodern in the sense that her multifaceted and fluid identity destabilizes the rigid boundary between subject and object. Her indeterminate nature challenges these dichotomies and heralds the advent of new female subjectivities that are not grounded in binary logic and are thus released from the hierarchical relations implicit in binarism.

Desire is linked to a new version of subjecthood, as delineated by Fevvers, and to feminist liberating powers. By the end of the novel, Fevvers defines herself as a "New Woman" (273) in relation to—not in opposition to—both Walser, as the object of her desires, and desire itself. Her linking of Walser's "beloved face" to "the vague, imaginary face of desire" (204) suggests that the novel posits desire as an elusive but life-affirming notion. The novel rejoins desire and love, which it depicts as divorced from sex in most instances—since it depicts sex as most often nothing more than pornography—and presents love and desire as containing emancipatory potentials. Carter ends *The Sadeian Woman* with the claim that "It is in this holy terror of love that we find, in both men and women themselves, the source of all opposition to the emancipation of women" (150). In *Nights at the Circus,* she takes a step further and creates a world in which human beings are freed through love and desire, by learning not to fear love and not to equate desire and sex with pornography. The novel's presentation of desire smacks of essentialism—desire as opposed to the culturally constructed, pornographic *mise en scène* of desire—and yet, since desire functions on a utopian level and as carrying liberatory potential, it may be a utopian rather than essentialist reformulation of desire.

The novel distinguishes between pornography and desire. The pornographic nature of the "museum of woman monsters" (55), in which Fevvers is forced to work for a time, lies in its *mise en scène* of sexuality. As the Angel of Death, Fevvers claims that she does not engage in sexual intercourse itself; she merely poses as one of the *"tableaux vivants"* (60) staged on "stone niches" in a "sort of vault or crypt" (61). The museum's male visitors indulge in a pornographic voyeurism; they don costumes and look at the female "prodigies of nature" arranged as spectacle (59). The gentleman who favors Fevvers, for example, never touches her but, rather, looks at her while "playing with himself under his petticoat" (71). The male engages in sexual actions without the female in this pornographic situation and thus remains in control; she serves merely as a visual stimulus. The novel's depiction of pornography as a staged representation of sexuality rather than as sexuality itself supports Marie-Francoise Hans and Gilles Lapouge's view of pornography as a "sexual spectacle, its reproduction or its representation, *the discourse on sexuality and not sexuality*" (24; my translation).

The museum of women monsters in Carter's novel reinforces the notion that pornography is a representation of male domination.[20] The museum is an artificial arena in which men occupy the position of dominance with no hindrances, since women are literally cast as museum objects to be viewed and consumed: Fevvers claims that the men visitors "hired the use of the idea of us [the women]" (70). Carter's depiction of the pornographic museum functions as a critique of male domination and the oppression of women; it supports her claims in *The Sadeian Woman* that pornography has a liberating potential, if it is used "as a critique of current relations between the sexes," and that "sexual relations between men and women always render explicit the nature of social relations in the society in which they take place and, if described explicitly, will form a critique of those relations, even if that is not and never has been the intention of the pornographer" (19–20). In other words, if pornography is a representation of male domination, then it is implicit that pornography can be used to criticize that very domination. As Susan Gubar has pointed out, the divergent feminist arguments about pornography suggest that "an explicitly misogynist representation cannot automatically be equated with a sexist ideology" (730). Indeed, *Nights at the Circus* depicts the misogyny inherent in pornography as a means of criticizing male domination and its sexist ideology in general.

Fevvers's assertion that the women freaks in the museum had "hearts that beat, like yours, and souls that suffer" (69) is an indictment of a society that objectifies women and treats them as less than human. The association of pornography and the dominant male-centered ideology surfaces through Fevvers's statement that "there was no terror in the house our [male] customers did not bring with them" (62). The novel depreciates male dominance with its depiction of men who are so fearful of losing their positions of mastery in the hierarchy of conventional heterosexual relationships that they are reduced to jerking themselves off while looking at women freaks in a damp basement. *Nights at the Circus's* strategy of turning pornography on its head manifests both feminist and postmodern impulses: feminist in the sense that it uses a conventionally misogynist discourse—pornography—to criticize the male-centered ideology that produces it; postmodern in its subversion of the supposed dichotomy established between pornography and daily life. Fevvers's assertion, for example, that it was "those fine gentlemen who paid down their sovereigns to poke and pry at us who were the unnatural ones, not we. For what is 'natural' and 'unnatural,' sir?" (61) both criticizes and calls into question the conventional dichotomy between that which is natural and that which is unnatural and thus exposes the opposition as an ideological construction. Within the world of the museum, sexual gratification occurs through staged means and is devoid of interpersonal connections or, in some cases, contacts. In the "Black Theatre," for example, the woman freak's task is to place "a noose around his [the client's] neck and give it a bit of a pull but not enough to hurt, whereupon he'd ejaculate" (61). The portrayal of the museum and its offerings thus demonstrates pornography's dehumanization of sex and sexuality.

The novel's depiction of pornography exceeds the bounds of the museum scenes, however, which heightens its criticism of male domination in its suggestion that sexual relations are for the most part pornographic in a culture that objectifies women. The attempted rape-murder by sword of Fevvers by a *gentleman* is a good case in point; it is a pornographic *mise en scène* of a sexual act. He makes her "Lie down on the altar" naked and approaches her with something that "was a sight more aggressive than his other weapon, poor thing, that bobbed about uncharged, unprimed," and that *"something was—a blade"* (83). This scene demonstrates the utter divorce between sexuality and interpersonal love and/or desire and the explicit link between sexuality and violence that exist in a male-dominated world. Fevvers's description of the gentleman's useless and passive penis both ridicules the notion that man's dominating position is grounded in his *natural* aggressiveness and exposes the means by which men dominate in actuality: through violence. The novel thus playfully reinforces the Lacanian notion that the privilege attributed to the male and the penis is grounded in "a confusion of the virile member with a phallic signifying function" (Ragland-Sullivan 290).

The gentleman dominates the situation only through his possession of a lethal sword, a phallic power that Fevvers appropriates—she has her own sword—to extricate herself from his power. Fevvers also uses her wings to escape the gentleman's grasp by simply flying out of his window and, therefore, uses a power that is not phallic in nature. The fantastic enables Carter to bypass and undermine phallic power and to posit other forms of power. Although flying away from an aggressor is not a practical solution for most women, Carter's use of the image indicates the liberating quality of strategies of empowerment that are not phallic and violent. Fevvers's use of her wings is a form of power similar to her use of storytelling, which she rids of its phallic associations—pen as penis—as well as of its reliance on strict distinctions between fiction and nonfiction; in both cases, self-empowerment is achieved through means that are nonviolent and that subvert Western binary logic.

The life stories of various abused women, which are retold by Fevvers within her own narrative, also contain depictions of events that are both part of everyday life and pornographic. Carter in this way makes explicit the link between pornography and the system that produces it. The story of the diminutive Wonder, one of the museum's women monsters, is punctuated by a description of how a company of comic dwarfs mistreated her: "I travelled with them seven long months, passed from one to another, for they were brothers and believed in share and share alike. I fear they did not treat me kindly, for, although they were little, they were men." The dwarfs' passing around of Wonder highlights the objectification of women inherent in Western culture. For the male dwarfs, Wonder is a commodity to be used by all and then discarded, "abandoned" (68). Mignon's story is more explicit in its depiction of the violence inflicted on women by men to assert their authority. Mignon is a battered circus wife, who is literally treated as an object: "the Ape-Man beat his woman as though she were a carpet" (115). She is also "abandoned to the mercies of a hungry tiger by her lover" (127), the Strong Man, when an escaped tigress intrudes upon their sexual encounter. Mignon's body itself, with its skin that was "mauvish, greenish, yellowish from beatings" and showed "marks of fresh bruises on fading bruises on faded bruises" (129), testifies to the horrifying violence that daily ensures male dominance.

The novel does not merely point out the oppression of women by a male-dominated system, however; it offers potential solutions. Mignon, for example, acquires self-confidence and steps beyond her role as eternal victim. Fevvers and Lizzie help clean her up and find her a new position free of "The cruel sex [that] threw her away like a soiled glove" (155). Mignon is teamed up with the Princess in the dancing tigers act: the Princess plays the piano and Mignon sings. The two women quickly become friends and lovers, cherishing "in loving privacy the music that was their language, in which they'd found the way to one another" (168). Mignon is strengthened through the music that she believes they have "been brought together, here, as women and as lovers, solely to make" (275). The novel thus offers lesbian relationships as a possibility for women to find love and purpose in a world in which violence dominates heterosexual relations and women are kept from assuming control of their lives and talents. Fevvers reacts to this flowering of Mignon by asserting that "Love, true love has utterly transformed her" (276), in the sense that love has enabled Mignon to reject the role of victim and create herself as an active subject.

The transformative powers of love and the potential of lesbianism take on a larger and more fantastic force in the novel's depiction of a Siberian asylum for women who murdered their husbands and the revolt of these prisoners sparked by the vitality of desire. Designed and run by a countess who "successfully poisoned her husband" and sought to assuage her conscience by serving as "a kind of conduit for the means of the repentance of the other murderesses," the prison is a "*panopticon*": "a hollow circle of cells shaped like a doughnut, the inward-facing wall of which was composed of grids of steel and, in the middle of the roofed, central courtyard, there was a round room surrounded by windows. In that room she'd sit all day and stare and stare and stare at her murderesses and they, in turn, sat all day and stared at her" (210). As Michel Foucault has pointed out in *Discipline and Punish,* the panoptic prison design makes it "possible to hold the prisoner under permanent observation" by setting up "a central point from which a permanent gaze may control prisoners and staff." The cost of this system of surveillance by observation is that it manages "to entrap the whole of penal justice and to imprison the judges themselves" (248–50). Carter playfully presents this paradox in the depiction of the countess who is "trapped as securely in her watch-tower by the exercise of her power as its objects were in their cells," since she must always keep watch over her prisoners: "the price she paid for her hypothetical proxy repentance was her own incarceration" (214). The wardresses are also imprisoned and watched, so that everyone within the system of the asylum is, in effect, a prisoner, regardless of her official position. Carter's depiction of the prison configuration implicitly serves as a parallel to the existing social structure, in which all human beings are effectively imprisoned.

In the prison chapter, the novel's omniscient narrative voice is totally separated from the voices of Fevvers and Walser, who are not present. Although the narrative does not condone murder, it analyzes the murderesses' acts as responses to the historically specific condition of women: "There are many reasons, most of them good ones, why a woman should want to murder her husband; homicide might be the only way for her to preserve a shred of dignity at a time, in a place, where women were deemed chattels, or, in the famous analogy of Tolstoy, like wine bottles that might conveniently be smashed when their contents were consumed" (210–11). The narrative voice's feminism surfaces in this discussion of the murderesses as victims of an inequitable system. The mock-rational tone emphasizes the absurdity of a world in which violence is the only recourse for women, since they are dominated and oppressed by men through violence. The narrative zooms in on one of the inmates, Olga, "who took a hatchet to the drunken carpenter who hit her around once too often" (211). Having "rehearsed in her mind the circumstances of her husband's death" and attributed them to things outside of her control, Olga "exonerated herself" (214, 215) and set out to communicate with the wardress who brought her food daily. The relationship between Olga and her guard, Vera, quickly moves from a touch of the fingers, to "a free if surreptitious exchange of looks," to an exchange of notes. Having no pen or pencil, Olga "dipped her finger" in "her womb's blood" to write an answer to Vera's "love-words" (216).

Olga's use of her menstrual blood to assert herself as an active subject challenges the traditional association of menstrual blood with dirtiness and inferiority to men. Later in the novel, Carter provides evidence of this conventional devaluation of anything to do with women's reproductive selves in the depiction of a tribal woman banished to a "primitive hut" outside the village to give birth to her child. Lizzie aptly describes the scene with the submissive "prone woman" and her baby alone in the freezing hut as a "tableau of a woman in bondage to her reproductive system" (282, 283).[21] Olga thus uses one of the most overt emblems of femaleness, traditionally used to set women apart as inferior to men, as a means of empowerment; she literally writes herself into subjecthood with her menstrual blood. This specific instance of a woman's assertion of power through an innovative writing process is linked to the novel's general presentation of creative storytelling as a strategy for empowerment and self-construction that challenges the established order.

Moreover, desire has generative powers within the world of the prison. It engenders love, which in turn feeds desire. The desire and love that develop between Olga and Vera spread to the other inmates of the asylum: "Desire, that electricity transmitted by the charged touch of Olga Alexandrovna and Vera Andreyevna, leapt across the great divide between the guards and the guarded. Or, it was as if a wild seed took root in the cold soil of the prison and, when it bloomed, it scattered seeds around in its turn. The stale air of the House of Correction lifted and stirred, was moved by currents of anticipation, of expectation, that blew the ripened seeds of love from cell to cell" (216–17). The novel depicts desire as a force strong enough to destroy the artificial divisions that culture establishes between human beings to uphold a given hierarchical social order. Desire and love become agents of hope that have potential liberating powers. Within the world of the prison, that potential is actualized when the women prisoners and guards rise up against the countess and escape the asylum.

The image of "an army of lovers" striking out on foot across the Siberian tundra to "found a primitive Utopia" is both fantastic and freeing. Carter's novel uses this extraordinary situation to assert the possibility of change: "The white world around them looked newly made, a blank sheet of fresh paper on which they could inscribe whatever future they wished" (217–18). The new sisterhood of women sets out to forge a new social order that excludes men and rejects the notion of "fathers" and "the use of the patronymic" (221). This new "republic of free women" is not totally independent of men, however, since the women are forced to ask a passing male traveler for "a pint or two of sperm" to ensure their community's survival. When Lizzie hears the traveler recount his meeting of the women, she sarcastically asks what they will do if they give birth to baby boys: "Feed'em to the polar bears? To the *female* polar bears?" (240–41). Lizzie's question highlights the impossibility of severing ties between the sexes if humanity is to continue, since both sexes are necessary for reproduction. While the narrative voice cannot be equated with Lizzie's specific words, Lizzie's challenging of the female utopia indicates that the novel does not view a separatist lesbian community as a final answer to the problems faced by women within a male-centered culture. The novel clearly seeks to go beyond separatism to a restructuring of the whole system in such a way that men would no longer dominate and women would no longer be oppressed.

The novel ends on the rejuvenating and liberating note of Fevvers's carnivalesque laughter, brought on by Walser's question as to why she went "to such lengths" to convince him that she was the "only fully-feathered intacta in the history of the world." She is delighted by this question, to which she gleefully retorts, "Gawd, I fooled you" (294). Fevvers's subjecthood is assured through Walser's question, since it proves that she has the power to construct her own version of herself. She attributes her ability to fool even a skeptic, such as Walser was at the start of the novel, to her spirited determination to define herself: " 'To think I really fooled you!' she marvelled. 'It just goes to show there's nothing like confidence' " (295). Laughter thus functions as a liberating strategy that is useful in the process of developing new versions of the subject.

Fevvers's loud, uncontrollable laughter problematizes the meaning of the novel's ending at the same time that it releases a liberating energy. It is an ambivalent form of laughter in that it exceeds its context and its meaning is plural and dynamic. Ambivalent laughter is a vital element of the carnival, described by Bakhtin as embracing both "death and rebirth" and as "directed toward something higher—toward a shift of authorities and truths, a shift of world orders" (127). Fevvers's laughter salutes the end of Walser's skepticism and disengagement, as well as her feelings of diminishment, and welcomes the fresh winds of change.[22] The laughter that physically ends Carter's novel thus creates a sense of beginning. Uncontained, it "spilled out of the window" and infects everyone and everything: "The spiralling tornado of Fevvers' laughter began to twist and shudder across the entire globe, as if a spontaneous response to the giant comedy that endlessly unfolded beneath it, until everything that lived and breathed, everywhere, was laughing" (294–95). This ending, which is also a beginning, offers ambivalent laughter as a means of approaching twentieth-century life, since Fevvers's laughter rings out as midnight passes and ushers in a new century.

Carter's exploration of carnivalistic laughter indicates that it can help propel feminist aims. Fevvers's laughter over her ability to fool Walser into believing that she is a virgin bird-woman challenges male domination as well as Western binary logic. Fevvers resists male-centered definitions of her by assuming control of her own self-construction and undermining the conventional opposition between reality and fiction. Her laughter thus disrupts the male-centered established order; it is a manifestation of release from the status quo that is directed toward an as yet undelineated feminist version of a new and better world. Ending the novel on a note of carnivalistic laughter does not diffuse the subversive nature of *Nights at the Circus;* rather, it provides a vital image, one that is divorced from Western rationality and logic, to carry the potential for change urged by the novel. Bakhtin's claim that carnivalistic laughter can "grasp and comprehend a phenomenon in the process of change and transition" (164) helps to explain why it is a useful vehicle for feminist fiction writers who wish not only to expose the ills of the established order but also to posit ways in which that order is being undermined and changed.

The novel's ending with laughter also anticipates potential new forms for feminist fiction. Bakhtin's argument that carnivalistic laughter possesses "Enormous creative, and therefore genre-shaping, power" (164) supports the notion that a feminist appropriation of carnival laughter opens up the way for the formation of new types of feminist fiction that would be subversive and liberating both at the level of narrative and of politics. Since ambivalent laughter and the carnivalesque in general bring together the ordinary, sensory, physical world and the visionary and thus allow a space for change and for the future without divorcing themselves from the material situation, they make ideal strategies for the furthering of subversive feminist aims.

By subverting expectations, carnivalization both exposes and challenges the established male-centered order and offers possibilities for change. But Carter is careful to keep her narrative grounded in the material situation by maintaining a balance between depictions of daily life and of fantastic occurrences, even if they are intermingled. While carnivalization propels forward the novel's more utopian feminism, other strategies, such as embedded stories-autobiographies and inverted norms, also serve subversive functions, notably as vehicles for the novel's Marxist feminism. A variety of strategies usually associated with postmodernism thus enable Carter to bring the two strands of subversive feminism together and to posit a feminism that blends their best qualities and avoids their pitfalls: *Nights at the Circus* adopts Marxist feminism's emphasis on the material situation, which utopian feminism tends to ignore; and it adopts utopian feminism's creative and hopeful dynamism, which Marxist feminism often lacks. By establishing a materialist, sociohistorical grounding for its utopian vision, of new women and men creating a world that would be better in feminist terms, the narrative explains why the present world is still far from being a feminist utopia and, yet, still offers some hope for the future.

Notes

1. In a related vein, Paulina Palmer locates "a key area of tension in Carter's writing" between "utopian elements" and "an equally strong emphasis on the analytic and the 'demythologising' " (179). I argue that the bringing together of these two impulses in *Nights at the Circus* creates not tension but rather a space where possibilities for change can be explored.

2. In one sense, then, Carter's novel is an example of what Alison Lee describes an the tendency within British postmodern fiction to "challenge Realist conventions from within the

very conventions they wish to subvert" (xii). Lee does not discuss how feminism and/or feminist fiction fit into her thesis.

3. Although he does not address feminism, Fredric Jameson cautions that, even in abstract theoretical accounts that appear to "lack agency," "agents of all sizes and dimensions are at work" in the sense that any "seemingly disembodied force is also an ensemble of human agents" that " 'make their history' " even if it is " 'not in circumstances of their own choosing' " ("Afterword" 382–83).

4. Similarly, Sally Robinson argues that Carter "disrupts an essentialist equation between biological sex and social gender" but at the same time "*foregrounds* gender as constitutive of subjectivity by tracing the processes by which 'official' women—that is, individuals sexed female—are socially and discursively constructed as Woman according to the needs of the dominant, 'official' sex, men" (77).

5. Along the same lines, Toril Moi argues that "To name is to exercise power" and that although "Definitions may well be constraining: they are also enabling" (37). Sally Robinson notes that Fevvers "places herself as the subject of her own story" (23).

6. Carol Siegel also notes that Fevvers is "hatched—in defiance of biological genre" (12).

7. Nancy Hartsock argues in *Money, Sex, and Power* that, within "masculinist ideology," "The body is both irrelevant and in opposition to the (real) self, an impediment to be overcome by the mind" (242) and that it is not surprising that the body and "material reality" are devalued by Western societies since these are the realms with which women are in closer contact (235–36).

8. Although this interest in mirrors recalls mannerism, postmodernism more thoroughly problematizes the dichotomy between appearance and reality by demonstrating that reality is always already represented and thus cannot be dissociated from appearance. Fevvers's identity is one that she has created for herself and cannot be separated from what she appears to be.

9. Fevvers in this sense has more in common with Amazon warrior women than with traditional Western conceptions of women.

10. My argument thus differs from that of Robinson, who argues that "While Fevvers is placed as the object of various male gazes in the text, she simultaneously places herself as the subject of her own story" (23). I am suggesting that Fevvers actively creates herself as subject *and* object; she is not passively "placed as the object of various male gazes." Later in her discussion, however, Robinson seemingly contradicts her earlier analysis when she suggests that "Fevvers takes full responsibility for engineering herself as spectacle and, thus, resists victimization" (125)—a formulation with which I thoroughly agree. In much the same way, Ricarda Schmidt argues that "the miraculous Fevvers is the inventor of her own singularity for which she seeks acclaim" (72). As Carol Siegel suggests, "Carter gives us woman as someone other than Other, someone who is not defined by and absorbed into the patriarchal power structure" (12).

11. That women are victimized daily is supported by FBI statistics on rape. For example, 1987 FBI statistics cited in *Crime in the United States: 1987 Uniform Crime Reports* indicate that, in the United States alone, there is "one *Forcible Rape* every six minutes" (6). The FBI reports define "Forcible Rape" as "the carnal knowledge of a female forcibly and against her will" and include "Assaults or attempts to commit rape by force or threat of force" (13). These figures are necessarily conservative, since many rapes and attempted rapes go unreported.

12. In a similar vein, Linda Hutcheon notes that Carter's novel "straddles the border between the imaginary/fantastic (with her winged woman protagonist) and the realistic/historical" (*Poetics* 61), but she does not pursue this line of analysis.

13. I am here using the term *ideology* in the sense defined by Michele Barrett as "a generic term for the processes by which meaning is produced, challenged, reproduced, transformed" (97).

14. As Hutcheon asserts, "women (as prostitutes, in particular) are never real; they are but representations of male erotic fantasies and of male desire" (*Politics* 32).

15.   This co-optation is particularly evident in attitudes and laws concerning women's reproductive capacities.

16.   Carter's clear theoretical awareness suggests that she knows Bakhtin's work and is using it for her own purposes. Paulina Palmer has like myself observed the connection between Carter's *Nights at the Circus* and Bakhtin's concept of carnivalization. In a discussion aimed specifically toward the novel's focus on "woman-identification and female collectivity" (200), Palmer argues that Carter adopts "carnivalistic perspectives" to perform "an analysis of patriarchal culture and the representation of female community" (197).

17.   In much the same way, the Amazon warrior woman has often been created as a figure that threatens the status quo.

18.   Hutcheon suggests in more general terms that in the fiction of writers such as Carter, "subjectivity is represented as something in process, never as fixed and never as autonomous, outside history. It is always a gendered subjectivity, rooted also in class, race, ethnicity, and sexual orientation" (*Politics* 39).

19.   Although she does not explicitly assert that Fevvers creates herself as both subject and object simultaneously, Ricards Schmidt does note that "Fevvers does not simply become men's passive object, for her wings ensure that she herself constitutes a formidable subject which others must react to. But as the eye metaphor indicates, she does nevertheless need the reaction of others to have her own conception of herself confirmed" (68).

20.   Susan Gubar argues that most feminists agree that "pornography represents male domination," even writers as dissimilar as "Millett and Carter" (730).

21.   Much Marxist feminist analysis highlights the connection between women's reproductive capacities and women's oppression.

22.   Rory Turner also links Fevvers's laughter at the end of the novel with Bakhtin's notion of ambivalent laughter, asserting that it "expresses a relationship to existence of all inclusive regeneration that is both mocking and triumphant" (57).

Works Cited

Bakhtin, Mikhail. *Problems of Dostoevsky's Poetics.* Trans. Caryl Emerson. Theory and History of Literature 8, Minneapolis: U of Minnesota P, 1984.

Barrett, Michele. *Women's Oppression Today: Problems in Marxist Feminist Analysis.* London: Verso, 1980.

Carter, Angela. *Nights at the Circus.* 1984. New York: Penguin, 1986.

———. *The Sadeian Woman: And the Ideology of Pornography.* New York: Pantheon, 1978.

Crime in the United States: 1987 Uniform Crime Reports. Washington, D.C.: Federal Bureau of Investigation, United States Department of Justice, 1987.

De Lauretis, Teresa. *Alice Doesn't: Feminism, Semiotics, Cinema.* Bloomington: Indiana UP, 1984.

Delphy, Christine. *Close to Home: A Materialist Analysis of Women's Oppression.* Trans. Diana Leonard. Amherst: U of Massachusetts P, 1984.

Finn, Geraldine. "Patriarchy and Pleasure: The Pornographic Eye/I." *Feminism Now: Theory and Practice.* Ed. Marilouise Kroker and Arthur Kroker. Montreal: New World Perspectives, 1985. 81–95.

Foucault, Michel. *Discipline and Punish: The Birth of the Prison.* Trans. Alan Sheridan. New York: Pantheon, 1977.

Fraser, Nancy, and Linda Nicholson. "Social Criticism without Philosophy: An Encounter between Feminism and Postmodernism." 1988. *Feminism/Postmodernism.* Ed. Linda Nicholson. New York: Routledge, 1990. 19–38.

Gubar, Susan. "Representing Pornography: Feminism, Criticism, and Depictions of Female Violation." *Critical Inquiry* 13 (1987): 712–41.

Hans, Marie Francoise, and Gilles Lapouge. *Les femmes, la pornographic, l'erotisme.* Paris: Editions du Seuil, 1978.

Hartsock, Nancy. "Foucault on Power: A Theory of Women?" *Feminism/Postmodernism.* Ed. Linda Nicholson. New York: Routledge, 1990. 157–75.

———. *Money, Sex, and Power: Toward a Feminist Historical Materialism.* 1983. Boston: Northeastern UP, 1985.

Hutcheon, Linda. *A Poetics of Postmodernism: History, Theory, Fiction.* New York: Routledge, 1988.

———. *The Politics of Postmodernism.* New York: Routledge, 1989.

Huyssen, Andreas. "Mapping the Postmodern." 1984. *After the Great Divide: Modernism, Mass Culture, Postmodernism.* Bloomington: Indiana UP, 1986. 178–221.

Jameson, Fredric. "Afterword—Marxism and Postmodernism." *Postmodernism/Jameson/Critique.* Ed. Douglas Kellner. Washington, D.C.: Maisonneuve, 1989. 369–87.

———. "Postmodernism, or The Cultural Logic of Late Capitalism." 1984. *Postmodernism, or, The Cultural Logic of Late Capitalism.* Durham: Duke UP, 1991. 1–54.

Lee, Alison. *Realism and Power: Postmodern British Fiction.* New York: Routledge, 1990.

Lyotard, Jean-Francois. *The Postmodern Condition: A Report on Knowledge.* Trans. Geoff Bennington and Brian Massumi. Minneapolis: U of Minnesota P, 1984.

McHale, Brian. *Postmodernist Fiction.* New York: Methuen, 1987.

Moi, Toril. "Postmodernist Theory: Feminist Postmodernism in the USA." *Criticism in the Twilight Zone: Postmodern Perspectives on Literature and Politics.* Ed. Danuta Zadworna-Fjellestad. Stockholm: Almqvist and Wiksell International, 1990. 34–46.

Palmer, Paulina. "From 'Coded Mannequin' to Bird Woman: Angela Carter's Magic Flight." *Women Reading Women's Writing.* Ed. Sue Roe. New York: St. Martin's, 1987. 179–205.

Ragland-Sullivan, Ellie. *Jacques Lacan and the Philosophy of Psychoanalysis,* Urbana: U of Illinois P, 1986.

Robinson, Sally. *Engendering the Subject; Gender and Self-Representation in Contemporary Women's Fiction.* Albany: SUNY UP, 1991.

Schmidt, Ricarda. "The Journey of the Subject in Angela Carter's Fiction." *Textual Practice* 3 (1989): 56–75.

Siegel, Carol. "Postmodern Women Novelists Review Victorian Male Masochism." *Genders* 11 (1991): 1–16.

Turner, Rory P. B. "Subjects and Symbols: Transformations of Identity in *Nights at the Circus.*" *Folklore Forum* 20 (1987): 39–60.

Revamping Spectacle:
Angela Carter's *Nights at the Circus*

MARY RUSSO

I begin with the description of a fictional poster depicting a young woman with wings shooting through the air like a rocket, a French circus poster hanging in the London dressing room of a famous aerialiste, "the most famous aerialiste of her day"—her day being the end, "the fag-end, the smoldering cigar-butt, of a nineteenth century which is just about to be ground out in the ashtray of history"[1]—a day, in other words, not unlike our own. In large letters, advertising her engagement in Paris, is her slogan: "Is she fact, or is she fiction?" The poster's sensational image of female flight is marked by a rather unusual angle of viewing:

> The artist had chosen to depict her ascent from behind, bums aloft, you might say; up she goes, in a steatopygous perspective, shaking out about her those tremendous red and purple pinions, pinions large enough, powerful enough to bear such a big girl as she. And she was a *big* girl. Evidently this Helen took after her putative father, the swan, around the shoulder parts (*NC*, 7).

The Helen in question, "Helen of the High-wire," sometimes called "the Cockney Venus," is the fabulous "Fevvers," the central character of Angela Carter's 1984 novel, *Nights at the Circus*.[2] As her stage names indicate (and all her names are stage names), Fevvers straddles high and low culture. A woman with wings, she is no ordinary angel—if there could be such a thing—but rather an exhilarating example of the ambivalent, awkward, and sometimes painfully conflictual configuration of the female grotesque. Everything about this creature is sublime excess: her size, of course, and those wings which strain and bulge beneath her "baby-blue satin dressing gown;" her six-inch-long eyelashes which she rips off gleefully one eye at a time, suggesting not only her deliberate production of unnaturalness, but also the prosthetic grotesque (a question of give and take); her taste for immense quantities of champagne with eel-pie and a bit of mash; and her overwhelm-

From *The Female Grotesque: Risk, Excess, and Modernity* (New York and London: Routledge, 1995): 159–81. ©. Reprinted by permission.

ing rancid smell ("something fishy about the Cockney Venus") (*NC*, 8).
"Heroine of the hour, object of learned discussion and profane surmise, this
Helen launched a thousand quips, mostly on the lewd side" (*NC*, 8).

> Fevvers begins her act under a heap of brightly colored feather behind tinsel
> bars while the orchestra plays "I'm only a bird in a gilded cage." Vamping, she
> strains at the bars and mews "part-lion and part-pussy cat" (*NC*, 14).

Walser, the skeptical young American reporter who is assigned to cover
her for a paper in the United States, smugly identifies this opening bit as
"kitsch." With great self-satisfaction, he notes that "the song pointed up the
element of the meretricious in the spectacle, reminded you that the girl was
rumored to have started her career in freak shows" (*NC*, 14). In fact, Fevvers
has performed in meretricious spectacles her entire life, beginning with the
tableaux staged in Ma Nelson's whorehouse and moving on to a less hos-
pitable institution, the Museum of Female Monsters, directed by the grue-
some Madame Schreck, who kept her anatomical performers in niches in an
underground cave, stacked like wine bottles, for private viewings.[3]

In fact, it is debatable whether any performance site is not meretricious
in this novel for Carter, who described herself as both a feminist and a socialist writer, and who seems to have gone beyond the more individualistic, psychic model of spectacularity which characterizes her short stories, such as
"The Flesh and the Mirror," to map an historical and even global notion of
spectacle similar to that described by Guy Debord in *Society of the Spectacle*. For
Debord, "the spectacle is not a collection of images, but a social relation
among people, mediated by images."[4] Spectacle in this sense is not an imma-
terial world apart, but rather the condition, divided, and producing division,
of late capitalism:

> the spectacle, grasped in its totality, is both the result and the project of the
> existing mode of production. It is not a supplement to the real world, an addi-
> tional decoration . . . It is the omnipresent affirmation of the choice *already
> made* in production and its corollary consumption (Debord, 6).

In a different though not incompatible sense, the concept of the "already
made" is central to postmodernist discourse,[5] where it refers to the characteristic mode of cultural reprise or intertextuality of which Angela Carter's work
is often taken to be an example.[6] Linda Hutcheon, for instance, in an essay on
the politics of parody, cites the production of Fevvers as a feminist parody of
Leda and the Swan as an example of subversive repetition.[7] Describing *Nights
at the Circus*, she writes:

> The novel's parodic echoes of *Pericles, Hamlet,* and *Gulliver's Travels* all function
> as do those of Yeats' poetry when describing a whorehouse full of bizarre
> women as "this lumber room of femininity, this rag-and-bone shop of the

heart"; they are all ironic feminizations of traditional or canonic male representations of the so-called generic human-Man. This is the kind of politics of representation that parody calls to our attention (*NC,* 98).

In *Nights at the Circus* alone, dozens of other examples of intertexts from
high and low culture might be cited, and not all of them by any means as
central to the European canon as Shakespeare, Swift, or Yeats.[8] Allusions
abound to the twentieth-century artistic and political avant-gardes, to Andrei
Bely's *Petersburg,* to Freud, Poe, Bakhtin, and to the Marquis de Sade who
remains perhaps the most striking influence throughout Carter's work.[9]
Equally important, popular culture, which had once produced its own version
of critical parody in carnival, reappears and is transformed in modes of display, performance, and reproduction which characterize its institutionaliza-
tion in the European circus, museums, journalism, and advertising. Nor does
Carter limit herself to male producers and performers. In what may be my
favorite bit of intertextual play, Fevvers looks into the mirror as she prepares
to go on stage in St. Petersburg and delivers Mae West's famous line, "Suck-
ers," from *I'm No Angel* (1993), which features the great female impersonator
dressed in circus garb as a lion tamer in an imposture of dominance and control.[10] This Hollywood image of Mae West as a "double-bluff" dominatrix is
refigured in the excesses and obvious artifice of Fevvers' body and her act.[11]
The cinematic frame is transposed to the frame of the mirror, an historical
backward slide from high technology to the artisanal production of the
female body "making-up."

Female narcissism itself as a canonical representation of the feminine is
parodied and revised in the frames, mirrors, and circus rings which accom-
pany the hyperbole of self-consciousness that is female masquerade. Carter
returns again and again in her writing to female narcissism as a scene of failed
transcendence.

"FLESH AND THE MIRROR"

In the short story, "Flesh and the Mirror," Carter's unnamed European heroine returns to Japan from a trip to England to find her lover absent. Of
course, she is not alone, because someone is always looking: "I am told that I
look lonely when I am alone." To overcome the particular loneliness of this
looked-at-ness, she sets out to restage the scene.[12] Again, in a paradigmatic,
imperialist gesture of recentering, she uses the "enigmatic transparency" and
"indecipherable clarity" ("Flesh and the Mirror," 69)[13] of Japan literally to
"reorient" herself, as subject and center of the world:

> And I moved through these expressionist perspectives in my black dress as
> though I was the creator of all and of myself, too, in a black dress, in love, cry-

ing, walking through the city in the third-person singular, my own heroine, as though the world stretched out from my eye like spokes from a sensitized hub that galvanized all to life when I looked at it ("Flesh and the Mirror," 68).

Yet even as a perfect heroine of her own little black costume drama, she is excruciatingly embarrassed by her acute consciousness of the old scripts she is using ("And wasn't I in Asia? Asia!") and the old, ridiculed models ("Living never lived up to the expectations I had of it—the Bovary syndrome.") Back in another hotel room with a stranger, the center is lost as the coordinates of the self disappear into a psychotic or "magic" mirror above the bed, the mirror without an embodied self: ("I was the subject of the sentence written on the mirror. I was not watching it.") The ambiguity of the mirror in this story is that it provides, on the one hand, a possible identity, and that, on the other, it binds the heroine to the mirror as flesh to image so that real experience takes place "elsewhere," when as in blindness or a kind of death, she is not able to look.

> Mirrors are ambiguous things. The bureaucracy of the mirror issues me with a passport to the world; it shows me my appearance. But what use is a passport to an arm chair traveler? Women and mirrors are in complicity with one another to evade the action I/she performs that she/I cannot watch, the action with which I break out of the mirror, with which I assume my appearance ("Flesh and the Mirror," 71).

Breaking out of the mirror, if only provisionally, effects a self-estrangement; in the terms of the story, she feels as if she had "acted out of character" and that her "fancy-dress disguise" had led her to a "modification of myself that had no business at all in my life, not in the life I had watched myself performing" ("Flesh and the Mirror," 72). In this story, all she can do is "light a fresh cigarette from the butt of the old one" ("Flesh and the Mirror," 72) in a gesture of involuntary repetition, and leave this room for another room where, after a while, the estrangement she has felt from her lover, her country, her body, and herself, appear normal. The difference is that the normal now is recognized as merely the habitual and the performative: *The most difficult performance in the world is acting naturally, isn't it?"* ("Flesh and the Mirror," 77, emphasis mine).

The heroine of *Nights at the Circus* begins in some ways where the heroine of "Flesh and the Mirror" leaves off, trying to act natural which, in her case, will mean acting flamboyantly artificial. Like all of Carter's creations she loops and somersaults backward as well as forward in the plot, expanding the spatial dimensions of female spectacularity but never leaving the mirror entirely behind. Female narcissism is still a dilemma in this book, but Fevvers, without reading Simone de Beauvoir, knows at least that she is not born a "natural" woman. In fact, she is not even born, but hatched. The lack of human origins confounds the expectations of Walser, who wonders why all of

London isn't searching, as he is, for her belly button. But Fevvers "does not bear the scar of loss." "Whatever her wings were, her nakedness was certainly a stage illusion."[14] Her body is not lacking but her trajectory, as I will describe it in relation to her act, is out of sync with the conventions of what is called human development. She starts and stops in the intervals between points, hovering on the brink of possibility, instead of going forward.[15]

WINGS OF CHANGE

A Klee painting named *Angelus Novus* shows an angel looking as though he is about to move away from something he is fixedly contemplating. His eyes are staring, his mouth is open, his wings are spread. This is how one pictures the angel of history. His face is turned toward the past.[16]

Never mind the diabolical explanations of air-foil you get in Pan-Am's multilingual INFORMATION TO PASSENGERS, I happen to be convinced that only my own concentration (and that of my mother—who always expects her children to die in a plane crash) keeps this bird aloft.
　　　　　　　　　　　　　　　—*Amanda Wing in Erica Jong's Fear of Flying.*

In an interview,[17] Carter identifies a crucial intertext which I would like to follow up in discussing Fevvers as a female grotesque, a passage written by the poet Guillaume Apollinaire which she had previously quoted in her controversial nonfiction work, *The Sadeian Woman:*

It was no accident that the Marquis de Sade chose heroines and not heroes," said Guillaume Apollinaire. Justine is woman as she has been until now, enslaved, miserable, and less than human; her opposite, Juliette, represents the woman whose advent he anticipated, *a figure of whom minds have as yet no conception, who is rising out of mankind, and will have wings and who will renew the world* (emphasis mine).[18]

Although Carter's critics have sometimes confused her own views of the "praxis of femininity"[19] with Sade or Sade's heroine, Juliette, who wraps herself in the flags of male tyranny to avoid victimization, Carter is quite explicit about Juliette's limits as a model of the future for women.[20] "She is, just as her sister is, a description of a type of female behavior rather than a model of female behavior and her triumph is just as ambivalent as is Justine's disaster." If Juliette is a New Woman, "she is a New Woman in the model of irony."[21] What Juliette gains in the way of freedom is the ability to occupy space, "transforming herself from pawn to queen . . . and henceforth goes wherever she pleases on the chess board. Nevertheless, there remains the question of the presence of the king, who remains the lord of the game." Juliette masters the destructive techniques of power, inflicting suffering rather than suffering herself; yet although she seeks to avoid the fate of her sister at all costs, the two figures of femininity are inversely connected to pain, pleasure, and death. The difference may be that Justine's narrative of female suffering and submission may seem more representative of an essentialistic formulation of feminine identity and the "condition of women," whereas Juliette's behavior is far in excess of any possible identification with other women because disavowal of any shared "femininity" is a condition of her dominance and her freedom.[22]

Nights at the Circus is unique in its depiction of relationships between women *as* spectacle, *and* women as producers *of* spectacle. To the extent that female countercultures are depicted in the novel, they are placed within larger social and economic histories and fictions. The point I want to make here is simply that to the extent that value is contested in the production of images of women in this novel, it is contested socially. One body as production or performance leads to another, draws upon another, establishes hierarchies, complicities, and dependencies between representations and between women. Conflict is everywhere. Female figures such as Madame Schreck, "the scarecrow of desire," organize and distribute images of other women for the visual market. Her disembodied presence suggests the extreme of immateriality and genderless politics; she may, as the narrator suggests, be only a hollow puppet, the body as performance *in extremis*.[23]

It is with great irony that Carter reproduces aspects of Juliette and the libertarian tradition in *Nights at the Circus*. In a series of critical counterproductions of the affirmative woman "who will have wings and who will renew the world," Fevvers in born and born again, as an act (in the theatrical sense) of serial transgression. I have described Fevvers as the figure of ultimate spectacularity, a compendium of accumulated cultural clichés, worn and soiled from circulation. Yet, poised as she is on the threshold of a new century, her marvelous anatomy seems to offer endless possibility for change. Seeing her wings for the first time, Ma Nelson, whose whorehouse gives Fevvers a comfortable girlhood, identifies in "the pure child of the century that just now is waiting in the wings, the New Age in which no woman will be bound down to the ground" (NC, 25).

Ironically, in the context of the whorehouse, this means only that Fevvers will no longer pose as Cupid with a bow and arrow, but will now act as the Winged Victory, a static performance of her femininity "on the grand scale," but hardly a pure or transformative vision. The magnificent Nike of Samothrace from the second century B.C., long thought to be the greatest example of Hellenistic sculpture, is deservedly famous for its activation of the space around it. Standing eight feet tall, the figure of the victorious goddess leans out into the spatial illusion of onrushing air, still in motion, barely touching the ground. This icon of classical culture was much reproduced as a collectible souvenir and model of classicism. Through the techniques of miniaturization and reproduction described in chapter three, Nike reemerged in the late nineteenth century as Victorian bric-a-brac. It is in this guise that she is reproduced and reenlarged by the young Fevvers, whose domestic portrayal (on the whorehouse mantel) of this art object-souvenir in the *tableau vivant* for male visitors would seem merely to set the terms for their accession to, and repeatable acquisition of, the other women who service them. Like Trilby, Fevvers poses as the advertisement and model for similar commodities; not exactly a prostitute herself, she nonetheless installs the myth of femininity as virgin space in the displaced aura of the art work, while suggesting the comfort of the already-used, the "sloppy seconds" of womanhood waiting, for a price, in the upper chambers.

THE POSE

The redundancy of such posing, its mimetic charge, is always already excessive, as Craig Owens[24] has pointed out in one of the most interesting essays on contemporary mimesis and the pose.[25] Owens tentatively isolates two different perspectives on the question of the pose: the social and the psychosexual. As an example of the social perspective, he cites the work of Homi Bhabha on the mimetic rivalry of colonial discourse as an "ironic compromise" between what Bhabha describes as "the synchronic *panoptical* vision of domination—the demand for identity, status—and the counter-pressure of the diachrony of history—change, difference."[26] From the social perspective, Fevvers' first pose looks down (here, from a domestic perch) as if reversing the power relations of the panoptical gaze with the power of aerial surveillance. The compromised circumstances of her pose within the topography of the "house" (already a mock family space, headed by a Madame) contributes further to the irony of the *tableau*.[27]

From the psychosexual perspective, this pose reveals the constraints of the masquerade of femininity, as described and analyzed by Mary Ann Doane.[28] Although Doane's first essay on masquerade had focused on female spectatorship rather than female spectacle, it would appear, as she acknowledges in her second essay on the topic, that the concept of masquerade is more promising as a way to understand femininity as spectacular production.

> To claim that femininity is a function of the mask is to dismantle the question of essentialism before it can even be posed. In a theory which stipulates the claustrophobic closeness of the woman in relation to her own body, the concept of masquerade suggests a "glitch" in the system . . . Masquerade seems to provide that contradiction insofar as it attributes to the woman the distance, alienation, and divisiveness of self (which is constitutive of subjectivity in psychoanalysis) rather than the closeness and excessive presence which are the logical

outcome of the psychoanalytic drama of sexualized linguistic difference. The theorization of femininity as masquerade is a way of appropriating this necessary distance or gap, in the operation of semiotic systems, of deploying it for women, of reading femininity differently ("Masquerade Reconsidered," 37).

But this shift leaves some problems unsolved. The theoretical drawbacks of appropriating the psychoanalytical model of masquerade as if it were the definitive feminist answer to the constraints of gender (or worse, as if the dismantling of essentialist models of femininity could *tout court* dispel the effects of the imposition of gender, making feminism unnecessary) are, in my view, increasingly evident in the disavowal of the female body as a site of political activism.

In the case of Fevvers as Winged Victory, there is redoubled irony in her grotesque body (already redundant with wings *and* arms) in exposure and retreat as her arms are released to represent the complete "original" of a dismembered female figure, an ideal of Beauty, while her feathery humps are spread out to the viewer only to be taken as useless, arty, attachments:

> Well, Ma Nelson put it out that I was the perfection of, the original of, the very model for that statue which, in its broken and incomplete state, has teased the imagination of a brace of millennia with its promise of perfect, active beauty that has, as it were, been mutilated by history (*NC,* 37).

To the redundancy of arms and wings, Ma Nelson (alias Admiral Nelson) adds even more; to complete the picture, she places a sword in the hands of Victory ("as if a virgin with a sword was the fittest guardian angel for a houseful of whores.") This finally is too much for the clients: "Yet it may be that a *large* woman with a *sword* is not the best advertisement for a brothel. For slow, but sure, trade fell off from my fourteenth birthday on" (*NC,* 32). Although blame for the demise of the whorehouse falls, in the last analysis, on the bad influence of Baudelaire ("a poor fellow who loved whores not for the pleasure of it but, as he perceived it, the *horror* of it"), business falls off when young men become impotent at the sight of the big girl becoming a big woman with too many appendages and a phallus—a Medusa with her own sword. And, of course, she has received the sword from a symbolic mother who is giving her best part, in the theatrical sense, to complete the pose of the living statue. Ma Nelson, a cross-dresser and a Madame, is also (not surprisingly) a feminist:

> "Yet we were all suffragists in that house; oh, Nelson was 'Votes for Women', I can tell you!"

> "Does that seem strange to you? That the caged bird should want to see the end of cages, sir?" queried Lizzie, with an edge of steel in her voice.

Lizzie's questions and commentary, which repeatedly interrupt the auto-biographical narrative that Walser hopes will pin down the truth about Fevvers, suggest an interrogation of female biography modeled on the stories of Cinderella or Snow White, filled with evil mothers and sisters and a Prince. Fevvers herself describes her coming of age as an apprenticeship in being looked at: "Is it not to the mercies of the eyes of others that we commit ourselves on our voyage through the world." And she does not wait for a Prince to take her away; on the contrary, her greatest fear is that his kiss would harden the white powder on her face and "seal me up in my *appearance* forever." (*NC,* 39). Her way out, as it were, is in the company of the other women who, if Fevvers is to be believed, were, when not working, learning to read and play instruments. Lizzie describes a world of female sociality set in a liminal time when, as with the French clock she carries with her, it is always noon or midnight—the time of change and of revolution. The portrait of the artist as a young mannequin ends with the Winged Victory keen on learning how to fly.

> We all engaged in our intellectual, artistic or political—Here Lizzie coughed—pursuits and, as for myself, those long hours of leisure I devoted to the study of aerodynamics and the physiology of flight . . . (*NC,* 40).

FLYING: LESSONS OF CLASS, GENDER, AND SEXUALITY

How did Fevvers really learn to fly? The Oedipal Walser, always searching for origins and empirical certainties, can only assume that a male impresario, some Svengali or other, has created Fevvers and her act. He cannot fathom the collaboration of Fevvers and her inseparable companion and foster mother, Lizzie, and it is this disbelief that leads him to wonder whether, after all, underneath the layers of masquerade, Fevvers may not be a man, throwing all questions of identity, authenticity, and origins onto the axis of gender.

> "Don't excite yourself, gel," said Lizzie gently. Fevvers' chin jerked up almost pettishly.
> "Oh, Lizzie the gentleman must know the truth!"
> And she fixed Walser with a piercing, judging regard, as if to ascertain just how far she could go with him. Her face, in its Brobdingnagian symmetry, might have been hacked from wood and brightly painted up by those artists who build carnival ladies for fairgrounds or figureheads for sailing ships. It flickered through his mind: Is she really a man? (*NC,* 35).

The figure of the aerialist, as I indicated in the first chapter in considering the work of Balint, Starobinski, and others, has repeatedly produced the question of gender for the male viewer. The female aerialist as masculinized or ambiguous in relation to gender appears in historical sources, as well as fiction and visual representation. Arthur Munby's famous photographs and diaries of Victorian working girls includes female gymnasts and acrobats whose masculine qualities he never fails to note.[29] Although, as Stallybrass and White have noted, Munby's voyeurism is usually characterized by the "conjunction of the maid kneeling in the dirt and the standing voyeur" (from high to low), the gaze upward (from low to high) can produce a similar effect: on the one hand, a reinforcement of male power and social standing and on the other a temporary reversal so that the male viewer appears childlike or at least diminished.[30] From Huysmans's Miss Urania to Cleopatra, the "big woman" in Tod Browning's *Freaks,* the aerialist and the female acrobat have been women represented through the eyes of a dwarfed, clownish, or infantilized man. In an unusual reversal, George Grosz's *Seiltänzerin* (1914), an aerial drawing of a female tightrope walker, shows a demonic clown looking up from far below at the large, muscular figure straddling the rope between her thighs as she strains to raise herself up onto one leg. This grotesque caricature of the Romantic ideal of ethereal Womanhood suggests, as well, an altered masculinity in the balance.

Carter's production of Fevvers as the aerial diva, enigmatic regarding gender, is only the latest version of this image, produced typically by male artists but occasionally and with surprising results by twentieth-century women artists and writers. The figure of the trapeze artist Frau Mann (alias the Duchess of Broadback) who appears in the first chapter of Djuna Barnes' *Nightwood,* is the repressed, lesbian prefiguration of a Fevvers—a possible body.[31] Her body is strong and muscular, and in the air, it appears "much heavier than that of women who stay on the ground." It is a body shaped through her work and the technology of aerial performance. Her legs, for instance, "had the specialized tension common to aerial workers; some of the bar was in her wrists, the tan bark in her walk." Like Fevvers, her very flesh seems sewn into her performance costume, making an artifice of nudity; Frau Mann, however, goes a bit further in this regard than Fevvers, in that her costume reweaves the crotch in a textual rezoning of the body as off-limits to men.

> The stuff of her tights was no longer a covering, it was herself; the span of the tightly stitched crotch was so much her own flesh that she was as unsexed as a doll. The needle that had made one the property of the child made the other the property of no man (Barnes, 13).

Nudity and clothing are a continuous surface, flattening the image of Frau Mann's body, and in a reversal of the usual fetishistic practice as described by Freud, redesigning the "phantasmagoric division between an inside and an outside" which characterizes the representation of the female body as invested with mystery or threat.[32] Whether this feminine surface sufficiently interferes with the (male) fetishist's desire to know and therefore have, or whether "the needle" in question is the projection of a lesbian morphology, there is definitely a *different* line of viewing and a different spectatorship suggested than that represented by Walser's suggestion that Fevvers really needs a tail: "Physical ungainliness in flight caused, perhaps, by the absence of a *tail*—I wonder why she doesn't tack a tail on the back of her cache-sexe; it would add verisimilitude and, perhaps, improve the performance."

The comparison of *Nights at the Circus* with Barnes' *Nightwood,* written in 1936, reveals a commonality of surrealist techniques and themes, as well as a mutual interest in the dispersion of carnivalesque materials in new social formations. *Nightwood* was introduced in the thirties by an extremely anxious T. S. Eliot, who feared that the characters in the novel would be regarded "as a horrid sideshow of freaks."[33] His evocation of the freak show as the trope to be shunned would seem to substantiate Allon White's claim that the remnants of carnival as cultural history reemerge as "phobic alienation" in bourgeois neurosis, since "bourgeois carnival is a contradiction in terms."[34] The metaphor of the freak show in Eliot's introduction (clearly a reference to the lesbian and transsexual themes of the novel) resonates oddly with the first chapter, "Bow Down," in which Felix (Baron Volkbein) is introduced as a dévoté of the circus and popular theater. The high/low dichotomies of class and gender give way as the "carnival of the night" temporarily subsumes difference. Volkbein's attachment to "that great disquiet called entertainment" mirrors his own aristocratic yearnings: "In some way they linked his emotions to the high and unattainable pageantry of kings and queens" (Barnes, 11). The entertainers, of course, in the carnivalesque tradition, mimic the pomp and titles of the upper classes. Felix's pleasure in the mock ritual of the "bow down" to the demimonde is palpable. At once degrading and liberatory, his social and sexual dissolution amidst the carnival of *Nightwood* recalls Aschenbach's encounters with the grotesque figures in *Death in Venice:*

> He moved with a humble hysteria among the decaying brocades and laces of the *Carnavalet;* he loved that old and documented splendour with something of the love of the lion for its tamer—that sweat-tarnished spangled enigma that, in bringing the beast to heel, had somehow turned toward him a face like his own . . . (Barnes, 11).

> The emotional spiral of the circus, taking its flight from the immense disqualification of the public, rebounding from its illimitable hope, produced in Felix longing and disquiet. The circus was a loved thing he could never touch (Barnes, 12).

In contrast, Walser is a male spectator oblivious to the transcendent powers of the circus. Though Carter's deeply historic novel is set at the end of the nineteenth century, Walser is much younger than the Baron, as a representative of the bourgeoisie. Of course, he is first of all an American on the brink of the "American Century," filled with all the common sense and the imperialistic instincts required to make him an ideal employee for Colonel Kearney (a P.T. Barnum clone). Secondly, he is a journalist and a professional debunker, sent to reveal the secrets of the trade, to sort, discard, and exploit the travesties of the circus as he will later plunder ethnographic materials in his ethnocentric explorations of other cultures. No aesthete or modernist intent on looking up to women or lamenting old myths, he tries instead, in what to him is the most effective democratic mode, to bring Fevvers down to his scale.

As model spectator, Walser is continuously in the dark when it comes to issues of gender and generation, especially the aspects of female homosociality which dominate the London section of the book. He cannot tolerate sexual ambiguity and he cannot recognize or place "older" women, particularly in foreign national contexts. The dialogical narrative of Lizzie and Fevvers, with its dissonant tonality, silences, and contradictions makes him increasingly anxious to place Fevvers and to illuminate those aspects of her anatomy and her story which are extraneous or implausible. The story of her first flight, which is simultaneously the story of her surrogate mother, Lizzie, and her "natural" mother, London ("London, with one breast, the Amazon queen") is told as a night fable (*NC*, 36). The nocturnal carnival which occasions intimations of the sublime for Felix borders on the terrifying for Walser, whose imagination is easily overwhelmed: "Although he was not an imaginative man, even he was sensitive to that aghast time of night when the dark dwarfs us" (*NC*, 37). Fevvers, if she is (and she certainly is in some sense) a bird, is not a natural flier:

> Like Lucifer, I fell. Down, down, down I tumbled, bang with a bump on the Persian rug below me, flat on my face amongst those blooms and beasts that never graced no natural forest, those creatures of dreams and abstraction not unlike myself, Mr. Walser. Then I knew I was not ready to bear on my back the great burden of my unnaturalness (*NC*, 30).

She learns to fly through cultural imitation (a fake Titian of Leda and the Swan), some library books, risks and falls, a momentary sense of hovering ("that sensation that comes to us, sometimes on the edge of sleep") (*NC*, 31), and finally, through the help of Lizzie's knowledge gleaned from observing pigeons learning to use their "aerial arms," she lets Lizzie push her into the air, risking not only death but the "terror of irreparable *difference*" (*NC*, 34).[35] She flies for the first time through the dark, into a liminal space in the hours before dawn on Mid-summer's Night, and then back to work, posing as Winged Victory.[36]

The elevation of the grotesque body to the nocturnal sublimity of a mid-summer's night is accomplished with great effort, and, like the narrative itself, it works as a collaborative effort between Fevvers and Lizzie. The model for flight is a lowly pigeon but the experience and its description are meant nonetheless to be sublime. Fevvers' flying style is as eclectic, grand, and ungainly as her voice and as indeterminate with regard to its origins. Walser's description of her voice reflects his own skepticism regarding the narrative of her first flight.

> Her voice . . . her cavernous, somber voice, a voice made for shouting about the tempest, her voice of a celestial fishwife. Musical as it strangely was, yet not a voice for singing with; it comprised discords, her scale contained twelve tones. Her voice with its warped, homely Cockney vowels and random aspirates. . . . Yet such a voice could almost have had its source, not within her throat but in some ingenious mechanism or other behind the canvas screen, voice of a fake medium at a seance (*NC, 43*).

This "throwing" of the female voice is an extremely telling acoustical image.[37] It is reminiscent of *Trilby* and of the seemingly disembodied telephone voice of Claire Niveau in Cronenberg's *Dead Ringers*. Located at the site of "perhaps, the most radical of all subject divisions—the division between meaning and materiality," the voice is that place of excess which precedes and follows the organization of meaning (Silverman, 44). The spatial image of the *thrown voice* further stretches the gaps or intervals between the body and language, like one of Fevvers' long, antisocial yawns. The body which produces this voice is not identical with it, any more than the sounds produced are identical in any positive sense with meaning. In relation to music as organized sound, "this voice is not for singing," meaning that it is "noisy" in the technical sense and exceeds the regimes of canonical Western music. As an instance of cultural noise, this voice, which is the voice of the novel as well as the voice of Fevvers, contains within it a particularly resonant blend of modernist scales, class and regionally inflected vowels and aspirates, and the "rough music" of carnival.[38] The "grain" of this voice, to use Roland Barthes expression, suggests a different cultural as well as a different musical history in which, as he suggested, "we would attach less importance to the formidable break in tonality accomplished by modernity."[39] Deeply historical as well as radically modernist in its trajectory, the voice of the "celestial fishwife"—the sonic female grotesque *par excellence*[40]—flies from the cavern, above the tempest, and to the heavens and down again to Cockney London, somber, full, and in its own way sublime.

To recapitulate briefly the relationship between the aerial sublime and the female grotesque, I want to return to Fevvers in the midst of her circus act. By way of reference, I turn to the paradigm of the trapeze act as analyzed by Paul Bouissac in his work on the semiotics of the circus. Once in the air, the act is a negotiation, with interruptions, between two stations, with a certain expenditure of energy by the velocity of flight (up to 60 mph), permitting the human body to offer a certain illusion of suspension. Bouissac fails to note that in the case of the female performer, her negotiation of space is often interrupted by a male performer who catches her. Fevvers in the air, however, travels alone.

An additional model of normativity for the flying act is provided by Thomas Aquinas who notes, writing of "real" angels, "their motion can be as continuous or as discontinuous as it wishes. And thus an angel can be in one instant in one place and at another instant in another place, not existing at any intermediate time." I am assuming that in relation to identity, Fevvers has equal claim to either of these models yet no full claim at all to either, since her act seems to dissimulate failure to occupy either time or space in these modes. Quoting the novel, from the point of view of the informed male spectator:

> When the hack *aerialiste*, the everyday wingless variety, performs the triple somersault, he or she travels through the air at a cool sixty miles an hour; Fevvers, however, contrived a contemplative and leisurely twenty-five, so that the packed theater could enjoy the spectacle, as in slow motion, of every tense muscle straining in her Rubenseque form. The music went much faster than she did; she dawdled. Indeed, she did defy the laws of projectiles, because a projectile cannot *mooch* along its trajectory; if it slackens its speed in mid-air, down it falls. But Fevvers, apparently, pottered along the invisible gangway between her trapezes with the portly dignity of a Trafalgar Square pigeon flapping from one proffered handful of corn to another, and then she turned head over heels three times, lazily enough to show off the crack in her bum (*NC*, 17).

For Walser, semiotician and connoisseur of the hoax, it is precisely the limitations of her act which allow him momentarily to suspend disbelief and grant her a supernatural identity, for no mere mortal could effect such incompetence in the air without dire consequences. Walser observes:

> For, in order to earn a living, might not a genuine bird-woman—in the implausible event that such a thing existed—have to pretend she was an artificial one? (*NC*, 17)

What is more interesting to me than this sophisticated insight which, after all, only goes so far as to permit him the pleasure of a naive spectator's night at the circus, is that Fevvers reveals what angels and circus stars normally conceal: *labor* and its bodily effects in the midst of simulated play and the creation of illusion. Her body dawdles lazily (the hardest work of all in the air) and yet, unlike her angelic sisters, she never seems to occupy discrete spots on her trajectory; she does not rest. She vamps in the musical sense, filling in the intervals with somersaults. The one time she is static in the air, perched on the swing, the rope breaks and she is stranded. What is revealed in her routine is at one level economic: the Victorian working girl is not the angel (in the house), and the novel is in many ways about working girls.[41] This is not to say that here finally a materiality has emerged from underneath an illusion, that with the appearance of work, we have a ground, that we are no longer, so to speak, in the air. Rather, I would read Fevvers' act as a reminder that the spectacle which conceals work is itself produced, and revamping spectacle shows up and diverts this cultural production.

THE INTERGENERATIONAL BODY (POLITIC)

Carter herself has remarked that "the creation of Fevvers necessitated the creation of her foster mother, Lizzie, a gnarled old leftist." Throughout the novel, Lizzie undercuts the high-flying rhetoric of the new age woman while working behind the scenes to effect a revolution. Her own body is unfetishized. She exists unadorned as a kind of maid or sidekick in the drama of the star performer, but her work is nonetheless indispensable. As a couple, Lizzie and Fevvers produce a real challenge to the male and heterosexual gaze of Walser, who is confused both by their narrative mode and by their apparent physical incompatibility, which he can only articulate as a question of scale, measured in height. From a distance, he sees them as "a blond, heroic mother taking her daughter home from some ill-fated expedition up west, their ages obscured, their relationship inverted."

Together, they figure an intergenerational grotesque of the kind which Mikhail Bakhtin evokes in his paradigm of the grotesque terracotta images of senile, pregnant hags. When Lizzie first sees that her young ward has wings, she does not uncritically welcome the new in the guise of youth, as Ma Nelson does; rather, she historicizes *herself*, and sees in Fevvers the "Annunciation of my own Menopause." When the figurative biological clock is communal, birth and rebirth are dialectical. This parody of the annunciation is of the critical variety which Linda Hutcheon has described in her work on postmodernism as signalling "how present representations come from past ones, and what ideological consequences derive from both continuity and difference" (Hutcheon, 93). The consequences of such an intergenerational conception is that the new is not immediately and transparently identified with the young. This interrupts the logic of what Debord describes as "false choice in spectacular abundance," the creation of arbitrary contrasts and competitions which seem natural or self-evident. Among these false choices is a certain commodification of generational difference:

> Wherever there is abundant consumption, a major spectacular opposition between youth and adults comes to the fore among the false roles—false because the adult, master of his life, does not exist and because youth, the transformation of what exists, is in no way the property of those who are now

young, but of the economic system, of the dynamism of capitalism. *Things* rule and are young.[42]

Again, my point is not to deny that there are such things as aging and generational difference; rather, the spectacle of the new is produced and can therefore be counterproduced. As Fevvers and Lizzie together reconfigure "the pure child of the new century," the "new" becomes a possibility that already existed, a part of the aging body in process rather than the property (like virginity) of a discrete and static place or identity. What appeals to me about this vamping onto the body (to use the word in a slightly archaic sense) is that it not only grotesquely de-forms the female body as a cultural construction in order to reclaim it, but that it may suggest new political aggregates—provisional, uncomfortable, even conflictual, coalitions of bodies which both respect the concept of "situated knowledges" and refuse to keep every body in its place.

It is tempting to read this novel and even Carter's entire *oeuvre* as a progression, as one critic sees it, from the alienation of the femininity of the "coded mannequin" to the liberatory prospects of the woman with wings.[43] Indeed, towards the end of the novel, Fevvers looks forward to the day when "all the women will have wings, the same as I":

> The dolls' house doors will open, the brothels will spill forth their prisoners, the cages, gilded or otherwise, all over the world, in every land, will let forth their inmates singing together the dawn chorus of the new, the transformed (*NC*, 285).

But Carter never lets this optimistic progressivism stand unchallenged:

> "It's going to be more complicated than that," interpolated Lizzie.
> "This old witch sees storms ahead, my girl. When I look to the future, I see through a glass, darkly. You improve your analysis, girl, and *then* we'll discuss it" (*NC*, 285–86).

Lizzie's view of the future is not forward-looking but rather—like the angel of history in a powerful and much-quoted passage from Walter Benjamin—a look backwards to see the future in the past, not as "sequence of events" but as "a catastrophe which keeps piling wreckage upon wreckage" (Benjamin, 257). To Lizzie and to the angel of history, "a storm is blowing from Paradise" (*NC*, 257). And there is no going back. In Benjamin's image, borrowed from Klee's painting *Angelus Novus*, the angel is caught by the storm with his wings blown open; the storm "propels him into the future to which his back is turned, while the pile of debris before him grows skyward. *This storm is what we call progress*" (emphasis mine) (Benjamin, 258).

Only if Lizzie's stormy comments are read as merely cynical or extraneous can the exchange be made to stand for a developmental antithesis in Carter's writing rather than an apocalyptic intersection of incommensurate discourses, resulting in a "blow-up" of the narrative and a breakup of two women's narrative partnership. To side provisionally with Lizzie, who represents an ever-present but minority voice in the novel, it is more complicated than that.

I would prefer to read their differences as part of an ongoing dialogue, filled with conflict and repetition—a difficult friendship and an improbable but necessary political alliance.[44] At this point in the novel, the conversation is about losses and making do. Fevvers has "mislaid her magnificence on the road from London; one wing is bandaged and the other has faded to drab. She is no longer commercially viable. God knows if she will ever fly again." Lizzie's anarchic power, "her knack for wreaking domestic havoc," is lost. As the designated heroine of the novel, Fevvers is trading in her wings for marriage with what she hopes will be a transformed Jack Walser ("I'll sit on him, I'll hatch him out. I'll make him into the New Man, in fact, a fitting mate for the New Woman"). And Lizzie, of course is skeptical: " 'Perhaps so, perhaps not,' she said, putting a damper on things."[45] For Lizzie, it is necessary to think twice "about turning from a freak into a woman" (NC, 283).[46]

This exchange between Lizzie and Fevvers is, like everything in the novel, inconclusive. As Susan Suleiman has written, Carter's strategy "*multiplies* the possibilities of linear narrative and of 'story,' producing a dizzying accumulation that undermines the narrative logic by its very excessiveness."[47] There is always something left over, something as untimely as subjectivity itself, that forms the basis of a new plan, perhaps another flight.

Like Fevvers' excessive body itself, the meaning of any possible flight lies in part in the very interstices of the narrative, as the many-vectored space of the here and now, rather than a utopian hereafter. The end of flight in this sense is not a freedom from bodily existence but a recharting of aeriality as a bodily space of possibility and repetition:

> There is a feeling of absolute finality about the end of a flight through darkness. The dream of flight is suddenly gone before the mundane realities of growing grass and swirling dust. . . . Freedom escapes you again, and the wings which were a moment ago no less than an eagle's and swifter, are metal and wood once more, inert and heavy.[48]

Notes

1. Angela Carter, *Nights at the Circus* (London: Chatto and Windus, The Hogarth Press, 1984). All subsequent references are to this edition as *NC*.

2. I am indebted to three extraordinary students who worked with me on senior theses which focused on the work of Angela Carter: Linda McDaniel and Jennifer Hendricks of Hampshire College, and Meg O'Rourke of Mt. Holyoke.

3. The topography of the Madame Schreck episode owes much to Edgar A. Poe, but there are historical precedents for the anatomical museum. See, for instance, Christiane Py and

Cecile Vedart, "Les Musées d'anatomie sur les champs de foire" *Actes de la recherche en sciences sociales,* no. 60 (November 1985), p. 3–10.

4.   Guy Debord, *Society of the Spectacle* (Detroit: Black and Red, 1983), p. 1.

5.   Fevvers construes her own primal scene from a possibly fake and certainly filthy ("as though through a glass darkly") painting of the Leda and the Swan by Titian (*NC,* 30).

6.   For an extremely important discussion of feminist writing in relation to the historical avant-garde in general and Dada/Surrealist parody in particular, see Susan Rubin Suleiman, *Subversive Intent: Gender, Politics, and the Avant-Garde* (Cambridge, Massachusetts and London: Harvard University Press, 1990).

7.   Linda Hutcheon, *The Politics of Postmodernism* (London and New York: Routledge, 1983).

8.   For a discussion of intertextuality and politics in her work, see Angela Carter, "Notes From the Front Line," in Michelene Wandor, ed., *On Gender and Writing* (London: Pandora, 1983), p. 71.

9.   In her interview with Helen Cagney Watts, Carter herself says that Sade was a primary influence. Helen Cagney Watts, "Angela Carter: An Interview with Helen Cagney Watts," in *Bète Noire* (August 1987), p. 162. In relation to Sade, see also David Punter, "Angela Carter: Supercessions of the Masculine," in his *The Romantic Unconscious: A Study of Narcissism and Patriarchy* (New York: New York University Press, 1990), pp. 28–42.

10.   Carter writes about Mae West, in *Nothing Sacred* (London: Virago, 1982). This impersonation of the impersonator is Fevvers' (and Carter's) stock-in-trade.

11.   The "double bluff" was not only sexual (a woman playing a man playing a woman playing a man), but also existential: she plays on the "freedom" given to older women. As Carter points out, Mae West started her Hollywood career in middle age. Her self-display played on the masquerade of youthfulness, the freedom of the discard who has nothing left to lose, and the impersonation of male power. "She made of her own predatoriness a joke that concealed its power, whilst simultaneously exploiting it. Yet she represented a sardonic disregard of convention rather than a heroic overthrow of taboo." (*The Sadeian Woman and the Ideology of Pornography* [New York: Pantheon Books, 1978], p. 62).

12.   Angela Carter, "The Flesh and the Mirror," in *Fireworks: Nine Profane Pieces* (London and New York: Penguin Books, 1987), p. 67.

13.   See, for instance, Roland Barthes, *Empire of Signs.* trans. Richard Howard (New York: Hill and Wang, 1982).

14.   This question is posed first to Walser by an Indian fakir. Walser sees his journalistic quest as a compilation of "Great Humbugs of the World" (*NC,* 11).

15.   As a male and heterosexual witness to Fevvers' naked artificiality, it is Walser's impossible task to "cover Fevvers' story" which means to expose her fiction.

16.   Walter Benjamin, "Thesis on the Philosophy of History," in *Illuminations,* trans. Harry Zohn (New York: Schocken Books, 1969), p. 257.

17.   See "Angela Carter, an Interview with Helen Cagney Watts," in *Bète Noire* (August 1987), pp. 161–175.

18.   Angela Carter, *The Sadeian Woman,* p. 79.

19.   See, for instance, Andrea Dworkin, *Pornography: Men Possessing Women* (New York: Perigree Books, 1979.), pp. 84–85. The phrase "praxis of femininity" is Carter's (*The Sadeian Woman,* p. 78).

20.   For an excellent discussion of Justine and Juliette in relation to criticism of Carter, see Elaine Jordan, "The Dangers of Angela Carter" in *New Feminist Discourses: Critical Essays on Theories and Texts* (London and New York: Routledge, 1991), pp. 119–131. I am in agreement with Jordan's "defense" of Carter (not, as she says, that Carter needs defending). For another view of Carter on Sade, see Susanne Kappeler, *The Pornography of Representation* (London: Polity Press, 1986), pp. 133–137. See also Andrea Dworkin cited in previous note. For a critical overview of the pornography debates within feminism, see B. Ruby Rich "Feminism and Sexuality in the 1980s" in *Feminist Studies,* vol. 12 (1986).

21. Carter, *The Sadeian Woman*, p. 79. For another influential and provocative account of the interests and pitfalls of Sade for contemporary feminists, see Jane Gallop, *Thinking Through the Body* (New York: Columbia University Press, 1988); see also, her *Intersections: A Reading of Sade with Bataille, Blanchot, and Klossowski* (Lincoln: University of Nebraska Press, 1981).

22. In relation to Juliet's character, Carter is quite unambiguous: "A free woman in an unfree society is a monster," (*The Sadeian Woman*, p. 27; also, quoted in Jordan, p. 121). Jordan makes the excellent point that both figures of antithetical feminity point towards something else in Carter and are meant to show up the limitations of these types as models of resistance.

23. For a very different use of the iconography of the emaciated female body, see for instance the puppetry of Lotte Prinzel, or in the context of feminist art, see Valie Export's performance work described in "Persona, Proto-Performance, Politics," *Discourse* 14/2 (Spring 1992), pp. 26–35.

24. Craig Owens, "Posing," in *Difference: On Representation and Sexuality Catalog* (New York: New Museum of Contemporary Art, 1985), pp. 7–17.

25. Owens identifies the pose as both an "imposition" and an "imposture." Since, in his view, sexuality is imposed (culturally) we might characterize Fevver's installation of femininity as a reimposition.

26. Owens also mentions the work of Dick Hebdige on the self-display of punk subculture. Of course, the social and the psychosexual merge in many examples of posing in contemporary cultural production. Jennie Livingston's very successful documentary film on camp balls and "vogueing," *Paris is Burning*, has racial, class, and sexual dimensions. Like Fevvers and the other women exhibits and performers in *Nights at the Circus*, the young performers in her film band together in "houses" which take the names of commercial fashion houses.

27. Ma Nelson has a further distinction. She cross-dresses as Admiral Nelson, commanding the whorehouse like a tight ship: "It was a pirate ship, and went under false colours . . . It was from the, as it were, topsail or crow's nest that my girl made her first ascent" (*NC*, 32). The Winged Victory of this barge, of course, is a ship's figurehead.

28. See Mary Ann Doane, *Femmes Fatales: Feminism, Film Theory, Psychoanalysis* (New York and London: Routledge, 1991), especially pp. 17–43. Doane's influential 1982 essay, "Film and Masquerade: Theorizing the Female Spectator" is reprinted in this collection along with the recent, "Masquerade Reconsidered." The first essay represents an attempt to dislodge the psychoanalytic discussion of masquerade as the norm of femininity and to see it, rather, as a defamiliarization and a "way out." Her second essay emphasizes the theoretical constraints and the socio-political implications of the concept of sexuality as masquerade in Riviere and Lacan. In relation to feminist theory and theories of the feminine, see especially her reply to Tania Modleski (pp. 40–43). Modleski's critique of Doane is contained in *The Women Who Knew Too Much: Hitchcock and Feminist Theory* (New York: Methuen, 1988), pp. 25–28.

29. Munby indicated in his diary that he intended to write a paper on female gymnasts. His interest in their sexuality is evident in most entries. For instance: "The only clothing she had on was a blue satin doublet fitting close to her body and having very scanty trunk hose below it; her legs, cased in fleshings, were as good as bare, up to the hip: the only sign of a woman about her was that she had a rose in her bosom, and another in her short curly hair . . . " (Entry dated 7 September, 1868) quoted in Michael Hiley, *Victorian Working Women: Portraits from Life* (Boston: David R. Godine, 1980), p. 116. See also, D. Hudson, *Munby: Man of Two Worlds: The Life and Diaries of Arthur J. Munby* (London: John Murray, 1972).

30. Stallybrass and White point out that the contradiction between the high social standing of the upper-class male and the low class standing of the maid is complicated by the physical comparisons of his weakness and her strength, and his childishness in relation to her role as nurse. Of course, a point to be made here is that Munby is controlling both the sightlines and the social configuration.

The Politics and Poetics of Transgression. (Ithaca: Cornell University Press, 1986), pp. 155–156. See also, L. Davidoff, "Class and Gender in Victorian England: The Diaries of Arthur J. Munby and Hannah Cullwick," *Feminist Studies,* vol. 5, no. 1, pp. 89–141.

31. Djuna Barnes, *Nightwood,* with an introduction by T. S. Eliot (New York: New Directions, 1961).

32. For an important, recent consideration of fetishism and the depth model of the female body in relation to curiosity, see Laura Mulvey, "Pandora: Topographies of the Mask and Curiosity" in *Sexuality and Space,* ed. Beatriz Colomina (New York: Princeton Architectural Press, 1992), pp. 58–59.

33. Barnes, xvi. Although Eliot does not mention the lesbian texts and in his plea that the book not be read as a "psychopathic study," his insistence that the "miseries that people suffer through their particular abnormalities of temperament" be understood not on the surface but in light of "the deeper designs . . . of the human misery which is universal."

34. Allon White, "Hysteria and the End of Carnival: Festivity and Bourgeois Neurosis," in *The Violence of Representation: Literature and the History of Violence,* ed. Nancy Armstrong and Leonard Tennenhouse (New York: Routledge, 1989), pp. 156–170.

35. She fears that her first flight will be her last and that she will pay for her hubris with her very life (*NC,* 36).

36. Fevvers herself interrupts the sublime narrative of night flight with the ongoing account of her working life (*NC,* 37).

37. See Kaja Silverman, *The Acoustic Mirror: The Female Voice in Psycho-analysis and Cinema* (Bloomington: Indiana University Press, 1988).

38. For a study of noise and cultural production in relation to carnival and twentieth century music, see Mary Russo and Daniel Warner, "Rough Music" *Discourse* 10.1 (Fall–Winter 1987–88), pp. 55–76. See also Jacques Attali, *Noise: The Political Economy of Music* (Minneapolis: University of Minnesota Press, 1985).

39. Roland Barthes, *Image-Music-Text,* trans. Stephen Heath (New York: Hill and Wang, 1977), p. 189.

40. The figure of the fishwife suggests the marketplace speech of carnival, the revolutionary power of the women of the French revolution, and the "fishwives" of Marx's *Eighteenth Brumaire.* Carter also elicits the olfactory image of fishy women in descriptions of Fevvers "perfume" in the first chapter.

41. For an account of the female circus performer as Victorian working girl, see Michael Hiley, *Victorian Working Women: Portraits From Life* (Boston: David Godine, 1980). The figure of the female acrobat raises the predictable questions of gender and propriety: "Ought we forbid her to do these things? . . . And, though it is not well to see a nude man fling a nude girl about as she is flung, or to see her grip his body in mid-air between her seemingly bare thighs. I think that an unreflecting audience takes no note . . . and looks upon these things and looks at him and her only as two performers. Still, the familiar interlacing of male and female bodies in sight of the public, is gross and corrupting, though its purpose be mere athletics" (p. 119).

42. Guy Debord, *Society of the Spectacle* (Detroit: Black and Red, 1983), p. 27.

43. Paulina Palmer's "From 'Coded Mannequin' to Bird Woman: Angela Carter's Magic Flight," in *Women Reading Women's Writing* (New York: St. Martin's Press, 1987), argues that the tension which exists between an impulse to analyze and demythologize gender and the impulse towards utopian celebrations of woman-centered culture is reflected in two "stages" of Carter's work. From Palmer's perspective, the image of the puppet or "coded Mannequin" is "replaced by the image of Fevvers' miraculous wings which she observes make her body 'the abode of limitless freedom' and the egg from which she claims to have been hatched." Hoffmann, Freud, and the uncanny are associated with texts published prior to 1978, those "marred by an element of distortion," and those later texts, including *The Bloody Chamber* and especially *Nights at the Circus,* are associated with "the expression of emotions which have a liberating effect." As an opening illustration of this dichotomy, she cites a passage (which I would

agree is crucial) from the conclusion of the novel, in which Fevvers, for the last time, gives an "enthusiastic if cliché-ridden speech heralding the new age of women's liberation" (Palmer, 179).

44.   The claim that "an emergence of a female counter-culture is celebrated" in the novel (Palmer, 180) is, in my view, true only as a prefigurative *possibility*. And many female types and institutional contexts are represented in the novel, implicating any definition of female counterculture in the histories and metahistories of violence and oppression by and of women. Fevvers herself eats caviar in a grand hotel, at the expense of the peasant woman, Baboushka. Countess P., Olga Alexandrovna, and Madame Schreck all partake in criminality and destruction.

45.   The prospects for life with Walser, the New Man, have seemed dim for most of my students. Although I have suggested alternative readings, on the numerous occasions when we have discussed his transformations as successively a brash American journalist, a fellow traveller with the clowns, a surrealistic anthropologist who "goes native," and a new age man, students tend to see him in all these roles as a "jerk"—something closer to the bad alternatives in Tania Modleski's *Feminism Without Women* than to the nondominant types in Kaja Silverman's *Male Subjectivity at the Margins.*

46.   Lizzie's greatest fear is that Fevvers will become the "tableau" of "a woman in bondage to her reproductive system, a woman tied hand and foot to that Nature which your physiology denies" (*NC,* 283). Carter never accedes to a definition of even motherhood as the "natural"; throughout the novel mothers are secondhand representations within fictions, images, and tableaux.

47.   Susan Rubin Suleiman, *Subversive Intent: Gender, Politics, and the Avant-Garde* (Cambridge: Harvard University Press, 1990), p. 137.

48.   Beryl Markham, *West with the Night* (Boston: Houghton Mifflin, 1942), p. 17.

Selected Bibliography

PRIMARY SOURCES

Novels

Shadow Dance. London: Heinemann, 1966. American edition: *Honeybuzzard.* New York: Simon and Schuster, 1967. New York: Penguin, 1996.

The Magic Toyshop. London: Heinemann, 1967. New York: Simon and Schuster, 1968. New York: Penguin, 1996.

Several Perceptions. London: Heinemann, 1968. New York: Simon and Schuster, 1968.

Heroes and Villains. London: Heinemann, 1969. New York: Simon and Schuster, 1969. New York: Penguin, 1981.

Love. London: Rupert Hart-Davis, 1971. Rev. ed. London: Chatto and Windus, 1987. New York: Penguin, 1988.

The Infernal Desire Machines of Doctor Hoffman. London: Rupert Hart-Davis, 1972. American edition: *The War of Dreams.* New York: Harcourt Brace Jovanovich, 1973. New York: Penguin, 1994.

The Passion of New Eve. London: Gollancz, 1977. New York: Harcourt Brace, 1977.

Nights at the Circus. London: Chatto and Windus, 1984. New York: Viking Penguin, 1985. New York: Penguin, 1993.

Wise Children. London: Chatto and Windus, 1991. New York: Farrar, Straus and Giroux, 1992. New York: Penguin, 1993.

Stories

Fireworks: Nine Stories in Various Disguises. London: Quartet, 1974. New York: Harper and Row, 1981. Harper Colophon, 1982.

The Bloody Chamber and Other Adult Tales. London: Gollancz, 1979. New York: Harper and Row, 1979. New York: Harper Colophon, 1981.

Saints and Strangers. English edition: *Black Venus.* London: Chatto and Windus, 1985. New York: Viking Penguin, 1986. New York: Penguin, 1987.

American Ghosts and Old World Wonders. London: Chatto and Windus, 1993.

Burning Your Boats: The Collected Short Stories. Introduction by Salman Rushdie. London: Chatto and Windus, 1995. New York: Henry Holt, 1996.

Nonfiction, Editions, and Translations

The Sadeian Woman: An Exercise in Cultural History. London: Virago, 1979. American edition: *The Sadeian Woman and the Ideology of Pornography.* New York: Pantheon, 1979. New York: Harper Colophon, 1980.

Nothing Sacred: Selected Writings. London: Virago, 1982. "Notes from the Front Line." In *On Gender and Writing,* ed. Michelene Wandor, 69–77. London: Pandora Press, 1983.

Wayward Girls and Wicked Women: An Anthology of Stories. Ed. Angela Carter. London: Virago, 1986.

The Virago Book of Fairy Tales. Ed. Angela Carter. London: Virago, 1990. American edition: *The Old Wives Book of Fairy Tales.* New York: Random House, 1990.

Sleeping Beauty and Other Favorite Fairy Tales. Ed. Angela Carter. Illus. Michael Foreman. London: Victor Gollancz, 1991. Boston: Otter, 1991.

Expletives Deleted: Selected Writings. London: Chatto and Windus, 1992. New York: Vintage, 1993.

The Second Virago Book of Fairy Tales. Ed. Angela Carter. Illus. Corinna Sargood. London: Virago, 1992. American edition: *Strange Things Sometimes Still Happen: Fairy Tales from around the World.* Winchester, Mass.: Faber and Faber, 1993.

Interviews

Carter, Angela. "Angela Carter." By Kerryn Goldsworthy. *Meanjin Quarterly* 44, no. 1 (1985): 4–13.

Carter, Angela. "Interview with Angela Carter." By Ana Katsavos. *Contemporary Fiction* 14, no. 3 (Fall 1994): 11–17.

SECONDARY SOURCES

Boehm, Beth A. "Feminist Metafiction and Androcentric Reading Strategies: Angela Carter's Reconstructed Reader in *Nights at the Circus.*" *Critique* 37, no. 1 (Fall 1995): 35–49.

———. "*Wise Children:* Angela Carter's Swan Song." *Review of Contemporary Literature* 14, no. 3 (Fall 1994): 84–89.

Brown, Richard. "Postmodern Americas in the Fiction of Angela Carter, Martin Amis and Ian McEwan." In *Forked Tongues? Comparing Twentieth-Century British and American Literature,* Ed. Ann Massa and Alistair Stead, 92–110. London: Longman, 1994.

Chedgzoy, Kate. "The (Pregnant) Prince and the Showgirl: Cultural Legitimacy and the Reproduction of *Hamlet.*" In *New Essays on "Hamlet",* Eds. Mark Thornton and John Manning, 249–89. New York: AMS, 1994.

Clark, Robert. "Angela Carter's Desire Machine." *Women's Studies* 14 (1987): 147–61.

Delbaere-Garant, Jeanne. "Psychic Realism, Mythic Realism, Grotesque Realism: Variations on Magic Realism in Contemporary Literature in English." In *Magical Realism: Theory, History, Community,* Eds. Lois Parkinson Zamora and Wendy Faris, 249–63. Durham and London: Duke University Press, 1995.

Gass, Joanne. "Panopticism in *Nights at the Circus.*" *Review of Contemporary Fiction* 14 no. 3 (Fall 1994):

———. "Written on the Body: The Materiality of Myth in Angela Carter's *Heroes and Villains.*" *Arkansas Review* 4, no. 1 (Spring 1995): 12–30.

Gamble, Sara. *Angela Carter: Writing from the Front Line.* Edinburgh: Edinburgh University Press, 1997.

Jordan, Elaine. "The Dangers of Angela Carter." In *New Feminist Discourses: Critical Essays on Theories and Texts,* Ed. Isobel Armstrong, 119–31. London: Routledge, 1992.

Kendrick, Walter. "The Real Magic of Angela Carter." In *Contemporary British Women Writers: Narrative Strategies,* Ed. Robert E. Hosmer Jr., 66–84. New York: St. Martin's Press, 1993.

Lappas, Catherine. " 'Seeing is believing, but touching is the truth': Female Spectatorship and Sexuality in *The Company of Wolves." Women's Studies* 25 (1996): 115–35.

Ledwon, Lenora. "The Passion of the Phallus and Angela Carter's *The Passion of New Eve." Journal of the Fantastic in the Arts* 5, no. 4 (1993): 26–41.

Linkin, Harriet Kramer. "Isn't it Romantic?: Angela Carter's Bloody Revision of the Romantic Aesthetic in 'The Erl-King.' " *Contemporary Literature* 35, no. 2 (Summer 1994): 305–23.

Matus, Jill. "Blonde, Black and Hottentot Venus: Context and Critique in Angela Carter's 'Black Venus.' " *Studies in Short Fiction* 28, no. 4 (Fall 1991): 467–76.

Michael, Magali Cornier. "Angela Carter's *Nights at the Circus:* An Engaged Feminism via Subversive Postmodern Strategies." *Contemporary Literature* 35, no. 3 (1994): 492–521.

———. *Feminism and the Postmodern Impulse: Post-World War II Fiction,* 171–208. Albany: State University of New York Press, 1996.

Palmer, Paulina. "From 'Coded Mannequin' to Bird Woman: Angela Carter's Magic Flight." In *Women Reading Women's Writing,* Ed. Sue Roe, 177–205. Brighton: Harvester, 1987.

Punter, David. "Angela Carter: Supersessions of the Masculine." *Critique* 25, no. 4 (Summer 1984): 209–21.

———. "Essential Imaginings: The Novels of Angela Carter and Russell Hoban." In *The British and Irish Novel since 1960,* Ed. James Acheson, 142–49. New York: St. Martins, 1991.

Robinson, Sally. *Engendering the Subject: Gender and Self-Representation in Contemporary Women's Fiction.* Albany: State University of New York Press, 1991.

Rose, Ellen Cronan. "Through the Looking Glass: When Women Tell Fairy Tales." In *The Voyage In: Fictions of Female Development,* Eds. Elizabeth Abel, Marianne Hirsch, and Elizabeth Langland, 209–27. Hanover and London: University Press of New England, 1983.

Rubenstein, Roberta. "Intersexions: Gender Metamorphosis in Angela Carter's *The Passion of New Eve* and Lois Gould's *A Sea Change." Tulsa Studies in Women's Literature* 21, no. 1 (1993): 103–18.

Sage, Lorna. *Women in the House of Fiction: Post-War Women Novelists,* 168–77. New York: Routledge, 1992.

Schmidt, Ricarda. "The Journey of the Subject in Angela Carter's Fiction." *Textual Practice* 3, no. 1 (1989): 56–75.

Sheets, Robin Ann. "Pornography, Fairy Tales, and Feminism: Angela Carter's 'The Bloody Chamber.' "*Journal of the History of Sexuality* 1, no. 4 (April 1991): 633–57.

Siegel, Carol. *Male Masochism: Modern Revisions of the Story of Love,* 135–62. Bloomington: Indiana University Press, 1995.

Smith, Patricia Juliana. "All You Need Is *Love:* Angela Carter's Novel of Sixties Sex and Sensibility." *Review of Contemporary Fiction* 14, no. 3 (Fall 1994): 24–29.

Suleimann, Susan Rubin. *Subversive Intent: Gender, Politics, and the Avant-Garde,* 134–40, 162–63. Cambridge and London: Harvard University Press, 1990.

Turner, Rory P. B. "Subjects and Symbols: Transformations of Identity in *Nights at the Circus." Folklore Forum* 20, no. 1–2 (1987): 39–60.

Wilson, Robert Rawdon. "SLIP PAGE: Angela Carter, In/Out in the Postmodern Nexus." *Ariel* 20, no. 4 (October 1989): 96–114.

Also see *The Review of Contemporary Fiction* 14, no. 3 (Fall 1994) for short articles on Carter.

Index

◆

The Volume Editor

Lindsey Tucker is professor of English at the University of Miami. She is Author of *Stephen and Bloom at Life's Feast: Alimentary Symbolism in James Joyce's "Ulysses"* (1984), and *Textual Escap(e)ades: Mobility, Maternity, and Textuality in Contemporary Fiction by Women* (1994).

The General Editor

Zack Bowen is professor of English at the University of Miami. He holds degrees from the University of Pennsylvania (B.A.), Temple University (M.A.), and the State University of New York at Buffalo (Ph.D.). In addition to being general editor of this G. K. Hall series, he is editor of the James Joyce series for the University of Florida Press and the *James Joyce Literary Supplement*. He is the author and editor of numerous books on modern British, Irish, and American literature. He has also published more than one hundred monographs, essays, scholarly reviews, and recordings related to literature. He is past president of the James Joyce Society (1977–1986), former chair of the Modern Language Association Lowell Prize Committee, and current president of the International James Joyce Foundation.